America's Century

America's Century

Perspectives on
U.S. History since 1900

edited by

Iwan W. Morgan and Neil A. Wynn

HM

HOLMES & MEIER
New York | London

For Jane and Humphrey

Published in the United States of America 1993 by
Holmes & Meier Publishers, Inc.
30 Irving Place
New York, NY 10003

Book design by Adrienne Weiss

This book has been printed on acid-free paper.

Library of Congress Cataloging-in-Publication Data

America's century : perspectives on twentieth-century American history
/ edited by Iwan W. Morgan and Neil A. Wynn.
    p.   cm.
  Includes bibliographical references and index.
  ISBN 0-8419-1303-X (cl : acid-free paper)
  ISBN 0-8419-1304-8 (pbk. : acid-free paper)
    1. United States—History—20th century.   I. Morgan, Iwan W.
II. Wynn, Neil A.
E741.A68   1993
973.9—dc20   91-29508
                                                                  CIP

Manufactured in the United States of America

Contents

Preface

This book was written to meet a number of demands. First, we wished to produce an up-to-date, single-volume study of twentieth-century America. Second, we felt that there was a strong need for a text that combined a broad narrative account of the period with some consideration of historiographical issues, and at the same time examined major thematic concerns. As a consequence this book consists of chronological chapters followed by select surveys of critical topics that merit special attention. Finally, we responded to the growing demand to focus on the internationalization of American history as articulated by the Organization of American Historians, and to show how American history was viewed from outside. In including comparative references we hope to demonstrate how American history has shaped other nations, and how other nations have helped to shape American history.

The first idea for this book sprang out of meetings and encounters at the British Association for American Studies annual conferences, and it reflects the continuing and growing British interest in the United States and its history. This interest is evident not only in British universities, but also in polytechnics and colleges throughout the United Kingdom and Europe.

Our editorial work was supported by our respective institutions through the provision of research time and other facilities. We are grateful, too, to all our contributors who produced chapters and revisions despite their heavy commitments over a long period of time. Both our families helped us with our work, bore with us patiently, and provided an atmosphere that added stimulation to our activity. The book is dedicated to our children.

Iwan W. Morgan
City of London Polytechnic

Neil A. Wynn
University of Glamorgan

America's Century

Introduction
America's Twentieth Century

——— *Iwan W. Morgan and Neil A. Wynn*

Twenty years or so ago, most history teachers had a common understanding of what the term "twentieth-century America" conveyed and could use it with reasonable confidence that their students shared their perception. During the 1950s and 1960s America's twentieth-century development was conventionally viewed in terms of inexorable progress toward economic abundance, modern big government, racial and social equality, and international primacy. Many would have agreed with the sentiments expressed in 1941 by Henry Luce when he said that "the twentieth century must be to a significant degree an American century." Today few people would speak so confidently about either the present or the past.

Teachers and students now have to grapple with a period that has appeared to lose coherence and symmetry. The central themes of U.S. history since 1900 have become less easily visible, and uncertainty has grown about its direction. Discontinuity and cyclical swings appear to be the main characteristics of a century that encompasses many diverse and seemingly contradictory developments—from Progressivism to the New Right, nativism to ethnic pluralism, economic depression to affluence, liberalism to conservatism, and isolationism to internationalism. Typifying this discontinuity and uncertainty, even the apparent passing of the Cold War and the collapse of communism in Eastern Europe raised questions about America's future role.

In the face of this apparent diversity, historical perspectives have narrowed. It has become increasingly common to view the century in at least two parts: the recent spate of books on "The United States since 1945" suggests that postwar America has a uniformity or coherence that separates it from the prewar era and provides a new point of historical reference to replace "twentieth-century America." Our book goes against this current trend, in the belief that modern America can best be understood from a perspective that spans the century as a whole. By identifying historical themes and forces that have continued to operate since at least 1900 the writers of this book wish to highlight the continuities, as well as discontinuities, of modern American history and so help to restore the notion of "twentieth-century America."

Our emphasis on a long-term overview does not preclude recognition of the fact that the twentieth century encompassed a series of shorter eras, each often with apparently distinctive characteristics, events, and personalities. Nonetheless there have been recurrent forces or processes that have persisted throughout the twentieth century, separating it from the nineteenth century and, at the same time, cutting across the lines of narrower periodization.

In his first annual message to Congress on December 3, 1901, President Theodore Roosevelt announced:

> . . . the tremendous and highly complex industrial development which went on with ever-accelerated rapidity during the latter half of the nineteenth century brings us face to face at the beginning of the twentieth century with very serious social problems. The old laws, and the old customs . . . are no longer sufficient.

The developments to which Roosevelt referred not only continued but indeed quickened in pace over the next ninety years, transforming the face of America. Much of the twentieth century can be seen as a continuation of, and a coming to terms with, the reality of the problems that Roosevelt identified. The new president touched upon the growth of industrial centers and new patterns of work, but he focused particularly upon the development of the big-business economy and the emergence of a corporate society in which government had to deal directly with business and unions. With even greater foresight he might have said more about urban and suburban growth—and decay; the growth of wealth and the problem of its distribution or concentration; rising social tensions and the pressure for further democracy and the extension of citizenship rights to women, blacks, and other underprivileged groups. All of these issues were surfacing and were recognized at the end of the nineteenth century, and they continued to be central features of America's twentieth-century development.

In response to the growth of the corporate economy Roosevelt increasingly advocated federal supervision and regulation of business. In beginning the growth in power of the centralized state and the presidency, Roosevelt could be said to have initiated the developments and debates that were to be a major feature of the twentieth century. At the beginning of the century the majority of American citizens had little direct contact with the federal government. There were no income taxes, no federal social welfare provision, little regulation of business, and the government had a budget surplus of $46 million. Over the next ninety years the federal government grew enormously in size and influence. In the late 1980s it employed more than three million civilian workers, spent over $500 billion on social welfare and operated a budget deficit in excess of $146 billion. Such figures only hint at the shift away from principles of laissez-faire toward a regulated capitalist economy, and they say nothing of the change within the institutions of government, particularly the growth of executive power, in response to wider social and economic change.

It is possible to identify at least four major functions undertaken by the expanding federal government over the course of the twentieth century. The Progressives launched the "regulatory state" to oversee the operation of the business economy, and the New Deal created the "guarantor state" which promoted public-welfare programs within the context of a private-enterprise economy. The modest welfare state of the 1930s was expanded and modernized under the Fair Deal and Great Society programs, and by the Republican administration of Richard Nixon. Some historians suggest that the New Deal also bred a "broker state" that promoted a plurality of conflicting demands from different groups on federal policymakers, but sought to respond to these according to principles of equity rather than solely in accordance with each group's power and influence. It has also been argued that the growth of American foreign involvements during World War II and, more particularly, during the Cold War led to the development of a "national security state" to manage defense and foreign affairs.

Significantly, as the twentieth century draws to a close, each manifestation of the state is under attack. Ronald Reagan's administration challenged the ethos of the "regulatory state" and the "guarantor state." Many commentators observed that the federal government, particularly the legislative branch, is so attuned to the particularist demands of interest groups that the "broker state" prevents the adoption of a truly national approach to America's problems. Finally, the passing of the Cold War leaves the future of the "national security state" in doubt. It may well be, therefore, that the twenty-first century will see major modifications in the character and role of the state.

The incremental nature of the state in "America's century" reflected broader changes in society itself. A few simple statistics indicate the scope of this transformation. The expansion of the American economy can be seen in the growth of GNP from $18.7 billion in 1900 to over $4,500 billion in the late 1980s. Population also grew from 76 million to over 246 million. In part this was due to a continuation of immigration—between four and five million immigrants have entered the U.S.A. in each decade after World War II—but it also represented a considerable natural increase. Despite ongoing immigration (and the greater proportion of Asian and Hispanic immigrants since the relaxation of restrictive nationality quotas in 1966), American population became more homogeneous as the percentage of foreign-born in the population fell from one-third to one-sixth. The distribution of this growing population also changed. In 1900 some 60 percent of Americans were still classed as rural; by the 1980s the figure was down to 20 percent, and the bulk of Americans lived in urban areas. Urban demography itself underwent change in the latter part of the century when there was also a move from city centers to suburbs, and from large cities to smaller ones. Throughout the century there were also regional shifts in population from East to West, South to North, and later from North to South or Southwest. In 1900 the physical center of the population was located southeast of Indianapolis; in 1990 it had shifted west into Kansas.

Part of this movement reflected the changing location and nature of industry as heavy industry was replaced by light industry, engineering gave way to electronics, and assembly lines were replaced by robotics. While the percentage of operatives and laborers in the work force fell from 50 percent in 1900 to 30 percent in 1970, the number of white-collar workers rose so that by 1970 they made up 50 percent of the total work force. The numbers of blacks and women in the labor force and the types of work they performed also changed, reflecting the variety of forces affecting their status in society.

Changes in America's international position were equally significant. An emergent world power in 1900, the United States has been the world's most powerful nation since 1945. From a position of almost no overseas involvement in 1900 (other than in the Philippines), by the mid-1970s America was party to forty-two alliances, including eight security treaties, and had over a million troops stationed in more than thirty countries around the world. In addition, the dollar was the world's major reserve currency and the prop of the international economic system from 1945 to 1971. However, just as American military power was questioned in the 1980s and 1990s, so too the rise of the yen and the deutschmark began to challenge the preeminence of the dollar.

A number of these developments could have been examined as separate unifying issues in their own right and this book could have been written wholly on a thematic basis; four chapters do focus on themes and issues that in our view especially merit separate attention. However, we have opted for a mainly chronological approach based on conventional period divisions in order to illustrate the variations in influence at different times of recurrent historical forces, and to show as well the changing responses of different participants to those forces. This approach will, we hope, give students a better understanding of the unity that underlies the apparent diversity of America's twentieth-century experience. At the same time such an arrangement recognizes the significance and impact of unique events such as wars and depressions, and the contribution of individuals from Theodore Roosevelt through to Ronald Reagan, or from Jane Addams through to Jesse Jackson.

The chronological approach used in this book also facilitates consideration of the historiographical debates that dominate twentieth-century American history. Virtually every important issue and personality has been subject, following initial assessment, to revisionist, counterrevisionist, and sometimes even postrevisionist interpretation. While historians have argued about the nature and aims of Progressivism, they have also disagreed about the myths and realities of the twenties; and while subjects like the New Deal, the origins of the Cold War, and the presidency of John F. Kennedy have been particularly fertile grounds of dispute, new issues such as the domestic impact of war—from World War I to Vietnam—or the changing roles of women now also figure prominently in historical exchanges.

Historians have constantly rewritten the American twentieth century as their perspectives changed and as each generation viewed the past from the vantage point of a new present. References to the main historiographical debates are included throughout this volume in order to illustrate the changing perceptions of the twentieth century and provide students with a yardstick against which to judge contemporary viewpoints.

Nevertheless, it remains true that each chapter is by an individual contributor reflecting a particular point of view or interest, and each may stand alone as a treatment of its period or topic. The opening chapter points to the first stumbling responses to the problems that emergent modern America faced as a result of industrialization, urbanization, and social inequalities. In breaking away from America's nineteenth-century laissez-faire traditions, Progressivism launched the twentieth-century trend of government action to resolve social problems. Similar developments were evident in other industrial nations, but whereas they tended to reflect the concerns of organized working-class groups and the influence of socialism, reform in the United States was couched much more in established terminology of social mobility, individualism, and liberty. Progressivism has tended to have a favorable historical image as a reform movement underpinned by a positive and optimistic view of the possibility of change. Alun Munslow's survey corrects this view by analyzing the variety of concerns and solutions proposed under Progressivism's banner, and indicates that attempts were made to create a set of values that would impose cultural unity on America's heterogeneous society. Some of the tensions and conflicts were undoubtedly resolved by political reform, and others by the 100 percent Americanism of

World War I, but some persisted into the twenties. The postwar period also witnessed the emergence of new problems, as Americans looked back to memories of a prewar past to grapple with problems of a rapidly changing present.

This dichotomy of change and reaction makes any description of the postwar decade as "conservative" too simplistic. While the twenties have been seen as a reaction to Progressivism, the resurgence of business Republicanism and the assault of rural nativism against urban cosmopolitanism were counterbalanced by the continuing trend of modernization in government, organizational structures, and the economy. Even Herbert Hoover's stumbling response to the Great Depression was closer in spirit to New Deal interventionism than to laissez-faire traditions. The complexities of the Jazz Age and its significance as a transitional era in America's twentieth-century development are underlined by Ian Purchase's questioning of the very periodization of that decade.

While the crisis of the Depression, rather like that of wartime, may well have brought a suspension of, or even a final resolution to some of the social conflicts of the previous decades, it raised again in a very direct way questions about the regulation and direction of the economy, the role of the state, and the development of social welfare. As Stuart Kidd makes clear, however, the New Deal is a difficult subject to interpret. Like Progressivism, it was a changing and dynamic phenomenon. While pointing to the achievements of Franklin Roosevelt's reform program, Kidd also indicates its imperfections and failures. The New Deal did not create a new state, and it was more evolutionary than revolutionary. But whatever its imperfections, and there were many, the New Deal did forge a new political consensus that was liberal and pluralist in character.

During and after World War II parts of the Roosevelt legacy became redundant and disappeared. Others were consolidated and provided the basis for the postwar welfare state. In so far as class and trade unionism were significant features of the 1930s, these were now largely accommodated within the political system. Instead, the liberal agenda began to change in recognition of the "American dilemma" of race relations for the first time in the 1940s.

Perhaps even more than other decades, the 1940s defy simple periodization. The decade therefore features in two overlapping chapters. Both point, however, to the impact of international affairs upon American society, first through direct involvement in World War II and then through the ideological confrontation of the Cold War. Neil Wynn suggests that while World War II had a considerable domestic impact on America, the political, social, and economic developments of this decade span the conventional dividing line of 1945. John Dumbrell links them to the supposedly sterile 1950s. Both authors point to the reinterpretations of their decades and of Presidents Truman and Eisenhower. While their presidencies saw the continued growth of federal government and a continuation of some New Deal policies, the late 1940s and 1950s also witnessed the growth of the "national security state" and an emphasis on conformity. The two essays indicate the complex nature of American politics and society at midcentury, and suggest that the era following World War II, like the 1920s, cannot be characterized simply in terms of reaction or reform.

After being consolidated in the postwar years, the New Deal legacy was significantly extended in the mid-1960s under Lyndon Johnson. The New Frontier–Great Society reforms also underlined the continuity of twentieth-century reform in sharing the same optimistic beliefs and addressing some of the issues initially tackled by Progressivism. Yet, as Iwan Morgan argues, the reform impulse was based on questionable assumptions, achieved only partial success, and was short-lived. Meanwhile Cold War liberalism reached a denouement with military failure in the Vietnam War. By the end of the 1960s the United States was entering a period of self-doubt, and reassessing the domestic and international position that had shaped its midcentury history.

One of the major concerns of modern America has been with the position of women and racial minorities. The central thrust of twentieth-century American women's history has been the pursuit of equality. Since 1900 women have increasingly moved out of the private world of the home into the public world of work and politics. However, as Jay Kleinberg demonstrates, gender equality has proved an elusive goal. Despite recent advances gender continues to be a powerful determinant of life chances and life-style: just as many African-Americans struggle to overcome built-in forces of discrimination, so too many American women remain the victims of ingrained male prejudice.

The different phases of American reform since 1900 had all, to varying degrees, raised the issue of black civil rights. In

Chapter 9 Neil Wynn argues that twentieth-century black history fell into four phases—an early period characterized by white racism coupled with important changes in black demography; a transitional era of growing black expectations and some recognition from federal government; an explosion of protest and reform from the mid-1950s to early 1970s; and finally a period of relative conservatism in which the issue of race relations appeared to fade as a matter of national concern.

At various points in the twentieth century both blacks and women have received support in their quest for equality from the Supreme Court—although more recently the Court has also acted to limit women's freedom in areas such as abortion. Historians have tended to neglect this institution in favor of studying presidents, parties, and political movements, but nonetheless the Supreme Court has been instrumental in shaping the twentieth century through its power to interpret and reinterpret the Constitution. As David Barling indicates in Chapter 10, judicial reinterpretation of the Constitution since 1900 has gone through four phases. Initial conservative opposition to the growth of federal government gave way to a transitional era that was followed by a full-scale commitment to extend rights to underprivileged groups, but recently there has been a shift back toward the strict-constructionist views dominant at the start of the century.

If the pursuit of equality is one of the dominant features of America's domestic history since 1900, its rise to superpower status appears to be the central theme of its international history. As Geoff Stoakes argues in Chapter 11, this trend has been the product of contending forces. The dichotomies between isolationism and internationalism, ideals and self-interest, anticolonialism and imperialism have consistently shaped American foreign policy since 1900. The interaction of these different forces has created a complex historical pattern that has seen the United States rise to prominence early in the century, enter a period of isolationist reaction thereafter, establish its international primacy during World War II and the Cold War, and finally enter a period of reassessment in the wake of Vietnam.

Relative international decline mirrored relative economic decline in the 1970s, and both challenged the assumptions about American power and abundance that had underlain the nation's twentieth-century experience until that point. As Iwan Morgan argues in Chapter 7, the United States entered an era of uncertainty in the 1970s as conventional solutions proved unable to resolve the new domestic and foreign problems. Even the confident conservatism of Ronald Reagan in the 1980s failed to restore the international and economic position that the United States had enjoyed at midcentury. Questions about budget deficits, the imbalance of wealth in American society, and the U.S. role in world affairs still remained to be answered when George Bush took office in 1989. Such recent trends suggest that only for a relatively brief time was the twentieth century truly "the American century."

This book may reflect something of an outsider's perspective on twentieth-century America. Under the influence of Frederick Jackson Turner and others, historians traditionally interpreted America's nineteenth-century experience in terms of uniqueness and emphasized its essential isolation from, and contrasts with, European history. It is difficult to sustain this approach for the twentieth century. The development of the entire Western industrial world, including that of the United States, has been shaped to some extent by the same forces and events: world wars, ideological divisions, the growing interdependence of the global economy, and changing international relationships. Owing to its different traditions, values, and socioeconomic structures, America's responses to these changes have sometimes been dissimilar to those of Western European countries. In particular the collectivist trends of the twentieth century did not generate a consistently strong working-class political or trade-union movement in America as it did in Europe (and as a result we have not assigned a separate chapter to "organized labor," but deal with "labor" in the generic sense in each chapter where appropriate). On the other hand there have been many similarities and links between developments in America and Western Europe—so much so that one might talk of an Atlantic culture if not of an Atlantic economy.

Throughout the century there has been a flow of ideas backward and forward across the Atlantic: "progressivism" was a term in common use in British politics before 1914, and Woodrow Wilson was said to be introducing a prime ministerial presidency in the United States; later in the century commentators were to talk of the presidential leadership of British prime ministers. Economic theorists were to influence policies in many countries: John Maynard Keynes probably was accepted more widely in the United States than in Britain, Milton Friedman perhaps more in Britain than the United States. During World War II America and Britain established a "special relationship" that continued into the 1950s, and was revived during the Reagan administration and then during the Gulf War of 1991. The civil-rights and women's movements have also had international dimensions. British suffragettes, for example, gave inspiration to their American sisters prior to 1914, while in the 1960s it was American feminism that provided the example for the rest of the world. African-Americans were influenced in their campaigns by the struggle against colonialism and the example particularly of Gandhi in India; blacks in South Africa, the West Indies, and Britain have in turn found inspiration in the United States. In popular culture, too, the flow was more than one way. Hollywood had, and continues to have, a worldwide impact; American popular music, including jazz and blues, influenced British and other performers such as the Beatles in the 1960s, who in turn found wider audiences in the United States.

As events in the late 1980s and early 1990s have made all too clear, it is now impossible to understand the history of the United States or any other country in isolation. While Eastern Europeans seek U.S. aid and Western Europeans copy American fashions, all industrial nations watch events in the Middle East anxiously or express concern about deforestation in Latin America or fishing policies in the Pacific. Even health crises such as AIDS and cholera have worldwide ramifications. Nonetheless, American society remains distinct from others in a variety of ways, and the contributors to this volume hope to identify and explain what is unique about America's experience and why the twentieth century became for so long the "American century." In so doing they provide an understanding, too, of the new sense of American limits that has helped to create a growing age of uncertainty. Whether that mood will persist will depend, no doubt, on a combination of internal and external factors. The decline of foreign "empires," particularly the Soviet bloc, and the shifting pattern of political and economic relations in Europe, the Middle East, Asia, and elsewhere provide a constantly changing international setting. It remains to be seen whether the United States will be able to respond to the domestic and foreign challenges, and whether the decline of the American "empire" is temporary or permanent.

1
The Progressive Era, 1900–1919

Alun Munslow

The twentieth century opened, as all new centuries do, with people looking back to the past and ahead to the future. The hopes and fears of many Americans were summarized by the eminent historian and philosopher Henry Brooks Adams who believed that the thinking man of 1900 stood "bewildered and helpless" in the face of the achievements of the old century, but that "the new American" born in 1900 would experience changes hitherto unimagined in the future. With remarkable foresight Adams predicted that this new American would be "the child of incalculable coal-power, chemical power, electric power, and radiating energy, as well as new forces yet undetermined." Furthermore, the twentieth-century American would have to think "in complexities unimaginable to an earlier mind [and] deal with problems altogether beyond the range of earlier society." The twentieth century, Adams concluded, would see a new universe that "would know no law that could not be proved by its anti-law."[1] In other words, the new century would be one of conflict and clouded uncertainty.

The years that followed have borne Adams out as Americans have faced the consequences of massive technological achievement, economic growth and collapse, internal change and conflict, and growing involvement overseas. Even as Adams wrote, Americans were confronting these issues for the first time. The opening decades of what was to become the "American Century" were marked by what another observer described as "a period of clamor, of bewilderment, of an almost tremulous unrest," as various groups and individuals were forced to question their perceptions of America, its past and its possible future.[2] The historian David Noble has even described the period beginning in 1890 as one of "profound cultural crisis."[3] This crisis was the result of the process of modernism; that is, the emergence of contemporary society as formed by industrialization and urbanization. To be modern in the twentieth century was, as Adams understood, to experience adventure, power, and novelty. This experience could strengthen national unity, but it could also divide the American people. The great paradox of modernity was its ambiguity, ambivalences, conflicts, contradictions, and disunities. Perhaps the major theme of the first era of American development in this century was that coherence, such as there was, came through the recognition of cultural fragmentation. To be American at the start of the twentieth century was to be part of a world in which, as Karl Marx had said, "all that is solid melts into air, all that is holy is profaned, and man is at last compelled to face with sober senses his real conditions of life and his relations with his kind."[4]

The sense of anxiety and crisis was not unique to America. In both the Old World and the New, the uncertainty of the new century in its first decades created a shared transatlantic experience of rapid social change. The Anglo-Irish poet William Butler Yeats undoubtedly captured the early-twentieth-century mood on both sides of the Atlantic when he wrote:

> *Things fall apart; the center cannot hold,*
> *Mere anarchy is loosed upon the world.*
>   "The Second Coming," 1921

James J. Kloppenberg has compared the cultural and philosophical responses to these changes in Europe and America and found continuities that produced, in his view, a common "politics of progressivism."[5] This entailed a shared belief in the necessity to develop the role of the state in the face of a new corporate capitalism and a concern for the welfare of the common people. While corporations themselves had already begun to provide for their workers' welfare, it was clear that the state had a major regulatory role to play.

It was from this ferment of ideas and contradictions that reformist socialism in Europe and its American equivalent, Progressivism, emerged and pointed out the philosophical direction that many were to follow through the rest of the century. In America this intellectual turmoil took the form of pragmatism— a system of thought that emphasized useful experimentalism and skepticism. Although developed in the latter part of the nineteenth century, pragmatic philosophy dominated social thought during the Progressive era. Found in the work of Charles Peirce, William James, and John Dewey, pragmatism imagined an open-ended universe with no eternal truths. Ideas had to be tested in the crucible of the real world in order to establish their utility rather than prove their truth. This relativism was the keystone of the new transatlantic perspective on modern society, in which cultural flux, emergent corporate, industrial power, and welfare liberal politics were the common themes.

Though more confident than Henry Adams of the accomplishments of the nineteenth century, many people remained concerned about the costs involved in the growth of America's economic power and emerging world political authority. Consequently Progressivism was essentially the reactions of many divergent social and economic groups to the massive changes brought by America's rapid industrialization. The new conditions of modernity, as evidenced in the uncontrolled expansion of the cities, the enormous waves of immigrants, and the beginning of the migration of blacks from the South to northern industrial centers, all combined to produce this sense of cultural and social crisis that called forth a movement of reform and regulation. This movement began in the cities but quickly expanded to include a broad range of activities within the states, and ultimately emerged at the federal level in Washington, D.C.

Eventually almost every group had its Progressives— farmers, industrial workers and artisans, small shopkeepers, small and large businessmen, bankers, the old mercantile elite, trade unionists, academics, local politicians, lawyers, and clerics. The issues they tackled were dictated by their different experiences of economic change. The reform agenda thus included the trusts, bossism, the character of taxation, conservation of natural resources, the conditions of work of laboring men, women, and children, the nature and functioning of trade unions, female suffrage, vice, crime, prohibition, the rights of blacks, and structural changes in the legal apparatuses of local, state, and federal government.

Because of the variety of concerns and approaches subsumed under the banner of Progressivism, its exact nature was debated at the time and by generations of historians since. The arguments have centered upon which social and economic groups dominated the movement, and on the nature of their objectives. According to Richard Hofstadter, many members of the reform movement came from the middle ranks of society who, squeezed on one side by new industrial magnates and on the other by the rising ranks of labor, were motivated by a desire to preserve and protect their economic and social status.[6] This interpretation has been much criticized by historians who have argued that the social costs of industrialism promoted a nonsectarian humanitarian call for reform in the advocacy of shorter hours of work in factories, a desire to protect women and children, and an attack on tenement slums. Equally, other historians have noted that many Progressives set about modifying the structure and operation of government without necessarily considering what was in their own best interests.

Some reformers were inspired by the desire to uphold traditional values, while others saw a need to adapt these to modern conditions. The Progressive ideology has been described by Eric F. Goldman as an essentially liberal movement in political terms, but Gabriel Kolko sees it as a conservative one.[7] Despite this difference, both agree that there was a questioning of the direction in which the new class of entrepreneurs appeared to be taking laissez-faire capitalism. Throughout it all, however, whatever the issue at whatever level of government, whether primarily humanitarian or political, reform was often viewed and undertaken as part of what has been designated as a quest for efficiency, a position recognized by writers such as Samuel P. Hays and Robert Wiebe.[8] Reflecting the optimistic notion that human society could be made more harmonious by rational planning, this quest was found in the conservation movement, the "time and motion" (factory efficiency) studies of Frederick W. Taylor, and the attempts to make local government less bureaucratic and cumbersome and more responsive to popular control. The cult of the expert and the professional, along with the notion of efficiency through regulation, became part of the very texture of Progressivism.

Yet another view of Progressivism sees it as a regulatory and reformist movement emerging out of changes in the nineteenth-century political system. Richard L. McCormick argues that as a result of elections in the mid-1890s in New York State, for example, modern issue-oriented political parties emerged. The politically corrupt party machines disappeared, allowing long hidden issues to be addressed, and in the process curbed abuses within the social system and the economy.[9] As the title of his book suggests, political realignment ultimately produced reform through regulation in New York State, and by implication what happened in one state may have occurred in others.

These different concerns reflected the changes that had taken place in America, for Progressivism was ultimately a product of the economic history of the late nineteenth century. As late as 1860, the American economy was agrarian-based, and ranked behind Britain, France, and Germany in industrial output. However, by 1919 America possessed the world's highest per capita income and manufactured more industrial goods than the other three economies combined. The most significant features of post–Civil War American growth were its rapidity and scale. This economic power was built upon a vast well of natural resources and an enormous internal market, developed through the expansion of the regional railroad system across the continent. Consequently the accumulation of capital was realized on a huge scale. The value of America's economic output in 1860 was less than $2.5 billion; by 1900 it was over $10 billion, and the contribution of manufacturing rose from one-third to one-half of the total. The growth of the economy was characterized by the development of monopoly capitalism—the trust. Between 1890 and 1903 the number of industrial combinations grew from twelve to over three hundred, and 1 percent of all companies produced 40 percent of manufactured output. It was this fact, perhaps more than any other, that aroused the fears and criticisms of the reformers.

The most significant fact of the industrial period was the rise of a class of entrepreneurial leaders who welded the new industrial order together: Gustavus Swift and Philip K. Armour

18

in meat packing; J. J. Hill and Edward Harriman in railroading; John D. Rockefeller in oil and petroleum products; J. P. Morgan in finance and investment; and Henry Clay Frick and Andrew Carnegie in iron and steel. This emergent-dominant industrial class created a new cultural hegemony of the propertied and well-to-do—the bedrock of a new business civilization—through the popular texts written by the leaders of the new industrial class like Carnegie's *Triumphant Democracy* (1886) and *Gospel of Wealth* (1901). Ideas of self-improvement were reinforced by others, like the black leader Booker T. Washington in his autobiography *Up from Slavery* (1911), as well as in the enormous range of dime novels written about the conquest of the West and the exuberant imperialist imperative of the age. Traditional beliefs like thrift, heroic materialism, self-help, and the plausibility of rags-to-riches success, economic individualism, and equality of opportunity were incorporated in a new context and became the staple ideological diet that fed the thoughts of the urban poor and dispossessed. Pulp literature was served to the masses by Richard Harding Davis who, in numerous short stories such as those in *Stories for Boys* (1891), plays, and novels such as *Van Bibber* (1892), captured the bourgeois spirit of achievement that ushered in the twentieth century—ideas that permeated the ideological fabric of society. His conservative values of hard work, patience, masculine virtue, courage, enterprise, and endeavor were also found in Horatio Alger's immensely popular and now better-known books. Alger wrote more than eighty books such as *Ragged Dick* and *Mark, the Match Boy*, which perpetuated the belief that in a free country poverty should be no bar to a man's advance.

The ideological justification for the new business hegemony was provided not only by leading businessmen like Carnegie, and popular writers like Davis and Alger, but also by intellectuals. William Graham Sumner, the Yale professor of sociology, in particular accepted the growing social inequalities produced through rapid industrialization as inevitable and good. He cast doubt upon the American liberal equal-rights tradition, derived from Jefferson, by presenting what he saw as the harsh reality of life under the new order—that Jeffersonian equality produced only the survival of the unfit, while true liberty meant inequality and the survival of the fittest. This uncompromising view of the benefits of the new business civilization was derived from Herbert Spencer's application to human society of Darwin's theories of the evolution of species. Influenced by such ideas, the advocates of the new industrial civilization had no qualms about the future. Indeed, they were confident that material progress would strengthen traditional American principles and promote social progress. As Andrew Carnegie wrote in his essay on wealth in 1889, while the law of competition "may sometimes be hard for the individual, it is best for the race, because it insures the survival of the fittest in every department."[10]

This equation looked far from proven in the industrial cities in 1900. For the majority of the urban industrial workers material progress was not translated into social progress. In welfare terms America lagged far behind Europe, even though by the turn of the century it was clear that the human costs of industrialization were high. The severe economic depression of 1893–96 produced considerable suffering, and with it worrying expressions of discontent in the form of strikes against wage cuts and "industrial armies" marching to lobby Congress. While economic distress had occasioned the first calls for reform from the farmers in the Populist movement of the 1880s, paradoxically the Progressive era itself was one of relative prosperity. Between 1897 and 1914 wholesale prices rose by 50 percent, a peacetime record, and the total value of currency in circulation rose by 60 percent. The financial infrastructure became highly sophisticated, fed as it was by the consumer boom in a new range of goods, from bicycles to metal burial caskets, electric lighting to telephones and automobiles. Nevertheless, the rapid growth of the economy could not hide the surge of economic inequality that left the majority of Americans poor and ill-housed. Even in periods of boom many workers were poorly paid and even the better paid could expect to experience at least some short-term unemployment. Boom or bust, few industrial workers could escape the overcrowding and squalor of city life that resulted from rapid urban growth.

The urbanization of America had occurred on a massive scale. In 1840 only 10 percent of the population was urbanized. In 1890 the figure had risen to 45 percent and much of the energy of urban reformers was absorbed by the problem of tenement slums. As early as 1890, housing reformer Jacob Riis wrote *How the Other Half Lives*, an exposé of slum life and conditions in New York's Lower East Side. Thanks to Riis and other reformers, the New York Tenement House Commission was established in 1900. Its report prompted the passage of the 1901 New York Tenement House Law which increased building standards and outlawed the "dumbbell" tenement design, which had permitted adjoining buildings to share a small central airshaft for ventilation.

A harrowing portrait of the problems of the urban poor was drawn by social worker Robert Hunter in his influential book *Poverty,* published in 1904. The position of women and children particularly evoked a strong sympathetic reaction among the middle classes after the social reconstructionist John Spargo published *The Bitter Cry of the Children* (1906) detailing the awful conditions in which children of the slums lived. Many saw the child as the central issue of humanitarian reform, at the same time the victim of poverty, disease, and crime, and yet the key to cultural hegemony through education in the middle-class virtues of sobriety, thrift, self-esteem, and self-help. Juvenile delinquency was understood as a social problem that required improved legal as well as correctional machinery, and the world's first juvenile court was set up in Chicago in 1899, followed by the establishment of the probation system in the 1900s, initially in Illinois and then nationally.

According to historian Arthur A. Ekirch, the urban humanitarian strand of Progressivism was a "crusade for social justice."[11] The range of humanitarian reform was not limited to slum dwelling but cast its net across all aspects of city and factory life. Nowhere was this better exemplified than in the work of perhaps the most significant humanitarian reformer of the Progressive decades, Jane Addams. With Ellen Gates Starr, Addams founded the first community center, or settlement house, in Chicago in 1889. Although Jane Addams was determined on such an enterprise even before, she was prompted to search for an appropriate location in America after seeing the work of Octavia Hill and Canon Samuel Barnett at Toynbee Hall among the urban destitute of London's East End in 1886. The Chicago settlement, Hull House, in turn became the model for the four hundred or so that were built and operated over the next thirty years in the United States.

An indefatigable worker among the native and immigrant poor, Addams wrote several books that attempted to describe and evaluate the conditions of tenement and city life, with particular reference to the exploitation of children and young women. By 1900 twenty-eight states had some basic regulation of child labor, and in 1904 the National Child Labor Commission was set up to investigate, draw up model child labor bills, and lobby Congress. In 1914, however, twenty-two states still allowed children under fourteen years of age to work, and sixteen states did not require employers to know the ages of the children they employed.

On balance, the urban social reform response was conservative, and achieved only limited successes. Few antislum reformers, for example, favored municipally owned housing, given its socialist overtones. It has been suggested that such conservative sentiment was a substantial obstacle to the provision of adequate housing for the poor, particularly when they fell upon hard times. What the humanitarian reformers had established beyond any doubt, however, was the connection between city life and the factory regime. In the polyglot American city, often the only connecting thread between the many ethnic and native groups was their experience of work.

The factory system produced a wage-dependent labor force, for the bulk of whom the factory was a curse. In 1914 the average working week was still fifty-five hours, while many industries, notably textiles, exploited female and child workers, the cheapest form of labor. The most important agency working to establish the legality of labor legislation for women was the National Consumer's League (NCL) led by Florence Kelley. Under Kelley's guidance the NCL gathered statistical evidence on women and children at work in industry, in the hope that the vast array of data might convince the courts and government of the need to act. In 1908 the NCL engaged the Boston lawyer and reformer Louis Brandeis to present its evidence in the case of *Muller v. Oregon* before the Supreme Court. The Court accepted his argument that an Oregon state law limiting the hours of labor of women in bakeries to ten hours was constitutional. Finally, in *Bunting v. Oregon* (1917) the Supreme Court declared in favor of a ten-hour law for both men and women. On the issue of the social welfare of workers, the Bureau of Labor investigated European schemes of social insurance, although little came of its work in legislative terms. Demands for health insurance failed, largely because the labor leadership was lukewarm in its support, and the medical profession was intransigent in its opposition.

In spite of economic inequality, and with few notable exceptions, American labor did not produce a European-style socialist response. Although the reasons why socialism failed to take hold stretch beyond the Progressive decades, the failure of the American laboring classes to create a class awareness is arguably one very good reason for the advent of the reform movement. Often those who claimed to be Progressives were united only by their opposition to socialist ideas, and their advocacy instead of "Americanism." In one sense the foundations of America's welfare state were laid in the Progressive era, but this was not achieved, as in parts of Europe at the same time, notably in Britain, through a powerful socialist movement.

The failure of socialism in America, the most fully developed capitalist nation, has been much debated. In a book published in 1906, the European philosopher Werner Sombart asked *Why Is There No Socialism in America?* and the subject of American "exceptionalism" has continued to vex labor historians ever since. In a recent assessment, Eric Foner argues that the assumption implicit in the title of Sombart's book is misleading. There was, and still is, an American socialist movement, but one with a history significantly different from European counterparts.[12] The issue, as Foner sees it, is why labor and union militance did not translate either into a separate workingmen's party or into a strong and successful class-based socialist movement. He disagrees with Sombart's view that American socialism crashed on "the reefs of roast beef and apple pie," in other words, that it had no relevance to a people of plenty like the Americans. Foner also takes issue with the argument used by some Progressives, and later refined by consensus historians such as Louis Hartz,[13] that America did not need socialism because of its unique historical experience. According to this theory, America's absence of a feudal past, along with the broad-based property ownership of frontier society that resulted from cheap land, made socialism redundant

Foner contends that America was not exceptional, first because there was no European norm but a myriad of socialist parties, few of which were truly revolutionary or even strictly socialist in ideology. Furthermore he points to the strength of socialism in America at the time Sombart was writing. The Socialist Party of America (SPA) was formed in 1901 and had almost 120,000 members by 1912. In the elections that year the SPA's presidential candidate, Eugene V. Debs, won 900,000 votes, 6 percent of the total cast, and more than twelve hundred Socialists achieved state or local office. This surpassed the electoral support for the Labour party in Britain at that time. Paradoxically this success reflected the fact that American liberalism did color American socialism in its emphasis upon equality, individualism, and independence. In using traditional terminology to articulate the case against the growth of corporate and state power the SPA was able to attract support from tenant farmers in Oklahoma and Texas, industrial workers in Chicago, immigrant workers in the Midwest, and middle-class intellectuals in the East. Debs himself was a perfect example of the American socialist. Once a Democrat, he progressed through Populism to socialism, and his appeal was always to emotion rather than ideology. Even so, Debs was rarely able to capture the support of the mass of American workers, and the relative success of 1912 was to be short-lived.

The history of trade unionism during the Progressive decades reveals the un-American nature of socialism. Samuel Gompers, leader of the American Federation of Labor, recognized that conflict between labor and capital was often unavoidable, but argued that this was a matter of economics rather than class. Nevertheless, there were instances during the Progressive period of genuine labor opposition to the hegemonic system of bourgeois-Progressive values. Militant western miners, for example, joined with other groups in 1905 to form the Industrial Workers of the World (IWW). Nicknamed the Wobblies, the IWW stressed a revolutionary program that included the abolition of the wage system, and promoted industrial unionism among the unskilled and immigrant workers who were excluded from membership of the AFL. The Wobblies were a clear break with America's ideological mainstream. Their objective was "One Big Union" in the fashion of European syndicalism, with the power to organize a general strike, paralyze society, and seize the government. Many Progressives were alarmed by the Wobblies and their reported acts of violence—so much so that the president of Harvard, Charles Eliot, claimed that only by their destruction might American liberty be saved.

Some historians have viewed the Wobblies as a legitimate and inevitable response to American industrialism and the true representatives of America's underclass. Others castigate the Wobblies, whose internal ideological disputes did much to limit their effectiveness. Ultimately they failed to create a genuine working-class consciousness, a viable socialist culture, or even a radicalized alternative to the dominant values. Strongest among migrant workers, miners, and lumbermen in the West and with only limited success in the East, the Wobblies never gained a mass membership. Their opposition to American participation in World War I, plus organized repression on the part of employers and "patriotic" groups, pushed them into decline. Their fate was sealed by the conviction of their leader, William D. ("Big Bill") Haywood, and other prominent Wobblies under the federal conspiracy and sabotage laws in 1918. The anticommunist Red Scare of 1919 completed the movement's demise, ending a colorful episode in the history of both trade unionism and opposition to the dominant bourgeois culture.

Insulated from direct contact with industry, the growing middle classes needed to be informed of the conditions experienced by workers. The human costs that were associated with the new order were brought to a wider public through the work of journalists, writers and academics. A new field of journalism developed in the form of the exposé. The writers involved in this form of investigative journalism, usually for the popular magazines like *Collier's* and *McClure's*, were called muckrakers—a term coined by President Theodore Roosevelt in 1906, and meant more in a pejorative than a complimentary sense. He feared the indiscriminate character of much muckraking journalism which he saw as counterproductive. Nevertheless, the muckrakers brought many issues before the public and produced strong and sympathetic reactions. This journalism, epitomized by the work of Ida Tarbell on the Standard Oil trust, John Spargo on child labor, and Lincoln Steffens on political corruption, was part of the broader flow of a new genre of modernist literature—naturalism.

The conjunction of massive capitalist industrialization and the experience of blind economic determinism resulted in a literature whose crudest manifestation was the propaganda novel. This literature explored everyday life in realistic and minute detail, examining the entrepreneur, factory and city life, speculation, and the exploitation and alienation of the new business culture. The strongest expression of this naturalism was found in the work of Theodore Dreiser, notably *Sister Carrie* (1900), *The Financier* (1912), and *The Titan* (1914). Another naturalist writer, Frank Norris, described with exhaustive accuracy the new industrial environment and the personal disintegration that resulted from the new economic pressures and the conflicts between competing economic interests in *McTeague* (1899), *The Octopus* (1901) and *The Pit* (1903). Upton Sinclair wrote one of the most compelling propaganda novels of the era, *The Jungle* (1906), which drew a frightening, if not always accurate, picture of life among the Packingtown workers in the Chicago stockyards. Its publication helped create the demand for the passage of the Pure Food and Drug Act and Meat Inspection Act in 1906. The former prohibited the manufacture and interstate sale of adulterated food, and the latter attempted to enforce sanitary regulations in the meat-packing industry.

The Progressive decades witnessed many cultural changes among several traditionally subordinate social and economic groups. In particular the role of women was affected, due primarily to the process of industrialization. Women worked not only in the new factories, but also in the expanding world of domestic service, and in clerical work and teaching. Marriage effectively ended the careers of most women who did not work in factories, revealing the class- and gender-based character of the lives of working women. The rise of the middle-class American woman was facilitated by entry into college. A sisterhood of bourgeois women developed during the period, notably among those who entered the community outside the home. Apart from Jane Addams, Ellen Gates Starr, and Florence Kelley, other famous examples of middle-class women who emerged from domesticity to become involved in public life were the settlement workers Lillian Wald and Julia Lathrop, the propagandist Rheta C. Dorr, the birth-control advocates Margaret Sanger and Charlotte Perkins Gilman, and the crusaders for improved public health Rachel Brooks Gleason and Pauline Wright Davis. There were others who pursued more radical lives like the farmers' leader Mary Ellen Lease, the labor leader Mother Jones, and the anarchist Emma Goldman. For many women the modern era was one of confusion and chaos. The question was whether to pursue the Victorian path of equality earned through feminine virtue, or to throw aside Victorian morality. For most women, of course, the answers remained unresolved and probably unresolvable.

The worst dilemma was that experienced by black women who not only suffered from established patterns of sexual prejudice, but additionally labored under race and class prejudice. Immigrant women also experienced the dual disadvantages of ethnic and class prejudice. The vast majority of African-American and immigrant women understood all too sharply the character of the extremes of wealth and poverty to be found in the urban environment. However, despite the community of interests among women in the face of economic and patriarchal exploitation, class distinctions were rarely overcome. Perhaps the most notable exception was the eventual extension of suffrage to women with the ratification of the Nineteenth Amendment to the Constitution in August 1920.

The experience of immigrant and black males in the industrial cities also reflected the spatial distribution of economic and political power. The influx of "new" immigrants from central, eastern and southern Europe, and of blacks from the South during the 1890s, for example, compounded the tenement-house problem. The pluralization of society was most pronounced in the northeastern and Great Lakes cities. Between 1900 and 1920 the proportion of first-generation foreign-born living in cities rose from 66 to 75 percent. Predominantly Catholic, Jewish, or Orthodox in religion, and most likely from peasant stock, the "new" immigrants differed considerably from the "old" immigrants from northern and western Europe, and from native white Anglo-Saxon Protestants. The consequent clash of cultures was revealed in the nativist anti-immigrant movement that demanded that "new" immigrants conform to the Anglo-Saxon core culture, or better still, should not be allowed entry at all. Even those Progressives who supported the liberal melting-pot theory of immigrant assimilation still required immigrant cultural modification before the foreign-born could participate in the creation of the new society.

It became increasingly clear, however, that in the cities the immigrants were neither conforming nor melting, but keeping their cultural heritage. This pluralization generated much anxiety among some groups who feared that immigrants not only imported radical politics and Roman Catholicism, but were also a genetic pool of inferior racial stock. There were many, like the sociologist Edward A. Ross and the eugenicists Madison Grant and Robert De Courcy Ward, who felt that the immigrants could not govern themselves. Consequent upon the entry of America into World War I a new xenophobia broke out, which culminated in the 1917 Literacy Test intended to restrict the numbers of foreign-born entering the country. Passed over President Wilson's veto, the test marked the final success of anti-immigrant feeling in the Progressive years. More draconian controls were to be introduced in the postwar years.

Another problem of assimilation concerned the movement north of hundreds of thousands of blacks. The Progressive decades marked the start of a major folk migration from the rural South prompted by the need for unskilled labor in the northern factories. Throughout the era the reform of race relations was never a high priority, despite the efforts of black leaders like Booker T. Washington and W. E. B. Du Bois, and white Progressives like Oswald Garrison Villard. Washington had already attempted to reach his own détente with southern leaders in the 1890s. His speech to a white audience at the Atlanta Exposition in 1895—referred to by critics like Du Bois as the Atlanta Compromise—was an effort to gain some time for blacks during one of the worst periods of race exploitation in American history. In his address Washington proclaimed that blacks would only earn their civil rights through time and by working with whites, but within a system of racial segregation. Unfortunately his speech was followed in 1896 by the *Plessy* v. *Ferguson* case in which the Supreme Court upheld the infamous "separate but equal" doctrine, and thereby wrote segregation into the Constitution.

The black leadership soon split between the accommodationist Washington and the more forthright Du Bois, who maintained that blacks had to reshape society through the education of the "talented tenth" of the race. As a result Du Bois established the Niagara Movement in 1905 to pursue his vigorous demands for equality. The failure of this all-black group led Du Bois to join the white-led National Association for the Advancement of Colored People (NAACP), founded in 1909. The NAACP and the National Urban League, a social welfare agency for blacks established in 1911, became the leading civil-rights organizations during the Progressive period, providing a platform for lobbying Congress, and offering advice and more tangible assistance to blacks in the emergent ghettos. Neither, however, was able to change the entrenched racism in society or alleviate living and working conditions for the vast majority of urban blacks, and their political influence was limited.

Theodore Roosevelt was regarded as the only major white politician who was a friend of the African-American, but that friendship was more apparent than real. Roosevelt's racism was manifest when he labeled black troops serving in Cuba during the Spanish-American War of 1898 as cowards and deserters. As president, he agreed, in 1906, to the dishonorable discharge of a battalion of black soldiers for allegedly taking part in a riot in Brownsville, Texas. Matters deteriorated under Roosevelt's successor, William Howard Taft, who saw no inconsistency between the Fifteenth Amendment and disenfranchisement. Even fewer blacks were appointed to federal office under Taft than under Roosevelt, and Taft did not oppose segregation in the federal service. Both Roosevelt and Taft recognized that electoral success for the Republican party no longer depended upon the black vote.

Given these circumstances it was hardly remarkable that the Democratic candidate for the presidency, Woodrow Wilson, received a majority of black votes in the 1912 presidential election. Nevertheless, Wilson's New Freedom, as his platform was called, was far from color-blind, and his first term inaugurated an officially sanctioned segregation in federal government. For Wilson and many Democratic Progressives, the price of getting the New Freedom through Congress with Southern Democratic votes was the sacrifice of the black Americans. Progressivism and segregation grew together; one of the great paradoxes of Progressive thought was the desire to assimilate the foreign-born but segregate the black.

Just as the economic and demographic transformation of the early twentieth century overwhelmed city dwellers, it also seemed that local urban democracy was under threat from the political machines and bosses. Although political corruption in the city was by no means a new phenomenon, what Arthur A. Ekirch calls the "forces of urban liberalism" responded with much greater vigor than before to "the demands of both political and social Progressivism" and "combined to advance the cause of reform and good government."[14] By the 1890s the primary political unit in the city, the ward, reflected the economic, population, and spatial changes of the age of industrialism. In Boston, for example, the downtown wards were the poorest, had the highest concentrations of immigrants, and were the most heavily industrialized. The wards on the periphery were the wealthiest, and had the fewest immigrants and no industry. By 1900 the American city was economically, geographically, and culturally divided as never before. The political reformers shared British commentator James Bryce's opinion that American cities were the worst governed in the world. Richard Hofstadter adds that the stimulus for reform was "the alienation of the professionals."[15]

For Hofstadter the impulse toward political reform, as with social reform, was the anxiety felt among the middle ranks of society about their status in the new order. The modern age of mass politics, industrialism, immigration, and urbanization had destroyed the old social order. As a consequence many political reformers attempted to establish bourgeois hegemony under the guise of a resurgent democracy made more amenable to popular control. By attacking the corrupt politicos who depended upon a constituency of both immigrant and native poor, many Progressives were not actually rescuing democracy but sustaining and entrenching their own position. Thus, the effort to extend the naturalization period of immigrants and so isolate them from the political system was intended not to broaden democracy, but to restrict it.

From the reformers' perspective, ward-based blocs of immigrant votes were the foundations of corrupt political machines. Bosses like George Washington Plunkitt of New York City or Tom Pendergast of Kansas City were attacked, along with corrupt businessmen, as destroyers of American democracy. Some historians have posed the question whether the bosses, corrupt though they were, served useful social functions. Many bosses actually supported the kinds of Progressive reforms that did not directly affect their position, but which may have benefited their working-class constituents. An example of the latter would be Democratic ward boss John Fitzgerald, grandfather of John F. Kennedy and twice mayor of Boston between 1905 and 1914, who embraced political reform as a way of retaining political power and bending the local Democratic party to his will.

Nonetheless, many Progressives saw bossism as a problem, and their attack upon it took two main forms. There were attempts to alter the structure of local government so as to make it more difficult to elect corrupt politicians, by abolishing ward-based elections, and instituting referenda, recalls, and initiatives to make politicians more responsive to the popular will. Second, efforts were made to persuade middle-class reformers to enter politics. The assumptions underlying this strategy are clear: not all sections of society were to be involved in municipal decision-making, and the cities' best interests were to be served by denying political power to the laboring classes, native and foreign-born. Reform charters such as that enacted in Boston in 1909 ended ward-based elections. Elsewhere, secret ballots were introduced. In some cities city-manager plans, which replaced the mayor-council system of government with elected commissions of experts, were adopted. Although such approaches were briefly in vogue, they were never widely accepted. Progressivism still relied on the traditional politics of personality, and several notable reform mayors were elected in the early twentieth century, including Samuel "Golden Rule" Jones of Toledo, Patrick Collins of Boston, and Tom Johnson of Cleveland. Whatever their forms of government, the cities were the legal creatures of the states, and reformers often had to fight for their city reforms through the state legislatures. As a consequence, many cities had "Home Rule" movements that were directed toward divorcing the city from the often restrictive control of state government in favor of local autonomy in services such as policing.

Although the crusade for social and political justice was largely metropolitan in origin, states also became laboratories of reform. The rise of the corporate state, in which the trusts and big business exerted preponderant influence on government, could often only be directly attacked at the level of the individual states, where most monopolies were incorporated. As a result, a number of reform governors were elected like John P. Altgeld of Illinois, Hazen Pingree of Michigan, Hiram W. Johnson of California, Robert M. La Follette of Wisconsin, Theodore Roosevelt and Charles Evans Hughes of New York, and Woodrow Wilson of New Jersey. Even in the South, where liberalism was generally less evident than elsewhere, Jeff Davis of Arkansas, Joseph W. Folk of Missouri, James K. Vardaman of Mississippi, and Hoke Smith of Georgia established Progressive reputations.

The most celebrated of the reform governors was La Follette of Wisconsin, who pushed through a multifaceted program that included direct primaries, stricter controls over state civil service, regulation of railroad rates, conservation measures, and increased corporation taxes. After his departure, but at his instigation, Wisconsin also became the first state to enact a progressive income tax. La Follette was also responsible for the so-called "Wisconsin Idea," entailing a close liaison between the state government and the state university which allowed for a fruitful exchange of reform expertise in the field of social and political reconstruction. The regulatory commissions that he established and staffed with experts also became an important ingredient in Wisconsin's experiment in scientific government.

Wisconsin's reforms were widely copied, and other states made significant innovations of their own. The direct primary, pioneered by South Carolina in 1896, spelled the end for the old convention system of choosing party candidates, which had proved susceptible to boss control. The direct primary was in use in all except three states by 1916. Led by Nevada in 1899, thirty states adopted preferential primaries for the election of senators, and the Seventeenth Amendment to the Constitution finally mandated direct election of senators in 1913. Many states also adopted initiative, referendum, and recall procedures, and some, such as Oregon in 1908, enacted sweeping corrupt-practices legislation. The results of the political reforms were not everything that Progressives had hoped for. Party bosses, more experienced politicians than reformers, were often able to dominate elections, and special-interest groups could use their economic power to thwart reforms proposed through initiative and referendum.

More significant were the state laws that dealt with social conditions. By 1916 nearly two-thirds of states had insurance for victims of industrial accidents, many had enacted factory inspection laws, and some granted aid to mothers with dependent children. Nearly every state established a minimum age for employment (varying from twelve to sixteen years) and imposed limits on the employment of children of eight to ten hours a day. In 1914 Arizona became the first state to establish old age pensions. Though the law was struck down by the courts, the principle was finally accepted in the 1920s. Nonetheless, only eleven states had old age pensions before 1929, and no state had unemployment insurance until 1932.

Increasingly, too, the states became the tier of government that tackled corruption through the creation of a democratically organized bureaucracy, whose function was the regulation of corporations. Government regulation of big business within a democratic welfare framework became one of the central features of American liberalism during the Progressive era. Reformers believed that regulation by disinterested experts was the best way to control the industrial leviathan. Literally hundreds of state boards and commissions investigating almost every aspect of public life were instituted during the Progressive years. They established principles for the regulation of employment and the slums, investigated the consumption of alcohol and the effects of mass immigration, and attempted to end the corruption of the statewide political machines.

In the end, however, it was clear that the main symbols of the new order, the trusts, could only be controlled through federal action. Although the states had passed local anti-monopoly laws as early as the 1870s, the ultimate response had to come from Congress. In 1887 it passed the Interstate Commerce Act and in 1890 the Sherman Antitrust Act—both attempts to regulate the growth and abuses of monopoly power. Unfortunately the Sherman Act was ambiguous, in that it made illegal conspiracies among companies acting "in restraint of trade" but did not mention manufacturing. A series of cases heard before the Supreme Court in the 1890s failed to define the act's intentions, and as a result it did not halt the continued growth of monopoly power.

After the depression of 1893–96 there was a further merger movement prompted by the growing sophistication of the market in stocks and shares. In 1901 the United States Steel Corporation came into being out of a combination of Carnegie's steel companies and the financial interests of J. P. Morgan. It was described as the first billion-dollar company. Public opinion was also roused by the stock-market panic produced by the conflict between railroad interests in 1901, and the eventual compromise that resulted in the creation of the Northern Securities Company. This holding company, which tied together the vast business empires of James J. Hill, E. H. Harriman, and

J. P. Morgan, was an attempt to create a national monopoly in the railroads. Fearful that its farmers would be charged excessive rates, the state of Minnesota immediately began a suit against the company in the Supreme Court. By then the Roosevelt administration was planning a federal suit. National interest was further stimulated by the creation of other monopolies in the production of beef, sugar, agricultural machinery, and alcohol.

It was to Theodore Roosevelt that the antitrust movement owed its national reputation. When he became president as a result of the assassination of William McKinley in 1901, he was only forty-three years old and famous for his exuberance. This "steam engine in trousers," as he was once described, had established his antitrust position as governor of New York. Roosevelt had a much more sophisticated view of corporate power than his sobriquet of "trustbuster" might suggest. Early on in his presidency he recognized that monopoly was an inescapable consequence of the emergent corporate economy. His solution to the problem of the trusts was regulation, not a futile attempt at destruction.

The Roosevelt administration's most famous attempt at regulation was the prosecution in 1904 of the Northern Securities Company. The case reached the Supreme Court which held that the company was in violation of the 1890 Sherman Anti-Trust Act and consequently against the public interest. Following this success Congress passed several regulatory acts designed to address Progressive antimonopoly concerns. The Hepburn Railroad Rate Act of 1906 allowed the Interstate Commerce Commission (ICC) to declare certain railroad rates illegal and enforce new ones. The Mann-Elkins Act of 1910 further strengthened the power of the ICC in controlling railroad rate policy, and extended regulation to telephone and telegraph companies.

Although attacks on the trusts continued with Roosevelt's successor, Taft, the high point for the movement to control corporate power came in 1913–14 with Woodrow Wilson's New Freedom policies. Wilson came to national prominence as a reforming governor of New Jersey, where he attacked the corrupt state political machine. In the 1912 presidential election, with Roosevelt representing the Progressive party, Taft the Republicans, and Wilson the Democrats, it became clear that Wilson rejected Roosevelt's New Nationalism platform. Unlike Roosevelt, Wilson did not accept the inevitability of the trusts and corporate power. Appealing to the premodern traditions of Jeffersonian individualism, Wilson argued that the trusts could be broken. How it was to be achieved was far less clear than Wilson's certainty that it could be done.

In theory Wilson's New Freedom policies reemphasized America's old precorporate values of free enterprise, free markets, and free competition. They recognized, however, that federal activism rather than traditional laissez-faire principles was essential for the achievement of these goals. Accordingly, Wilson sought not only to curb the trusts, but also to reform the tariff system and introduce currency and banking reform. Although Wilson's comprehension of these issues in Progressive terms may have been limited, he nevertheless knew he had to control corporate power.

Committed as he was to the notion of free market, it was the tariff that engaged Wilson's immediate attention upon entering office. Thanks mainly to his efforts, the Underwood Tariff became law in October 1913, cutting duties from 37 percent to 27 percent and extending the list of free items. While not opening the United States to free trade the Underwood Tariff at least halted the established trend toward high levels of protection for U.S. industry and the trusts. The loss of revenue from duties was partially offset with the introduction of federal income tax, levied under the newly ratified Sixteenth Amendment. This had some progressive features in that the burden rose in accordance with income, but the top rate was only 7 percent on incomes above $500,000 (the base rate was 1 percent on families with an annual income of $3,000, which excluded most Americans).

Wilson's antitrust policy manifested the contradictory strands of Progressive thought concerning the problem of business monopoly. In line with his New Freedom campaign, his initial concern appeared to be trust-busting, and he supported the Clayton Act which toughened the Sherman law by prohibiting interlocking directorates, specifying unfair trade practices, and excluding trade unions from its controls. However, Wilson had already shifted ground to give priority to regulation. Legislation enacted in September 1914 established a new regulatory body, the Federal Trade Commission, which was empowered to define unfair trade practices and issue cease and desist orders in cases of unfair competition. The commission's main power lay in public investigation and in its apparent acceptance of big business, suggesting that Wilson now agreed with the New Nationalist philosophy. Compromises in other areas came in response to various political pressures and reveal Wilson more as a pragmatist than as a man of moral principle.

Never a strong social justice Progressive, Wilson originally opposed federal laws that would protect children at work, provide subsidies for farmers, or enact female suffrage. But he reversed his position on each of these issues when the midterm election results came in. Following the Republican gains in 1914, Progressive-inspired legislation poured out of Congress with presidential approval. These included the La Follette Seamen's Act of 1915 to protect the rights and conditions of merchant seamen; a workmen's compensation law for federal employees in 1916; the Keating-Owen Child Labor Act of 1916, which excluded goods manufactured by children under fourteen from interstate commerce; and the Adamson Act of 1916, which provided an eight-hour day for federal workers on the railroads. In addition, the Federal Farm Loan Act of 1916 brought the Populist dream of cheap rural credit to reality. Wilson even supported votes for women from 1916, and female suffrage was finally achieved throughout the United States with the passage of the Nineteenth Amendment in 1920.

The view of Wilson as a coy Progressive is confirmed by the history of the Federal Reserve Act of 1913, which marked the first major reform of the banking system since the Jacksonian era of the 1830s. The act established twelve regional Federal Reserve banks to hold the reserves of member banks. Through alterations in the reserve requirements, or by varying the interest charged for loans, the Federal Reserve could affect money supply and credit as economic conditions required. Although influenced by the work of his adviser Louis D. Brandeis, Wilson was prompted less by Progressive zeal in promoting the legislation than by bankers themselves seeking an infusion of order in the increasingly chaotic world of finance. The act was a compromise between bankers, agrarian interests, and reformers, and it failed entirely to satisfy any group. The shortcomings of the new system were revealed by the crash of 1929. Nevertheless, the act was the first step toward federal economic management which would become a fundamental feature of twentieth-century America.

The presidencies of Roosevelt and Wilson represent major shifts in the character of American government. Regulation, the centerpiece of their reform programs, indicated the form that government was to take for the rest of the century. In this respect, America mirrored Britain and Germany where the growth of the regulatory state also produced substantial changes in the bureaucratic scope and style of government. In the American case, the initial proliferation of state regulatory agencies was followed by similar developments at the federal level. The Federal Trade Commission and Federal Reserve Board were the two leading examples of the new agencies that had supervisory powers over the marketplace. Others, most notably the Department of Commerce and Labor created in 1903 and divided into two separate departments in 1913, were primarily information-gathering bodies. However, their very existence testified to the importance accorded to commerce and labor by government, and the information they provided assisted other bodies in the task of regulation.

The development of the regulatory state was in part a by-product of the cult of the expert and efficiency, but it was also an inevitable part of the process of cultural hegemony exercised by the new industrial elite. The dominance of the new business classes was best served not by the establishment of a repressive state, but by creating complex modern bureaucratic structures that influenced and directed people's lives.

The Progressive state, with the independent regulatory commission as its principal instrument, recognized and counterbalanced the rise of the modern corporate economy. In essence it adapted to government the principles of Fordism, a term derived from the methods of Henry Ford, the most significant entrepreneur of the early twentieth century. *Fordism* refers to the corporate form of business organization and production refined by a detailed division of labor, the application of Frederick W. Taylor's principles of scientific management, and Henry Ford's own special insight that mass production entailed mass consumption. In short, Fordism as applied by Progressive reformers represented the rational, modernist democratic state, which would impose order on chaos through a new regulatory governmental system.

In presidential terms both Roosevelt and Wilson were activists who established the twentieth-century view of the presidency as a potent interventionist force in government. The Republicans under Roosevelt were pushed increasingly toward an acknowledgment of the power of the corporate state, and the Democrats under Wilson came to recognize that their traditional states' rights legacy required substantial modification. This was not achieved easily—Roosevelt split his party over the issue in the election of 1912 and Wilson had personal difficulties in coming to terms with it. In all, the Progressive era was the seedplot not only for the political divisions that were to emerge after World War I, but more significantly, for the evolution of the nature of government represented by the New Deal in the 1930s and beyond.

Although Progressivism was essentially a series of social, political, and cultural responses to domestic American economic development, there were equally profound changes taking place in America's international relations. It was during the Progressive decades that the United States finally acknowledged its world role. This process began well before 1900.

American expansionism had focused on continental empire for much of the nineteenth century, but it turned into a salt-water imperialism in the 1890s. Several different forces operated to propel America into its twentieth-century world role. The belief in the need for overseas markets to serve the massive output of America's heavy industry, and the desire to protect those economic interests once established, were powerful factors. A national sense of mission to extend to other nations the benefits of American democracy was also significant. The 1898 conflict with Spain over Cuba was couched in terms of a war on behalf of self-determination, but in practice the war was really a sop to a growing popular jingoism. Spain's refusal to give Cuba its independence was the signal that eventually forced McKinley to act. The peace treaty that ended the brief Spanish-American War gave the United States new possessions, notably the Philippines. Not everyone welcomed the acquisitions, and many Progressives spoke out against what appeared to be a breach with America's isolationist and democratic traditions.

The war over Cuba made clear the necessity for an American-controlled canal across the Central American isthmus. After a convenient revolt against Colombian rule in 1903, a canal treaty was signed with Panama and Roosevelt's "highway of civilization" was eventually opened to traffic in 1914. This helped expand American trade with the Far East immeasurably, but America's interest in China had been well established much earlier. Fears that Europe might divide up China prompted Secretary of State John Hay in 1899 to suggest the Open Door policy, whereby all the major Western powers would have equal access to the Chinese market. Other international events brought America onto the world stage. The war between Japan and Russia allowed a willing Roosevelt to accept the role of arbitrator in 1905 at Japan's request.

Roosevelt's realistic appraisal of power politics, which produced a working relationship between America and Japan, was lost on his successor. William Howard Taft and his secretary of state, Philander C. Knox, tried unsuccessfully to revive the Open Door policy by stimulating American private investment in the Far East. This "dollar diplomacy" was ultimately rejected by Woodrow Wilson who disapproved of both Roosevelt's pragmatic "big stick" and Taft's dollars. Nevertheless his evangelical interventionism in the Caribbean and Central and South America, notably in Nicaragua, Haiti, the Dominican Republic and even in Mexico, exceeded that of Roosevelt and Taft together. Wilson's actions, although justified by the moral rhetoric of upholding international law, were often closely associated with the need to protect American economic interests.

Both economics and morality played a part in bringing the United States into World War I, but when the European war began in 1914 most Americans were surprised and initially happy to stay neutral. The war inevitably created domestic upheavals, not least by emphasizing ethnic divisions. However, the majority of Americans felt a cultural affinity with the Western Allies—Britain, France, Italy, and Belgium. Distrust of German militarism overcame feelings of Anglo-Saxon solidarity, and in 1917 the policy of unrestricted submarine warfare confirmed popular convictions that Germany was a warmonger. Despite Wilson's protestations of neutrality, the United States became increasingly supportive of the Allies. The sinking of the *Lusitania* in May 1915 produced a strong U.S. reaction, par-

ticularly as American lives were lost. Despite German as-
surances, other ships were also sunk and the war became the
chief issue in the 1916 presidential election. In the event,
Wilson won a narrow victory on a platform of peace and Progressivism over the Republican candidate, Supreme Court Justice Charles Evans Hughes. The resumption by Germany of
unrestricted submarine warfare, however, ended Wilson's hopes
of bringing about a negotiated peace between the belligerents,
and in April 1917 he asked Congress to declare what for him
was a righteous war. Conscription followed and within two
months American soldiers were in France. Within six months
3.5 million Americans were under arms, and given the massive
American commitment victory was ultimately assured. At home
the war proved to be a significant factor in the close of the
Progressive movement.

The connection between America's involvement in the
war and the end of Progressivism has long engaged the attention of historians. Traditionally, the war was seen as the
"nemesis of reform," but some historians argue that the war
simply accelerated the decay in Progressivism that was already
occurring after the climacteric of the 1912 election and Wilson's
first term. Others suggest that the conflict turned America away
from its preoccupation with reform by placing a new national
agenda before the public, and that the demands of patriotism
reduced the relevance of Progressivism.

The relationship between war and social change is highly
complex. In one recent examination of the war's impact on
American society it has been argued that "whole sections of the
community found their lives transformed by the war."[16] The
war brought full employment, a rise in real wages, an increase
in union membership, and recognition of labor in the War Labor
Board and in other wartime agencies. Although the war effort
produced a huge expansion in government activity, the ends of
government had changed. The prosecution of war replaced the
regulation of corporate power as the primary objective. Often
with the cooperation and involvement of businessmen, the
federal government assumed greater powers than ever before,
and through bodies such as the War Industries Board and the
Food Administration, directly influenced economic activities.
Government agencies determined priorities in terms of raw ma-

terials and manpower, drew up minimum standards of hours and wages for war workers, established codes to protect women in work, and even began the first federal housing program in congested war-boom towns. Some prewar issues, such as Prohibition, immigration restriction, and votes for women, were resolved during or shortly after, and partly because of, the war. On the other hand, racial tension was exacerbated by wartime migration and black military service, and labor violence increased as strikes were stigmatized as unpatriotic and disloyal. While the AFL became incorporated in the war effort, the IWW and the Socialist Party of America became victims of repression under espionage and sedition legislation. Conformity was further encouraged by the Committee on Public Information which shaped and "nationalized" public opinion and encouraged the mood of intolerance that, under the guise of Americanism, spilled over into the Red Scare of 1919. Concern for social justice was not compatible with the predominantly conservative era that followed.

While the wartime and postwar hysteria was in some ways a reaction against the change and upheaval of the war years, it also reflected the tensions and conflict evident in America in the preceding two generations. The first decades of the twentieth century were given coherence by the cultural flux resulting from America's need to come to terms with both its history and its future. The processes of modernization following the Civil War had created a society upon new economic foundations. This produced a unique ideological challenge to traditional concepts of laissez-faire. In the views of historians such as Hofstadter and Ekirch, the Progressive response was to pioneer the American welfare state, not out of a desire for socialism or big government, but rather to sanitize socialism and, of necessity, use government to check the growth of corporate power. In the end, although the Progressive era produced few solutions for the nation's dilemmas, it remains significant as the period when America began to address the consequences of corporate economic power and the metropolitanization and pluralization of twentieth-century society. Progressive reformers increasingly acknowledged the need for a bureaucratized and interventionist state apparatus to cope with the social and economic problems of the new industrial order. Many also accepted the need for America's rise to world power. As such they charted the course that American liberalism would follow at home and abroad for much of the twentieth century.

Notes

1. Henry Adams, *The Education of Henry Adams* (New York, 1907), pp. 487, 496—98.

2. Walter E. Weyl, *The New Democracy* (New York, 1914), p. 1.

3. David W. Noble, *The Progressive Mind, 1890—1917* (Chicago, 1970), p. 4.

4. Karl Marx and Friedrich Engels, *Manifesto of the Communist Party* (London, 1888), p. 46.

5. James J. Kloppenberg, *Uncertain Victory: Social Democracy and Progressivism in European and American Thought, 1870—1920* (New York, 1986), p. 299.

6. Richard Hofstadter, *The Age of Reform* (New York, 1955), pp. 135—66.

7. Eric F. Goldman, *Rendezvous with Destiny: A History of Modern American Reform* (New York, 1956); Gabriel Kolko, *The Triumph of Conservatism: A Reinterpretation of American History, 1900—1916* (New York, 1963).

8. Samuel P. Hays, "The Politics of Reform in Municipal Government in the Progressive Era," *Pacific Northwest Quarterly* 55 (1964): 157—69; Robert H. Wiebe, *The Search for Order 1877—1920* (New York, 1967).

9. Richard L. McCormick, *From Realignment to Reform: Political Change in New York State, 1893—1910* (Ithaca, N.Y., 1981).

10. Andrew Carnegie, "Wealth," *North American Review* (June 1889): 656—66.

11. Arthur A. Ekirch, *Progressivism in America: A Study of the Era from Theodore Roosevelt to Woodrow Wilson* (New York, 1974), pp. 67—89.

12. Eric Foner, "Why Is There No Socialism in the United States?" *History Workshop Journal* 17 (1984): 57—80.

13. Louis Hartz, *The Liberal Tradition in America* (New York, 1955).

14. Ekirch, *Progressivism in America*, pp. 90—91.

15. Hofstadter, *The Age of Reform*, p. 148.
16. Neil A. Wynn, *From Progressivism to Prosperity* (New York and London, 1986), p. xviii.

Bibliography

The best general introductions to this period remain Samuel P. Hays, *The Response to Industrialism: 1885–1914* (Chicago, 1957); Richard Hofstadter, *The Age of Reform: From Bryan to FDR* (New York; 1955); and *The Progressive Movement 1900–1915* (Englewood Cliffs, N.J., 1963). More detailed introductions include Robert Wiebe, *The Search for Order, 1877–1920* (New York, 1967); David W. Noble, *The Progressive Mind, 1890–1917* (Chicago, 1970); Arthur A. Ekirch, Jr., *Progressivism in America: A Study of the Era from Theodore Roosevelt to Woodrow Wilson* (New York, 1974). For more recent treatments see T. J. Jackson Lears, *No Place of Grace: Antimodernism and the Transformation of American Culture* (New York, 1981); Nell Painter, *Standing at Armageddon* (New York, 1987); and John Milton Cooper, Jr., *Pivotal Decades: The United States, 1900–1920* (New York, 1990). Within a smaller compass there are several pamphlets/articles that are essential introductory reading, notably John Buenker, "The Progressive Era: A Search for a Synthesis," *Mid-America* 51 (1969): 175–93, David P. Thelen, "Social Tensions and the Origins of Progressivism," *Journal of American History* 56 (1969): 323–41, and J. A. Thompson, *Progressivism*, British Association for American Studies, Pamphlet No. 2, 1979. See also T. J. Jackson Lears's important article "The Concept of Cultural Hegemony: Problems and Possibilities," *American Historical Review* 90 (1985): 567–93.

On industry, the trusts, and the effects of late-nineteenth-century economic change, see Alan Trachtenberg, *The Incorporation of America: Culture and Society in the Gilded Age* (New York, 1982), and on the nature of the corporate state see Gabriel Kolko, *The Triumph of Conservatism: A Reinterpretation of American History, 1900–1916* (New York, 1963); James Weinstein, *The Corporate Ideal in the Liberal State: 1900–1918* (Boston, 1968); Eric F. Goldman, *Rendezvous with Destiny: A History of Modern American Reform* (New York, 1956); Samuel P. Hays, *Conservation and the Gospel of Efficiency* (Cambridge,

Mass., 1959); and R. Jeffrey Lustig, *Corporate Liberalism: The Origins of Modern American Political Theory, 1890–1920* (Berkeley and Los Angeles, 1982). On social reconstruction see Robert H. Bremner, *From the Depths: The Discovery of Poverty in the United States* (New York, 1956), and Paul Boyer, *Urban Masses and Moral Order in America, 1820–1920* (Cambridge, Mass., and London, 1978). On comparisons with Europe and the transatlantic perspective see James J. Kloppenberg, *Uncertain Victory: Social Democracy and Progressivism in European and American Thought, 1870–1920* (New York, 1986).

On the history of labor see Philip S. Foner, *History of the Labor Movement in the United States* (New York, 1965), and on socialism Irving Howe, *Socialism and America* (San Diego, Calif., 1985); James Weinstein, *The Decline of Socialism in America, 1912–1925* (New York, 1967); and Melvin Dubofsky, *We Shall Be All: A History of the Industrial Workers of the World* (New York, 1969). The best recent article on socialism is by Eric Foner, "Why Is There No Socialism in the United States?" *History Workshop Journal* 17 (1984): 57–80. The debate on consensus versus hegemony is best introduced in T. J. Jackson Lears's article "The Concept of Cultural Hegemony," cited above, but Louis Hartz remains the next stop, *The Liberal Tradition in America* (New York, 1955). On the literature of the Progressive decades and muckraking in particular see Louis Filler, *Crusaders for American Liberalism* (New York, 1939). On the literature of the Progressive era see Michael Spindler, *American Literature and Society: William Dean Howells to Arthur Miller* (London, 1983), and Arun Mukherjee, *The Gospel of Wealth in the American Novel* (London, 1987).

The expansion in recent years of the material on women is daunting. Most accessible are Aileen Kraditor, *The Ideas of the Women's Suffrage Movement, 1890–1920* (New York, 1965); William L. O'Neill, *Everyone Was Brave: The Rise and Fall of Feminism in America* (Chicago, 1969); Ann Douglas, *The Feminization of American Culture* (New York, 1977); Ruth Bleier, *Science and Gender: A Critique of Biology and Its Theories on Women* (New York, 1984); Angela Davis, *Women, Race and Class* (New York, 1981); Margaret Forster, *Significant Sisters: The Grassroots of Active Feminism: 1839–1939* (London, 1984); and Nancy Woloch, *Women and the American Experience* (New York, 1984).

The position of the foreign-born during the Progressive decades is treated admirably in John Bodnar, *The Transplanted: A History of Immigrants in Urban America* (Bloomington, Ind., 1985). On nativism see John Higham, *Strangers in the Land: Patterns of American Nativism: 1860–1925* (New York, 1963). An excellent examination of the immigrant urban experience and contribution to a major industry is James R. Barrett, *Work and Community in the Jungle: Chicago's Packinghouse Workers, 1894–1922* (Urbana, Ill., and Chicago, 1987). For the black during the period see August Meier, *Negro Thought in America, 1880–1915: Racial Ideologies in the Age of Booker T. Washington* (Ann Arbor, Mich., 1963); David Gordon Nielson, *Black Ethos: Northern Urban Negro Life and Thought, 1890–1930* (Westport, Conn., and London, 1977); and Robert L. Allen, *Reluctant Reformers* (New York, 1975).

Political corruption has always interested historians, and the best introduction is Frank Mann Stewart, *A Half Century of Municipal Reform* (Berkeley, Calif., 1950); see also Alexander B. Callow, *The City Bosses in America* (New York, 1976). There are many local and state studies of the Progressive decades, notably David P. Thelen, *The New Citizenship: Origins of Progressivism in Wisconsin, 1885–1900* (Columbia, Mo., 1972); Samuel T. McSeveny, *The Politics of Depression: Political Behavior in the Northeast, 1893–1896* (New York, 1972); and Richard Jensen, *The Winning of the Midwest: Social and Political Conflict 1888–1896* (Chicago, 1971). On national politics and the changing character of government the key texts are George E. Mowry, *The Era of Theodore Roosevelt and the Birth of Modern America, 1900–1912* (New York, 1958); Arthur S. Link, *Woodrow Wilson and the Progressive Era: 1910–1917* (New York, 1954); and Richard L. McCormick, *From Realignment to Reform: Political Change in New York State, 1893–1910* (Ithaca, 1981). On America's emergence as a world power see Foster R. Dulles, *America's Rise to World Power, 1898–1954* (New York, 1955); Howard K. Beale, *Theodore Roosevelt and the Rise of America to World Power* (New York, 1956); and Arthur S. Link, *Wilson the Diplomatist* (New York, 1957). Recent studies of the effects of World War I include Neil A. Wynn, *From Progressivism to Prosperity* (New York and London, 1986), and David M. Kennedy, *Over Here: The First World War and American Society* (New York and Oxford, 1980).

2

Normalcy, Prosperity, and Depression, 1919–1933

Ian Purchase

Seventy years on, a review of the American 1920s suggests some revealing comparisons with our own times. Both eras follow the end of major international conflicts—World War I and the Cold War. Both begin the search for a new world order to stabilize international relations. In each case the ending of hostilities appears to vindicate the American national mission. The "war to end all wars" saw the triumph of liberal democracy, and in the early 1990s the collapse of communism in the Soviet Union and its satellite regimes in Eastern Europe has left liberal capitalism without a major ideological challenger. In both instances the need for a new world order brings economic issues to the foreground, above all the role of the United States in stabilizing the world economy and in managing the flow of international investment. This role was arguably more central in the 1920s than it has been in the early 1990s.

Comparisons go further. The processes of economic development, accelerated by technological innovation and communications revolutions as remarkable as those of the late nineteenth century, change organizational structures, production methods, and the relations between producer and consumer, producer and government. In the 1920s change focused on the development of a national economy and oligopolistic corporations. More recently, it has centered on the creation of an international economy and multinational companies. These changes, among others, provoke renewed consideration of the role of government, federal and state, in the operation of a private-enterprise economy. The 1920s were the successor to Progressivism's overhaul of nineteenth-century laissez-faire principles, while the 1990s are the legatees of the Reagan administration's attempt to overturn the welfare state of the New Deal and the Great Society. Beneath the surface of political rhetoric in both periods lie some fundamental questions about the relationship between government and governed. Should government embody and enact a consensus of national values or should it establish and police a national arena within which contending values can interact and thereby strengthen the quality of national life and institutions? Is the primary commitment of government to the interests of the individual or to those of the community?

The prevalent political mood of both periods is characterized by a conservatism that is innovative as well as reactionary. The uneasy coexistence of tradition and change and the relentless modifications of social institutions, habits and lifestyles, linked in a complex, long-term relationship with economic change, provoke and sustain a recurrent debate about cultural values in both eras. Demographic change, particularly that brought about by migration and immigration, results in ethnocultural tension between dominant white groups and subordinate racial and ethnic groups: African-Americans and recently arrived immigrants from southern and eastern Europe in the 1920s and, more recently, African- and Hispanic Americans. In each period the displacement of social groups also generates a sense of cultural crisis evident in the powerful revival of religious fundamentalism and demands for social prohibitions.

There are, of course, some significant differences too. The world role of the United States is significantly greater now than it was then. Its governmental functions are more varied and complex. The American economy is less buoyant and dominant now than in the 1920s when the United States was both the world's major industrial manufacturer and the major producer of agricultural commodities. And contemporary corporate and political leaders, looking toward America's twenty-first century, are less confident of the nation's future than were the apostles of the century's third decade, which they called the New Era. Rooted in their experience during World War I, many economists, businessmen and politicians advocated a "new era" for the American economy. According to William Barber, their ideas developed between 1921 and 1928 as an "implicit model." The model proposed that national economic performance could be improved through "informed manipulation" and empirical method, and that the development of a distinctive and superior American standard of living would benefit humanity.[1]

These introductory comparisons establish some central themes for a review of the American twenties. The period marked the decline, but not the end, of some traditional attitudes and institutions and the rise, but not the full development, of modernizing mechanisms within an expanding economy. In some instances, older ideas and practices were given a new lease on life and legitimacy. It was a period of transitions, as often complacently praised as they were strongly attacked.

The transitional nature of the decade is well illustrated by the political personalities of the three Republican presidents whose administrations spanned the decade. Warren G. Harding (1921–23), Calvin Coolidge (1923–29) and Herbert Hoover (1929–33) have been traditionally viewed as three of the least effective holders of presidential office due to idleness, incompetence, or ideological disposition. Harding has been portrayed as genial and corrupt with little capacity to conceptualize, let alone resolve, the issues confronting his administration. Coolidge, on the other hand, has been characterized as a taciturn do-nothing, overly compliant with the self-serving interests of big business. And Herbert Hoover, in the words of historian Richard Hofstadter, was "the last presidential spokesman of the hallowed doctrines of laissez-faire liberalism, and his departure from Washington marked the decline of a great tradition."[2]

More balanced presidential reputations have emerged with historical revision. Warren Harding's personality and political allegiances reflected old-time, small-town Ohio loyalties. He was gregarious, affable, and politically cautious, but he also recognized that a modernizing economy made new demands on government. His cabinet and policies reflected this duality. Political appointments included long-standing cronies such as

Harry Daugherty (attorney general) and Albert Fall (Interior) and, despite conservative opposition within the party, four able and effective cabinet officers: Andrew Mellon (Treasury), Charles Evans Hughes (State), Henry C. Wallace (Agriculture), and Herbert Hoover (Commerce). While his administration bowed to conservative pressure for protectionism, tax reductions, and limited government, Harding also supported the activist policies of his able cabinet members in negotiating postwar international settlements, promoting efficient government, and tackling some of the longer-term economic problems revealed by the depression in the early twenties.

Calvin Coolidge's New England small-town origins proved to be a political asset in an increasingly urban and sophisticated age. According to historian Ellis Hawley, Coolidge was "almost a folk hero" because "he became a symbol of integrity and simplicity in an age of organisation, extravagance, and threatening change."[3] Although there was a good deal of continuity with the Harding administration in terms of policies and personnel, Coolidge emphasized the more conservative elements of Harding's fiscal measures. Tax reductions benefited the wealthy on the grounds that this would stimulate investment and generate more economic activity and greater general prosperity. This "trickle-down" economic theory can be viewed as a precursor of the supply-side economics popular in the 1980s. Indeed, Ronald Reagan—surely a folk hero for his own times—was an admirer of Coolidge. The correspondence is even closer since Coolidge, like Reagan, was unable to keep federal expenditure down. Despite its laissez-faire image, the Coolidge administration maintained the transition toward modern government.

Revisionist history has generally attributed the increased activity of the federal government to the energy and inspiration of Herbert Hoover. Indeed, Hoover has been viewed as the chief architect of the New Era. As one of his cabinet colleagues tartly remarked, Hoover was secretary of commerce and "under secretary of everything else." He sought to extend the role of government as facilitator, organizing national conferences of expert opinion, increasing his department's role as a gatherer and publicist of new ideas, and promoting standardization and trade associations in order to eliminate waste and create efficient competition. Advocating a new voluntarism, he stressed the need for cooperation among interest groups and recognized that a consensus among labor, industrial management, and farmers was dependent upon economic growth. Hoover's voluntarism drew on the deep-rooted American values of self-reliance and individualism, and the new ideology was a combination of modernity and tradition. Unquestionably modern was his conviction that a consumer economy was emerging to replace an older producer economy, and this belief was evident in his energetic attempts to improve working conditions and raise wages in order to enhance purchasing power. And, believing that economic growth was essential to the development of the society that he envisaged, he was a keen promoter of an expansionist foreign trade policy.

Hoover formulated, in theory and in practice as cabinet officer and president, the only fresh reworking of liberal ideology to emerge in the New Era. In this task he had supporters such as Henry Wallace—who was often a bureaucratic rival as well—and opponents such as Andrew Mellon. His conception of the associative state neatly reconciled the development of an efficient, bureaucratic governmental machinery with traditional principles of self-management by state governments and private bodies. The model for the associative state lay partly in the wartime regulatory boards of the Wilson administration. Indeed, Hoover succeeded in placing many wartime members of these boards who were favorable to his ideas on the major federal regulatory commissions. Identifying collective interest groups, the federal government was to work cooperatively with private organizations. However, federal agencies with a more combative attitude to business practice, notably the Interstate Commerce Commission, remained resistant to Hoover's persuasion.

The success of the associative state was limited. It appeared to work effectively during the short depression at the outset of the decade and during the period of growth that followed, but not during the prolonged depression after 1929. This was partly because the associative state recognized only organized economic interest groups—even labor to some degree—but this excluded unorganized sectors of the population and social interest groups from its attention. Moreover, true to his principles, Hoover refused to use governmental power to regulate and coerce. This weakened some of his presidential initiatives in combating depression, for which he has been frequently criticized. Ironically, however, Hoover's vision has attracted favorable attention from both left and right. The New Left historian William Appleman Williams has praised Hoover for preserving the principles of voluntarism and community action against the invasive encroachments of the corporate state.[4] Conversely, Hoover's model of association has proved valuable in the conservative revamping of the federal government in the 1980s.

It was not only the federal government that became more activist during the 1920s. Many state governments did so too, following the lead of Hoover and Wallace. They extended professional services to corporations and private organizations and were more active in the field of social welfare than Washington. Efficient and scientific management was sought by states as varied as conservative Maryland and progressive Wisconsin. State expenditure amounted to 75 percent of all public spending during the decade, and it doubled between 1922 and 1932. The bulk of state spending went on highway construction and education, and much of the necessary revenues was raised through bond flotations and the increasingly popular—and regressive— sales tax. However, state fiscal conservatism ran deep. In the 1930s many state treasuries paid off debts incurred in the twenties rather than adopt deficit spending in order to meet the needs of the destitute and to regenerate local economies. States did not experiment with venture capital and collaborative investment as many were to do in the 1980s. Undoubtedly advances were made in state administration during the 1920s, but the record of the following decade suggests that further improvement was called for. The implementation of New Deal measures was hindered by fiscal conservatism, constitutional limitations to effective action, the need for legislative reapportionment, and localized partisan politics, which were often corrupt and boss-dominated.

The transitional nature of the decade is also evident in foreign policy. On the one hand the forces of tradition were powerful, particularly in the aftermath of a world war that had heightened nationalist fervor and ethnic loyalties and hostilities. The Versailles peace settlement had frustrated ambitions for arrangements that would both establish a stable world order and permit the United States its traditional unilateral freedom of action. Public opinion and congressional judgment were therefore most frequently in favor of military and diplomatic withdrawal, trade protectionism, and the restoration of unilateralism. On the other hand, administration policymakers persistently sought to build a new world order based on arms limitation, international arbitration, and economic development. Here, they presaged some of the major axioms of later twentieth-century American foreign policy.

The foundations of New Era foreign policy were laid by Charles Evans Hughes and were developed by his successors as secretary of state, Frank B. Kellogg and Henry L. Stimson. Hughes, with President Harding's support, concluded a series of bilateral peace treaties with the Central Powers that incorporated most of the major provisions of the Treaty of Versailles. He went on to negotiate membership of the World Court, but this was blocked, like the subsequent attempt by Coolidge and Kellogg, because the Senate attached too many conditions to membership. In an effort to achieve military stabilization, and in particular to restrain the rising power of Japan, Hughes called the major powers to the Washington Conference in 1921. A series of treaties emerged the following year that limited naval armaments, established a framework for peaceful cooperation in the Pacific and Far East, and guaranteed equal economic access to China, thus endorsing America's traditional Open Door policy.

A further attempt was made by Coolidge and Kellogg in 1927 to limit the construction of naval warships, but it met with little response from rearming nations. Following an initiative from the French foreign minister, Aristide Briand, a multilateral agreement—the Kellogg-Briand Pact—was concluded in 1928. Its signatories agreed not to use war as a means of advancing, rather than defending, their national interests. Although a welcome expression of international goodwill, its substance was slight—a point not lost on President Coolidge. International responses to Japanese incursions in Manchuria in 1931 were weak despite the violations of the diplomatic agreements of the decade. President Hoover realized that sanctions would be ineffective, and Stimson declared on behalf of the administration that the United States would not recognize any gains made by Japan. As a result, greater strategic importance was attached to the American military presence in the Philippines.

Hughes was also responsible for laying the groundwork for a new policy toward Latin America. A series of bilateral agreements was concluded that cleared the way for a renunciation of the use of American force in the hemisphere—thus voiding the Roosevelt Corollary of the Monroe Doctrine—and the injection of American investment to stimulate economic development. The new policies were threatened by Coolidge's dispatch of troops to Nicaragua in 1926 and by worsening relations with Mexico. However, successful diplomacy by Coolidge's envoy, Stimson, in Nicaragua and by Ambassador Dwight W. Morrow in Mexico paved the way for a more ambitious Pan-American policy. This was signaled by the goodwill tour of the region by President-elect Hoover and later extended by Franklin D. Roosevelt's Good Neighbor policy.

Although New Era diplomats began to open significant new initiatives in foreign policy, they were unable to fulfill their promise. Lack of support from Congress and a broadly isolationist public partly explains this. So does the commitment of European nations to their own, often narrowly conceived, national interests. But the New Era also failed to develop adequate mechanisms to sustain and control foreign policy. Hughes and Hoover hoped to channel American overseas investment into development that would benefit the recipient nation as well as the home investor. The inadequacy of their advisory controls resulted in imprudent speculative investment that helped to destabilize Europe and Latin America. To put this in perspective, however, it should be noted that overseas trade and investment in the 1920s amounted to only 5 percent and 3 percent respectively of GNP. The success of the New Era must ultimately be judged by its domestic policies.

This analysis has so far suggested some important continuities in the decade, but domestic events suggest some subtle changes taking place within the period. Four phases can be identified: 1919–21, characterized by postwar social and economic instability; 1922–25, the years of most rapid economic growth and social change which the novelist F. Scott Fitzgerald identified as the Jazz Age; 1925–29, a period of economic stabilization and social retrenchment; and 1929–33, marked by the deepening and debilitating catastrophe of the Great Depression.

Of all the transitions in the decade that from war to peace

proved the most traumatic. It released great depths of anger, frustration, and anxiety. Americans were taken by surprise by the ending of hostilities in 1918. Many, even among the well-informed, had expected the war to continue for months, perhaps years. The war economy and its attendant government controls had only just begun to work at peak capacity when rapid demobilization threw both into reverse. The effects of this reversal were worsened by President Woodrow Wilson's decision not to develop a policy of postwar reconstruction and to allow the economy to redirect itself. The speed of this turnaround partly explains the period of acute dislocation in the winter of 1918–19. Wartime government agencies were wound down, factories were closed or changed production, and farmers faced diminishing markets. Demobilization exacerbated not only the tensions and dislocations of the war period itself but also the deeper strains evident within the economy and society. As a result, the immediate postwar period exposed many of the problems and issues that would be addressed in the 1920s.

Inflation had been kept in check by wartime price controls but it rose sharply by 50 percent during 1919. Consumers sought items denied them during the war, credit became more freely available, and foreign markets continued to be buoyant, stimulated by U.S. government loans to the war-ravaged countries of Europe. The economy boomed during 1919, but the tightening of credit later in the year by the Federal Reserve Board and a cutback in federal expenditure led to deflation and a severe recession that lasted until the late fall of 1921. Unemployment rose to 11.7 percent of the work force (19.5 percent of nonfarm employees) in 1921 with between four and six million persons out of work. Once prices had been lowered, inventories liquidated, and credit stabilized to avoid speculation, the economy recovered rapidly in 1922 on the strength of continuing consumer demand. Nevertheless, the effects of inflation and recession exacerbated the social instability of the postwar period.

The war had stimulated new industries, internal migration, and the employment of women, creating new social patterns in expanding cities and imposing new demands on local as well as federal government. Few of these changes had time to become accepted as part of everyday life. The war had also led to a series of forced alliances between uneasy partners. In particular, the major wartime governmental regulatory agencies were often staffed by businessmen who were ideologically opposed to government intervention in the free market. Organized labor, which had benefited from increased wages and higher status in wartime, was a reluctant collaborator in the process of federal regulation of employment. Further problems resulted from the renewal of old ideological disputes that had been repressed or redirected by wartime propaganda. This combination of factors led, almost inevitably, to outbreaks of public disorder and popular hysteria in 1919–20, triggered by the demobilization of two million soldiers and a series of strikes and bombings.

While around four million workers were involved in strike activity, public attention focused upon the general strike in Seattle, the steelworkers' strike against the unrelenting management of U.S. Steel, the police strike in Boston, and the bituminous coalminers' strike. Labor gained few concessions. The disclosure of a series of mail bombs in late April 1919 led to riots as May Day marchers were attacked by antiradical protesters in many large industrial cities. These events were only part of what has been termed the Red Scare, during which organized labor, particularly the more radical Industrial Workers of the World, socialists and anarchists came under heavy attack. The scare culminated in the deportation of nearly nine hundred supposed subversives and radicals in late 1919 and early 1920 as a result of a campaign directed by Attorney General A. Mitchell Palmer. Although the hysteria died away by mid-1920, it left organized labor demoralized in its wake and shattered the fragile strength of socialism for the next decade.

Blame for the Red Scare has traditionally been laid on Attorney General Palmer. However, the causes lie wider and deeper. It has been suggested that the scare was used by conservative business groups committed to restoring the open shop and management domination of the work force. The Espionage Act of 1917 and the Sedition Act of 1918 had proved useful instruments against radicalism. Most state governments, too, had passed laws against criminal syndicalism, and California and New York were particularly active in using such legislation. Congress had also been assiduous in hunting out subversives. More deeply, the Red Scare tapped rich veins of xenophobia stimulated by prewar immigration and by postwar anxiety about the uncertain condition of international affairs. The rise of Bolshevism loomed as a perceived threat to stability at home and abroad.

The virulent nativism of the postwar years, historian John Higham has argued, had long cultural roots in the ideology of Anglo-Saxonism.[5] This had been expressed by imperialistic nationalism at the turn of the century, the Protestant antipathy to Roman Catholicism as an alien and subversive creed, and the traditional hostility to political radicalism which fed on a popular culture of anti-intellectualism. Antiradicalism, he suggests, was reinforced in the war and postwar years by anti-Semitism. Jews were subjected to a quota system in the recruitment policies of major Ivy League universities and colleges from 1915 and were barred from municipal office in New York City. While these prejudices were most frequently populist and were astutely played upon by Hiram Wesley Evans, Imperial Wizard of the Ku Klux Klan, when he identified his supporters as "the plain people," they obtained a degree of intellectual and social respectability in the early part of the period. Madison Grant's *The Passing of the Great Race* (1916) articulated anxieties about the decline of the "Nordic" race in scholarly terms. A member of a distinguished New York family, Grant went on to support eugenics and immigration control. Moreover, his book was only one of a series of studies that invited Americans to view their cultural heritage as under threat of enervation and decline.

Phenomena such as the Ku Klux Klan, Prohibition, and immigration restriction were vehicles within the arena of public affairs for the conscious as well as covert propagation of the cultural values and social order of white Anglo-Saxon Protestantism. Sociologists Seymour Lipset and Eric Raab have argued that the proponents of conservative world views in the period sought a "status substitution" by which cultural authority compensated for a loss of social power in an increasingly cosmopolitan society.[6] The Ku Klux Klan never achieved a national power base, but was strongly entrenched in several state party organizations and governments in the South, Midwest and Pacific Northwest. Although strongest among small-town dwellers, it had a sizeable membership in many large cities, particularly among recent rural migrants and those living in neighborhoods vulnerable to social change. Tolerated but seldom openly condoned by national politicians, the Klan's membership rose to around four million before internal scandals and public indifference led to its decline in mid-decade.

Immigration restriction left a more permanent mark upon twentieth-century American history. Although Wilson vetoed a literacy test bill aimed at limiting immigration in 1917 (but passed by Congress), Harding approved the Emergency Quota Act of 1921. Though later extended, the measure failed to fulfill its framers' intentions and immigration exceeded 700,000 in 1924. Consequently, the National Origins Act of 1924 imposed tighter quotas and shifted the census base on which the quota was calculated in order to favor immigration from northern and western Europe. This discriminatory measure sought to base future immigration on the ethnic profile of mid-nineteenth-century America. It sharply reduced the so-called "new" immigration from southern and eastern Europe and ended immigration from Asia. Newcomers from the Slavic and Latin countries of Europe were the particular targets of popular hostility, and ethnicity remained a lively issue in the politics of the 1920s. Subsequently, immigration dropped to around 300,000 per annum, and the act remained the basis of U.S. immigration policy until new legislation in 1966 reopened America's "golden door" to all peoples.

Immigration control proved a more permanent victory than the prohibition of the manufacture, sale, and transportation (though not consumption) of alcohol. The Eighteenth Amendment, long advocated by the Anti-Saloon League, was passed by Congress in December 1917, partly as a war measure, and achieved ratification by January 1919. Congress passed the Volstead Act over President Wilson's veto in the following October. Prohibition featured large in the popular culture of the period and fostered new vocabularies and social institutions as varied as the speakeasy and the federal enforcement agent. It can be seen as a symbolic crusade that united those who felt their social dominance threatened by the new urbanism. Prohibition was directed by the representatives of white Anglo-Saxon Protestantism, who came from established urban middle-class families, the newer professions such as social work, and small-town and rural America, against the nexus of machine politics, ethnicity, and power located in and symbolized by the city saloon. However, although the drinking habits of the working classes were curtailed at first, general levels of consumption rose again from the mid-twenties, and Prohibition has generally been deemed a failure in that it created more ills than it cured. It inaugurated new levels of sophistication in the organization of crime, and gangsterism invaded the urban social fabric as well as the news headlines.

Gang wars inspired by Prohibition were one form of urban violence in the postwar years. Another, shorter-lived at the time but recurrent in the longer term, was the series of race riots that erupted in Chicago, Washington, D.C., and Omaha in 1919. Race relations continued to be strained throughout the decade, and contributed to the continuing debate about the role of urban culture in America's modernizing society. This debate was sharpened by the revelation of the 1920 census that urban dwellers comprised 51.4 percent of the total population.

Urbanization had a dramatic effect upon American consciousness in the 1920s. It can be argued that the emerging metropolis forged a new relationship between the city, suburbs, and rural hinterland and had become a new social and economic entity. The largest population increase occurred in satellite cities and large metropolitan centers. These grew at a rate of 27 percent between 1920 and 1930, compared with 16.1 percent in the country as a whole. Even more marked was the growth of suburban populations, facilitated by rising automobile ownership and highway construction. In 1920 there were sixty-eight cities with populations exceeding 100,000; by 1930 there were ninety-two. Rising urban land values underscored the significance of this expansion. The urban area of the United States—one-fifth of 1 percent of all land—was valued at $25 billion in 1920 and at $50 billion in 1926. Meanwhile farmland fell in value from $55 billion to $37 billion. Speculative urban development, from skyscrapers in major cities to empty real estate in Florida, fed a land and construction boom in the first six years of the decade.

Significantly for future growth, urban planning became more prevalent. The federal government, spearheaded by the newly created Division of Building and Housing in Hoover's Commerce Department, promoted planning and model zoning laws. By 1930, 981 cities had zoning laws that regulated land use and building construction. The Regional Planning Association of America brought together architects, planners, housing experts, and sociologists to devise regional city environments, drawing on the English garden city model developed by Ebenezer Howard. Radburn, New Jersey, was its most important experimental development. Private developers were also innovative. Jesse C. Nichols, a leading realtor, led the way with his Country Club District, which eventually covered 10 percent of Kansas City, Missouri. A restricted residential development in which the quality and functions of community life were closely monitored, it served as a model for many subsequent suburban communities. Nichols also established the first decentralized shopping center in 1922—the forerunner of today's ubiquitous suburban shopping mall. However, while zoning laws aided middle-class home owners and realtors and stabilized suburban communities, they did little to help those in poor housing, particularly in the inner cities. A survey in 1930 revealed that over 25 percent (six million) of America's urban homes lacked basic sanitary amenities.

The plight of urban areas was all too often the result of the flight to the city. Urban growth was predominantly fueled by migration from rural areas. The four cities of New York, Chicago, Detroit, and Los Angeles alone absorbed 4.5 million migrants between 1920 and 1930, and it has been estimated that nearly two million persons left the land each year between 1922 and 1929. The north-central and Pacific-coast states, as well as growth regions in the South and Midwest, benefited most from this migration. California drew its migrants (scathingly called "locusts" by native inhabitants) mainly from the central and northern Midwest, Pennsylvania, and New York. Many of the rural migrants to other states were Southern blacks. The black population became urbanized at nearly twice the rate of whites. By 1930 20 percent of all blacks lived in the Northeast and Midwest, and of these 88 percent were urban dwellers. Even in the South the number of black Americans living in cities more than doubled to three million between 1900 and 1930. The scale of internal migration exceeds that of the Depression era and suggests the extent to which rural society had to remake itself or at least reconsider its relationship with modern civilization. Farmers fought hard to protect their cultural and economic interests against encroaching urbanism while taking advantage, at the same time, of its material and technological innovations.

Thus the immediate postwar years defined, often in extreme and violent form, many of the issues that confronted

American society in the twenties: power relationships between contesting groups in a modernizing society; the effects of demography upon the national infrastructure; the role of the economy, and particularly business, in determining national priorities; and the role of government, divested of its emergency wartime powers. The early years of the twenties largely determined the terms in which the decade would discuss these issues, and the brief administration of Warren G. Harding, spanning depression and prosperity, has become a focus of close historical scrutiny.

Harding's landslide victory in the presidential election of 1920 may have changed the topography of American politics less than was once thought. The domestic policies of the Wilson administration were, by intent and default, moving in the direction of deregulation that Harding was to follow. Like Wilson, both Harding and Coolidge experienced difficulties in getting legislation through Congress due to internal party wrangles, the vigorous parliamentary tactics of Progressive Republicans, and the voting strength of special-interest groups, particularly the farm bloc. The business lobby was also strong and proved resilient even when under presidential pressure. The Republican ascendancy was not firmly controlled from the White House. Faced with postwar economic problems, Harding—with Hoover's encouragement—worked hard to help business, mediated between employers and workers in the coal-mining and railroad strikes of 1922, and was persistent, and eventually successful, in forcing U.S. Steel to reduce its working day from twelve to eight hours.

Harding continues to be identified as a president who subordinated the interests of government to those of business. For labor historians he conceded too much to business in mediating the strikes of 1922, and business interests were further accommodated by his reductions in federal expenditure and support for the sharp rise in tariffs—most notoriously the Fordney-McCumber Act of 1922. On the other hand, the revisionist historian Robert Murray points with approval to Harding's refusal to reduce taxation on the wealthy to the extent that Andrew Mellon wished, and to underwrite farmer production with federal credit on the grounds that to do so would favor a special interest.[7] The search for more efficient government continued, most notably with the Accounting and Budget Act

(1921), which placed fiscal policy more firmly within the control of the executive. Although its full significance was not evident at the time, this was a crucial development of presidential power. It laid the basis for fiscal planning and the presentation of an executive budget. Moreover, Harding's administration proposed needed reforms of the federal bureaucracy, including the creation of a new Department of Public Welfare, and inaugurated measures for the improvement of the national infrastructure, among them the development of civil aviation, highways, and the regulation of radio. Although Harding died suddenly in 1923 before these measures were enacted, Coolidge fulfilled most of the remaining agenda.

The Harding administration had to meet the demands of rapid prosperity and social change as well as recession. From early 1922 until 1924 the economy expanded more rapidly than at any other period in the decade. Wage rates rose sharply and the extension of credit in the decade peaked in 1923–24. New forms of cheap credit, particularly installment payments, and stable prices greatly increased purchasing power within the economy. Indeed, price stability was one of the notable features of the economy in the twenties, made possible by the remarkable growth in productivity. While the manufacturing labor force remained at the same level between 1919 and 1929, output rose by 60 percent. Farm productivity also rose, but here the rewards were more uncertain.

The farmer had long been central to the American economy and national political ideology. Farm exports had given the United States a favorable balance of trade in the late nineteenth century. Even at this time, however, declining commodity prices indicated overproduction and farm husbandry seldom looked to the long-term health of the land. Despite a boom during World War I, farming began to take second place to manufacturing in the economy. Under Henry Wallace in the early twenties, the Department of Agriculture encouraged scientific cultivation and cooperative marketing. Later in the decade, farmers were encouraged to limit production, but no incentives were offered and no controls were exercised. The New Era administrations failed to solve the problems of overproduction, but none of their successors up to the present day have succeeded in the task.

Farmers felt strongly disadvantaged in the twenties, and historians have generally supported this representation of farming conditions. They echo many of the criticisms made of Republican policy by lobby groups such as the American Farm Bureau and National Grange, and ignore the protection offered by higher tariffs and the extension of government underwriting of farm credit. Farms had benefited from the war effort with higher prices for staple crops. Acreages under cultivation—often of marginal land—had increased, and the increase had continued during the speculative postwar boom. When crop prices and land values collapsed as a result of depression, farmers were left with increased mortgage debts and as prices continued to slide, a declining income with which to service their obligations. Moreover, the parity ratio between the prices that farmers received for their crops and what they paid for goods and services worsened, feeding farmers' grievances. Agriculture was undoubtedly faced with major structural changes brought about by insolvent tenancy, consolidation of farm holdings, mechanization, and increasing specialization—particularly among truck farmers who met the needs of a newly nutrition-conscious urban population. Farmers therefore repeatedly pressed for government to adopt measures by which prices could be maintained or raised. The most favored plan later in the decade was McNary-Haugenism, named after its Congressional proponents. This advocated government purchase of surplus production and its subsequent release at home when crop yields fell or abroad if a domestic surplus continued. Coolidge and Hoover refused to support such an open-ended commitment of government resources.

This prevailing view of a depressed farm sector has been challenged by economic historian Peter Fearon, who has argued that farm income grew steadily in the decade and that farmers were ready buyers of consumer durables.[8] He also contends that the parity ratio was a false guide to the relative well-being of farmers since its base years (1910–14) were ones of exceptional and stable prosperity for agriculture. Moreover, the ratio did not fully account for all forms of income and resources from which farmers benefited. Such an argument necessarily questions the conventional proposition that a weak farm sector was one of the causes of the depression that followed the crash of 1929.

However, economic expansion during the period was undoubtedly powered by manufacturing and the growing service industries. By the late 1920s American manufacturing accounted for over 40 percent of the world's total output. Economic growth and instability produced a variety of structural, managerial, and production changes. Indeed, the 1920s are a critically important era in the development of modern American capitalism. Experiments in mass production, scientific management, marketing, and corporate structuring, underway in the Progressive period, now made further advances. A modern business system emerged that survived the Depression and laid the foundations for the later growth of the corporate economy in the fifties and sixties. This would only undergo significant revision when an unprecedented combination of problems afflicted the economy in the seventies.

Large corporations increased in size as a result of an unprecedented number of mergers by vertical integration and through the pyramidal organization of the holding company. The new corporations such as Ford, Eastman Kodak, and Sears, Roebuck were so big that they could often finance their own development. Forced by these developments to reconsider its own role, the finance sector released money earmarked for industrial investment into consumer credit and speculative stock investment. In addition, smaller and less capital-intensive businesses responded to growth and instability by forming trade associations, designed to coordinate operations, short of price-fixing, within a market sector. In contrast to the prewar era, both consolidation and cooperation were now encouraged by the federal government, and they were endorsed by a conservative Supreme Court under Chief Justice William Howard Taft, giving legal sanction to the methods used by business to create a strong national economy.

Entrepreneurial management, which owned as well as directed a company, was still the most common form of business enterprise, particularly among smaller firms. However, even this type of business was more likely to employ personnel managers and new production techniques, especially standardized parts and the assembly line. Henry Ford represented entrepreneurial management most successfully in the decade. However, the "visible hand" of management became more sophisticated as some of the biggest corporations experimented with new, oligopolistic structures during the twenties. Led by corporations such as Du Pont, General Motors, Standard Oil, and United States Rubber, new administrative structures separated central from line management in order to enhance rapid and aggressive responses to particular market sectors. By mid-decade such structures were being adopted in the retail and service sectors, particularly among flourishing and merging advertising companies and retail chains such as Atlantic and Pacific (A & P). They underwent refinement and more widespread adoption over the next generation.

Large corporate managements were successful in countering demands for the closed shop but also offered better working conditions and social benefits to their employees. Although brutal measures were still frequently used during labor disputes, a form of welfare capitalism emerged in the 1920s. This development was evidence not only of more sophisticated personnel management but also of the weakness of organized labor. Membership of the American Federation of Labor fell from 5 to 3.5 million in the 1920s, partly due to relative prosperity in the work force, but also due to the setbacks experienced in the wave of postwar strikes. In addition, labor leadership was either corruptly engaged in maintaining its own power or out of touch with its members and too anxious to speak the language of managerial progressivism.

Employment conditions in the decade are a matter of some dispute. Early interpretations pointed to full employment and rising prosperity, but labor historian Irving Bernstein has suggested a less promising view.[9] There were high levels of seasonal and technological unemployment, and in spite of the overall buoyancy of employment there was considerable variation and unevenness across employed groups, industries, and regions. The need for cheap labor was met by rural migration and by the recruitment of women into the work force, particularly in the newer service industries. The number of employed women rose between 1920 and 1930 from 8.3 million to 10.6 million, over 3 million of whom were married women. Proportionately fewer women found their way into the professions than in the previous decade, and women were almost always paid less than men for the same job. Unskilled labor did not do so well in the 1920s, and the wage gap between unskilled and skilled widened steadily, reversing wartime trends. Moreover, suggests Bernstein, the supposed reduction in working hours was more apparent than real because workers needed to maximize working hours and wages in order to keep up with the demands of a consumer and leisured society.

The speed of economic change was checked temporarily by recession in 1924. Other events during that year also invited some national stocktaking. A series of scandals emerged following Harding's death: Colonel Charles Forbes was convicted of fraud in his administration of the Veterans Bureau; Secretary Fall was imprisoned for the corrupt leasing of the Navy's oil reserves at Elk Hills, California, and Teapot Dome, Wyoming; and Attorney General Daugherty was forced to resign as a result of Congressional investigation of illicit dealings that benefited his family and cronies. Coolidge handled these exposures coolly, not wishing to taint himself or his chances of election as president.

His chief political opponents, however, were in no condition to threaten his return to the White House. The Democratic national convention of 1924 was one of the most divisive in the party's history and reflected the cultural conflicts of the New Era. There were two major rivals for the presidential nomination. William Gibbs McAdoo, Wilson's son-in-law and secretary of the treasury in the Wilson administration, drew support from the rural South and West, Protestant fundamentalists, nativists—including the Klan—and Prohibition supporters. By contrast Governor Alfred E. Smith of New York stood for a broader, pluralist interpretation of American citizenship and a sensitivity to urban values and needs. The deadlocked convention compromised on the 103rd ballot in selecting John W. Davis, a corporation lawyer and former solicitor general, as its presidential candidate. The protracted and discordant events in Madison Square Garden were the result of a disunited party seeking a new political and ideological base. It did not begin to find one until 1928. Nor could the Progressive party, fighting its last election with Senator Robert La Follette of Wisconsin as its presidential candidate, provide a viable alternative. In large part an alliance of insurgent Progressive Republicans and those hoping to establish the equivalent of the British Labour party, this third party's appeal was too marginal to threaten Coolidge.

The year 1924 marked the beginnings of a new equilibrium and retrenchment incorporating some of the social and ideological changes that had emerged during the early years of the twenties. The Ku Klux Klan declined from mid-decade, and religious fundamentalism was humiliated in the media coverage of the Scopes trial at Dayton, Tennessee, in 1925. A recurrent phenomenon in American history, religious fundamentalism in the 1920s was complex in nature. It had roots in urban as well as rural society and derived much of its force from intense ideological and institutional conflicts within a variety of Protestant denominations. The social objectives of fundamentalism were justified by strict biblical interpretation and were directed against attempts by liberal Christian organizations to adapt beliefs and religious institutions to the social needs of modern society through the Social Gospel movement. It lacked the kind of political agenda established by religious fundamentalism in the 1980s. Instead, individual fundamentalists most often sought their political objectives through the Prohibition movement and the Ku Klux Klan. On the other hand, revivalists such as Billy Sunday and Aimee Semple McPherson were as adept at exploiting the persuasive power of the media as their recent counterparts. The assertion of moral order also had its intellectual adherents in the New Humanism, whose spokesmen in Harvard and Princeton cited universal ethical laws and human reason in support of their views. The reassertion of traditional moral values was tacitly recognized by Hollywood when, after a series of sex and drug scandals involving film stars between 1921 and 1923, it established the Motion Picture Producers and Distributors of America Inc. under former postmaster general Will Hays to regulate the business practices and censor the moral standards of the film industry.

Calvin Coolidge was temperamentally suited to a period of retrenchment. Aware of popular moods and capable of articulating them persuasively, he was not an innovator or a legislative activist. Perhaps his greatest success was in fusing mainstream Republicanism with the progressive managerial ideology of the New Era, demonstrated by his much-quoted statement that "the business of the United States is business; he who builds a factory builds a temple." Coolidge's view of government was more quiescent than those of Harding and Hoover, but he was unsuccessful in reducing federal expenditure. His political intentions were most clearly indicated by the Revenue Act of 1926, which cut income tax in all categories and sliced surtaxes by 50 percent. One-third of all taxpayers were thereby exempted from tax payments and $350 million was released for discretionary expenditure.

One adverse effect of the Revenue Act was to worsen the growing maldistribution of personal income. In 1922 the wealthiest 1 percent received 12 percent of all personal income; by 1929 its share was 13.9 percent. In the nonfarm population the disposable income of the top 1 percent grew by 63 percent between 1923 and 1929; in contrast, that of the lowest 93 percent shrank by 4 percent. According to one study in the period, a family required an income of $2,000 in 1929 to ensure a basic standard of living, but, it was calculated, 60 percent of American families lived below this level. Moreover, real wages did not keep pace with the rise in productivity and thus profits went disproportionately to owners and stockholders.

Several important consequences resulted from this maldistribution of income. First, low-income families came under increasing pressure as they sought to achieve the standard of living established as a norm in the consumer society of the twenties, and many sought relief through increasing the number of family wage-earners and extending their credit liabilities. In the event of depression, low-income families would be particularly hard hit by unemployment and the contraction of credit. Second, real wealth was confined to a relatively small sector of the population whose spending power sustained the consumer boom. Real prosperity was therefore narrowly based and vulnerable to any cutback in consumer expenditure. And, third, the high level of wealth achieved by the most affluent could not be absorbed entirely by consumption. It found its way into speculative investment, particularly on the stock market, and capital investment. The results were inflated stock values and excessive production capacity.

There were signs of flagging consumption in the recession of 1927, but demand picked up in the following year with growing dependence upon credit. By mid-decade three-fourths of all automobile purchases were credit-financed, and households were bombarded with increasing levels of consumer advertising in newspapers and periodicals. Annual per capita advertising expenditures rose from five dollars in 1919 to over nine dollars in 1929. The automobile remained the commodity for which families were prepared to sacrifice most. Car registrations tripled between 1919 and 1929 and by the latter year 23 million cars were owned in a population of less than 30 million families, of whom probably one million owned two automobiles. Consumer durables were also the targets of family consumption. Just over 17 million homes—mostly urban—were wired for electricity by 1928. Some 15 million of these had electric irons, half that number had vacuum cleaners, 5 million had washing machines, and less than a million had refrigerators. The onset of the Depression progressively affected consumer spending. Between 1929 and 1931 the net profits of food companies fell by 41 percent, while those of companies supplying other household items fell by nearly 80 percent. The number of registered automobiles, on which just over 10 percent of the national income was spent in 1929, declined by one million in the same period. Nevertheless, gasoline sales remained steady, indicating the indispensability of the car for work and pleasure.

Changes in consumption were also related to demographic shifts and were often mediated by the family. Changes were uneven across class, generational, racial, ethnic, and regional boundaries, but family size was generally decreasing, due either to contraception and more public information about "sex hygiene" or to changes in behavior patterns. With fewer children—three rather than five became the norm—and with more advice on child-rearing offered by child psychologists, the middle-class family tried to adjust to the competing demands of a modernizing society, often with stress and confusion. Increasingly, the family conceded its training and socializing roles to the education system and the peer group. With prolonged adolescence and education a youth culture developed in the 1920s, which established its own behavioral codes and social styles, and prepared the young for the normative values of a competitive, consumer society.

The family largely defined the social and economic roles of most women, often at considerable personal cost, as sociologists Helen and Robert Lynd found in *Middletown* (1929), their classic study of Muncie, Indiana.[10] Divorce rates in Middletown were twice as high as the national average, which stood at one divorce for every six marriages by 1930. While new household gadgets made family management easier, they did not necessarily lessen the overall time spent on household tasks, and women came under increasing pressure to take paid employment outside the home. Whether this was due to economic necessity, as the Women's Bureau argued at the time, or due to a dual commitment to the family and to the acquisition of the life-style of a leisured, consumer society, as historian Winifred Wandersee has suggested, is a matter for debate.[11] The evidence of the Lynds suggests that women experienced difficulty in creating personal and social roles for themselves outside home and family, although other studies suggest that women succeeded in securing better welfare provision during the decade. At best, the decade appears to be one of uneven advances for women.

Coolidge's review of the state of the nation in December 1928 was serene and complacent, emphasizing the prospect of continuing prosperity. Indeed, "Coolidge prosperity" had won the presidential election for Herbert Hoover by a landslide larger than Harding's in 1920. It had been degrees of emphasis rather than matters of substance that had differentiated the Republican and Democratic party platforms, and both candidates had distinguished records as administrative progressives. Much of the campaign had focused on the character of the Democratic candidate, Alfred E. Smith, whose immigrant origins and Lower East Side upbringing, Catholicism, Tammany Hall connections, and dislike of Prohibition were all cast by his opponents as disqualifications for office. Smith's well-financed campaign rescued the Democratic party from its post-1924 limbo, but claims that it marked the emergence of the Roosevelt voter coalition must be treated with caution. The electoral alliance of the rural South and urban North was not fully established until the 1936 election.

Hoover's inaugural address set out an ambitious program of government action: extending prosperity by encouraging business and labor to work together to increase productivity and purchasing power; vigorous development of the nation's infrastructure and public services; conservation; and the strengthening of vital institutions such as the home. Hoover envisaged a "New Day"—the dawning of a new age of prosperity under American capitalism. He entered the White House with confidence in himself and his policies, but his certainty turned to rigidity under the adverse pressures of the Depression. This inflexibility underlay his determination to exercise full control over policy-making, his reluctance to take advice when it conflicted with his own convictions, his sensitivity to criticism, and his lack of political rapport with Congress and the public. It also did much to cast Hoover—falsely—in the mold of a Republican conservative. Ironically, in defending his presidential record after leaving office Hoover only succeeded in identifying himself with the stand-pat Republicanism that he had so despised in Coolidge, thus damaging his own historical reputation.

The Hoover record has been dominated by the Great Depression and his administration's inability to promote recovery. As a result, some of the "Great Engineer"'s achievements have largely passed unnoticed. Federal expenditure on highways and public works increased sharply, the national parks system was extended, ambitious hydroelectric power schemes were initiated, and plans for improving the nation's housing and child care were advocated to largely unresponsive Congressional, state, and local politicians. The Research Committee on Social Trends, appointed by Hoover, established the data from which national welfare policies could be developed, although it did not report until 1933. Nor can Hoover's problems with Congress be wholly attributed to his lack of political skill. Congressional indifference and antipathy, particularly after the Democrats gained control of both houses in 1930, were also to blame.

Neither president nor Congress knew how to counter the effects of the depression that was initiated by the Wall Street "crash" of 1929. Prices on the New York stock market rose by 40 percent in 1927 and 35 percent in 1928, and stood at 400 percent above their 1924 level before the great bull market slid and then collapsed in September and October 1929. This decline continued until the summer of 1932, when prices had returned to their 1924 level. The collapse in confidence demonstrated by the crash was endemic within the economy as a whole. The Federal Reserve Board's index of manufacturing production halved between 1929 and 1932. Income from agriculture, fisheries, and forestry fell from $8.3 billion to $3.3 billion in the same period. The high failure rate of banks reduced their number from 25,568 in 1929 to 14,771 in 1932. Investment levels showed a similarly precipitous collapse. Employment held up briefly under the Hoover administration's encouragement to employers to sustain their work force and wage levels, but then unemployment increased by four million a year from 1930 onward. Nearly 13 million workers—one in four of the work force—were out of work by 1933. Living standards dropped for all but a few, but statistics do not record in human measure the devastating costs of the Depression, particularly for the poor.

What caused the Depression is still wide open to debate, and one noted commentator, economist Peter Temin,[12] has frankly proposed that its causes cannot be disentangled. However, three explanations seem to dominate the debate: a crisis in the international economy; a decline in demand due to lowering levels of investment (the Keynesian model); and a cutback in the money supply due to rises in interest rates (the monetarist model).

Since the Great Depression was international in scope, an explanation that looks to factors outside the United States has appeal. Herbert Hoover was a strong advocate of the argument that the causes lay abroad, identifying particularly the British devaluation of sterling, growing protectionism, and the series of European banking failures in 1931. Since the Depression grew more severe at home in 1930 and 1931, this explanation seemed persuasive, particularly to Republicans anxious to exonerate themselves from responsibility. It is more likely, however, that the European crisis only revealed the basic lack of soundness in the international economy. In their efforts to pay heavy war debts, the European nations had come to rely increasingly upon U.S. loans, and American lending and investment had often been injudicious. The debtor nations' ability to repay had also been reduced by high tariffs in the United States. Their declining purchasing power had, in turn, weakened American exports. Hoover's twelve-month moratorium on war debt repayments and his attempts to make American investment abroad more responsible were moves in the right direction, but his approval of the Smoot-Hawley Tariff Act in 1930, which raised already high tariff rates, only provoked increased protection from America's trading partners. It seems reasonable to conclude, therefore, that the international economic crisis contributed to the depth and length of the Depression, but does not explain its specific character in the domestic economy of the United States.

Explanations that emphasized the decline in domestic demand were preeminent until the supply-side economics of monetarism grew popular in the late seventies and eighties.

Keynesian arguments have stressed the unequal distribution of income, the weakness of agriculture, the apparent saturation of demand in critical sectors such as automobiles and residential construction in the late twenties, and the curtailment of investment in response. For them, the role of the stock-market crash is critical insofar as it created unreasonable pessimism in 1930, which restricted consumer spending and investment and thus extended the Depression. A recent variant of the Keynesian position has been developed by the economic historian Michael Bernstein. He argues that "dramatically new demand patterns and investment opportunities" were emerging in the twenties, particularly in new service-sector industries such as chemicals, consumer durables and food processing. The Depression severely disrupted these new demand patterns, and they took a long time to recover. [13] Monetarists, on the other hand, have emphasized that in an economy where banking was unstable and the government, through the Federal Reserve Board, had allowed the money supply to expand, the raising of interest rates by the Federal Reserve Board in 1928–29 in order to dampen stock-price inflation was harmful. The sharp contraction in credit led to a series of bank panics and a reduction in the money supply that forestalled recovery.

The Hoover system essentially relied upon private agencies to carry out public policy, and public policy was to be created by rational discussion among experts. This was the quintessential New Era vision of the associative state, but it precluded direct and extensive federal action to restore the economy. In order to stop the contraction of credit, the Hoover administration adopted a series of measures to underwrite credit for farmers, home buyers, and the banking system. None of the measures was sufficiently expansionist to revive confidence, and their effects were undermined by deflationary policies such as the tax increases in the Revenue Act of 1932. The nation's banking system was in recurrent crisis as a result. Early administration resistance to the extension of trade associations to foster cooperation and recovery, because of the danger of price-fixing and cartelization, was belatedly reversed by 1932. While expenditure on public works grew each year, Hoover favored a more disciplined injection of public money into the economy in order to revitalize critical industries. This was achieved by the creation of the Reconstruction Finance Corporation (RFC) in

1932 which was authorized to lend up to $2 billion to banks and financial institutions. The RFC was criticized for helping needy corporations while failing to assist destitute citizens. In late 1932 the RFC was only granting credits—not making outright grants—to state governments that could no longer pay for relief out of state and private funds. Indeed, the Hoover measures of 1932 marked the limits as well as the inventiveness of the New Era.

The Great Depression was a hard test of the new ideas and institutions that had been developing in the twenties, particularly since many of them had not reached maturity. The agencies and bureaucracies created to extend the facilitating role of government were limited in scale and were often frustrated by indifference and hostility within the executive and Congress. Within the economy some important organizational transitions were underway, but these were far from complete. Corporate managerial practices and trade association agreements were in many ways at an experimental stage of development. Service industries were only beginning to assert their new power within a consumer economy. And farming was slow in coming to terms with the economic implications of the technological and social changes of the period.

Was the New Era, as Ellis Hawley has remarked, a search that failed?[14] In the shorter term, the election of Franklin D. Roosevelt and the pursuit of more direct federal solutions in the New Deal would suggest that it was. But the longer view, which takes account of a flourishing corporate economy since World War II and the failure of liberalism to build a state apparatus that could command and serve a permanent national consensus, may give us pause to consider that postwar America has been as much the legatee of the New Era as of the New Deal.

In a decade of sharp transitions, similar in scale and speed to our own, it was inevitable that much remained incomplete—even incoherent—to those who witnessed them. Josephine Herbst, a shrewd critic and writer, gave telling expression to this sense of flux:

> But is there such a thing as the twenties? The decade simply falls apart upon examination into crumbs and pieces which completely contradict each other in their essences. . . . Even individual characters cannot be stud-

ied in a state of static immobility. It was all flux and change with artistic movements evolving into political crises, and where ideas of social service, justice, and religious reaction had their special spokesmen.[15]

And the distinguished historian Charles Beard asked in 1927 whether American civilization in the new machine age stood at "the dawn, not the dusk, of the gods." Looking back from the perspective of the late twentieth century, it seems evident that an uncertain dawn had broken. New ideas and institutions were being developed but not without forceful opposition and the residual power of inertia. Information systems—governmental, popular and academic—were being devised to reduce the gap between change and an understanding of its direction and processes. But there is some truth in Donald McCoy's charge that Americans "were not adequately equipped to recognize the implications of the increasingly swift developments of their society and time. . . . They dropped old ideas too slowly and did not devise enough valid new concepts or apply them skillfully enough."[16] Above all, Americans experienced the period differently, dependent upon age, sex, income, race, ethnic origin and geographical location. This begins to explain both the volatile expectations of the era and Herbst's observation that it falls apart into contradictory crumbs and pieces.

Notes

1. William J. Barber, *From New Era to New Deal: Herbert Hoover, the Economists, and American Economic Policy, 1921–1933* (Cambridge, 1985), p. 2.

2. Richard Hofstadter, *The American Political Tradition and the Men Who Made It* (London, 1962), p. 282.

3. Ellis W. Hawley, *The Great War and the Search for a Modern Order* (New York, 1979), p. 77.

4. William Appleman Williams, *The Contours of American History* (Cleveland, 1981), p. 437.

5. John Higham, *Strangers in the Land: Patterns of American Nativism 1860–1925* (New York, 1977), pp. 264–99.

6. Seymour M. Lipset and Eric Raab, *The Politics of Unreason: Right-Wing Extremism in America 1790–1977* (Chicago, 1978), pp. 110–45.

7. Robert K. Murray, "Herbert Hoover and the Harding Cabinet," in *Herbert Hoover as Secretary of Commerce: Studies in New Era Theory and Practice,* ed. Ellis W. Hawley (West Branch, Iowa, 1974), pp. 19–42.

8. Peter Fearon, *War, Prosperity and Depression: The U.S. Economy 1917–1945* (Deddington, Oxford, 1987), pp. 25–42.

9. Irving Bernstein, *The Lean Years: A History of the American Worker 1920–1933* (Boston, 1960), pp. 47–82.

10. Robert S. and Helen M. Lynd, *Middletown: A Study in Contemporary American Culture* (New York, 1929), pp. 121–30.

11. Winifred D. Wandersee, *Women's Work and Family Values 1920–1940* (Cambridge, Mass., 1981), pp. 89–92.

12. Peter Temin, "Notes on the Causes of the Great Depression," in *The Great Depression Revisited,* ed. Karl Brunner (Boston, 1980), pp. 125–36.

13. Michael A. Bernstein, *The Great Depression: Delayed Recovery and Economic Change in America 1929–1939* (Cambridge, 1987), pp 57–63.

14. Hawley, *The Great War and the Search for a Modern Order,* pp. 226–29.

15. Josephine Herbst, "A Year of Disgrace," in *The Noble Savage,* ed. Saul Bellow and Keith Botsford (Cleveland, Ohio, 1961), p. 160.

16. Donald B. McCoy, *Coming of Age* (Harmondsworth, 1973), p. 144.

Bibliography

Historiographical essays are a useful starting point in reviewing the ways in which historians have approached the period. Valuable analyses have been published by Henry F. May, "Shifting Perspectives on the 1920s," *Mississippi Valley Historical Review* 43 (1954): 404–27; Burl Noggle, "Configurations of the Twenties," in *The Reinterpretation of American History and Culture,* ed. William H. Cartwright and Richard L. Watson, Jr., (Washington, 1973), pp. 465–90, and "The Twenties: A New Historiographical Frontier," *Journal of American History* 53 (September 1966): 299–314; and Don S. Kirschner, "Conflicts and Politics in the 1920's: Historiography and Prospects," *Mid-America* 48 (1966): 219–33.

The legacy of early histories of the period can be discerned in Arthur M. Schlesinger, Jr., *The Age of Roosevelt*, Vol. 1, *The Crisis of the Old Order, 1919–1933* (Boston, 1956); John D. Hicks, *Republican Ascendancy, 1921–1933* (New York, 1960); and William E. Leuchtenburg, *The Perils of Prosperity, 1914–1932* (Chicago, 1958). The latter text incorporates some of the interpretive shifts of the fifties, but some of its sharper analyses of political changes are obscured by an epigrammatic style that owes much to Frederick Lewis Allen. A more recent survey with a good bibliographical essay that draws intelligently on revisionist scholarship is Ellis W. Hawley, *The Great War and the Search for a Modern Order: A History of the American People and Their Institutions, 1917–1933* (New York, 1979). The essays collected in John Braeman et al., eds., *Change and Continuity in Twentieth-Century America: The 1920's* (Columbus, Ohio, 1968) provide valuable insights into significant political and social phenomena in the period.

The cumulative impact of the war and postwar period are persuasively assessed by Neil A. Wynn, *From Progressivism to Prosperity: World War I and American Society* (New York, 1986). The characteristics of nativism are analyzed in John Higham, *Strangers in the Land* (New Brunswick, N.J., 1955); and Stanley Coben, "A Study in Nativism: The American Red Scare of 1919–1920," *Political Science Quarterly* 79 (March 1964): 52–75; and those of Prohibition by Norman H. Clark, *Deliver Us from Evil* (New York, 1976). The varied manifestations and motivations of the Ku Klux Klan have been closely studied, and Kenneth T. Jackson, *The Ku Klux Klan in the City, 1915–1930* (New York, 1967), opens with a useful historiographical review. Religious fundamentalism in the decade has been examined in Norman F. Furniss, *The Fundamentalist Controversy, 1919–1931* (New Haven, Conn., 1954), and its ideological opponent has been analyzed in William R. Hutchinson, *The Modernist Impulse in American Protestantism* (Cambridge, Mass., 1976). Rural-urban tensions of the period have received critical scrutiny in Don S. Kirschner, *City and Country: Rural Responses to Urbanization in the 1920's* (Westport, Conn., 1970).

The major revisionist study of the Harding presidency is Robert K. Murray, *The Harding Era: Warren G. Harding and*

His Administration (Minneapolis, Minn., 1969). Less favorable evaluation is made in Eugene P. Trani and David L. Wilson, *The Presidency of Warren G. Harding* (Lawrence, Kans., 1977). The best study of Coolidge is the revisionist account by Donald B. McCoy, *Calvin Coolidge: The Quiet President* (New York, 1967). Works on the career of Herbert Hoover abound. Those that predate or refute revisionist interpretations include Albert U. Romasco, *The Poverty of Abundance: Hoover, the Nation, the Depression* (New York, 1965), and Edgar Robinson and Vaughn Bornet, *Herbert Hoover: President of the United States* (Stanford, Calif., 1975). Major revisionist studies include the biography by David Burner, *Herbert Hoover: A Public Life* (New York, 1978); Joan Hoff Wilson, *Herbert Hoover: Forgotten Progressive* (Boston, 1975); and Martin L. Fausold, *The Presidency of Herbert C. Hoover* (Lawrence, Kans., 1985).

Much revisionist thought on the New Era's politics and foreign policy stemmed from Richard Hofstadter's "Herbert Hoover and the Crisis of American Individualism" in *The American Political Tradition and the Men Who Made It* (London, 1962), pp. 279–310; and two essays by William Appleman Williams, "The Legend of Isolationism in the 1920's," *Science and Society* 18 (Winter 1954): 1–20, and his chapter on Herbert Hoover in *The Contours of American History* (Cleveland, Ohio, 1961). The outcomes of revisionist thinking can be found in Joan Hoff Wilson, *American Business and Foreign Policy, 1920–1933* (Lexington, Ky., 1971); Michael J. Hogan, *Informal Entente: The Private Structure of Cooperation in Anglo-American Economic Diplomacy, 1918–1928* (Columbia, Mo., 1977); and Robert N. Seidel, *Progressive Pan-Americanism* (Ithaca, N.Y., 1973). Useful surveys are Selig Adler, *The Uncertain Giant, 1921–1941* (New York, 1965), and L. Ethan Ellis, *Republican Foreign Policy, 1921–1933* (New Brunswick, N.J., 1968).

The American economy during the period has received extensive treatment. A classic work is George Soule, *Prosperity Decade: From War to Depression, 1917–1929* (New York, 1947). More recent surveys include Jim Potter, *The American Economy Between the World Wars*, rev. ed. (London, 1985), and Peter Fearon, *War, Prosperity and Depression: United States Economy, 1917–45* (Deddington, 1987). On the origins of the Great Depression, Peter Fearon, *The Origins and Nature of the Great Slump, 1929–1932* (London, 1979), and Charles P. Kindleberger, *The World in Depression, 1929–1939* (Berkeley, Calif., 1973), provide accessible views of the international context. J. K. Galbraith, *The Great Crash* (Boston, 1955) presents a largely Keynesian case, while the monetarist argument is presented by Milton Friedman and Anna J. Schwartz, *A Monetary History of the United States, 1867–1960* (New York, 1963), and critically evaluated by Peter Temin, *Did Monetary Forces Cause the Great Depression?* (New York, 1976). Both the latter studies are technical.

The growing institutional links between government and the economy and the growth of a managerial society are examined in Robert F. Himmelberg, *The Origins of the National Recovery Administration: Business, Government and the Trade Association Issue 1921–1933* (New York, 1976); William J. Barber, *From New Era to New Deal: Herbert Hoover, the Economists, and American Economic Policy, 1921–1933* (Cambridge, 1985); and Guy Alchon, *The Invisible Hand of Planning: Capitalism, Social Science, and the State in the 1920s* (Princeton, N.J., 1985). The development of new corporate structures is delineated in Alfred D. Chandler, Jr., *The Visible Hand: The Managerial Revolution in American Business* (Cambridge, Mass., 1977) and their manipulation of changing ideological and social habits is analyzed in Roland Marchand, *Advertising the American Dream, 1920–1940* (Berkeley, Calif., 1985). The attempts of business to accommodate to new social conditions are examined in Stuart D. Brandes, *American Welfare Capitalism, 1880–1940* (Chicago, 1976), and Morrell Heald, *The Social Responsibilities of Business: Company and Community* (Cleveland, Ohio, 1970).

A good survey of the agricultural economy is M. K. Benedict, *Farm Policies of the United States, 1790–1950* (New York, 1957). More detailed studies include James H. Shideler, *Farm Crisis, 1919–1923* (Berkeley, Calif., 1957); Theodore Saloutos and John D. Hicks, *Agricultural Discontent in the Middle West, 1900–1939* (Madison, Wis., 1951); and Gilbert C. Fite, *Cotton Fields No More: Southern Agriculture 1865–1980* (Lexington, Ky., 1984). The best survey of labor conditions is still Irving Bernstein, *The Lean Years: A History of the American Worker, 1920–1933* (Boston, 1960). The question of the distribution of income is addressed in C. F. Holt, "Who Benefited from the Prosperity of the Twenties?", *Explorations in Economic History*

14 (1973): 147–65; and Frank Stricker, "Affluence for Whom? Another Look at Prosperity and the Working Class in the 1920s," *Labor History* 24 (1983): 274–90. The varied economic roles of women are considered in Leslie W. Tentler, *Wage-Earning Women: Industrial Work and Family Life in the United States, 1900–1930* (New York, 1979); Winifred D. Wandersee, *Women's Work and Family Values, 1920–1940* (Cambridge, Mass., 1981); and Patricia M. Hummer, *The Decade of Elusive Promise: Professional Women in the United States, 1920–1930* (Ann Arbor, Mich., 1979). The continuity of social feminism is considered in J. Stanley Lemons, *The Woman Citizen: Social Feminism in the 1920s* (Urbana, Ill., 1973), and a recent synthesis is Dorothy M. Brown, *Setting a Course: American Women in the 1920s* (Boston, 1987).

Although a wide range of social and cultural phenomena, often critical in determining popular and professional views of the decade, has been beyond the scope of this chapter, it may be useful to note some important texts dealing with these areas of experience. Still invaluable to historians of the period are Robert S. and Helen M. Lynd, *Middletown: A Study in Modern American Culture* (New York, 1929), and the *Report of the president's committee on . . . Recent Social Trends in the United States* (New York, 1933). Excellent studies on the intellectual and artistic changes under way early in the century are Henry F. May, *The End of American Innocence: A Study of the First Years of Our Own Time, 1912–1917* (New York, 1959), and T. Jackson Lears, *No Place of Grace: Anti-Modernism and the Transformation of American Culture, 1880–1920* (New York, 1981). A useful survey of professional and popular thought in the twenties, although somewhat limited by its theme and the demands of generalization, is Roderick Nash, *The Nervous Generation: American Thought, 1917–1930* (Chicago, 1970). The first two chapters also contain a good historiographical review of popular and professional accounts of the decade. Several essays in Warren Susman, *Culture as History: The Transformation of American Society in the Twentieth Century* (New York, 1984), contain perceptive insights into cultural values in the period.

3

The Great Depression and the New Deal

Stuart Kidd

During recent years, the New Deal's legacy of a strong state serving the interests of the disadvantaged and underprivileged appeared beleaguered in the face of the claims of the New Conservatism of the 1980s that it represented the idealism of a misguided past rather than the realism of an engaged present. Undoubtedly Herbert Hoover would have gained satisfaction from the Republican party's belated revenge upon the Democrats' New Deal. For not only has the range of the state's responsibilities been reduced within the past decade, but the very notion of a strong state has been denounced as un-American, echoing Hoover's own beliefs in the 1930s. For liberals, on the other hand, the retraction of the state's responsibilities in fields such as welfare is disturbing, and they challenge the notion that a strong, welfare-oriented state is inherently un-American. They point to the inexorable development of the reforming impulse from the Populist movement of the 1890s, through Progressivism, the New Deal, the Fair Deal, and the New Frontier, to the Great Society program of the 1960s. For them, the strong, humane state is the epitome of enlightened twentieth-century Americanism, and they regard the New Deal as a crucial stage in its development.

The New Deal emerged out of the Great Depression of the 1930s, and while the Depression was not a peculiarly American phenomenon, liberals suggest that the New Deal was a distinctive American response to it. While some Americans in the 1930s were inspired and excited by experiments in economic planning and political management in authoritarian states such as the Soviet Union and Italy, the capitalist system and the democratic basis of American society survived the rigors of the Depression. Arthur Schlesinger, Jr., believed that the Great Depression constituted "a profound challenge to the pragmatic nerve" which the New Deal met by rejecting catastrophic perspectives in favour of "activism," "gradualness," and "piecemeal experiment."[1] One need not accept Schlesinger's eulogy of American liberalism to agree with his central point about the distinctiveness of the New Deal. Whatever its limitations, the New Deal did manage to avert a major political transformation in the United States through a more innovative political economy than was the case in other democratic states, such as Britain and France, which generally adopted policies of conservative retrenchment.

The New Deal emerged out of a crisis for American capitalism. In 1933 the administration of Franklin D. Roosevelt inherited a critical economic situation that had developed since October 1929, but which had its sources in both the maldistribution of income and the structural problems of the American economy during the 1920s. The volume of industrial production had declined by almost half its level of 1929, while construction activity, often cited as an indicator of an economy's health, was only one-eighth of its 1929 level. New residential housing starts declined from 937,000 units in 1925, the peak year of the previous decade, to 93,000 in 1933, the lowest number of starts since the 1880s when reliable records are first available. Certain sectors of the economy were particularly affected by the Depression. Agriculture, which had suffered from excess capacity since World War I, experienced average price declines of 60 percent between 1929 and 1933. In the year 1933 alone, 10 percent of the nation's farms were sold, most through forced sales and mortgage foreclosures. Financial institutions, which provided the motor for American capitalism, were in disarray. Between 1929 and 1934, ten thousand deposit banks failed, and on March 4, 1933, the day of Franklin Roosevelt's inauguration, thirty-eight states had closed their banks. On the same day the New York Stock Exchange suspended operations.

Most notably the Roosevelt administration inherited 13

million unemployed Americans who constituted about 25 percent of the work force. Estimates of unemployment for the 1930s are notoriously unreliable since the federal government did not undertake rigorous statistical accounting until 1940. It is frequently and tragically stated that during the Depression the federal government had more comprehensive information on pigs than on unemployed people. Any realistic assessment of unemployment must further take account of underemployment: of the amount of part-time work and the extent to which workers were obliged to accept employment that did not utilize their skills or expertise. One survey of unemployment in Philadelphia during April 1931 revealed that beyond the 25.5 percent without any job, 13.8 percent worked part-time. The incidence of unemployment also appears to have had a generational dimension. A partial census of 1937 revealed that while the overall unemployment rate was 16.4 percent, for fifteen-to-nineteen-year-olds it was 36.5 percent.

Such a clinical presentation of the evidence does not serve to convey the tragedy of the Depression which remains most effectively rendered by press photographs of Hoovervilles on the shoreline of New York's East River or of five-cent apple sellers on the intersections of city streets. The federal government established its own photographic program within the Farm Security Administration. Many of the 270,000 images reveal the extent of poverty, transience, and social dislocation occasioned by the Depression. Some of the most dramatic concern dust-bowl migrants for whom drought compounded existing problems of low agricultural prices and the consolidation of farms. Even before the publication of John Steinbeck's *The Grapes of Wrath* (1939), government photographers such as Arthur Rothstein and Dorothea Lange had alerted Americans to the nature of these developments. Rothstein's famous *Dust Storm* image presents a father and his sons struggling through a dust dune which almost submerges an outhouse of their farm, while Lange's *Migrant Mother* portrays a beleaguered mother in a pea pickers' camp in California anxiously contemplating an uncertain future. The folk singer Woody Guthrie immortalized the circumstances of the "soldiers in the dust." In his autobiography he describes his departure from Pampa, Texas, in heroic terms through the reconstruction of a conversation with the truck driver who is giving him a ride:

"Woody! Where ya headin?" . . .
"Cal'fornia," I said. "Hustlin' outta this dam dust!"
"Fer piece down th' road, ain't it?"
"Enda this dam highway! Ain't a-lookin' back!"[2]

There was a tendency for creative intellectuals during the 1930s to sentimentalize and ennoble "the people" and their sufferings, whether in the form of Guthrie's defiant boast that "dust can't kill me," the stoic determination of Lange's stranded mother, or Jane Darwell's dignified portrayal of Ma Joad in John Ford's screen version of *The Grapes of Wrath* (1940). There is much substance in the argument that this tendency romanticized the appalling. Ann Marie Low, who was a student in North Dakota during the mid-1930s, described the dust bowl in her diary as a more somber and disturbing experience: "The drought and dust storms are something fierce. As far as one can see are brown pastures and fields which, in the wind, just rise up and fill the air with dirt. It tortures animals and humans, makes housekeeping an everlasting drudgery, and ruins machinery."[3] Lorena Hickok, a "confidential investigator" for the New Deal's relief administrator, Harry Hopkins, reported on the lived realities of the "Okies" in California during 1934:

> On the outskirts of Bakersfield is a place called "Hoover City"—a jungle of tents, cardboard houses, built out of cartons, no sanitation whatever. In "Hoover City" live 100 families, wretchedly—itinerant farm workers, oil workers out of jobs, unemployed of all sorts. It's a terrible place. . . . What *are* we going to do with these people?[4]

The end of Guthrie's "highway" for some Okies was personal tragedy: a sad and ironic inversion of the American ethic of westward movement.

The West and its inhabitants were not the sole victims of the Depression. In his second inaugural, Franklin Roosevelt recognized the scope and magnitude of the crisis when he claimed that "one-third of a nation" was "ill-housed, ill-clad, ill-nourished." In 1938 he identified the South as "the nation's number one economic problem," and the National Emergency

Council's subsequent *Report on Economic Conditions of the South* pointed to the inadequate standard of living in the region. Of particular concern was the declining plantation system and its handmaiden, sharecropping. Over 1.7 million families, or about 8.5 million individuals, were dependent upon some sort of tenancy arrangement in the South. They constituted approximately one-quarter of the South's total population and accounted for half its farmers. At the bottom of the tenancy pyramid was the sharecropper who farmed twenty to fifty acres, shared his crop equally with his landlord in lieu of a cash rent, and was often chronically in debt to local merchants. Erskine Caldwell's gothic portrayal of Jeeter Lester and his family in *Tobacco Road* (1932) symbolized the desperation of the cropper in the Depression decade. Yet "low" comedy does not appear an appropriate medium to convey the plight of a class with little land and less capital, who farmed soils that were often as impoverished as the means used to cultivate them were outmoded. In the mountain counties state relief directors estimated that between 30 percent and 60 percent of the population received relief, and ironically, may have suffered no consequent decline in their standard of living. In 1934 a field worker for the Federal Emergency Relief Administration described a district in western Tennessee as "table land. Thin soil. Terrible housing. Illiteracy. Evidence of prolonged undernourishment. No knowledge of how to live decently or farm profitably even if they had decent land."[5] For sharecroppers accustomed to hard times the Depression was a catastrophe. While "five-cent cotton" placed intolerable strains on already unacceptable standards of living, mechanization and the consolidation of agriculture deprived croppers of their conventional means of making any living at all. During the late 1930s sharecropping began to disappear under a "tidal wave of tractors."

In an industrial society, some of the most visible effects of the Depression were evident in the cities where most Americans lived and worked. The bread lines, apple sellers and shantytowns became sad features of the urban landscape during the early phase of the Depression. In New York City an average of 5,000 people a day visited the Free Employment Bureau, while in mid-January 1931, eighty-one distribution points provided free meals for 85,000 people. During the early 1930s between 300,000 and 800,000 New Yorkers were jobless—a double tragedy because of the extent of unemployment and the imprecision with which it was estimated. Although the standard of living for those in full employment may have improved during the Depression due to declining prices, many were cast into abject poverty. Economic stagnation and rising unemployment resulted in a shrinking tax base for city governments and, by the early summer of 1932, major industrial cities such as Philadelphia and Detroit were unable to meet their responsibilities for relief.

The economic and social crisis was paralleled by a crisis of authority within American society, not dissimilar to those in western Europe during the interwar years. Unlike the crises in France, Germany, and Italy, however, the crisis in the United States was a product of previous accomplishment rather than of inherent political and ideological division, military defeat, or the structural weaknesses of its political system. During the 1920s American capitalism had appeared capable of creating a society of abundance. The economy grew at a rate of 5 percent a year and real wages increased by 40 percent in the six years before 1929. By the year of the Great Crash one in six Americans owned an automobile. Will Rogers's pithy aphorism that America was the first country to go to the poorhouse in an automobile suggests a reason for the particular American crisis of leadership: the abrupt reversal of optimistic expectations.

The business leaders who had received cultural canonization during the 1920s were in disrepute after the stock-market crash of October 1929. Many subscribed to the fatalism of classical economic theory which assumed not only the inevitability of economic slumps but the undesirability of ameliorative action. It was apparent to many Americans not only that these custodians of the national future were unable to produce economic recovery through their own efforts, but that their actions had contributed to the economic collapse. In 1932 a Senate committee and its counsel, Ferdinand Pecora, revealed instances of malpractice by respected investment bankers in handling their clients' funds during the 1920s, and discovered, moreover, that they had evaded their social responsibilities during the economic crisis by minimizing their tax payments. Many of the visionary architects of the "temples" to the American way such as the utilities magnate Samuel Insull, who had been acclaimed by Calvin Coolidge in the 1920s, were within a decade associated rather with jails.

This disenchantment with business leadership was complemented by a disillusionment with political authority. Although historians such as Ellis Hawley and Joan Hoff Wilson have revised traditional views of Hoover as the last of the rugged individualists, it remains true that Hoover was not prepared to use the full powers of the federal government to counter the economic crisis. While he was neither a standpat conservative nor a naïve optimist, his devout commitment to residual American values compromised the effectiveness of his programs and deprived him of the appearance of being an active and humane chief executive. Although the American people did not overwhelmingly reject Hoover in 1932, Franklin Roosevelt, his principal opponent, won a resounding victory. While 15,758,901 Americans voted for Hoover, his Democratic opponent received 22,809,638 votes.

If the contemporary speculation about whether the United States was on the brink of a revolution was farfetched and fanciful, there can be no doubt that the early phase of the Depression constituted a crisis for the American establishment. In the latter decades of the century we have become inured to militant farmers in Europe blocking highways and ports to prevent food shipments, and angry American Vietnam veterans demonstrating for recognition, compensation, and the verification of comrades missing in action. Consequently we may not appreciate the significance of either the disruptive actions of the Farmers' Holiday Association or the protest of the Bonus Marchers and its violent finale. At the time many intellectuals believed that the conditions were propitious for radical change: the breakdown of financial, production, and distributive mechanisms; the enlargement of the proletariat as unemployment increased, and the emergence of a repressive regime that needed to resort to force to maintain its authority.

The election returns of 1932 do not confirm this impression. Norman Thomas, for the Socialist party, and William Z. Foster, the Communist party's candidate, failed to poll a million votes between them. Despite the economic crisis, Thomas won fewer votes than Eugene Debs in 1912. Paradoxically, while the Great Depression confirmed much of socialist theory, the Socialist party collapsed during the decade. In 1936 Thomas received 187,342 votes, the lowest total received by a Socialist party candidate since 1900, while in the same year party membership declined to six thousand, the lowest figure since the party's founding. There are numerous reasons for the demise of the Socialist party in the 1930s but the most telling is the electoral appeal that placed the Democratic party in the vanguard of progressive change and gave it the power to effect such change. As Norman Thomas frequently recalled, the New Deal was to appropriate much of the Socialist party's platform of 1932.

The Communist party did experience growth during the Depression. Its membership increased from seventy-five hundred in 1930 to fifty-five thousand in 1938, plus about thirty thousand unregistered members in youth groups and trade unions. The party attracted support due to the Popular Front strategy, initiated by Stalin in 1935, which ordered Western Communist parties to cooperate with democratic and liberal groups in a united front against fascism, and because of the Soviet Union's support for the Republican cause during the Spanish Civil War (1936–39). However, despite its influence in the labor union movement and within government projects during the 1930s its importance as an organized political force should not be overstated. In 1936 Earl Browder could muster only 80,181 popular votes in the presidential election, while in 1940, in the wake of the Nazi-Soviet Pact, this declined to only 48,579. The Communists suffered along with the Socialists from the New Deal capturing the ground of the Left.

While the New Deal may serve to explain the failure of radical parties in the 1930s, it does not explain why they were not more successful in the election of 1932. The American electorate was not voting for the New Deal because it could not be anticipated in the vague, evasive, and often contradictory statements made by Roosevelt in his presidential campaign. Neither were the election results simply a repudiation of Hoover and a preference for Roosevelt, a charismatic and engaging political figure in comparison. The two-party system, whatever its inherent strengths, does not confine the nature of electoral behavior regardless of the economic and social context. In fact broader influences were at work in the form of the electoral realignment activated by Al Smith's campaign in 1928, in which the Democratic party attracted the votes of socialism's natural constituents: urban, ethnic, working-class groups.

During the 1930s the Democratic party became the national majority party, breaking the dominance that the Republican party had held since the 1890s. It was the New Deal rather than the Depression that consolidated Smith's gains and transformed the party into the normal majority party. In 1932 although Roosevelt won over 1.5 million more votes in cities than his Republican opponent, he failed to win twelve cities with populations of over 100,000. In 1936 he won ten of them and maintained the Democratic party's strength in cities that had been strong for Smith in 1928, despite the fact that he had ousted Smith as the party's leader. The election of 1936 also signified the incorporation of black Americans into the New Deal coalition, for while the majority of blacks had remained loyal to the party of Lincoln in 1932, they voted three-to-one in favor of Roosevelt in 1936. Organized labor voted overwhelmingly for Roosevelt in view of the New Deal's record on labor reforms and relief measures. In 1936 the CIO formed Labor's Nonpartisan League for Roosevelt, thereby departing from organized labor's policy of political nonalignment established by Samuel Gompers during the nineteenth century.

This constituency, together with the "solid South," which cast 76 percent of its vote for Roosevelt in 1936, elected FDR for an unprecedented four terms. These substantial changes in the party's composition and character buttressed Roosevelt despite the return of many rural voters to the Republican party in 1940, his controversial third-term decision, and his provocative conduct of foreign policy which antagonized isolationist opinion.

It is widely held, to the point where it has become almost an article of faith, that the New Deal preempted the development of more radical political forces. However, the broad statistical outlines of the economic history of the 1930s do not fully explain the popularity of Franklin D. Roosevelt and the New Deal for the American electorate or the acclaim that the New Deal and its maker have received from subsequent historians. The Roosevelt administration inherited nearly 13 million Americans unemployed but after seven years the New Deal had not managed even to halve the jobless total; over 8 million Americans, or 14.6 percent of the work force, remained unemployed. Also, despite a range of counterdepression strategies the American economy was unable to reach the 1929 level of industrial production until 1940.

However, the principles and precedents established by the

New Deal have proved as important for academic historians in evaluating its significance as the achievement of any immediate, short-term objectives. Many contend that the New Deal constituted a crossroads, or a watershed, in America's historical development. Carl Degler described it as "The Third American Revolution," as significant as the War of Independence and the Civil War in the changes that it inaugurated.[6] As the Great Depression represented the culmination of the processes of industrialization and urbanization that had transformed American society since the Civil War, the New Deal represented the maturation of the state's response to these developments: to control them in the national interest. This involved departures from the limited state of the nineteenth century and related assumptions about the desirability of the "free market," the sanctity of private property, and the virtues of American individualism. The changes wrought by the New Deal endured and by the 1960s had become central to the social and economic patterns of American life.

The New Deal reshaped the "private economy" prevailing in the United States, and introduced a mixed economy in which government, organized labor, and other interest groups joined business executives in economic decision-making. The federal government's commitment to a managed economy was of central importance and was reflected by several developments that substantially increased the state's economic functions. Although the Roosevelt administration was ill at ease with an unbalanced budget, and subscribed to Keynesian fiscal policy as much by coincidence as by intention, the New Deal ran a deficit throughout the 1930s, which was vital for relief and work provision for the unemployed. The New Deal's highest annual deficit—$4.42 billion in 1936—appears very small by today's standards and it is estimated that the New Deal's expenditures would have needed to have been five to ten times greater to affect demand significantly enough to promote recovery through the Keynesian formula. Furthermore, in fiscal 1938 the Roosevelt administration reduced the deficit to less than half that of the last year of Hoover's presidency. The result was the so-called Roosevelt recession of 1937–38 in which over 2.5 million Americans were added to the ranks of the unemployed.

Especially during the early Roosevelt period many New Dealers believed that economic revival would be promoted through structural reform rather than through fiscal policy. According to Richard Kirkendall, the New Deal sought to integrate agriculture within a "collectivist type of capitalism." This involved an increase in the regulatory functions of government over American agriculture and the promotion of farmers' own organizations. Production control was the New Deal's principal response to the excess capacity that had existed in agriculture since World War I. The Agricultural Adjustment Act of May 1933 encouraged farmers to reduce output by offering subsidies in return for their taking land out of production. The farmers' subsidies were derived from a processing tax, and when this was declared unconstitutional by the Supreme Court in 1936, were paid directly from the government's general revenue. Both the Soil Conservation and Domestic Allotment Act of 1936 and the second AAA of 1938 maintained the production control formula by changing the rationale of the policy from economic management to resource conservation, thus evading the constitutional question of whether the federal government could control production per se. The act of 1938 also supplemented production allotment with surplus control through the "ever-normal granary" which provided loans to farmers to store crops during abundant years. Although, as with unemployment, it was World War II rather than the New Deal that solved the agricultural crisis of the 1930s, the New Deal transformed the relationship of the state to the agricultural sector.

While the principal beneficiaries of these programs were large farmers and their organizations such as the Farm Bureau Federation, the New Deal's agricultural policy did not serve the exclusive interests of the large commercial concerns. Both the Resettlement Administration, created in 1935, and its successor of 1937, the Farm Security Administration, were intended to benefit small farmers and tenants, and their activities included the provision of low-interest loans to facilitate farm purchase or improvements and the establishment of subsistence-homestead communities to resettle destitute and marginal farmers. Statistically, the achievements of these agencies appear impressive. Tenant purchase loans were made to over 47,000 farmers, 145,000 were given help to reduce their debts, 300,000 farm families participated in producers/consumers cooperatives, and about 80,000 FSA clients benefited from the agency's health-care programs. Nevertheless, this assistance was small compared to the need. In the South alone there were 1.7 million tenants in 1935. Here, as elsewhere in the New Deal, public policy was constrained by existing social and political realities. Southern commercial interests, in particular, deeply resented the federal government's interference in the plantation system and with the rules of class, race, and caste that underpinned it.

The principles of government intervention and regulation within the economy were applied also to industry. The Roosevelt administration was ambivalent about the issue of industrial concentration and appeared to veer from an attitude close to Theodore Roosevelt's New Nationalism to a policy resonant of Woodrow Wilson's New Freedom by the later years of the decade. While the National Industrial Recovery Act of 1933 gave trade associations the authority to set standards to stabilize and regulate their commercial sectors exempt from the antitrust laws, in 1938 the New Deal embarked upon an antitrust program under Thurmond Arnold, and established the Temporary National Economic Committee to investigate the extent of monopoly in the United States. However, the New Deal's shift was one of emphasis, not of substance, and was in accord with the principle of federal regulation of business activity established with government supervision of the codes of fair competition formulated by the trade associations under the NIRA.

Many contemporaries—like many subsequent historians—appeared relieved that the Supreme Court invalidated the NIRA in *Schechter* v. *U.S.* (1935). However, the NIRA was a bold and complex venture that linked industrial stabilization, through codes of fair competition, with labor reforms and public-works expenditure. It contained a theory of recovery that was dependent upon synchronizing the efforts of the trade associations to rationalize business conditions through output and trade practice agreements with the increased economic demand that maximum hours, minimum wages, increased trade union activity, and a $3.3 billion appropriation for public works were expected to produce. In the event the Public Works Administration, directed by Harold Ickes, was too cautious in implementing projects to be able to "prime the pump" of economic demand to the degree required. Furthermore, as the National Recovery Review Board reported in 1934, the code authorities had become dominated by big business and the codes they produced served to restrict production and maintain prices to the detriment of independents. In both aspects the National Recovery Administration was undermined by the inadequacy of the federal government's administrative resources to implement a program of such scale and scope. Had it been successful, the NIRA would have had significant implications for the American political economy, with rational economic management being conducted within a democratic framework. The NRA's failure was due to a lack not of vision but of capacity. However, such a vision required readjustments in both the competitive ideal and the powers of the state that would have been unacceptable to many Americans.

While it was World War II rather than the New Deal that solved the problem of unemployment, the New Deal introduced the principle of government responsibility to ensure maximum employment which was subsequently codified in the Employment Act of 1946. The New Deal's relief programs were continuous throughout the 1930s, and imperative in 1933 due to the extent of unemployment and the inability of either local governments or private charities to cope with the relief burden. In 1934 eight million households were dependent on the federal government.

Because the federal government had no agencies specifically responsible for relief the Roosevelt administration had to create them. Whereas Hoover had only been prepared to make loans to the states for relief purposes, the Federal Emergency Relief Administration, established in May 1933, made outright and matching grants of federal funds to states to distribute food supplies, provide educational assistance, maintain transient camps, and encourage rural rehabilitation programs. While FERA provided direct relief to the needy, the program was not considered adequate to meet relief requirements during the forthcoming winter and in November 1933 an emergency agency was created under FERA's auspices, the Civil Works Administration. During the five months it existed it employed four million Americans on 180,000 federal, state, and local work projects. To maximize its effectiveness, it concentrated its funds on labor-intensive projects that were usually locally supervised. Although 80 percent of the administration's expenditures were devoted to wages rather than materials, relief recipients were not given mere make-work projects. CWA workers built 3,700 children's playgrounds and 450 landing areas at airports, and one-third of the budget was devoted to providing 250,000 miles of new and improved roads.

The distinction between direct relief and work relief was an important one in the New Deal's programs. Direct relief was regarded as a dole which, in Roosevelt's words, acted as "a narcotic, a subtle destroyer of the spirit." Work relief, however, was considered a constructive way station between unemployment and private employment, and payments were deliberately fixed below prevailing wage levels in the private sector to facilitate the transition. The most notable example of this approach to work relief and the New Deal's most significant agency in this sphere was the Works Progress Administration. Founded in 1935, it spent $11.5 billion during its eight-year life span, employing over eight million workers, nearly three-fourths of whom were employed in engineering and construction. The WPA improved 572,000 miles of the national road system and built 67,000 miles of new streets, 78,000 new bridges and viaducts, and 8,000 parks. Despite these achievements there were distinct limits to the WPA's vision since it ignored the opportunities offered for manpower training. As James Patterson writes: "Most WPA jobs paid poorly and operated on the very dubious middle-class premise that all blue-collar workers were alike—equally able to perform any manual labor, no matter how demanding or unfamiliar."[7]

The WPA's activities were not limited to construction. The four arts projects organized within Federal One, the project established by the WPA in 1935, supported American artists and American art during a period when private patronage and demand had slumped. Within six months of its founding, Federal One employed 40,000 people and was to cultivate the talents of a range of creative intellectuals who would achieve eminence in later years, such as the novelists Richard Wright and John Cheever, the painters Jackson Pollock and Willem de Kooning, and the film director John Huston.

The New Deal's relief programs also addressed the needs of unemployed young people. One of the New Deal's most dramatic ventures was the foundation of the Civilian Conservation Corps, the first alphabetical agency to be created, in March 1933. By the time it was terminated in 1942, the agency had enrolled 2.5 million unemployed young men between the ages of eighteen and twenty-five to work on projects involving reforestation, prevention of soil erosion, national park development, and flood control. Besides being a relief measure, the CCC was an early indication of the New Deal's concern with resource management and conservation, which would be developed in subsequent agencies such as the Tennessee Valley Authority, the Resettlement Administration, the Farm Security Administration, and the Soil Conservation Service. The National Youth Administration was founded in 1935 and by the end of 1941 had provided 1.8 million young people with "out-of-school work programs" and aided 2 million students by providing work programs that financed their education.

Carl Degler claimed that a "guarantor state" emerged in the 1930s whereby the federal government promoted general welfare interests within the context of a private business culture.[8] The Social Security Act, signed by Roosevelt in August 1935, was perhaps the New Deal's most outstanding individual achievement in this respect. Unemployment insurance would be provided by a federal payroll tax on employers of more than eight workers and would be administered by the various states. Provision was made for matching federal and state funds for the states to aid the indigent (the crippled, the blind, dependent children, etc.), while the federal government assumed responsibility for old age insurance on the basis of a tax levied equally on employers and employees. For a society that had extolled the virtues of the work ethic and private charity, these were significant developments indeed.

The "guarantor state" extended to the protection and preservation of residential and farm property but revealed the limits of the New Deal's liberalism. While the New Deal assumed a potential conflict between private property and the public interest, this was one of scale and not of fundamental principle. The private mortgage market was supported by both the Home Owners' Loan Corporation, founded in June 1933, and the Federal Housing Administration, created in June 1934. By the middle of 1936 corporation loans covered one million mortgages. Farmers derived similar benefits. By the end of 1935, the Farm Credit Act of June 1933 and the Farm Mortgage Refinancing Act of January 1934 arranged federal refinance for one in five farm mortgages, while the Farm Mortgage Moratorium Act of August 1935 provided for a three-year moratorium against foreclosure, subject to court approval. In these spheres the New

Deal's concept of private property was positively Jeffersonian. On the other hand, the New Deal's commitment to public housing was limited. Between 1933 and 1937 the PWA's Housing Division sponsored fifty-one public projects in thirty-six cities housing 22,000 families at a cost of $150 million. In September 1937 the United States Housing Authority was established and received an initial appropriation of $500 million to provide financial assistance to state and local housing authorities to build rented accommodation for the lowest-income citizens. By 1941 only 350 USHA projects had been initiated, which accounted for 130,000 homes. Clearly, such a limited commitment was inadequate to meet the requirements of urban renewal and rehousing. Nevertheless, it should be recognized that the New Deal's major public housing campaign occurred during a period of Congressional conservatism and against a backcloth of local opposition to public housing. The Roosevelt administration had no magic wand with which to put its policies into effect and, as elsewhere, national and local resistance contributed to limiting the scope of the program.

Historical writing about the New Deal generally accepts the premise that the growth of the state during the 1930s served to challenge the prerogatives of private wealth and power. The New Deal is therefore viewed as part of the American liberal tradition which sought to advance the interests of the community against those of the business classes. Concerns expressed by organizations such as the Liberty League and the National Association of Manufacturers were not misplaced because of the New Deal's attempt to restrict the scope of private wealth and power in the interests of the general welfare.

Regulation of the special interests was a major concern of the New Deal. From the very outset the Roosevelt administration intervened dramatically to bolster the banking system. Roosevelt's proclamation of a national bank holiday, which permitted the Treasury Department to evaluate banks before they were allowed to reopen, was reinforced subsequently by legislation of a more permanent character. The Banking Acts of 1933 and 1935 were intended to restore confidence in the banking system by guaranteeing savers' deposits, divorcing the business of banks from speculation, and rationalizing the Federal Reserve system to give its board greater authority to make monetary policy effective during economic recessions. The New Deal's banking policy sought to give the banking system a preventive function with regard to the business cycle, as opposed to the contributory role it had played in causing the depression of the 1930s. Similarly, the Federal Securities Act (1933) and the Securities Exchange Act (1934) sought to outlaw the kinds of unethical and imprudent practices that had contributed to the Wall Street crash. The 1934 law created the Securities and Exchange Commission to regulate new issues and trading practices.

In the sphere of public energy the New Deal clashed frequently with the utilities. With the Tennessee Valley Authority, created in May 1933, the New Deal accomplished what had been impossible during the 1920s: the federal development of the Muscle Shoals project to cover the entire Tennessee basin. By 1945 the system consisted of nine dams on the main river and eleven on its tributaries. The authority intended to promote wide-ranging regional development through flood control, land use, and reclamation, but most importantly through the generation of hydroelectric power whose rates would serve as a yardstick for private companies. The project involved the cooperation of seven state governments and represented the conviction that electricity was not amenable to local control. In the field of rural electrification the New Deal undertook to provide services to areas that private utilities had neglected on grounds of cost and risk. Established in 1935, the Rural Electrification Administration provided electricity to 780,000 farmers in 1941 and accounted for 75 percent of all new rural installations. Whereas only 10 percent of American farmers were supplied with electricity in 1933, 35 percent enjoyed its benefits by 1941. The New Deal sought to regulate public utilities as well as supplement them. The Public Utility Holding Company Act of 1935 threatened dissolution to electricity and gas conglomerates that could not demonstrate their efficiency, social usefulness, and local importance.

It should be noted that these reforms were not necessarily inimical to the interests of the capitalist class since government regulation was considered by many indispensable to the stability of the capitalist system itself. Historians from the left such as Ronald Radosh and Gabriel Kolko have suggested that the New Deal's reforms were perfectly consonant with the interests of the capitalist class. Indeed, Radosh believes that a corporate liberal elite was instrumental in framing and promoting many of them.[9] Neither did the New Deal's policies always conform to its rhetoric. Although Roosevelt asserted in his tax message of June 1935 that "the duty rests upon the government to restrict [large] incomes by very high taxes," the subsequent Wealth Tax Act increased taxes by only $250 million and did not significantly redistribute wealth. The New Deal's labor reforms, however, were less welcome to the business community, although Radosh and other dissenting historians would claim otherwise. They represent the other side of liberal historians' "anti-business" coin. Not only did the state intervene in the traditionally private conduct of labor-management relations but it provided the means for the working class to advance its own interests through collective action.

The New Deal sought to use the state's power to provide basic standards for the American working population through maximum hours and minimum wages introduced in the NIRA of 1933 and reiterated in the Fair Labor Standards Act of 1938. However, the principal significance of the New Deal was its encouragement to labor organization. First established in Section 7(a) of the NIRA and reinforced in 1935 in the National Labor Relations Act (Wagner Act), the workers' rights to join a union free from employer interference and to have that union negotiate on his or her behalf provided a tremendous stimulus to union organization. Not only did union membership increase from barely three million in 1933 to almost nine million in 1939, but the New Deal's collective bargaining initiatives stimulated the growth of organization in the mass-production, unskilled industries. This led to the growth of a major splinter union confederation, initially established within the AFL in 1935 as the Committee for Industrial Organization, expelled in 1936, and becoming formally independent in 1938 as the Congress of Industrial Organizations under the leadership of John L. Lewis, head of the United Mine Workers.

Labor's advances during the 1930s were not accomplished without considerable friction in labor-management relations. Strike activity sharply increased during the New Deal period. Irving Bernstein places the year 1934 alongside 1886 and 1894 as having "a special quality in American labor history."[10] About 1.5 million workers were involved in over eighteen hundred strikes during that year. The major issue in these work stoppages was union organization and recognition. Throughout the summer Minneapolis was racked by the teamsters' strike for union recognition, which involved considerable civil disorder due to violent clashes between the strikers and both the antiunion Citizens' Alliance and the police. On the West Coast, longshoremen, acting unofficially, managed to shut down virtually every port on the shoreline. This culminated in a general strike in San Francisco between July 16 and 19.

The peak year for strikes during the 1930s, however, was 1937, when over forty-seven hundred work stoppages took place, involving nearly two million workers. The large majority of these strikes were about union recognition and were most spectacular in the automobile industry where workers illegally occupied factories in sit-down strikes at General Motors and Chrysler. The principal beneficiary of this upsurge of industrial unionism was the CIO, whose membership totals rivaled and sometimes surpassed those of the AFL during its early years. Due to the organizing drives of the CIO and their stimulating effects upon the AFL, the percentage of the labor force organized rose from 7.4 in 1936 to 17.7 in 1941.

Employer resistance to unionization was considerable and belies the argument of some of the Left that the New Deal's labor reforms were welcomed by employers as a means of diverting working-class discontent into safe, conservative, bureaucratic channels. Employers resisted unionization by violent means, whether in the form of a Citizens Army in Minneapolis or through the use of armed police as in San Francisco or in Chicago. In the latter city, ten demonstrators were killed at Republic Steel on May 30, 1937, in what became known as the Memorial Day Massacre. During 1937 two developments significantly softened employer resistance. In December a Senate subcommittee chaired by Senator Robert M. La Follette, Jr., exposed the range of antiunion techniques used by employers, including strikebreakers, vigilante groups, espionage agents, and the blacklist. Of greater importance was the Supreme Court's decision in the Jones and Laughlin Steel Corporation case which affirmed the constitutionality of the Wagner Act and hence deprived employers of any excuse not to comply with its terms.

Given the extent of employer resistance to unionization, together with the Roosevelt administration's own concerns about militant unionism, it may seem reasonable to argue that labor's gains were the products of its own struggles rather than gifts from the state. Indeed, Frances Fox Piven and Richard A. Cloward have contended that labor's gains were greatest when the working class was at its most militant and the state was put on the defensive. However, it is incontestable that the New Deal provided the context in which these struggles could be successful.[11]

Following James MacGregor Burns, some liberal historians claim that the Roosevelt administration developed a "broker state" which promoted a plurality of conflicting demands upon policymakers, but directed the state's policy not according to a group's influence or power alone, but according to predetermined principles of equity and justice.[12] It sought to invest new meaning to American values such as democracy, equality of opportunity, and voluntary cooperation through intervention to provide constraints upon private action, direct support to those without the resources to help themselves, and, in particular, to confer "countervailing power" upon nondominant groups so as to redress the collective advantages of corporate wealth. Hence brokerage responded to power and sought to develop it in a countervailing manner, but always within an idealistic framework and within the terms of the Roosevelt administration's broader concerns and strategies to secure economic recovery.

African-Americans were variously disadvantaged by this broker-politics scenario. Specific, focused aid to the black community was inhibited by the political risks to a Democratic administration that valued the support of the white supremacist South. President Roosevelt's refusal to support a federal antilynching bill was based on his reluctance to undermine the bedrock of Democratic support in the region. Frequently, as Raymond Wolters has suggested, black interests were at variance with the Roosevelt administration's recovery strategies and were expediently sacrificed.[13] The minimum wage deprived southern black workers of their one competitive advantage in selling their labor, while federal subsidies for production control served to encourage landlords to dispense with tenants, and the planter-dominated county committees that distributed federal subsidies often prevented tenants from receiving their just allocations. Furthermore, the original Social Security Act did not apply to agricultural laborers or domestic servants, major occupations for black Americans in this period, and the decentralized nature of the WPA's public-works projects allowed local, and often racist, forces to determine who would benefit from employment and the eventual completed projects.

The benefits that African-Americans derived from the New Deal were as members of a disadvantaged class rather than as a racial minority. Yet the 1930s may be described as the seedbed of the civil-rights changes twenty and thirty years later. The establishment of the principle of government intervention on behalf of the disadvantaged had significant implications, as many white Southerners recognized in the 1930s. While it is true that the TVA and CCC maintained segregated work camps in the South, and that the RA and FSA provided limited benefits to black tenants and sharecroppers, the fact remains that the New Deal did interpose the federal government between the subordinated southern black population and the white ruling class and, as such, created the potential for the state to become a significant force in determining the South's conduct of its race relations.

The "broker state" was particularly sensitive to political considerations that could influence the direction of the New Deal's programs. Some historians subscribe to the "two New Deals" thesis, which holds that the Roosevelt administration reoriented its political strategy during 1935 in more progressive social directions. Under pressure from either the "Right" of the Liberty League, or the "Left" of demagogues such as Huey Long, Francis Townsend, and Father Coughlin, the New Deal moved to the "left." The "broker state" is not, therefore, viewed as a static, monolithic entity, but as one that adapted to changing political, economic, and social circumstances and perceptions during the Depression decade.

New Dealers may have overestimated the threat posed by Huey Long. The senator from Louisiana's Share-the-Wealth Movement probably exaggerated the extent of its support: 27,000 clubs with eight million members. Nonetheless, Long's proposal to provide each American family with a five-thousand-dollar endowment by restricting the size of fortunes and re-distributing wealth had inevitable appeal to voters and pointed to a structural absence within the New Deal's own programs. The same can be said for Dr. Francis E. Townsend's Old Age Revolving Pensions Plan. The plan proposed to pay senior citizens two hundred dollars each month on the condition that they spend it within thirty days in order to boost economic demand and promote revival. Townsend Clubs were spawned throughout the United States, claiming a membership of 3.5 million, and able to collect 20 million signatures for their petitions. To dismiss these schemes as impracticable is to ignore the chord they struck in the American consciousness, which was heard clearly by the New Dealers themselves.

Presiding over this "broker state" was Franklin D. Roosevelt, who, many historians believe, performed a crucial historical role. Roosevelt and Hoover assume an antinomial relationship in much historical writing: the experimentalist versus the dogmatic ideologue; the humanist versus the technocrat; the interventionist versus the rugged individualist, and so on. Some liberal historians have also engaged in counterfactual speculation about the likelihood of a great period of American reform issuing from the presidency of a John Nance Garner, Al Smith, or Newton D. Baker, Roosevelt's principal rivals at the Democratic convention of 1932. The doubts of many suggest an underlying assumption that great men do make history and that the New Deal is one of the leading examples of this.

The figure of Roosevelt has both personal and institutional significance. The "squire" from Hyde Park and former governor of New York derived his charisma from a personality that transcended his class background, a strength of presence that was the greater because he was crippled with poliomyelitis, and an adaptable rhetorical ability that could move an inaugural audience as well as a farm family listening to one of his "fireside chats" on the radio. Unlike Hoover, he understood the need for the president to communicate to the people and, in particular, to reassure Americans about the intentions of their government. Perhaps it has become an overworn and sentimental cliché to cite the eulogy delivered by the black workingman during Roosevelt's funeral procession in 1945: "He hope'd me." However, this was the public image that Roosevelt cultivated from his first inaugural when he claimed that "the only thing we have to fear is fear itself."

Roosevelt's electoral popularity was at its height in 1936. Whereas Hoover had won six states in the election of 1932, Alf Landon won only two in 1936, which signaled the extent to which the Republican party had been overwhelmed in the first years of Roosevelt and the New Deal. During Roosevelt's first term the Republicans faced substantial Democratic majorities in both houses of Congress and lacked any consensus about how to sustain a credible political response to the New Deal. Divisions between the progressive forces represented by Landon and the old guard conservatism of Hoover were especially debilitating. As Donald R. McCoy writes of the election of 1936: "The overall impression was that there were two Republican parties in the field, one requesting an opportunity to run the New Deal right, the other waging a crusade against any form of New Deal."[14]

During his first term Roosevelt enjoyed a "tractable Congress" that supported his proposals and granted the president and his agencies significant executive power. This was the basis upon which Roosevelt expanded presidential leadership and power to an unprecedented degree. However, Roosevelt's presidency was not "imperial," and there were definite limits to his own power and that of his office. Both political and institutional forces checked presidential power. Once the immediate economic crisis of 1933 had been negotiated, the huge majorities of the Democrats in Congress promoted the reemergence of factionalism that was inherent in the party. In 1936 the Democrats outnumbered Republicans by three to one in both houses of Congress. Such generous majorities permitted rural and southern Democrats to express their latent hostility to the New Deal's welfare and spending programs. Beginning in 1936 with the utilities and taxation bills, conservative Democrats, in concert with Republicans, began to oppose the New Deal's legislation with increasing effectiveness.

The logic of this situation might have been a party realignment whereby the Republican party incorporated dissident Democratic elements, leaving the Democratic party as the political home for the urban, progressive masses. Roosevelt's intervention in the Congressional elections of 1938 may have been intended to accomplish this. However, this attempt to "purge" selected conservative Democrats during the primaries was a failure and merely served to reinforce the intransigence of conservative elements within his party. Political considerations restricted the powers of the president and the scope of the New Deal.

The limits of presidential power also had an institutional

dimension that may be understood as a reassertion of legislative authority after four years of executive dominance. In particular, Roosevelt's attempt to alter the composition of the Supreme Court in 1937 was widely interpreted as a dangerous interference with the constitutional principle of the separation of powers. The challenges to the New Deal posed by the Supreme Court both in its capacity of judicial review and as an issue forced by Roosevelt were much more serious than the combined efforts of Long and the Liberty League.

During 1935 and 1936 the Court invalidated a number of New Deal measures including the NIRA and the AAA. Roosevelt's response was that the justices' strict constitutional interpretation of the federal government's rightful powers was more appropriate to a "horse-and-buggy" age than to the complex economy of twentieth-century America. Whatever the merits of the argument, his attempt to resolve the impasse between the New Deal and the judiciary by altering the composition of the Court lacked political tact and perception. Rather than propose a constitutional amendment to this end, on February 5, 1937, he asked Congress directly for legislation that would empower him to appoint an additional justice for each sitting justice over the age of seventy years and six months, up to a maximum of six. While the intention was to secure a majority on the Court that was favorable to the New Deal's legislation, the "court-packing plan" was considered by many critics a violation of the Court's traditional independence and hence a dangerous breach of constitutional separation of powers. Even Roosevelt's electoral popularity and personal intervention could not ensure success for his proposals. Roosevelt claimed that he lost the battle but won the war over court reform because subsequent Supreme Court rulings on the New Deal's legislation were favorable. However, this was merely making the best of a serious political defeat. More than any other factor, it was Roosevelt's "court-packing plan" that consolidated conservative opposition to the New Deal.

Roosevelt was not omnipotent, despite his popularity. Neither was the state created by the New Deal monolithic, despite its enormous expansion. While the New Deal changed many of the relationships of the federal system of government, it is also true to say that it was a captive of them. Federal aid to the states rose from $217 million in 1932 to $2 billion in 1935. States were anxious to obtain federal patronage but equally deter mined to maintain local control of its administration. Hence the New Deal often faced the anomalous situation in which states welcomed federal funds but disapproved of the programs for which they were intended. FERA, social security, and the NYA all involved matching federal/state funding. In the case of FERA, the federal government provided over 70 percent of all expenditure on public relief in 1934 and 1935 and had difficulty persuading some states to contribute their shares. The government was forced to federalize relief administration in six states. Furthermore, when the federal government withdrew from providing direct relief in 1935 many states did not take up the responsibility. Thirteen states provided no relief while twelve others spent under fifty cents a month on each of their charges. The record of the states in consolidating the New Deal, in the spheres of labor reform and industrial regulation, fell short of many New Dealers' expectations, and although some states did enact "Little New Deals," they financed them through sales taxes, a regressive mode of taxation.

Through many of its programs the New Deal established direct relationships between the federal government and the cities that circumvented the states. Even here local resistance could undercut the effectiveness of the New Deal's programs. Public housing, for example, was opposed by a broad coalition of interests, including landlords, real estate agents, and mortgage bankers. Twenty-four of the PWA's fifty-one public-housing projects were built on empty land and did not require slum clearance due, to a large extent, to the influence of unsympathetic local interests. There were real limits to the nationalizing tendencies generated by the New Deal, and the period has been aptly characterized as one of "federalism in transition."

The New Deal's limits also have a temporal aspect. It is generally accepted that after 1938 the New Deal was no longer innovative and that New Dealers concentrated on maintaining and expanding existing programs. This was due, in part, to the strength of Congressional conservatism and also to the distractions of world politics at this time. However, as Robert S. McElvaine observes, the Roosevelt administration proposed "few new departures" after 1937, and this suggests that the New Dealers had reached their own limits.[15]

How do we assess the significance of the New Deal? The most influential interpretations of the New Deal were developed in the 1950s and early 1960s, in the wake of McCarthyism and on the tide of the new liberal consensus of Kennedy's New Frontier and Johnson's Great Society. Liberal historians celebrated the virtues of the strong, interventionist state devoted to humane and just social reconstruction, symbolized in the figure of a charismatic and vigorous popular leader. These liberal historians were idealists for whom the history of twentieth-century America was stamped by fitful but unstoppable progress toward a more just and equitable society. For them the New Deal is of more than historical interest; it is the fount of the ongoing effort to achieve social justice.

Their critics on the left have not shared liberals' admiration for the New Deal and its accomplishments. The New Left emerged during the 1960s disillusioned with the capacity of contemporary American liberalism and determined to reappraise the sources of the liberal tradition. Dissenting scholars such as Barton Bernstein, Howard Zinn, William Domhoff, Ronald Radosh, and Theda Skocpol have emphasized the shortcomings of the New Deal's programs, the congruities between the New Deal's reforms and corporate interests, and the coincidences between a strong state and the maintenance of capitalism in a period of crisis. While they may disagree about whether the engine of reform was located in the corporate boardroom or in the executive departments of government they collectively suggest that a primary objective of the New Deal was to preserve the capitalist system and the social order dependent upon it. If the capitalist class was obliged to concede some of its traditional autonomy to federal regulation during the 1930s, the capitalist system itself was sounder in 1940 than when Roosevelt took office. Although the working class made substantial gains from the New Deal, by the end of the Depression decade its potential threat to the capitalist order had been significantly reduced. Clearly, some of the New Left's arguments have been overstated, yet they remain important reference points from which to gauge the limitations of liberal reform.

In the light of the New Conservatism of the 1980s, the optimism of liberal scholars may be thought to have been unfounded and the frustrations of the New Left to have been hopelessly utopian. Americanism in the 1980s had connotations more resonant of the 1920s than of the 1930s. This orientation is likely to be reinforced by momentous global developments as we enter the last decade of the century. The transformation of the state's role and authority in Eastern European countries, together with the restructuring of their collectivist economies on capitalist lines, may suggest that individualism, private property, and democracy are universal prerequisites for the attainment of a satisfactory standard of living. Even the last bastions of communism do not appear secure from challenge. Although thwarted, the students' movement of 1989 on behalf of democracy in China may indicate a significant ground swell for change which may be realized in the near future. Perhaps it will be the twenty-first century that will fulfill Josiah Strong's ambition for the current one: that Shanghai should become like Kansas City. Significantly, the American values that may excite the democratizing communist blocs and will affirm the New Conservatism in the West are those that the New Deal so vigorously questioned in degree if not in substance.

However, we should not be beguiled by the histories of other states to the neglect of the lessons of our own. It is difficult to envisage a satisfactory conservative interpretation of the Great Depression that included photographs of the unemployed, homeless, and destitute of the Hoover years and argued the case for the limited state. If economic fluctuations are beyond the precise control of any form of public policy, the moral issues of economic crisis will undoubtedly reappear in the future, and we should hesitate to write the New Deal's obituary at this point. For like Mark Twain's, it may be premature.

Notes

1. Arthur M. Schlesinger, Jr., "Sources of the New Deal: Reflections on the Temper of a Time," *Columbia University Forum* 2 (Fall 1959): 11–12.

2. Woody Guthrie, *Bound for Glory* (London, 1977), p. 188.

3. Ann Marie Low, *Dust Bowl Diary* (Lincoln, Neb., 1984), p. 101.

4. Harry Hopkins, in *One Third of a Nation: Lorena Hickok Reports on the Great Depression*, ed. Richard Lowitt and Maurine Beasley (Urbana, Ill., 1981), p. 310.

5. Paul E. Mertz, *The New Deal and Southern Rural Poverty* (Baton Rouge, La., 1978), p. 4.

6. Carl N. Degler, *Out of Our Past: The Forces That Shaped Modern America* (New York, 1984), p. 412.

7. James T. Patterson, *America's Struggle against Poverty 1900–1980* (Cambridge, Mass., 1981), p. 65.

8. Degler, *Out of Our Past*, p. 450.

9. Ronald Radosh, "The Myth of the New Deal," in *A New History of Leviathan: Essays on the Rise of the American Corporate State*, ed. Ronald Radosh and Murray Rothbard (New York, 1972), pp. 146–87.

10. Irving Bernstein, *Turbulent Years: A History of the American Worker, 1933–1941* (Boston, 1969), p. 217.

11. Frances Fox Piven and Richard A. Cloward, *Poor People's Movements: Why They Succeed, How They Fail* (New York, 1979).

12. James McGregor Burns, *Roosevelt: The Lion and the Fox* (New York, 1956), pp. 183–208.

13. Raymond Wolters, *Negroes and the Great Depression: The Problem of Economic Recovery* (Westport, Conn., 1970).

14. Donald R. McCoy, *Coming of Age: The United States during the 1920s and 1930s* (Harmondsworth, 1973), p. 264.

15. Robert S. McElvaine, *The Great Depression: America 1929–1941* (New York, 1984), p. 307.

Bibliography

The trauma of the Depression is strongly conveyed by those who experienced it directly. Hank O'Neal's *A Vision Shared: A Classic Portrait of America and Its People, 1935–1943* (New York, 1976) contains an excellent collection of photographs from the FSA project. Life at the northern and southern ends of the Great Plains is recounted in Ann Marie Low, *Dust Bowl Diary* (Lincoln, Neb., 1984) and Woody Guthrie, *Bound for Glory* (New York, 1943), while a distressing insight into southern poverty is provided by the observations of Margaret Bourke White and Erskine Caldwell, *You Have Seen Their Faces* (New York, 1937). Lorena Hickok's reports have been collected in Richard Lowitt and Maurine Beasley, eds., *One Third of a Nation* (Urbana, Ill.,

1981) and Studs Terkel's *Hard Times: An Oral History of the Great Depression* (New York, 1970) contains many and varied first-hand accounts of the era. For historical treatments of the Depression's regional effects, see Donald E. Worster, *The Dust Bowl: The Southern Plains in the 1930s* (New York, 1979); Paul E. Mertz, *The New Deal and Southern Rural Poverty* (Baton Rouge, La., 1978), and Barbara Blumberg, *The New Deal and the Unemployed: The View from New York City* (Cranbury, N.J., 1979). The social theme within American culture during the 1930s is treated in William Stott, *Documentary Expression and Thirties America* (New York, 1973); Richard H. Pells, *Radical Visions and American Dreams: Culture and Social Thought in the Depression Years* (New York, 1973), and David P. Peeler, *Hope Among Us Yet: Social Criticism and Social Solace in Depression America* (Athens, Ga., 1987).

The New Deal's achievements are most emphatically proclaimed in Carl N. Degler, *Out of Our Past: The Forces that Shaped Modern America*, 3rd ed. (New York, 1984), pp. 412–50, and Arthur M. Schlesinger, Jr., *The Age of Roosevelt*, 3 vols. (Boston, 1957–60). William E. Leuchtenburg is more guarded in his excellent *Franklin D. Roosevelt and the New Deal* (New York, 1963), while Robert S. McElvaine updates liberals' evaluations in *The Great Depression: America, 1929–1941* (New York, 1984) by taking account of the people's views. A recent, authoritative work is Anthony J. Badger's thematic treatment, *The New Deal: The Depression Years, 1933–1940* (New York, 1989).

For a range of perspectives from the left that evaluate the significance of the New Deal very differently, see Barton J. Bernstein, "The New Deal: The Conservative Achievements of Liberal Reform," *Towards a New Past: Dissenting Essays in American History* (New York, 1968); Ronald Radosh, "The Myth of the New Deal," in *A New History of Leviathan: Essays on the Rise of the American Corporate State*, ed. Ronald Radosh and Murray N. Rothbard (New York, 1972); and Theda Skocpol, "Political Response to Capitalist Crisis: Neo–Marxist Theories of the State and the Case of the New Deal," *Politics and Society* 10 (1980): 155–201.

The politics of the period are treated in James M. Burns, *Roosevelt: The Lion and the Fox* (New York, 1956), and John M. Allswang, *The New Deal and American Politics: A Study in*

Political Change (New York, 1978). James T. Patterson has contributed tremendously to our understanding of the decade. See *Congressional Conservatism and the New Deal* (Lexington, Ky., 1967), and *The New Deal and the States: Federalism in Transition* (Princeton, N.J., 1969). For the state of the political parties see Arthur M. Schlesinger, Jr., ed., *History of U.S. Political Parties*, vol. 3 (New York, 1973), and outside the mainstream, Alan Brinkley, *Voices of Protest: Huey Long, Father Coughlin, and the Great Depression* (New York, 1982).

The New Deal's approaches to industrial regulation are brilliantly explored by Ellis W. Hawley, *The New Deal and the Problem of Monopoly: A Study in Economic Ambivalence* (Princeton, N.J., 1966), and Theodore Saloutos, *The American Farmer and the New Deal* (Ames, Iowa, 1982) incisively examines agricultural policy. On agriculture, see also Richard S. Kirkendall's essay in John Braeman, Robert H. Bremner, and David Brody, *The New Deal*, vol. 1 (Columbus, Ohio, 1975). A classic study of labor in the 1930s is Irving Bernstein, *Turbulent Years: A History of the American Worker, 1933–1941* (Boston, 1969). The history of black Americans during the decade is treated with differing emphasis by Harvard Sitkoff, *A New Deal for Blacks: The Emergence of Civil Rights as a National Issue* (New York, 1978) and Raymond Wolters, *Negroes and the Great Depression: The Problem of Economic Recovery* (Westport, Conn., 1970). On fiscal policy, see Herbert Stein, *The Fiscal Revolution in America* (Chicago, 1969) and for a collection of interesting essays on topics such as relief, the cities, and women, see Harvard Sitkoff, ed., *Fifty Years Later: The New Deal Evaluated* (New York, 1985).

4

The Forties: Wartime and Postwar America, 1940–1948

Neil A. Wynn

Unlike the other decades in twentieth-century American history, the 1940s are not usually seen as a single coherent period. Instead, historians tend to divide this decade into two distinct and even contrasting parts: the Roosevelt and World War II years from 1941 to 1945, and the postwar Truman years through to 1952. Indeed the period is often seen in terms of the contrasts between the presidents and their achievements, with Roosevelt's apparent success in wartime mobilization and international cooperation, particularly with the Soviet Union, being compared with the conflict and uncertainty at home and the beginning of the Cold War in foreign affairs under Truman.

This division may, however, be no more than a historical convenience, for it is possible to establish continuities both within the 1940s between the war and peace years, and between the 1940s and preceding and succeeding decades. While the particulars may differ, it can be argued that general trends such as the growth of presidential power and federal government begun in the thirties continued through the war years and beyond, and moreover that the basic principles of the New Deal were consolidated and extended. Yet at the same time the forties were a period of transition, witnessing decisive social and economic change that in large measure determined the shape of the decades to come. In other words, it can be suggested that modern America emerged not, as many recent writers claim, after 1945, but even before that, amid the hiatus of World War II.

The impact of World War II on American domestic affairs was for a long time ignored by historians. That is no longer the case. While writers such as Richard Polenberg, John Morton Blum, and Richard Lingeman have pointed to the overall significance of the war years, others have examined the differing effects of the conflict on women, labor, blacks, civil liberties, and the media; one of the latest studies is of gay men and women in World War II. Indeed we might now be said to be in a revisionist phase, with the focus on the permanence of wartime change, questioning the extent to which one might agree with Polenberg's view that "Pearl Harbor marked more than the passing of a decade; it signified the end of an old era and the beginning of a new."[1]

The American war experience differed from that of other countries. The United States suffered none of the devastation experienced by European or Asian nations. Only 400,000 American troops were killed, and 600,000 wounded or missing in action, a negligible figure when compared with the tens of millions who died elsewhere. While the other Allied powers emerged from the war shocked and exhausted, America suffered so few traumas that a retired Red Cross worker could tell historian Studs Terkel that the "war was fun for America."[2]

One fact is certain: World War II ended the Depression. When the conflict in Europe began in 1939 there were still approximately ten million unemployed in America, but as the country moved from being the "arsenal of democracy" to become an active participant this situation quickly changed. American industry boomed during the war as a result of massive Allied war orders and federal defense spending. The GNP rose from $91 billion in 1939 to over $200 billion by 1944, and more new industrial plant came into being during the first three years of the war than in the previous fifteen years of peace.

Industrial growth brought increased employment, and by 1942 there were labor shortages in some parts of the nation. Manpower shortages led to increased employment opportunities, longer working hours, higher wage rates and higher earnings. During the war average real wages rose 50 percent.

This is not to say that everyone got rich during the war—far from it. Many Americans remained trapped in poverty even in this boom period, and others on fixed or limited incomes saw their earnings eroded by inflation. Those people with enlarged incomes often found it difficult to spend their money, as cutbacks and rationing led to shortages or restrictions on consumer goods.

While rationing had an egalitarian aspect in that theoretically at least, it affected everyone equally, the war also brought some leveling in income distribution. Reported incomes for the top one-fifth of the population increased 23 percent; those of the bottom fifth rose by almost 70 percent. Although such figures hide disparities in wealth that existed in other forms, it is still true that many Americans were better clothed and better fed during the war than they had been in the thirties. For most Europeans the contrasts were stark—when GIs began arriving in Britain they were often described as "overfed, oversexed, and over here"!

Such disparities were to continue after the war when America emerged not only with its economy intact, but with $26 billion in new factory plant and huge capital reserves. Wartime shortages and government war bonds meant that Americans had saved $140 billion. At the war's close this money and the bottled-up demand of frustrated consumers combined to fuel the affluent society that quickly emerged after postwar reconversion. This transition was aided by foreign policy initiatives such as the Marshall Plan, the expansion of the armed forces after 1947 with the onset of the Cold War, an expansion of credit, and a variety of domestic government policies. As a consequence of all these forces the GNP stood at $284 billion in 1950, and the average gross family income had risen to $4,444 a year.

In addition to economic change, the war brought considerable change in American government. The need to mobilize and supply a military force of some fifteen million required considerable central direction. Military planning and operations, often in collaboration with foreign powers, needed speed, efficiency, and secrecy. As a result, the war brought about a massive increase in the power of the president and an enormous expansion in the role of federal government. The War Powers Act of 1941 and 1942 enabled President Roosevelt to place executive functions in new agencies and to allocate priorities and resources throughout the economy as necessary. A new bureaucracy emerged beginning with the War Resources Board, a planning body established in 1939 and quickly superseded by the Office of Production Management (1941) and the War Production Board (1942). The WPB, headed by Donald M. Nelson of Sears, Roebuck, was theoretically the supreme war agency responsible for allocating industrial supplies, setting production quotas, and overseeing industry generally. The board was, however, never all-powerful. Roosevelt reserved final authority to himself, and when Nelson's indecisiveness created difficulties the president, in true Rooseveltian style, delegated others to carry out some of the agency's functions.

While various individuals were given responsibility for the production of oil, rubber, or other urgently needed materials, new bodies were created to deal with the many aspects of wartime organization. Paul V. McNutt, former governor of Indiana and head of the Federal Security Administration, now headed a War Manpower Commission to handle the competing demands of industry, agriculture, and the armed forces. An Office of Price Administration was created to stabilize prices and rents and control profiteering. A War Labor Board was established to adjudicate in disputes disrupting war production. The Office of Defense Transportation centralized scheduling and organization of railroads and other transport, but limited itself to coordination rather than the direct control used in World War I. Other agencies dealt with civilian defense, scientific research and development, and war information.

More than thirty new agencies were created and an Office of War Mobilization under James F. Byrnes had to be established to coordinate them all. The federal civil service doubled during the war, and although reduced in peacetime, at over two million it still remained more than twice the size of the prewar establishment. The 1949 Reorganization Act enabled Roosevelt's successor, Harry S. Truman, to eliminate some of the unnecessary agencies and slim down government—at the same time it also improved executive coordination and control of agencies.

Military decision-making and the personal role of the presidents in foreign affairs served further to enhance the role of the executive and the development of an "imperial presidency." Indeed, such was the wartime expansion of executive agencies that some people suggested that Congress was redundant to the war effort, and others even proposed the suspension of party politics in order to present a united front and achieve more efficient wartime government. Despite such ideas, however, politics continued as usual. It was felt to be important to uphold constitutional arrangements, not only for reasons of domestic morale, but also to demonstrate the strength of democratic institutions to the world. There was neither coalition nor national government in America during the war, and not only did Congress continue to amend or oppose legislation throughout the war, but Congressional and presidential elections were also held in 1940, 1942, and 1944.

Although Roosevelt was reelected for third and fourth terms—and it may well be that the war helped to ensure his victories by discouraging ideas of change while the conflict was still continuing—he did face opposition. His margins of victory declined from the heights of the thirties, and Republican Congressional victories strengthened the conservative anti–New Deal coalition that had been evident before 1940. In the immediate postwar elections of 1946 the Republicans captured control of both House and Senate, a feat not achieved since 1930.

This shift to the right in America was in sharp contrast to the British experience where the gain in support for the Labour party culminated in its election victory of 1945. Elsewhere in Europe parties to the left of center gained generally. However the experience of the United States was so dissimilar as to make comparison misleading. Britain, for example, had been under the leadership of the essentially Conservative National Government since 1931, and whereas the United States had witnessed major reform in the prewar decade, Britain had not. In addition, of course, Britain had suffered major destruction and hardship during the war which increased rather than decreased the demands for a program of economic and social reform. In America the electorate had experienced twelve years of change and of increasing government regulation under Democratic leadership, and the swing to the Republicans was a reflection of this.

In America the wartime political trend, coupled with the disappearance of New Deal agencies and of New Dealers and the rehabilitation of businessmen through their leadership in the battle of production, encouraged contemporaries to write of a "waning of the New Deal" and to bemoan the end of reform.

Roosevelt himself gave credence to such views when he said that "Dr. New Deal" would be replaced for the duration by "Dr. Win the War." Furthermore, he refused to support proposals for a national health scheme or to countenance inflationary increases in minimum wage rates. Congress, too, resisted attempts to reform the social security and unemployment insurance programs and froze the rate of social security contributions, thus postponing a scheduled increase. Congressional opposition watered down FDR's proposal to increase the tax burdens of the rich and of corporations, and also had sufficient strength to pass antiunion legislation over his veto in 1943.

While it was true that the reform drive did not appear to be strong during the war, it must be remembered that the New Deal had already apparently been running out of steam and that little new in the way of legislation had been achieved since 1938. Nonetheless, the war did bring about the demise of a number of prominent New Deal agencies—the Civilian Conservation Corps in 1942, the Works Progress Administration and National Youth Administration in 1943. However, there was little need for such bodies given military mobilization and full employment. In this sense the New Deal did not continue because it was no longer necessary. If the New Deal was just a series of ad hoc responses to particular problems, when those problems disappeared so too did much of the New Deal. But of course the New Deal was much more than this. Basic underlying principles had been established with long-term reforms during the thirties, and these not only remained in effect but were also reinforced by wartime experience.

Massive government spending to finance the war effort persuaded many people finally of the logic of Keynesian economic policy. If the government could spend a total of $330 billion in wartime, it seemed only reasonable that it should spend a fraction of that amount to ensure prosperity in peacetime. Coupled with the real fear of a return to Depression conditions once the war was over, such thinking ensured that there would be some commitment to continued direct central government regulation of the economy. This was recognized by FDR in his 1944 message to Congress in which he called for a second Bill of Rights based on certain economic truths in order to establish "a new basis of security and prosperity." Even Thomas E. Dewey, Roosevelt's Republican opponent in 1944, accepted that government would continue to have a role in social security, farm price regulation, banking insurance, and the recognition of labor. The question now was about the size of government and the extent of its involvement, not about whether there should be any involvement at all.

The Employment Act approved by President Truman in 1946 recognized the federal government's commitment to ensure the economic well-being of the country, but was limited by Congressional amendment. The act provided only that the government do "everything practicable" to bring about "maximum" (not full) employment, and the only machinery provided to do this was a Council of Economic Advisors. Nonetheless the act laid the basis for annual economic programs, and Truman demonstrated his leadership in economic matters through his attempts to deal with problems of postwar inflation.

If the war served to accelerate acceptance of certain New Deal ideas, it also demonstrated the extent of some the New Deal's failures. Through Selective Service the war revealed the effects of the Depression on the health and welfare of the American people. Some 50 percent of Selective Service registrants were rejected for armed service on grounds of poor health. Large numbers were also rejected because of educational deficiencies. Such revelations did not result in immediate legislation, but did help to place health and education high on the agenda for future reform. Immediate action was taken by the army which, forced to lower standards to overcome manpower shortages, implemented its own remedial medical program affecting some two million men. Basic literacy and training programs were also launched by the military. As had been the case during World War I, many service personnel left the forces in better shape than they had entered—provided of course that they were not killed or wounded in battle.

The most obvious reward for armed service, provided one survived (and in fact survival rates were very high—civilian workers ran greater risks of death or injury), was the Selective Servicemen's Readjustment Act of 1944. Known as the GI Bill of Rights, the act provided a readjustment allowance for all servicemen, loans for home, business, or farm purchase, and grants and subsistence support for those returning to school or college. Not intended as a program of social welfare, in the long run the act had almost the same effect. By 1950 one-third of the entire population had benefited from one aspect or another of the veterans' program. Nearly eight million veterans took advantage of education loans alone. Not for nothing did one of Studs Terkel's interviewees remember "The GI Bill, the American Dream."3

The GI Bill was clearly intended as compensation for the disruption suffered by those in the armed forces, but there was dislocation for those at home too. Most obvious was the movement of population as Americans headed toward military camps or to the centers for war production in the North and West. Over twelve million people moved out of state between 1940 and 1947, and another thirteen million moved within state lines. More than one million moved to California alone, the location of half the nation's shipbuilding and aircraft industries and the growing center of the military-industrial complex that came into being during the war.

While many of the Okies were now absorbed into the shipyards outside Los Angeles and San Francisco, numerous southerners also found employment in the auto and aircraft plants around Detroit. Smaller towns and cities also experienced enormous growth—Seneca Falls, seventy miles southwest of Chicago, grew in population from twelve hundred in 1940 to sixty-six hundred in 1944 as workers came in to build landing craft on the river shore. Not surprisingly, a great many places were unable to cope with this sudden influx and suffered as a consequence of the overcrowding that followed. When Ford established a new plant at Willow Run thirty miles outside Detroit, a trailer park sprang up to house 32,000 people in conditions that were far from ideal; another 15,000 immigrants to Detroit lived in dormitories, lodgings or hotels. While in Seattle people were reported to be sleeping in the streets, in many cities multiple occupation of single rooms, and even of single beds shared under a shift system of "hot-beds," was common.

Such conditions forced the government to expand social welfare programs as wartime measures. In 1942 a National Housing Administration was established with a budget of $2.3 billion. It was to provide over two million housing units during the war, far in excess of those built under the U.S. Housing Administration. Rent controls affecting 86 million people were also introduced in defense areas. In 1941 an Office of Defense Health and Welfare was established to administer federal funds provided for community improvements, medical provision, and nursery care. Federal, state, and local spending on health increased from several million to over one billion dollars. While some of this may be discounted due to inflation, there was nonetheless a 50 percent increase in the number of hospital beds and generally better medical provision.

Housing shortages and related health problems did not disappear, and health, education, and housing were all elements of Harry Truman's postwar proposals and his Fair Deal program. In September 1945 the new president outlined a twenty-one-point program in an address to Congress. It included full-employment policies, fair-employment laws, housing and health measures, and a continuation of social security. The Fair Deal called for an increase in minimum wage levels, strengthening of antitrust measures, continued farm price support and rural electrification, the extension of TVA schemes to other rivers, increased public housing, health insurance, federal aid for educational improvements, and civil-rights legislation. Truman's legislative achievements included the Employment Act of 1946, the raising of minimum wage levels from forty cents an hour to seventy-five, the extension of social security to another ten million people and increased benefits, and the National Housing Act of 1949 which proposed the building of over 800,000 units of public housing. Most dramatic of all were Truman's actions in the area of civil rights.

For African-Americans the 1940s were important years, although it did not immediately appear that this would be the case. The growth of the war industries before 1941 had little effect on blacks. While white unemployment dropped quickly after 1939, it remained high for blacks. In 1940 there were only 240 blacks working in the *entire* aircraft industry. In the armed forces blacks were segregated in the army, excluded from the air corps and marines, and limited to the roles of messmen and galley workers in the navy. A combination of black protest, wartime necessity, and changing government policy brought some improvements in this situation. Black leaders won concessions in military policy in the 1940 election year, and the threat of a march on Washington led by A. Philip Randolph in 1941 resulted in an executive order prohibiting discrimination in defense industry. However, it was not until after 1942 that growing manpower shortages produced real changes in black employment, and only toward the end of the war was there any substantial change in military policy. As singer B. B. King said, "I used to sing gospel songs until I joined the Army—then I sang the blues."[4]

Still, one million African-Americans served in the armed forces, and before the war's end blacks were admitted to the marines and air corps, and to all branches of the navy which then began moving toward integration. Even the army experimented with integration under the pressure of the Battle of the Bulge in 1944, and although this ended with the victory in Europe, it provided an important precedent for future action. Whatever the limitations, the high rate of reenlistment among blacks at the end of the war was an indication both of the opportunities offered by armed service and of the barriers still faced in civilian life.

As was the case with the military, wartime demands for manpower brought changes in the employment of blacks at home. By 1944 8 percent of war workers were black, and the total number of blacks in the labor force rose by one million during the war. The number in skilled and semiskilled positions almost doubled, but even so black workers were largely confined to unskilled, hot, and heavy jobs.

In both military and civilian life racial progress met with resistance and sometimes violence. Press reports and rumors of assaults on black servicemen inflamed tensions created by the persistence of discrimination in employment and housing particularly in towns and cities experiencing growth in black and white populations. The migration of blacks exceeded that of whites in percentage terms as 1.8 million moved to different states during the war. In some cities the black population grew by over 100 percent. Competition over accommodation, jobs, and transportation added to the strains and worries of wartime, and in 1943 these tensions erupted in over 240 race riots or incidents in forty-seven different cities. The most violent clash occurred in June in Detroit, one of the most congested cities during the war, and a hotbed of racial antagonisms. After five days of violence twenty-five blacks and nine whites were dead. In August a rather different form of riot broke out in New York when blacks in Harlem exploded in rage against discrimination and attacked white-owned property. Five blacks died and five million dollars' worth of damage was done before the violence subsided. This was the last major riot of the war, and the last of its scale until the 1960s.

The absence of major racial disorder in the postwar era was due to a number of factors, one of which was Truman's action in the civil-rights field. When he became president the omens were not good: Truman's senatorial record on civil rights had not been strong, and many blacks had misgivings about the Missourian. However, he was to take actions on their behalf that far surpassed those of Roosevelt.

Shocked by details of postwar racial violence which included the lynching of two men and their wives and the blinding of a returning black soldier, Truman issued an executive order creating a Civil Rights Commission in 1946. The following year, in the first ever public presidential address to the NAACP, standing on the steps of the Lincoln Memorial, he spoke out against mob violence and declared that the national government must show the way in combatting racial violence. The Civil Rights Commission reported that same year and called for protection for blacks against lynching, the integration of the armed forces, and an end to segregation and discrimination in public life. Truman was to include most of these recommendations in his civil-rights message to Congress in February 1948.

Actions, of course, speak louder than words. In July 1948 President Truman issued two executive orders to bring about the beginning of integration in the armed forces and an end to discrimination in the civil service. It has been suggested that such actions were merely political exercises to win crucial black votes away from Henry Wallace's Progressive party, and it is clear that political considerations were involved in Truman's advocacy of civil rights. But if political factors were the only reasons for his stand, then Truman was taking a finely calculated gamble and must have been a shrewder judge than some historians would allow. Southern Democrats, predictably, reacted angrily to Truman's measures and to the inclusion of a strong civil-rights plank in the Democratic party platform at the 1948 convention—although this was the work of Hubert Humphrey, not Truman. Several southerners left the convention and formed the breakaway States' Rights party or Dixiecrats. As a result, Truman faced the election without either the more conservative or more liberal wings of his party.

Factors other than the purely political clearly influenced Truman. A petition presented to the United Nations Commission on Human Rights, tabled for the NAACP by the Soviet Union, showed that America's racial policies had become a matter of international concern. Equally significant was the militance of blacks who made clear their unwillingness to tolerate continued official discrimination. A. Philip Randolph and others threatened to lead a campaign of civil disobedience if segregation in the armed forces continued, and they clearly had considerable support.

Whatever the cause, Truman won the election in 1948 with a majority of the black vote. The Dixicrats carried only four states and received a mere 22 percent of the southern vote. Southern strength in Congress was such, however, that with Republican support they could block proposed legislation on lynching, poll taxes, and fair employment that Truman presented to Congress in 1949. The administration was more successful in the judicial area where Justice Department officials had some influence on the Supreme Court rulings against restrictive housing covenants. From then on the Federal Housing Administration refused to mortgage any property covered by restrictive covenants, although many of its broader policies still upheld segregation.

While Truman's actual tangible achievements may have been few, there had been a move from mere acquiescence to black demands to more outright positive support for civil rights in both the executive and the judicial branches of federal government by 1950. Certainly there was sufficient progress for blacks to look forward optimistically, and these expectations were sustained, too, by continued economic improvements.

Other racial groups were not as fortunate as black Americans. Wartime pressures combined with deep-seated race hatred in California, and in 1943 Mexican youths wearing flamboyant "zoot suits" were the object of attacks by servicemen in Los Angeles. More dramatic was the anti-Japanese feeling that surfaced on the West Coast after 1941. Despite the overwhelming loyalty of Japanese-Americans, concerted efforts were made to have them removed from their homes. The very absence of evidence against them was put forward as a demonstration of their deviousness or cunning. In a no-win situation, the Japanese-Americans were the victims of the perpetrators of the attack on Pearl Harbor and of a racial fear that had its roots in the nineteenth-century view "once a Jap always a Jap."

In February 1942, urged on by Secretary of War Henry L.

Stimson and Secretary of the Navy Frank Knox, President Roosevelt acceded to local pressures and issued an executive order authorizing the prescription of military areas and removal of people deemed to be a threat from those areas. Only one group was affected—more than 110,000 Japanese-Americans were rounded up and placed in "relocation" camps in California, Wyoming, Arkansas, Utah, and Arizona where they were held until 1944–45. Paradoxically, only 3,000 of the 150,000 Japanese-Americans on Hawaii were interned, no doubt because they made up one-third of the total population of the islands, and were vital to the economy there. As a result of their treatment, some five thousand Nisei (American-born Japanese) renounced their American citizenship. However, another 12,000 served in the military, and the two Japanese-American battalions that fought in Italy were the most decorated units in the U.S. Army.

Some seven thousand Japanese were repatriated to Japan after the war had ended but the majority started life anew in the U.S.A. Only 58 percent returned to the West Coast, the remainder becoming more widely dispersed than before the war. Some attempt to make restitution for lost property was made under the Evacuation Claims Act of 1948, but only $38 million of the estimated $400 million claimed was repaid. Although the Japanese seemed to be quickly reintegrated into American life, their experience in the war remained a bitter memory. In 1989 Congress approved the payment of $20,000 to each of the estimated 62,000 Japanese-American internees still alive, with payments due to start in 1991.

The experience of women in the war appeared to differ markedly from that of racial groups, but while some writers have claimed that the war was a watershed which brought a radical transformation in the position of women, others have questioned the extent and significance of such change. Indeed D'Ann Campbell in *Women at War with America* suggests that the war in many ways reinforced the "suburban ideal of companionate, child-centered marriages with little scope for careerism," the model against which so many were to rebel in the sixties.[5] However, the picture is probably not that simple.

The prewar limitations affecting women were considerable and were apparent with the onset of war. In 1941 a survey of seven aircraft factories found the total female labor force to number 143; in the shipbuilding industry the number was a mere 36. By 1943 the numbers had risen to 65,000 and 160,000 respectively, and in total the female work force rose from thirteen million to twenty million. During the war the proportion of females in the labor force rose from 25 percent to 36 percent.

Large numbers of women moved into heavy industry and were symbolized in press and propaganda by the overall-clad figure of Rosie the Riveter. Equally newsworthy were the 350,000 women who served in the armed forces in the Women's Army Corps (WACs) and Women Accepted for Volunteer Emergency Service (WAVES). However, more women were working in clerical and white-collar jobs, in government, banking, and sales. More significantly, while women service personnel were predominantly single and in their twenties, the type of women working in civilian occupations changed markedly as married and older women joined the labor force. Over 60 percent of the new women workers were married, and 75 percent were thirty-five or older. While this trend continued after the war, others did not.

Discrimination against women among unions, employers, and government persisted through the war. Women were excluded from most senior positions, had little part in the policy-making process, and despite official espousals of equal-pay policies, generally earned 40 percent less than men. Propaganda sanctioned and encouraged the idea of working wives, but at the same time stressed the temporary nature of wartime female employment. At the end of the war women were urged to return to traditional roles of housewives and mothers even though the great majority of women workers indicated a desire to remain in wage-earning work. At the war's end 2 million women were laid off and their proportion of the labor force declined to 29 percent. However, with postwar economic growth this crept back up slowly, and was never to return to prewar levels. Some of the new patterns of female employment also continued beyond the war.

It is not easy to discern what was happening amongst American women in the immediate postwar years. Little has been written of them in this period, and women were to many males—and historians—as blacks often were to whites—invisible. Certain wartime trends continued: by 1950 52 percent of women working outside the home were married, and the percentage of married women working had doubled. Equally, the number of female employees aged between forty-five and fifty-four grew: by 1950 they made up 40 percent of all women in wage-earning work. These "gains" were, however, concentrated in what had become traditional areas of women's work—typing, teaching, nursing, sales, and domestic service. Women usually worked in a segregated environment with few male co-workers beside them, and in 1950 women's median earnings were only 53 percent of men's. As Chafe points out in *The Unfinished Journey*, whatever change had occurred was "within a structure of assumptions and values that perpetrated massive inequality between the sexes."[6]

If the experiences of women in the war years were mixed, consequences for trade unions were equally ambiguous. On the one hand the war brought massive growth and assured the survival of union organizations; on the other hand it saw a loss of militance as unions were incorporated into the decision-making process and as workers became consumers—haves, rather than have-nots. This process was to continue after the war under the twin forces of affluence and the ideological pressures of the Cold War.

At the start of the war both the AFL and the CIO issued no-strike pledges. In return they were granted recognition on government boards and labor-management committees, and in the form of maintenance of membership clauses in war contracts that helped boost and protect union membership. The number of workers in unions rose from eight million to over fourteen million, and a twelve-man National War Labor Board was established in 1942 to adjudicate in disputes and supervise wage settlements. It resolved 18,000 disputes and approved 415,000 settlements affecting 20 million workers. Nonetheless, rising prices and restrictions on wage increases to control inflation led to increasing outbreaks of strike action. In 1943, three million workers were involved in disputes including those in steel and rail. The most protracted conflict was with the miners led by the ever-fiery John L. Lewis. Lewis's determination, even in the face of threats of prison or the introduction of military control of the mines, won concessions for his members, but along with other strikes, this probably alienated sections of public opinion. Opposition to such apparently disruptive action led to the passage of the War Labor Disputes or Smith-Connally Act over the president's veto in 1943. Requiring cooling-off periods, strike ballots, and registration of membership, the act was to be the model for later legislation and it marked the move toward the formalization and bureaucratization of labor relations which became a feature of the postwar years. The other side of that coin was the move toward more complex work contracts including not just pay agreements, but also fringe benefits such as paid holidays and health-insurance schemes.

Although it is often easy to see these developments with hindsight, the postwar position of labor still seemed uncertain. There was considerable fear that the war would be followed by a return to the Depression, and some observers estimated likely unemployment to be anywhere between five and ten million people. In the event this fear proved unfounded. Despite the rapid demobilization of the armed forces and the closure of many war industries, there was no massive unemployment. This was due to the continuation of some government controls, the return of many women workers to the home, the speedy conversion of industry to peacetime production, the effects of the GI Bill, the Marshall Plan, and consumer demand. The main problem Truman had to deal with at home was inflation and the industrial strife it produced.

With the lifting of some government controls, rising prices and the surge in consumer demand combined to produce demands for wage increases. In 1946 over five thousand strikes involving 4.5 million workers threatened to disrupt economic recovery. Unlike the strikes of the thirties, these were no longer chiefly about union recognition, but were about the extent of union power in industry, and particularly whether organized labor would have a say in management decisions. Truman's response to the strikes was tough, threatening federal takeovers and the introduction of the draft in the steel and mining industries. The threats were not implemented and indeed most unions won increases in line with guidelines laid down by presidential fact-finding boards. When Congress introduced antiunion legislation with the Taft-Hartley Bill in 1947, Truman, mindful of his need of union support, vetoed it. Congress passed the bill anyway.

According to Robert Zieger, the Taft-Hartley Act and the unions' muted response to it "marked a turning point for organized labor."[7] However, other writers have pointed out that participation in the War Labor Board, and the closer relationship with government and the Democratic party, had already brought a mellowing of union attitudes. These developments continued after 1947 as union leaders resisted confrontational policies and widespread strikes as counterproductive to their aims. Instead, they worked to obtain better contracts from employers and to achieve legislative change through the Democratic party. Radical politics were increasingly disavowed, and as the Cold War intensified unions purged Communist elements and became increasingly conservative. In 1950 the CIO expelled eleven unions because of their supposed Communist leadership. George Meany, the man who was to head the AFL-CIO when they combined in 1955, could boast that he had never been on strike in his life.

For many observers the decline in union activism was just part of the failure to continue or resume New Deal policies, and indicative of Truman's poor leadership. Indeed, historians have not dealt kindly with Roosevelt's successor. Perhaps because his desktop sign read "The buck stops here," Truman has been held responsible for the onset of the Cold War and for failing to prevent the spread of McCarthyism at home; he has been seen as a failure who abandoned FDR's liberal inheritance, or as a schemer who professed support for policies but did not follow through.

Such judgments may be too harsh. The difficulties facing the new president were enormous. In international affairs Americans had to come to terms with a new world order and to work out their responses to it; at home they faced the problems of reconversion, the possibility of high unemployment, and questions concerning the continuity of domestic policy. One could sympathize with Truman when he recalled that he felt as if the moon, stars, and all the planets had fallen on him with Roosevelt's death.

The new president did not, after all, operate from a position of strength. Initially he had no popular mandate and was, moreover, bound to suffer in comparison with his predecessor in terms of charisma and popular following. The weakness of his position was increased by the Republican Congressional majorities that existed after 1946, and the conservative coalition that continued to exist even after 1948. Nor was the general climate of opinion conducive to radical departures, even if Truman had been prepared to support such moves. Indeed it is possible to see his famous upset victory in 1948 as a conservative vote in favor of neither an attack on the New Deal nor any further moves to the left. In such circumstances it is well perhaps to reconsider the achievements of the man from Independence.

It may be that Truman suffered from a certain snobbery and resentment from among the New Deal liberal and academic circle rather like that which Lyndon Johnson was to experience after Kennedy's death. Certainly the feisty former haberdasher lacked some of the social and political graces of a Roosevelt. Truman was not only not such a good speaker, lacking the bugle note in his voice, but also less receptive to new ideas. The fact that a number of Roosevelt's cabinet members, including Perkins, Morgenthau, Ickes, and Wallace, resigned in 1945 or 1946 seemed to bear out this view. However, all had held office for a considerable time and were entitled to a rest just as Truman was entitled to choose his own advisers; equally the differences with Ickes and Wallace revealed a divergence of ideas in both domestic and international policies and suggested a more conservative approach from Truman in both cases. Whatever these changes in personnel indicated, Truman still publicly announced a reform program from the start, and was to reiterate it in 1948 in his Fair Deal message.

As already stated, Truman's Fair Deal was a clear statement of the president's intention to continue Roosevelt's reform tradition and to enlarge upon it. In many ways a rearticulation of Roosevelt's 1937 inaugural address, it went further in including broader and specific references in areas such as civil rights and health reform. While little of the new legislation proposed was enacted, Truman's presidency did, nonetheless, see the consolidation of the basic New Deal social welfare program. Moreover, the Fair Deal laid out the agenda for future reform, and was to be picked up again in the 1960s.

That Truman's accomplishments were so few can be explained in part by the political factors already discussed, but other more fundamental reasons must also be considered. In the first instance the situation of the 1940s was not the same as that of the Depression era. The New Deal had been established when many were in need and cooperative and collective action on a large scale seemed necessary. This was not the case in the 1940s. The postwar American GNP grew rapidly with a 200 percent increase in productivity between 1947 and 1956 based upon new technology (the beginnings of computerization), automation, the developing aerospace, chemical, and electronics industries, and the growth of research and development.

Socioeconomic changes followed these industrial developments: the proportion of the work force classed as white-collar rose from 30 percent in 1940 to 37 percent in 1950, and continued rising. Increasingly America was again seen as a classless or essentially middle-class society in which affluence, as indicated by car ownership (27 million in 1940, 40 million in 1950), house ownership, and television viewing, was already widespread. Matters like home ownership and health care were not now seen as the concern of government programs but of individuals themselves. Many families now had more to spend on medical insurance or to invest in housing. While companies such as Blue Cross and Blue Shield, or company insurance schemes grew, demand for housing was to be met by the growth of suburban, low-cost, mass-produced housing developments initiated by people like William Levitt and financed with loans under the GI Bill or more generous mortgage schemes from the FHA.

The affluent society was already evident before 1950, but so too were some of the problems associated with it. The growth of suburbia brought an apparent (but often exaggerated) uniformity, with families of roughly the same size living in roughly the same type of house, driving to work in roughly similar cars, to do the same kind of work. Equally Americans were said to be striving to imitate their neighbors—the conformity of affluence was captured in the cliche "keeping up with the Joneses"—and it is well to remember that *The Lonely Crowd*, David Riesman's classic study of the new "other-directed" society motivated by impersonal forces such as advertising, was published in 1950.

Not all Americans were part of this emerging pattern. Many remained in blue-collar jobs, living in cities or older suburbs, or still working and living in rural areas. Many, of course, were still poor. As Richard Polenberg has pointed out in *One Nation Divisible*, distinctions of class, race, and ethnicity persisted even in the suburbs or were often replaced by new divisions based upon roles within the community.[8] Nonetheless, the prevailing ethos of the postwar years was one of conformity—a conformity of affluence, but also of insecurity.

Despite the prevailing affluence, many Americans remained uncertain about the future. The fear of a return to depression was never too distant, and in addition America now faced a new world role and a new conflict in the Cold War. The confrontation with the Soviet Union was one that few could understand, and setbacks in foreign affairs were particularly difficult to accept given America's undoubted military and economic superiority. The fact that the decade ended with involvement in another armed conflict, albeit a "police action," in Korea, only served to aggravate these doubts and to heighten these feelings. This, in turn, provided the background not only for a mood of conservatism, but also for the paranoia of McCarthyism which gripped the country, and created a mood that can only be described as repressive. In such a climate certain reforms became "ideologically" unacceptable, and the miracle may be not that Truman achieved so little, but that he managed to do so much.

For some historians the relative decline in reform after World War II was inevitable, a reflection of the pattern of reform and reaction that seemed to operate throughout American history. However, rather than there being any fixed cycle determining a swing back from public action to private concern as Arthur Schlesinger suggests,[9] we should recognize the impact of particular events. Thus while World War II transformed the economic context for political action, the Cold War shifted the basis of ideological debate, and both served to reduce, but not destroy, the reform dynamic. Yet at the same time the Cold War brought new forces into play and raised new concerns, no more so than in matters of foreign policy. Just as the decade began dominated by foreign affairs, so it ended. The effects of the Cold War were to be as significant as those of World War II itself, and lasted into the 1950s. While some of the personalities changed, many issues continued from one decade to the next, and the postwar years stand as a vital link in this process.

Notes

1. Richard Polenberg, *War and Society: The United*

States 1941–1945 (New York, 1972), p. 4.

2. Studs Terkel, "The Good War": An Oral History of World War II (London, 1985), p. 10.

3. Ibid., p. 142.

4. B. B. King, "Sounding Out," B.B.C. Television, January 31, 1972.

5. D'Ann Campbell, Women at War with America: Private Lives in a Patriotic Era (Cambridge, Mass., and London, 1984), p. 4.

6. William H. Chafe, The Unfinished Journey: America since World War II (New York and Oxford, 1986), p. 85.

7. Robert H. Zieger, American Workers, American Unions, 1920–1985 (Baltimore and London, 1986), p. 114.

8. Richard Polenberg, One Nation Divisible: Class, Race, and Ethnicity in the United States since 1938 (New York, 1980).

9. Arthur M. Schlesinger, Jr., The Cycles of American History (New York and London, 1989), p. 27.

Bibliography

There are very few books dealing with the 1940s as an entity. Some general surveys do begin either with the war or the New Deal, e.g., Richard Polenberg's social history, One Nation Divisible: Class, Race, and Ethnicity in the United States since 1938 (New York, 1980); Ralph F. DeBedts, Recent American History: 1933 to the Present, 2 vols. (Homewood, Ill., and London, 1973); Alonzo L. Hamby, The Imperial Years: The United States since 1939 (London and New York, 1976); and Frederick F. Siegel, A Troubled Journey: From Pearl Harbor to Reagan (New York, 1984). Accounts of postwar America that deal well with the late forties (and sometimes have an introduction on the war years) include William H. Chafe, The Unfinished Journey: America since World War II (New York and Oxford, 1986); William E. Leuchtenburg, A Troubled Feast: American Society since 1945 (Boston and Toronto, 1982); and Lawrence S. Wittner, Cold War America: From Hiroshima to Watergate (New York, 1979).

The American home front during World War II is now thoroughly examined in almost every aspect. Richard Polenberg's War and Society: The United States 1941–1945 (New

York, 1972) was one of the earliest studies in this area and remains the essential text, complemented by his documentary collection, *America at War: The Home Front 1941–1945* (Englewood Cliffs, N.J., 1968). John Morton Blum's *V Was for Victory: Politics and American Culture During World War II* (New York and London, 1976) is also stimulating while Richard Lingeman's *Don't You Know There's a War On? The American Home Front* (New York 1970) is lively and informative. Alan Clive's *State of War: Michigan in Wartime* (Ann Arbor, 1979) is an excellent local study that gives a good impression of a war-boom community. Studs Terkel's oral history, *"The Good War": An Oral History of World War II* (London, 1985) has a number of interesting reflections on Americans' war experiences at home and abroad.

War, government, and propaganda are thoroughly examined in Allan M. Winkler, *The Politics of Propaganda: The Office of War Information 1942–1945* (New Haven, Conn., and London, 1978), and Clayton R. Koppes and Gregory D. Black, *Hollywood Goes to War: How Politics, Profits and Propaganda Shaped World War II Movies* (New York, 1987).

Various social groups have been dealt with in individual monographs. For labor, see Nelson N. Lichtenstein, *Labor's War at Home: The CIO in World War II* (Cambridge and New York, 1982). For blacks see Neil A. Wynn, *The Afro-American and the Second World War* (New York and London, 1976); A. Russell Buchanan, *Black Americans in World War II* (New York, 1977); and Richard M. Dalfiume, *Desegregation of the U.S. Armed Forces: Fighting on Two Fronts, 1939–1953* (Columbia, Mo., 1969). The treatment of Japanese-Americans is fully examined in Roger Daniels, *Concentration Camp USA: Japanese-Americans in World War II* (New York, 1971), and Peter H. Irons, *Justice at War: The Story of the Japanese-American Internment Cases* (New York, 1982). Women and the war are the subject of D'Ann Campbell, *Women at War with America: Private Lives in a Patriotic Era* (Cambridge, Mass., and London, 1984); Karen S. Anderson, *Wartime Women* (Westport, Conn., 1981); and Leila J. Rupp, *Mobilizing Women for War: German and American Propaganda, 1939–1945* (Princeton, N.J., 1978). A recent addition to works on the social impact of the war is Allan Berube, *Coming Out under Fire: The History of Gay Men and Women in World War II* (New York, 1990).

One of the most important pieces of wartime legislation, the GI Bill of Rights, and the debates surrounding it, are the subject of Davis R. Ross, *Preparing for Ulysses: Politics and Veterans during World War II* (New York and London, 1969).

The domestic issues of the early Truman years are well covered in Alonzo L. Hamby, *Beyond the New Deal: Harry S. Truman and American Liberalism* (New York, 1973); Robert J. Donovan, *Conflict and Crisis: The Presidency of Harry S. Truman 1945–1948* (New York, 1977); and Joseph C. Goulden, *The Best Years, 1945–1950* (New York, 1976). J. Joseph Huthmacher, ed., *The Truman Years: The Reconstruction of Postwar America* (Hindsdale, Ill., 1972) is a useful collection of essays.

Recent general texts such as those by Chafe, Leuchtenburg, and Polenberg mentioned above are also good on this period.

Specific issues are dealt with in Richard O. Davies, *Housing Reform during the Truman Administration* (Columbia, Mo., 1966); William C. Berman, *The Politics of Civil Rights in the Truman Administration* (Columbus, Ohio, 1970); and Donald R. McCoy and Richard T. Ruetten, *Quest and Response: Minority Rights and the Truman Administration* (Kansas City, 1973).

5

Cold War America, 1945–1960

_____ *John Dumbrell*

At the end of World War II the twentieth-century promise of American power and prosperity was on the verge of fulfillment. The United States emerged from the war, which had seen its gross national product increase in real terms by 56 percent, as unquestionably the world's most powerful nation. Potential rivals in Europe and Asia either had been defeated, had sustained internal devastation or, like Britain, were beginning to witness the dismemberment of their colonial empires. The "psychology of supremacy," heralded in 1941 by Henry Luce's concept of the "American Century," was to dominate U.S. attitudes between 1945 and 1960. On the other hand, anxieties and insecurities that accompanied the new sense of American power profoundly shaped the national experience in these years. The awesome nature of American responsibilities in the postwar order caused concern. There was also unease about external and internal threats to America's security and national purpose, a feeling that at times manifested itself in irrational paranoia. Perhaps above all, Americans had to adjust to living under the shadow of the destructive potential of atomic weaponry which had been demonstrated by the bombing of Hiroshima and Nagasaki in 1945.

The process of national adjustment to America's new role underpinned the emergence of the Cold War consensus, which dominated the political and intellectual life of the period. Rooted in postwar prosperity, this consensus embodied a firm commitment to America's democratic institutions and private-enterprise system. American capitalism no longer embraced unequivocally the values of rugged individualism and unrestrained free enterprise. It had inherited from the New Deal a partial commitment to managerialist state interventionism. In this slightly modified form, American capitalism was seen as the most prolific generator of prosperity in the history of the world. It provided the model for other countries to imitate. The major threat to all this, of course, was seen to be communism: supposedly a monolithic force, centered on Moscow, possessing the potential to undermine freedom, democracy, and prosperity. In this environment, both liberals and conservatives united in their condemnation of communism and in their opposition to leftist revolutions abroad. Liberals, indeed, often felt a greater need than conservatives to establish their anticommunist credentials. They sought to demonstrate that a staunch commitment to American values could be combined with support for liberal policies at home. The irony of all this was that the very measures taken to combat communism themselves came to present a threat to the freedoms that were being defended. The foreign policy of the period was also characterized by an uncritical and counterproductive tendency to identify the U.S. national interest with global anticommunism.

The Cold War consensus also extended to the nature of the post–New Deal political and economic settlement. After the upheavals of the Great Depression and of World War II, there was no great appetite for doing away with the New Deal state. The real test of this came in 1953, with the inauguration of the first Republican president since Herbert Hoover. In fact, Dwight D. Eisenhower accurately judged the public mood when he confided to his brother Edgar his view that any party that tried to dismantle the New Deal would be destroyed. Of those who sought to return the federal government to its pre-Depression role, Eisenhower stated: "their number is negligible and they are stupid."[1] While Republican conservatives like Senator Robert A. Taft of Ohio did continue to attack the New Deal itself, consensual debate between 1945 and 1960 focused instead on whether the New Deal should be extended into new areas, or simply consolidated. The New Deal state would not be dismantled. Rather, it would evolve in a manner appropriate to a political and economic order geared to the ascendancy of Cold War security concerns. As it emerged from its militarization during World War II, the New Deal state was to be transformed, apparently on a permanent basis, into the Cold War or national security state. It was characteristic of the period, for example, that where domestic programs were expanded (as in the establishment of the National Science Foundation in 1950, or the 1958 National Defense Education Act), this was done as part of the national security program.

In the defense sector, the later 1940s saw major shifts in the development of the apparatus of the American state. Under the influence of anticommunism, the concept of "national security" came to supersede the very notions of "defense" and "foreign policy." The National Security Act of July 1947 created the unified Department of Defense under the civilian leadership of James V. Forrestal. It centralized surveillance under the aegis of the Central Intelligence Agency and set up the National Security Council to provide the president with a means of cutting through bureaucratic rivalries and coherently assessing future options. National security was interpreted as the basis for continued presidential domination of foreign policy-making, even in peacetime. National security became the focus for developing U.S. dependence on atomic weapons. Defined as a permanent feature of an apparently endless Cold War, it ensured that defense spending remained at levels that constituted a built-in stimulus to the U.S. economy: a stimulus, however, that created massive vested interests and diverted resources and energies from other areas.

The constant invocation of national security and the communist threat was an important part of President Truman's efforts to maximize Congressional and public support for his costly and interventionist foreign policy. The Truman administration's policy toward Europe was, in its own terms, a great success. By 1950, the $17 billion appropriated by Congress for the Marshall Plan were already spurring Western Europe on the path to economic recovery. Along with the North Atlantic Treaty Organization (ratified by the Senate in 1949), this economic aid effectively created a set of alliances within Western Europe based upon U.S. leadership. Potential opposition in Congress had been won over to support of the Marshall Plan and of NATO by recognition of the Soviet threat to Western Europe. Only thirteen senators, including Taft, voted against ratification of the NATO treaty. Meanwhile, the eleven-month airlift of supplies into West Berlin finally induced the Soviets to raise their blockade of the city in May 1949. The resolution of the crisis effectively culminated in the creation of the Federal Republic of Germany as a political entity securely within the U.S. sphere of influence.

Nevertheless, success in Western Europe was balanced by failures elsewhere in 1949, which left Americans feeling deeply insecure. U.S. financial aid could not prevent the overthrow of the Nationalist regime by communist armies in China, and in September came the announcement that the Soviet Union had successfully tested an atomic bomb. Both developments fueled bitter Republican attacks on the administration, including charges of treachery in high places. Truman's response to these reverses was to order a thorough defense review, whose findings formed the basis for National Security Council memorandum 68 (NSC-68) of April 1950. This document, which advocated a quadrupling of defense expenditure to wage a global struggle against communism, set the direction of U.S. Cold War policy for the next twenty years. Though never formally accepted by Truman, its recommendations were legitimized by the outbreak of war in Korea, which raised international tensions to a new level. Annual military spending had averaged $13–14 billion in the late 1940s, but the Korean conflict of 1950–53 saw budgets reaching $42 billion. In both institutionalizing the national security or "warfare" state and raising fears about domestic communist subversion, the Korean conflict was a major turning point. It set a precedent for the presidential conduct of undeclared war in Southeast Asia and cost nearly 55,000 American lives. The idea of fighting "limited," "brushfire" wars across the globe was an important corollary of Cold War containment strategies. Yet it was severely tested in Korea. As in Vietnam later, the U.S. public generally, and the Republican party in particular, were uneasy about the idea of a limited war, with victory being defined in the largely negative terms of containment rather than liberation.

Recent scholarship on the Korean conflict has revealed the extent to which the Truman administration itself considered widening the struggle. Most historians now tend to accept that Truman was ill-advised in not seeking a formal declaration of war in the summer of 1950, and also that his ordering of troops across the thirty-eighth parallel in October 1950 was misconceived. The conflict saw a number of dramatic episodes that galvanized opinion at home: Truman's initial commitment of troops after the June 1950 reports of a North Korean invasion of South Korea; General Douglas MacArthur's September landing at Inchon; the open involvement of Red Chinese troops on the North Korean side in November; and the firing of MacArthur as U.S. military commander in April 1951. The general had never accepted the logic of limited wars, and his open criticism of Truman's conduct of the war amounted to a direct attack upon civilian control of the military. The president had little choice but to dismiss him, and hope that the fierce Republican reaction to the firing would eventually ebb away.

The spectacular episodes and incidents of the Korean War simply punctuated a struggle that dragged on into a bloody stalemate almost reminiscent of World War I. The frustrations of the war caused the administration to consider use of the atomic bomb. They also provoked frenzied Republican attacks on the integrity of Truman and Secretary of State Dean Acheson. Buffeted by a series of corruption scandals, the Truman presidency petered out—Truman stood down after losing the 1952 New Hampshire primary to Senator Estes Kefauver of Tennessee—amid an atmosphere of helplessness and war-weariness.

Truman's domestic policies were largely overshadowed by momentous foreign policy developments. The ambitious program for extending New Deal liberalism, outlined early on in his presidency by Chester Bowles, made little headway. It was hindered by Republican gains in Congress, by southern Democratic opposition to black civil rights, and by the growing concentration upon foreign affairs and domestic anticommunism. Truman's Fair Deal reform program was put on the back burner during the Korean War. By this time, across the Atlantic Ocean, the major institutions of the British welfare state had been put in place by the post-1945 Labour government under Clement Attlee. In the United States, however, efforts to promote national health insurance and to expand hospital construction (along with, for example, other programs like the Brannan Plan to stabilize farm prices) all failed to win Congressional approval. Some advances were made in the civil-rights area, but mainly as a result of piecemeal executive action rather than in the form of legislation. Executive orders were issued in 1948 to combat discrimination in the federal civil service and segregation in the armed forces: and, indeed, Truman's Committee on Equality of Treatment and Opportunity in the Armed Services did make significant progress by 1953. However, the presidential commitment to civil rights was often dilatory and reactive, with Congress regularly being used as a scapegoat for lack of progress. Especially during the Korean War, black leaders found Truman reluctant to take even purely executive action against segregation within defense contracting firms. In late 1951, Truman did eventually create the President's Committee on Government Contract Compliance, a body principally concerned with publicizing and monitoring segregation rather than actually forcing desegregation.

Nonetheless, the Truman period did at least see, especially with the adoption of a strong civil-rights plank in the 1948 Democratic platform, the clear incorporation of race-relations reform into the liberal agenda. Generally, however, it was a period when New Deal reformism was consolidated rather than extended, and in which the cause of reform was inhibited and defined by anticommunism and the requirements of the national security state. Franklin D. Roosevelt had governed with a degree of informality and favored ad hoc initiatives. The Truman years, by contrast, saw moves towards greater formalization and institutionalization of a political system dominated by big-spending federal government and a highly visible, activist presidency.

At a personal level, Truman had many positive qualities. The picture of him as an ordinary man standing in the giant shadow cast by Roosevelt is misleading. Truman's treatment of political opponents, notably Progressive party presidential candidate Henry A. Wallace during the 1948 election, could verge on the unscrupulous. Nonetheless, his extraordinary success in that election demonstrated his ability both to project himself as a political leader in his own right and to gauge shifting trends in public opinion. While recognizing his strengths, it is difficult to acquit Truman of the related charges of insensitive anti-Sovietism and of complicity in the emerging horrors of the second Red Scare.

Truman himself despised Senator Joseph McCarthy and the wilder Republican professional anticommunists. He opposed the 1950 McCarran Act, which was passed over his veto; this required the official registration of left-wing organizations and outlawed the employment in defense plants and the admission to the United States of communist sympathizers. Nevertheless some revisionist historians have charged that in deliberately inflating the Soviet threat in order to gain support for his foreign policy, Truman set the stage for McCarthyism. His civil-service loyalty program, inaugurated in 1947, is often depicted as serving as the model for subsequent witch-hunts in other areas. By 1956, the program had led to 2,700 dismissals and 12,000 resignations. In reality, however hard he tried, Truman could not control the insidious hysteria of the Red Scare which he himself had done much to promote. His crude red-baiting of Wallace and the Progressives in the 1948 election further coarsened the standards of political debate.

The hysterical, internally directed anticommunism that gripped the United States in the decade after 1945 constituted the domestic side of the Cold War coin. Red-baiting provided a vocabulary by which enemies could be denounced, careers furthered, political battles conducted, and group rivalries advanced. As Arthur Miller wrote in the introduction to Act I of *The Crucible:* "Long-held hatreds of neighbors could now be openly expressed, and vengeance taken. . . ."[2] Witch-hunts and anticommunist vendettas extended into and shaped numerous areas of American life: popular culture, the arts, teaching, journalism, the legal profession, and the unions, among many others.

Most accounts of the McCarthyite phenomenon posit three main villains: the House Committee on Un-American Activities, J. Edgar Hoover, and Senator Joseph R. McCarthy himself. The committee had been established originally in 1938 under the chairmanship of conservative Texas Democrat Martin Dies. After 1945, under subsequent chairmen like Mississippi Democrat John E. Rankin and New Jersey Republican J. Parnell Thomas, the committee began to exploit and contribute to the new Cold War atmosphere. The Hollywood inquisitions, culminating in widespread blacklisting of suspect writers, directors, and actors, and the sentencing for contempt of the "Hollywood Ten," revealed the extent of the committee's philistine vindictiveness. The persecution in 1948 of former State Department official Alger Hiss, and his eventual imprisonment for perjury, was the committee's major cause célèbre. It paved the way for McCarthyism and unleashed passions that bear comparison with those raised by the Dreyfus case in France in the 1890s. Robert Bingham and Max Ascoli wrote in the liberal journal *The Reporter* on August 30, 1949: "Two trials were conducted at the same time in the same courtroom: one against Alger Hiss . . .; the other against the ghost of liberalism in the 1930s."[3] The former New Dealer Hiss was accused of passing classified State Department documents to Soviet agents in the late 1930s. Committee member Richard M. Nixon, a California Republican, rose to public prominence through his attacks on Hiss and his discovery, through Whittaker Chambers, of the "pumpkin patch papers" allegedly misappropriated by Hiss.

Where the committee was flashy and wayward, the FBI, headed by J. Edgar Hoover, was relentless and relatively clandestine in its hounding of suspected communist sympathizers. Hoover, a tireless advocate of anticommunist conspiracy theory, wielded huge influence within the Justice Department during the early Cold War period. It seems likely that Truman was not even briefed concerning Hoover's grandiose schemes to harass and arrest leftist sympathizers. The FBI informer network operated in a manner more appropriate to totalitarian dictatorships than liberal democracies. The bureau went to extraordinary lengths to accumulate information on left-leaning figures in the public eye, like the artist Rockwell Kent and the singer Paul Robeson. R. J. Lamphere, a former FBI agent, sees Hoover's dogged pursuit of, for example, the Rosenbergs as actually tending to be undermined by the wilder and more theatrical Congressional anticommunists. (Julius and Ethel Rosenberg were executed in 1953 for allegedly passing atomic secrets to Soviet agents.)

Among Congressional anticommunists, none were wilder or more histrionic than Joe McCarthy. The bullying, alcoholic Republican senator from Wisconsin certainly cannot be held responsible for orginating the movement that bears his name. In a sense, he contributed almost as much to the decline of McCarthyism as to its emergence and ascendancy. Notably, his 1954 attacks on the army, broadcast on national television, revealed him as an ill-informed ranter and led to his censure by the United States Senate later in the year. Although he operated principally through a combination of bluster and unsubstantiated accusation, McCarthy, too, had his informants. (He claimed access to a "loyal American underground"—people like Frances

G. Knight—in the supposedly communist-dominated State Department.) Albeit for a relatively brief period, McCarthy appeared to embody the threat to the rule of law and to the remnants of earlier civility in American public life.

To some extent, the celebrated episodes in the second Red Scare—the Hollywood investigations, the Hiss and Rosenberg cases, the trial of Communist party leaders, McCarthy's 1950 charges concerning communists in the State Department, the persecution of China expert Owen Lattimore—have drawn attention away from the thoroughgoing manner in which McCarthyism penetrated American society as a whole. In particular, political movements of the Left were largely destroyed and the labor movement transformed. A series of laws passed between 1950 and 1954 effectively silenced the Communist party of the U.S.A. (CPUSA) and other left-wing organizations. The CPUSA leadership made arrangements to continue an underground existence, with a precarious apparatus being set up in Mexico. The tactics of McCarthyism—guilt by association, suspicion equaling proof—ensured that the noncommunist Left either perished along with the CPUSA, or rushed to establish its anticommunist credentials. On the labor front, left-wing figures like the veteran West Coast longshoremen's organizer Harry Bridges were persecuted; private firms instituted their own anticommunist "industrial security" programs; and leftist unions were expelled from the Congress of Industrial Organizations (CIO). Labor leaders like Philip Murray of the CIO sought to build links with liberal Democrats as a way of opposing Republican attacks on labor, rather than defending left-wing unionists. In the event, attempts by labor leaders to demonstrate their anticommunism and forge new alliances did not inhibit the passage of Republican-sponsored labor legislation. The Taft-Hartley Act, passed in 1947 over Truman's veto amid hysteria generated by the wave of strikes that followed the end of World War II, constituted a drastic departure from the generally pro-labor legislative inheritance from the 1930s. The proto-McCarthyite context of the Taft-Hartley Act was clearly illustrated in the provision that compelled union organizers to forswear allegiance to communism as a prerequisite for access to the National Labor Relations Board.

Academic controversy about McCarthyism has centered largely on the question of whether it should be regarded as a mass- or elite-based movement. Accounts written in the 1950s and 1960s tended to portray McCarthyism as a species of popular irrationalism, particularly virulent among groups in American society that were anxious about their own status. The demagogic abilities of McCarthy were emphasized, with anticommunist liberals like Truman and Adlai E. Stevenson being seen as promoters of civilized values. During the 1970s a reaction against this view took place, most cogently expressed in the work of historians to the left of the liberal anticommunist tradition. It was argued that hysterial anticommunism was sponsored by business and political elites in order to attack the influence of the Left and to mobilize public support for the policies of the Cold War. Liberal Democrats, just as much as the Republican Right, were held responsible.

The complexity of the forces that came together to produce McCarthyism, both at the national and the state level, should caution us against glib generalization. The movement was clearly shaped by the resurgence of Congress and the Republican party after years of relative powerlessness. The reaction of East European ethnic groups against Soviet domination of their homelands was clearly a factor, as was a widespread resentment at the status enjoyed by the new federal civil-service elite created by the New Deal. McCarthyism also raised serious issues, as well as bogus ones: for example, the issue of excessive governmental secrecy and Congressional access to information. Attempts to test general interpretaions of McCarthyism at the state or regional level have inclined to point up the intricate complexity of the factors at work. Anticommunism in Texas was fostered by elite groups (like the Houston "Minute Women") concerned to protect vested interests. Californian McCarthyism was embedded in the domestic politics of the state, with local groups reacting to failures of U.S. policy in China and Korea. In the Midwest, the movement was more in the nature of an outgrowth of native conservatism.

Both at the local and national levels the evidence of mass support for the anticommunist crusade is slight. Certainly, people were worried about spies and the loss of atomic secrets. Truman both stimulated and fed off public worries about Soviet expansionism in the late 1940s. Such fears did not, however, automatically translate into support for paranoid anticommunism. Elites either failed to protect endangered freedoms or themselves joined the McCarthyite bandwagon. The Supreme Court under Chief Justice Fred M. Vinson, for example, effectively conspired in the suspension of the First Amendment to the Constitution. Presidents Truman and Eisenhower, although they both personally opposed McCarthy, also played their part. The latter's Executive Order 10450 actually extended the loyalty program. His appointments, notably to the Federal Communications Commission, also regularly included McCarthyites.

By the late 1950s the virulent phase of McCarthyism had passed. The nation settled into postwar stability and the worst of the Cold War threats appeared to diminish. However, the legacy of McCarthyism persisted: in the enshrinement of anti-communism at the heart of modern liberalism, in the weakness of domestic left-wing movements, and in real doubts about the ability and willingness of political leaders to protect democratic freedoms under difficult circumstances.

McCarthy's censure by the Senate in 1954, along with the ending of the Korean conflict and the inauguration of the new president in 1953, has often been interpreted as signaling the inception of a new period of political tranquility: the Eisenhower era. In fact, perceptions of President Eisenhower and of America in the 1950s are to a large extent inseparable. Positive views of one tend to reinforce positive views of the other. Impressions of the president and the period he dominated tend to fall into two categories. On the one hand, there are the complacent, self-satisfied fifties: a decade of mediocrity and materialism, conformity and philistinism, presided over by an amiable bumbler who preferred golf to government. On the other, the fifties have appeared to some veterans of the upheavals of the 1960s and 1970s as an oasis of calm certainty, a decade of solid economic achievement and relative harmony. In this light, Eisenhower appears as a benevolent wizard, the master strategist operating to great effect behind a facade of reassuring ordinariness and passivity.

Early views of Eisenhower as an ineffectual political tyro, who allowed the United States to fall behind the USSR in scientific and military technology, cannot realistically be sustained. They were largely the product of Kennedy partisanship in the 1960 presidential contest. Examination of Ike's military career hardly bears out his reputation for genial indifference to personal ambition. Many White House associates found his personality to have its abrasive side. He did intervene in issues, such as to encourage the Senate censure of Joe McCarthy, in ways that were not entirely obvious to contemporaries. While the degree of independence enjoyed by Secretary of State John Foster Dulles remains controversial, Eisenhower was far from being the puppet of staffers and cabinet members. He was certainly no prisoner of the Pentagon, as was seen in his efforts to restrain military spending through the New Look defense program and his departing remarks about the military-industrial complex. Eisenhower was also a skillful politician, as he showed in handling Congress, notably in converting conservative Republicans to accept his internationalist foreign policy aims in 1953–54. Though he affected to dislike politics, he was the first president to establish a legislative liaison staff in the White House.

Eisenhower's achievements and skills did, however, have their limits. He often appeared indecisive. This characteristic was especially evident in matters involving the Republican party. He made little effort to convert his personal popularity into support for GOP candidates at all levels of government. Ike was, of course, no regular Republican loyalist, having had no party affiliation prior to 1952. Later, exasperated at the prospect of Congressional committee chairmanships being held by the party's old guard, he told Republican National Committee chairman Leonard Hall that he was considering running as a Democrat in 1956! His equivocal attitude, after his 1955 heart attack, to Vice President Nixon's future also smacked of indecision, and threatened to damage the Republican cause.

Significantly, the negative side of Eisenhower's record extends to the two areas that were to dominate the politics of the 1960s: Vietnam and civil rights. It is true that the United States did not go to war at the time of the French defeat in Vietnam in 1954. Nonetheless, the commitments that were made to the artificial entity of South Vietnam between 1956 and 1960 established a momentum which, although not irreversible, provided a crucial backdrop to the tragic decisions of the following decade. During the late 1950s, U.S. personnel—military intelligence, diplomatic, and economic assistance officers—insinuated themselves into the interstices of the Saigon regime. On civil rights, Eisenhower appeared more concerned with America's image abroad and with problems of public order in the

Southern states than with the rights of blacks. E. Frederic Morrow, appointed in 1955 as the first black administrative assistant to the president, rapidly became disenchanted, confessing that he felt ridiculous in trying to defend the administration's civil-rights record. The White House seemed reluctant to defend the Supreme Court's school desegregation decisions. The sending of federal troops into Little Rock, Arkansas, in 1957 appears to have been occasioned primarily by concerns about public order in the wake of the insubordination of segregationist Governor Orval E. Faubus. Attorney General Herbert Brownell's civil-rights proposals were significantly weakened by the president and the cabinet, and culminated in the highly limited civil-rights acts of 1957 and 1960.

The contemporary debate about the Eisenhower presidency concerns not only the nature of his leadership and the extent of his successes, but also revolves around the problem of defining "Eisenhower Republicanism." Ike has often been seen as presiding over a further institutionalization of the New Deal, even extending it slightly. Certainly, he pressed successfully in 1954 for the extension of social security to some 10 million people previously uncovered. Further extensions were made in 1956 and 1958. Ike's health reinsurance proposals of 1954, though not enacted by Congress, gave weight to his own description of himself as a liberal on "human issues." Federal money would have been invested in the rehabilitation of the disabled and in hospitals, with a reinsurance service designed to encourage nongovernment health insurance. The 1954 Housing Act, calling for government construction of 140,000 dwellings over a four-year period, reflected the extent—modest by the standards of the Democrats, but real nonetheless—of Eisenhower's commitment to public housing. The organization of the Department of Health, Education, and Welfare, subsequent to its establishment by Congress in 1953, seemed also to symbolize the administration's support for an interventionist federal welfare role. The Eisenhower years were also crucial in institutionalizing the expanded presidential role inherited from prior Democratic administrations.

Somewhat in contrast to his public image, President Eisenhower grappled energetically with the problem of controlling the bureaucracy. The creation of a category of "political" Schedule C appointments, at bureau-head level and below, was designed to give the president greater leverage over potentially obstructive policy-making sectors of the civil service. However, one reason why Eisenhower was so concerned to impose control on the bureaucracy was precisely because his priorities were indeed more conservative than those of his Democratic predecessors. In many areas Eisenhower displayed a pro-business conservatism that Democrats in the bureaucracy, as elsewhere, would tend to oppose. His instincts tended in particular to favor a series of retreats in the federal government's role in economic development. During his presidency, federal control was weakened in the fields of atomic energy and exploitation of oil-rich "submerged lands." Ike's eagerness to limit the growth of the Tennessee Valley Authority led to a potentially damaging conflict-of-interest problem (the Dixon-Yates case of 1955). Presidential fondness for appointing people with a business background encouraged Adlai Stevenson, Democratic presidential candidate in 1952 and 1956, to speak of car dealers replacing New Dealers. The Eisenhower–Ezra Taft Benson farm policy also clearly ran against the grain of the New Deal, in its concern to cut federal intervention. Although he did support spending increases to combat the expected post–Korean War deflation, Eisenhower always thought of himself as a fiscal conservative. Iwan Morgan describes him as "at best a passive and half-hearted Keynesian."[4] Ike succeeded in balancing his budget, a major aim of his economic policy, three times in eight attempts. Examination of federal spending patterns, however, reveals not only Eisenhower's relative parsimony, but also the huge impact of the expanding national security state. The New Look did have some effect. Thus, in calendar year 1960, defense spending was lower in real terms than in any year since 1951. Yet there was no question as to where priorities lay. During Eisenhower's occupation of the White House, defense expenditures constituted a higher percentage of total federal outlays than during either the Vietnam War or President Reagan's massive defense buildup in the early 1980s.

Some historians have sought to emphasize Eisenhower's fundamental conservatism. Gary W. Reichard, for example, sees Eisenhower's domestic policies as representing the "reaffirmation of Republicanism," rather than the "New" or "Modern Republicanism" which the president affected largely for public-relations purposes.[5] In fact, "Modern Republicanism" was a highly unsatisfactory concept; it upset those who preferred traditional GOP shibboleths and seemed to contradict many of Eisenhower's own policy preferences. Robert G. Griffith has traced the lineage of Eisenhower's position to the corporate ideal of the Progressive era, Herbert Hoover's "associative state," and the corporatist phase of the New Deal.[6] Eisenhower lent a significantly conservative cast to notions of a "corporate commonwealth" committed to social harmony under the direction of a managerialist state.

Eisenhower had a deep personal commitment to fairness, to balance, and to intervening only when intervention was unavoidable. The omnibus tax bill of 1954 thus tried to balance concessions to business with a rejection of demands to cut corporate taxes. He used his power under the Taft-Hartley Act to intervene in strikes much less than Truman. Eisenhower could also be unpredictable, as in the early, short-lived appointment of trade unionist Martin P. Durkin, an opponent of Taft-Hartley, as secretary of labor.

The Eisenhower–John Foster Dulles foreign policy followed the trail laid during the Truman years. That its achievements were largely negative—not going to war—should not be taken as too great a criticism. While the effects of a nuclear war are unimaginable and incalculable, the Korean and Vietnam conflicts demonstrated the horrors of even "limited" wars. In July 1953, United States negotiators achieved a settlement in Korea, reestablishing the North-South division and settling the prisoner-of-war disputes. Committed in the 1952 election platform to "end neglect" of the Far East, Dulles and Eisenhower secured a defense treaty with Nationalist China after the shelling of offshore islands from the mainland in 1954. With a new crisis erupting in the Taiwan Strait in 1959, Ike's China policy combined hard-line rhetoric with a desire to avoid armed conflict. The administration also sought to exploit and widen Sino-Soviet splits.

In regard to small countries and winnable objectives, however, Eisenhower could act dramatically and ruthlessly. With U.S. oil interests at stake, the CIA moved in 1953 to restore the power of the shah in Iran. Repercussions of the coup were long-lasting and were later to dominate the final year of Jimmy Carter's presidency. In Guatemala, the takeover of United Fruit Company assets by the reformist regime of Jacobo Arbenz evoked a similar American response. The CIA conspired with friendly Central American governments to oust Arbenz in 1954.

These events would be remembered and invoked during the 1979 Sandinista revolution in Nicaragua. When John Kennedy entered the White House in 1961, he found a covert CIA operation being planned against Fidel Castro's communist government in Cuba. In 1958, some 14,000 U.S. troops were ordered to Lebanon to combat left-wing forces and send warning signals to regimes in Iraq and Egypt.

The failure to achieve an arms control argeement with the Soviet Union is often regarded as a major flaw in the Eisenhower record. Early overtures from the USSR, made after Stalin's death, were unlikely to make headway, given the anticommunist mood at home. Similarly, the shooting down of an American U-2 spy aircraft in May 1960 foreclosed prospects of any rapprochement with Soviet leader Nikita Khrushchev. Nonetheless, opportunities may have been lost in the mid-1950s, especially at the 1955 Geneva summit. Ike's arms control and peace proposals (notably the Open Skies and Atoms for Peace initiatives) were genuine attempts to enhance the cause of peace, but were essentially unlikely to form the basis of any realistic understanding with the Soviets. As it was, the arms race warmed up toward the spending explosion of the early 1960s. Eisenhower's legacy in American strategic thought was a rather confusing mixture of massive retaliation and flexible response. The United States and the USSR both exploded hydrogen bombs in 1954. The panic that greeted the launching of the Soviet space satellite Sputnik in 1957 also dented Eisenhower's attempts to hold down defense spending.

The Eisenhower legacy, therefore, was not simply one of peace and prosperity. The covert CIA operations, the failure to ease Middle East tensions, and the growing involvement in South Vienam all stored up problems for the future. The executive's handling of the Taiwan crises and the Eisenhower Doctrine in the Middle East represented an implicit attack on the foreign policy powers of Congress, and had implications for the future conduct of policy in Vietnam. The public and political mood of the late 1950s was also fractious and uncertain. The Sputnik launching generated intense (and generally unfair) criticism of the administration's scientific and technological policies. The sight of Castro and Khrushchev embracing at the United Nations building in New York raised anxieties in the wake of the U-2 incident. Allen Drury's novel *Advise and Consent* vividly described public reactions to the Sputnik launch:

". . . in the sudden burst of Soviet science in the later fifties, the golden legend crumbled . . . a too complacent and uncaring people awoke to find themselves naked with the winds of the world howling around their ears. . . ."[7]

Like President Reagan a quarter of a century later, President Eisenhower achieved popularity and the trust of the American public. Also like Reagan, however, Ike often looked for easy answers and appeared, particularly in his second term, to be somewhat out of tune with public expectations. For the time being, perhaps the best verdict on Eisenhower is that offered by William L. O'Neill: "Eisenhower did his best to make time stand still, and for a little while it did."[8]

The notion of the fifties as a period when time stood still is, of course, an intentionally paradoxical one. The fifteen years following the end of World War II saw momentous social and demographic changes. Between 1945 and 1960 the total population grew from 139.9 million in 180 million. The nearly 30 million increase between 1950 and 1960 represented the largest period of population growth over any decade in American history. In 1945, 56.6 percent of the population lived in towns and cities; in 1960, the figure was 69.9 percent. The per capita Gross National Product rose from $1,526 in 1945 to $2,788 in 1960. By 1960, 75 percent of American families owned a car, and 87 percent owned a television set. The consumer boom was accompanied by a credit explosion. Betwen 1946 and 1957, credit used to finance automobile purchase increased in value fifteen times over. Housing construction was concentrated in the burgeoning suburbs. Between 1948 and 1958, some 13 million new homes were built, 11 million of them in the suburbs. In fact, by 1960 almost one out of every three Americans lived in the suburbs of towns and cities. With rising living standards and huge advances against diseases like polio, life expectancy for whites rose from 66.8 years to nearly 71 years by 1960; the respective figures for nonwhites were 57.7 years and 63.3 years. By the mid-1950s a substantial majority of Americans considered themselves "middle class." With the expansion of the service economy, white-collar workers were held by 1956 to outnumber blue-collars. According to U.S. Bureau of Census definitions, white-collar employment rates jumped by four percentage points between 1950 and 1960. "Professional" sector employment rose three points.

Huge changes were taking place in the nation's economy.

Industries and jobs were moving southward and westward. Texas and California, in particular, grew in economic power along with the new petrochemical, electronics, and above all defense-oriented industries. Wall Street prices began to rise once again on a scale not seen since the 1920s. Corporate concentration gathered apace. By 1960, the two hundred largest corporations controlled over half of all U.S. business assets. The Eisenhower administration made no protest as, between 1950 and 1960, the fifty biggest U.S. corporations took over some 471 competitors. As the decade drew to a close, General Motors, Ford, and Chrysler between them produced about 95 percent of all U.S.-made automobiles. Some massive corporations resembled quasi-independent nation-states and were rapidly aspiring to multinational status. The organized labor movement continued to grow slowly in size, but was undergoing a relative decline of power. In fact, the 1950s saw the clear emergence of those economic shifts—from manufacturing to service industries, from Northeast to Southwest—that were to plague the movement for the next thirty years.

In what senses, therefore, may the fifties be seen as an era when time stood still? As one level, time stood still to the extent that these social changes encouraged an unimaginative conformity and suspicion of new ideas. The suburban white male of the 1950s, for example, is regularly depicted as the conformist "organization man": intolerant and blandly orthodox in his beliefs and opinions. Contemporary observers like John Keats portrayed the suburban wife as living a life of desperate vacuity behind the picture window. David Riesman saw the suburbanite as "seldom informed, rarely angry and only spasmodically partisan."[9] Vance Packard described the "forces of the times"— notably "big housing developments, big advertisers, big trade unions, and big corporate hierarchies"—as "conspiring to squeeze individuality and spontaneity from us."[10]

This is not to deny that the suburbs had their positive side, and that they were more complex and varied than they appeared in many hostile accounts. Mass housing construction, together with the availability of loans (especially under veterans legislation) brought home ownership within the compass of families previously confined to the low-cost rented sector. But as surburbs multiplied, inner cities declined. Inner Boston's population fell from 801,444 in 1950 to 697,197 in

1960. Up until the late 1950s, new housing developments were also generally white-only. Purchasers of houses in the mushrooming Levittowns were often required to sign radically exclusive transfer contracts. Inner-city populations were becoming increasingly low-income and black: a social change with momentous implications for the ensuing decade.

In the suburbs, on the other hand, visible indicators of prosperity could be seen by all: in the craze for consumer durables, in the appearance of vast shopping malls, and in the way in which cities were becoming increasingly built around the needs of the automobile. Especially after 1948, when Cadillacs acquired tail fins, the style of car—and the annual model change—assumed new importance for consumers. In 1955 each of the three major auto producers introduced radical new models, and the annual sales figures for new cars rocketed to almost eight million. The vast highway construction programs of the later 1950s (characteristically tied in with the need of the national security state to move military traffic swiftly) exemplified the new order. The very visibility of prosperity and change tended, however, to obscure the persistence of actual and relative deprivation. In 1959, the Census Bureau indicated that between 20 and 40 percent of American families were below the poverty line, depending upon how one defined it. In an unfortunate echo of Herbert Hoover in 1928, Adlai Stevenson announced at the 1956 Democratic convention that the grinding reality of poverty was slowly disappearing. It was left to the early 1960s for poverty to be "rediscovered" as a national (rather than a marginal or regional) concern.

Time stood still to the degree that the cultural and intellectual atmosphere stifled debate and exuded caution and complacency. Eric F. Goldman in 1959 saw himself as living in "a heavy, humorless, sanctimonious, stultifying atmosphere, singularly lacking in the self-mockery that is self-criticism."[11] Nothing contributed more to the atmosphere of narrow conformity than the dead hand of McCarthyism and of blinkered anticommunism. Cold War themes dominated even children's TV and the Western. One commentator describes the cowboy heroes of the 1950s as "mythic outriders of freedom, defeating the enemies of democratic civilization."[12] Popular culture did exhibit a capacity for articulating, very often in a displaced Cold War context, anxieties that underlay apparent complacency. The vogue for science fiction and monster movies may be interpreted in this light, as may, in a sense, the religious revival associated with evangelists like Billy Graham.

How justified, in fact, is the reputation of the 1950s for stultifying conformity? Obviously, we should guard against accepting the stereotypes of "organization man" and "suburban wife" too uncritically. Changing female employment patterns—by 1960, 40 percent of all women over sixteen were employed—do not support the latter stereotype, for example. The fifties experience of, in particular, students and women appeared, from the perspective of the 1960s, to be drab and inhibiting: the "ungeneration." Sixties student leader Todd Gitlin later wrote of "the dead, drab fifties."[13] However, as Gitlin himself shows, the later movements did not spring up overnight. Michael Harrington has identified the fall of 1958 as the time when, with the decline of McCarthyism and Martin Luther King's movement on its way in the South, "the sixties were beginning to stir within the fifties."[14] The theme of rebellion against conformity was obviously a vital aspect of the culture that produced James Dean, the beat novelists and poets, Abstract Expressionist painters like Jackson Pollock, and early rock and rollers like the young Elvis Presley.

The received view of political ideas in this decade is one of convergence. With Daniel Bell proclaiming the end of ideology, Cold War intellectuals and consensus historians are seen as turning to defenses of elitist managerialism and celebrations of American pragmatism. John Kenneth Galbraith's *American Capitalism* (1952) described an economy that was virtually self-regulating, subject only to delicate Keynesian fine-tuning by political managers. There is some substance to the view of intellectual activity in this period as being characterized by an unusual degree of consensus. However, received views of the period do not convey the subtle differences between Cold War intellectuals (nor, of course, their differences with critics of consensus like C. Wright Mills). Louis Hartz's *The Liberal Tradition in America* (1955), for example, is often taken as typical of the consensus school in its celebration of pragmatic liberalism and individualistic capitalism. But, as Robert B. Fowler has argued, Hartz attacked "the conviction of postwar liberalism that its values had little to do with ideology and were instead skeptical, pragmatic and open-ended."[15] Similarly, the fact that there was a Cold War consensus did not mean that there was no debate at all over national priorities—for example, between Eisenhower and Stevenson—and over the proper scope of federal power. It is also important to appreciate the very limited degree to which the decade represented a new era of good feelings. The early and late 1950s were not characterized by political tranquility. As Stephen Ambrose has pointed out, nostalgia for the "fifties" is really nostalgia for the relatively brief period between July 1953, when the Korean War ended, and the fall of 1957, when the Little Rock and Sputnik crises shattered the political calm of mid-decade.[16]

Literature of the 1950s dealt only obliquely with McCarthyism, as in Arthur Miller's *The Crucible* (1953). Instead, writers became interested in psychological themes. The beat writers of the later 1950s began to champion self-consciously aberrant behavior, and to concern themselves with "abnormal" states of mind, either as alternatives to "normality" or as its "real" face. Working more consciously within a received literary tradition, Robert Lowell wrote, in "Memories of West Street and Lepke," of Boston in the "tranquillized Fifties": where even the scavenger "in the back alley trash cans" has "two children, a beach wagon" and is "'a young Republican.'"[17]

In a sense, it is strange that a period that saw such massive social and demographic change, along with the consolidation of a globalistic foreign policy and of the post–New Deal, national security state, should have a reputation for dullness. Nonetheless, although their impact and extent probably have been exaggerated, the Cold War consensus and prosperity did inhibit creative energies. They temporarily camouflaged tensions that were being generated by social changes and by the reluctance of the federal government to tackle deep-seated problems. As it indulged in a prolonged debate over the national purpose in the late 1950s, the United States appeared to be treading water. The "tranquillized Fifties" were about to confront the vitality and energy, both constructive and destructive, of the new decade.

Notes

1. Fred I. Greenstein, *The Hidden-Hand Presidency: Eisenhower as Leader* (New York, 1982), p. 50.
2. Arthur Miller, *The Crucible* (New York, 1953), p. 7.

3. Max Ascoli, ed., *Our Times* (New York, 1960), p. 153.

4. Iwan W. Morgan, *Eisenhower versus "The Spenders": The Eisenhower Administration, the Democrats and the Budget, 1953–60* (New York, 1990), p. 179.

5. Gary W. Reichard, *The Reaffirmation of Republicanism: Eisenhower and the Eighty-third Congress* (Knoxville, Tenn., 1975), esp. pp. 227–37.

6. Robert G. Griffith, "Dwight D. Eisenhower and the Corporate Commonwealth," *American Historical Review* 87 (1982): 87–122.

7. Allen Drury, *Advise and Consent* (New York, 1959), p. 36.

8. William L. O'Neill, *American High: The Years of Confidence, 1945–1960* (New York, 1987), p. 211.

9. David Riesman, "The Suburban Dislocation" in *America as a Mass Society*, ed. Philip Olsen (London, 1963), pp. 303–4.

10. Vance Packard, *The Status Seekers* (New York, 1960), pp. 357, 358.

11. Paul S. Holbo and Robert W. Sellen, eds., *The Eisenhower Era* (Hinsdale, Ill., 1974), p. 8.

12. J. Fred MacDonald, *Television and the Red Menace: The Video Road to Vietnam* (New York, 1985), p. 143.

13. Todd Gitlin, *The Sixties: Years of Hope, Days of Rage* (New York, 1987), p. 1.

14. Michael Harrington, *Fragments of a Century* (New York, 1972), pp. 88–89.

15. Robert B. Fowler, *Believing Skeptics: American Political Intellectuals, 1945–1964* (Westport, Conn., 1978), pp. 284–85.

16. Stephen E. Ambrose, *Eisenhower the President, 1952–1969* (New York, 1984), p. 425.

17. Robert Lowell, *Life Studies* (London, 1959), p. 57.

Bibliography

On the period generally, see Paul A. Carter, *Another Part of the Fifties* (New York, 1983); J. Ronald Oakley, *God's Country: America in the Fifties* (New York, 1986); William L. O'Neill, *American High: The Years of Confidence, 1945–1960* (New

York, 1987); Gary W. Reichard, *Politics as Usual: The Age of Truman and Eisenhower* (Arlington Heights, Ill., 1988); and John P. Diggins, *The Proud Decades: America in War and in Peace, 1941–1960* (New York, 1989). Reliable accounts of Truman's presidency are: Alonzo L. Hamby, *Beyond the New Deal: Harry S. Truman and American Liberalism* (New York, 1973); Robert Donovan, *Conflict and Crisis: The Presidency of Harry S. Truman, 1945–1948* (New York, 1977) and *Tumultuous Years: The Presidency of Harry S. Truman, 1949–1953* (New York, 1982); Donald R. McCoy, *The Presidency of Harry S. Truman* (Lawrence, Kans., 1984); and William E. Pemberton, *Harry S. Truman: Fair Dealer and Cold Warrior* (Boston, 1989).

Truman's foreign policy is discussed by Daniel Yergin, *Shattered Peace: The Origins of the Cold War and the National Security State* (Boston, 1978); John L. Gaddis, *Strategies of Containment: A Critical Appraisal of Postwar American National Security Policy* (New York, 1982); and Norman A. Graebner, ed., *The National Security: Its Theory and Practice, 1945–1960* (New York, 1986). The best study of the Korean conflict is Burton I. Kaufman, *The Korean War: Challenges in Crisis, Credibility and Command* (Philadelphia, 1986).

The best overviews of McCarthyism are Richard M. Fried, *Nightmare in Red: The McCarthy Era in Perspective* (New York, 1990), and Michael J. Heale, *American Anti-Communism: Combating the Enemy Within, 1830–1970* (Baltimore, 1990). The "status" school is exemplified by Richard Hofstadter, *The Paranoid Style in American Politics* (New York, 1965) and Seymour M. Lipset and Earl Raab, *The Politics of Unreason: Right-wing Extremism in America, 1790–1970* (London, 1971). For elite-based views, see Athan G. Theoharis, *Seeds of Repression: Harry S. Truman and the Origins of McCarthyism* (Chicago, 1971), and Robert G. Griffith and Athan G. Theoharis, eds., *The Specter: Original Essays on the Cold War and the Origins of McCarthyism* (New York, 1974). The two best biographies of McCarthy are Thomas C. Reeves, *The Life and Times of Joe McCarthy: A Biography* (New York, 1982) and David M. Oshinsky, *A Conspiracy So Immense: The World of Joe McCarthy* (Philadelphia, 1983). Other important works dealing with domestic anticommunism are David Caute, *The Great Fear: The Anti-Communist Purge under Truman and Eisenhower*

(London, 1978); Kevin O'Reilly, *Hoover and the Un-Americans: The FBI, HUAC and the Red Menace* (Philadelphia, 1983); and J. Fred MacDonald, *Television and the Red Menace: The Video Road to Vietnam* (New York, 1985). For regional studies, see James T. Selcraig, *The Red Scare in the Midwest* (Ann Arbor, Mich., 1982); Don E. Carleton, *Red Scare! Right-wing Hysteria, Fifties Fanaticism and Their Legacy in Texas* (Austin, 1986); and Michael J. Heale, "Red Scare Politics: California's Campaign Against Un-American Activities 1940–1970," *Journal of American Studies* 20 (1986): 5–32.

For Eisenhower revisionism the seminal work is Fred I. Greenstein, *The Hidden-Hand Presidency: Eisenhower as Leader* (New York, 1982). The traditional view has recently been restated by Piers Brendon, *Ike: The Life and Times of Dwight D. Eisenhower* (New York, 1986). Stephen E. Ambrose, *Eisenhower the President, 1952–1969* (New York, 1984), and Chester J. Pach, Jr., and Elmo Richardson, *The Presidency of Dwight D. Eisenhower,* rev. ed. (Lawrence, Kans., 1990), are the best studies of Ike's presidency. Domestic policy issues are dealt with by: Gary W. Reichard, *The Reaffirmation of Republicanism: Eisenhower and the Eighty-third Congress* (Knoxville, Tenn., 1975); Robert G. Griffith, "Dwight D. Eisenhower and the Corporate Commonwealth," *American Historical Review* 87 (1982): 87–122; Robert E. Burk, *The Eisenhower Administration and Black Civil Rights* (Knoxville, Tenn., 1984); and Iwan W. Morgan, *Eisenhower versus "The Spenders": The Eisenhower Administration, the Democrats and the Budget, 1953–60* (New York, 1990). For foreign policy, see Townsend Hoopes, *The Devil and John Foster Dulles* (New York, 1974); Richard A. Melanson and David Mayers, eds., *Reevaluating Eisenhower: American Foreign Policy in the 1950s* (Urbana, Ill., 1987); and two studies by H. W. Brands, Jr., *Cold Warriors: Eisenhower's Generation and American Foreign Policy* (New York, 1988), and "The Age of Vulnerability: Eisenhower and the National Insecurity State," *American Historical Review* 94 (1989): 963–89.

Contemporary studies that usefully convey the mood and concerns of the 1950s are David Riesman et al., *The Lonely Crowd: A Study of the Changing American Character* (New York, 1950); William H. Whyte, *The Organization Man* (New York, 1956); John Kenneth Galbraith, *The Affluent Society*

(Boston, 1958); Vance Packard, *The Status Seekers* (New York, 1960); and Philip Olsen, ed., *American as a Mass Society* (London, 1963). Important recent studies of social and cultural trends include: Robert H. Bremner and Gary W. Reichard, eds., *Reshaping America: Society and Institutions 1945–1960* (Columbus, Ohio, 1982); Eugenia Kaledin, *Mothers and More: American Women in the 1950s* (Boston, 1984); Elaine Tyler May, *Homeward Bound: American Families in the Cold War Era* (New York, 1988); Robert B. Fowler, *Believing Skeptics: American Political Intellectuals, 1945–1964* (Westport, Conn., 1978); Richard H. Pells, *The Liberal Mind in a Conservative Age: American Intellectuals in the 1940s and 1950s*, 2nd ed. (Middletown, N.Y., 1989); and Nora Sayre, *Running Time: Films of the Cold War* (New York, 1982).

6

The Sixties: From the New Frontier to Nixon, 1960–1972

_____ *Iwan W. Morgan*

The 1960s marked a significant watershed in modern American history. The decade began with hope and promise, but ended in disillusion, division, and defeat. The postwar liberal consensus, based on confidence in economic growth, the efficacy of moderate reform, and ultimate victory in the global struggle against communism, reached its peak during the presidencies of John F. Kennedy and Lyndon B. Johnson, and then went into decline. Richard M. Nixon's accession to the White House was accompanied by a new sense of the limits of America's international power. It also signified the ebbing of the liberal tide that had produced the New Frontier and Great Society programs, the greatest outburst of reform since the New Deal. By the late 1960s liberalism was on the defensive against a conservative resurgence that would later culminate in the election of Ronald Reagan.

The actual nature and significance of the sixties have been much debated. The decade has a cult image of activism, protest, and inspirational leadership, but recent scholarship has tended to demythologize the era. The vision of the nation's leaders, the scope of reform, and the extent of support for change have come into question. Even the concept of "the sixties" as a distinctive era has been challenged, in recognition of the fact that history does not fit neatly into decades. The main legislative reforms were confined to the years from 1963 to 1966, while the impetus for change had its origins in the late 1950s, when demands arose for new federal programs to resolve domestic problems. Nor was protest an intrinsically sixties phenomenon. Civil-rights activism dated from at least 1955, and the largest ever anti–Vietnam War demonstration took place in Washington, D.C., in 1971.

The 1960 presidential election, conventionally the starting point for historical analysis of the sixties, underlined the ambiguous beginnings of the era. By then the national mood of well-being characteristic of the mid-1950s was in decline. The civil-rights movement was stirring, the economy was in recession, intellectuals worried that consumer-culture values had sapped national energies, and American prestige had been dented by a series of foreign policy reverses. In tune with these developments, Kennedy promised activist leadership to "get the country moving again" and meet the challenges of a new decade. In contrast, his Republican opponent, Vice President Nixon, ran on the record of the Eisenhower administration. Kennedy's narrow victory by 0.2 percent of the popular vote, the smallest winning margin since 1888, showed that the desire for change was not dominant and that satisfaction and complacency were still strong.

Kennedy brought a new style to the presidency with an emphasis on youth, vigor, and urgency, thus encouraging the change in the national mood. In addition to being the first Roman Catholic president, he was, at forty-three, the youngest man ever elected president and the first president born in the twentieth century. The Kennedy administration recruited a number of young technocrats and academics, reputedly the "best and brightest" of a new leadership generation, to serve in government. The president and his men (women received no important appointments) exuded confidence in their ability to resolve the nation's problems. Coming from a generation reared on American triumphs—victory in World War II, the containment of communism in Europe, and the economic transformation from depression to affluence—they saw no limits to what the United States could achieve.

To ensure that the nation had the strength of purpose to

fulfill its potential, Kennedy's style of leadership relied on moral exhortation, demands for sacrifice, and creating a feeling of perpetual emergency. This was best exemplified by the words of his inaugural address, "Ask not what your country can do for you; ask what you can do for your country." In office he allowed presidential press conferences to be televised live as a means of molding national opinion. Kennedy's mastery of this medium made him, in effect, the first television president. According to one analyst, "It was under and because of Kennedy that television became an essential determinant—probably the essential determinant—of a president's ability to lead the nation."[1] Kennedy was also the first American president whose leadership style spawned foreign imitators, particularly among the new generation of leaders who came to power in Western Europe in the 1960s. Social Democrat Willy Brandt rose to prominence in West Germany in part through his particular appeal to youth. Britain's Labour Prime Minister Harold Wilson relied to such a great extent on television and personal imagery (such as promising to get his country moving again through "the white heat of the technological revolution") that he was accused of supplanting prime ministerial with presidential government.

However the substance of Kennedy's achievements was less glittering than his image. Historiographical opinion about his presidency has gone through three phases. Early assessments, written soon after Kennedy's assassination in Dallas in 1963, eulogized him, but a revisionist view later emerged when policies associated with the dead president reaped a bitter harvest. With the passage of time a more balanced viewpoint has gained credence. While accepting that he had many political and personal shortcomings, historians now acknowledge the significance of Kennedy's charismatic and emotional impact. He helped stir the nation out of complacency, conveyed a sense of caring for the underprivileged unmatched by any of his successors, and invoked in many young Americans a commitment to activism. It can also be argued that the Kennedy promise showed signs of substance in his final year, during which he questioned some Cold War orthodoxies and showed more committed leadership on domestic issues, notably civil rights.

Greatest controversy surrounds Kennedy's foreign policy. Critics accuse him of escalating the Cold War and overextending America's international commitments. A further charge is that he expanded the "imperial presidency" by vesting principal responsibility for foreign policy-making in the National Security Council (NSC), a small body capable of responding with more speed and secrecy to presidential desires than the State Department, which was also subject to greater Congressional scrutiny. In contrast, sympathetic historians credit Kennedy for initiating Soviet-American détente, securing the first-ever arms control treaty, and recognizing the nationalist aspirations of the Third World. It is difficult to accept their implicit argument that he launched American foreign policy in new directions. As Secretary of State Henry Kissinger remarked in 1975, the Kennedy period is better seen as "the last flowering of the previous era rather than as the beginning of a new era."[2]

Kennedy's actions were largely shaped by inherited doctrines and policies. He shared the aspirations of global hegemony that had guided American foreign policy since World War II. He typified Cold War liberalism in his conviction that peace and national security were mutually dependent on the United States always being strong enough to resist the aggrandizement anywhere in the world of a monolithic, Soviet-dominated international communism. Acceptance of Eisenhower's domino theory motivated his expansion of American commitments in Southeast Asia, while the 1961 attempt to overthrow Cuban leader Fidel Castro was based on a CIA plan inherited from the previous administration. Kennedy's primary goal was to restore America's Cold War superiority, which many Democrats feared Eisenhower had surrendered in the late 1950s. To this end, he initiated the largest arms buildup in peacetime history prior to the Reagan era, took action against the expansion of communist influence in Third World countries like the Congo, Laos, and South Vietnam, and risked nuclear confrontation over Soviet policy toward Berlin and Cuba.

The Cuban missile crisis of October 1962 remains the occasion when the world came closest to nuclear war. On learning that the Soviet Union had emplaced nuclear missiles in Cuba, Kennedy ordered a naval blockade of the island to compel their removal and considered an air strike to destroy them when the Russians proved obdurate. A belated compromise, whereby the Soviets removed the missiles in return for a U.S. pledge never to invade Cuba, averted the danger of war. Paradoxically, by alerting the superpowers to the danger of brinkmanship, the crisis led to a decline of tension. In 1963 a limited nuclear test ban treaty was signed, the hot-line telephone was installed between the Kremlin and the White House to prevent accidental conflict, and Kennedy speeches began to manifest the spirit of superpower détente. However, the thaw did not extend to the Third World, which had become the major battleground of the Cold War after Soviet premier Nikita Khrushchev's endorsement in 1961 of "wars of national liberation" to promote communism through guerrilla struggles in countries emerging from colonialism.

Kennedy relied in part on idealism to win the "hearts and minds" of underdeveloped nations. He created the Alliance for Progress, a flawed effort to promote social reform in Latin America with U.S. economic aid, and the Peace Corps, which mobilized college-educated American youth to serve as community workers in developing countries. Nevertheless his administration placed greater emphasis on military power. It strengthened conventional ground forces, developed the elite Green Beret corps, and intensified counterinsurgency training in preparation for "brushfire wars" against communist guerrilla insurgencies. The testing ground for this strategy was South Vietnam, where American troop presence escalated under Kennedy from under 1,000 to over 16,000. However, the results proved disappointing, because the Americans were defending the corrupt, dictatorial, and inefficient Diem regime. Many Kennedy admirers argue that he would not have sanctioned further U.S. involvement had he lived. Given his beliefs concerning the domino theory, the monolithic nature of international communism, and the significance of the Third World, this view is difficult to support.

Kennedy was far more cautious in domestic affairs. His narrow election victory did not provide a mandate to challenge the informal Congressional coalition of Southern Democrats and Republicans that had stymied reform legislation since the late 1930s. The New Frontier, which was basically an extension of the New Deal–Fair Deal agenda, did not propose radical innovation, but Kennedy shelved much of his program rather than risk fighting losing battles with Congress. Economic policy was the main exception to this rule. In expanding federal responsibility for economic management, Kennedy made his most distinctive and innovative contribution to American liberalism.

Despite general prosperity, the economy had only achieved an annual growth rate of 2.5 percent under Eisenhower, barely half the Truman-era rate, and had suffered recurrent recessions. Under the tutelage of Walter Heller, chairman of the Council of Economic Advisers, Kennedy eventually became a devotee to the "new economics." In contrast to orthodox Keynesianism, which only prescribed budget deficits during a recession, this doctrine advocated "fine-tuning" the full employment economy with fiscal and monetary stimuli to maximize economic growth. Until Jimmy Carter, all of Kennedy's successors followed his lead in utilizing the so-called full-employment budget as the instrument of economic expansion. Instead of balancing the actual budget, this placed more emphasis on balancing the economy by calculating expenditures in relation to the hypothetical receipts if the economy were operating at full potential. As a result, deficits became a way of life for the federal government. Whereas the Truman and Eisenhower administrations had operated surplus budgets as anti-inflationary devices during periods of prosperity, only once has the federal budget been balanced since 1960. Under Kennedy the fiscal revolution that had started in the 1930s completed its course.

Tax reduction was the core of Kennedy's growth strategy. The 1962 Revenue Act was a supply-side measure, which increased business depreciation allowances to encourage new investment and plant modernization. More significantly, in 1963 Kennedy proposed a massive tax cut of $11.5 billion, mainly on personal incomes, which was enacted soon after his death. The result was the takeoff of the longest economic boom in American history, with the growth rate reaching 6.5 percent in 1964. With confidence in the modern economy at its peak, the "new economics" became the new orthodoxy. This success greatly enhanced the cause of reformism. Faith in government's technical ability to manage the economy was greatly strengthened, paving the way for federal antipoverty programs. Economic growth boosted federal revenues, generating funds for new spending programs. It also produced a harvest of popular support for the Democrats in the 1964 elections. Most significantly, it set the tone for many of the reforms of the 1960s. Kennedy economics freed American liberalism from its long but half-hearted concern to redistribute wealth. Expansion of the private economy was expected to ensure full employment and to spread the benefits of prosperity to all Americans, even those on low incomes. Confidence in the sufficiency of the incremental resources of growth made the redistribution of wealth and power redundant. Symbolizing this, to secure approval for tax reduction from deficit-conscious conservative congressmen, Kennedy willingly abandoned accompanying proposals for modest tax increases on high incomes.

Largely reliant on the efficacy of private enterprise, neither the New Frontier nor, later, the Great Society sought to reform capitalism itself. In 1962 Kennedy had a public confrontation with the United States Steel Corporation after it contravened federal anti-inflation price guidelines, but business-government relations were fundamentally harmonious in the 1960s. There was no outcry against the increasing trend of economic concentration, even though twentieth-century liberalism had espoused antitrust doctrines since the Progressive era. As in the 1950s, the need for large sums of capital to develop ever more sophisticated technology and the growing interdependence of the economy favored the large corporations. The top eighty-seven corporations increased their share of total industrial assets from 26 percent to 46 percent during the 1960s. By 1972 3.3 percent of American corporations controlled 70 percent of corporate assets and 75 percent of profits. Conglomerates (single corporations with multiproduct interests) increased in number; by 1970 the two hundred largest industrial corporations were active in over two thousand product markets. The late 1960s saw the largest wave of corporate mergers in American history prior to the 1980s, 80 percent of these resulting in conglomeration. Multinational corporations were also expanding: the foreign capacity of American firms grew by 471 percent between 1958 and 1968, compared with a domestic increase of 72 percent. This development provoked some expressions of fear in Western Europe about an American economic takeover. At home, meanwhile, the GNP rose from $520.1 billion in 1961 to $1,054.9 billion in 1972, fulfilling the most optimistic predictions for growth. Against this background the Democratic administrations of the 1960s regarded economic concentration as a worthwhile price for the increased output of the corporate economy.

One issue, however, could not be resolved through economic growth. By 1960 the extension of civil rights to blacks was the greatest moral imperative facing American democracy. Though a civil-rights supporter, Kennedy doubted that Congress could be persuaded to enact substantial legislation to outlaw the Jim Crow system of formal segregation and racial discrimination that was enshrined by state laws and traditions throughout the South. Initial administration strategy, directed by the president's brother, Attorney General Robert F. Kennedy, relied on enforcement of voting rights provisions in existing legislation rather than seeking new legal powers or mounting a direct challenge to states' rights through executive action. The long-term aim was to expand the Southern black electorate so that it could eventually destroy Jim Crow through the ballot box. Impatient with this timidity, civil-rights activists seized the initiative and dragged the hesitant Kennedys along in their wake.

In response to direct-action protest, the administration gradually escalated federal involvement to protect the rights of demonstrators and activists. Eventually marshals and troops were dispatched to enforce compliance with Supreme Court desegregation rulings by the state universities of Mississippi and Alabama, respectively in 1962 and 1963. Nevertheless the administration was reluctant to operate outside a narrow legal framework. When Kennedy finally introduced civil-rights legislation in 1963, his modest bill encompassed voting rights violations and school desegregation but not equal rights and fair employment. Disappointed black activists and their white allies stepped up protest activities, culminating in the demonstrations organized by Martin Luther King in Birmingham, Alabama, reputedly the South's most segregated city. Police brutality against the marchers, graphically recorded by television, horrified national opinion and convinced the president that civil rights was a moral obligation that could no longer be pursued through a strategy of patient advance. In June 1963 he announced that his priority now was legislation giving blacks full legal equality.

Although Kennedy did not live to see the bill become law, he was the first president to use his full powers, albeit hesitantly, to aid blacks. It was in doing so, Alonzo Hamby observes, that he "built most meaningfully on the liberal tradition he had inherited."[3]

The civil-rights revolution had an immense international

impact, particularly in Northern Ireland, where it encouraged Roman Catholics to engage in peaceful protest against the discriminatory practices of the Protestant majority. Comparisons between the two movements must be made with caution, owing to the nationalist dimension involved in Ulster, but the political resolution of America's civil-rights crisis contrasts sharply with the descent into sectarian violence and the permanent presence of British "peacekeeping" troops in the province since 1969. The inaction of the British government toward the Protestant-dominated Northern Ireland parliament during the peaceful phase of Catholic protest puts the Kennedy administration's actions in better light.

Kennedy's successor, Lyndon Johnson, had a record as Texas senator and Senate majority leader in the 1950s of placing party unity above reform. However, he worked wholeheartedly to complete and extend Kennedy's agenda, displaying greater mastery of legislative tactics than any postwar president. In large part, Johnson's personality shaped his presidency. Nursing a massive ego, he wanted to achieve political domination and a place in history as a great leader who promoted a reform program bigger even than the New Deal. On the other hand, deep personal insecurity, stemming from childhood experience, made him anxious to avoid conflict. His skills in conciliation and compromise had made him a successful Senate leader. Adopting the same approach as president, he projected himself as America's Big Daddy who would fulfill the nation's needs and bring consensus out of division.

Skillfully exploiting national remorse following Kennedy's assassination, Johnson prevailed on Congress to enact a host of previously blocked bills, particularly the Civil Rights Act of 1964. The death knell for formal segregation, the act outlawed racial discrimination in public places, prohibited discrimination on grounds of race and gender in employment, and gave the federal government strong enforcement powers. Though it failed to eliminate state government disenfranchising devices, this deficiency was made good by the Voting Rights Act of 1965, enacted in response to a new wave of civil-rights protest in the South. Between 1964 and 1968, the South's black electorate increased by over one million voters, heralding the end for Dixie's lily-white Democratic party, but also making Republicanism an appealing alternative to Southern conservatives. The latter trend was evident in the 1964 election, when Barry M. Goldwater, the most conservative GOP presidential cándidate since Calvin Coolidge, became the first Republican to carry the Deep South since Reconstruction. However, the rest of the nation overwhelmingly endorsed Johnson, who was reelected with the largest share of the popular vote in history (61.1 percent). Presidential coattails also carried many new Democrats into Congress, breaking the thirty-year hold of the conservative coalition and giving Johnson enough votes to enact the Great Society programs.

Johnson's Great Society marked a substantial expansion of the "guarantor state" initiated by the New Deal. A host of new welfare-related programs was enacted. The Medicare program, created in 1965, provided health insurance for the aged under social security, while the corollary Medicaid program allocated federal matching funds to state health programs caring for indigent welfare recipients. The 1965 Elementary and Secondary Schools Act, the first ever general aid-to-education legislation, provided federal funds to local school districts through a formula involving the number of low-income children in the county. Housing legislation established a rent supplement program for impoverished tenants in 1965 and subsidized a construction program of low-income housing for sale and rent in 1968. The 1966 Model Cities Development program provided federal aid to revitalize inner-city neighborhoods. Rural problems were also recognized; in 1965, Appalachia, one of the nation's poorest regions, was given redevelopment aid.

At the same time the Great Society gave liberalism a new dimension through its quality-of-life concern. Antipollution and landscape preservation legislation marked important advances in federal responsibility for environmental protection. The national park system was substantially expanded, benefiting conservation and leisure activities. Consumer rights, freedom of information, automobile safety, and highway standards all came within the Great Society's purview. Federal aid for higher education was greatly increased, and support for the arts was institutionalized through creation of the National Endowment for the Arts and Humanities.

After civil rights, Johnson's main domestic goal was to eradicate poverty. Official estimates numbered the poor at 39 million in 1959 (21 percent of the population), but Michael

Harrington's best-selling 1962 book, *The Other America*, put the figure at 50 million.[4] Racial minorities, the aged, female-headed families, and residents of depressed regions were the main groups comprising the poor. Whites made up 70 percent of the poor, but poverty was most heavily concentrated among blacks. In 1965 43 percent of black families lived in poverty. Despite postwar prosperity, average black income was only 53 percent of white per capita income in 1962, the same as in 1947. Shocked at the extent of poverty in the affluent society, Johnson made it his personal mission to eliminate the problem.

There were three fundamental means of attacking poverty: a massive expansion of the public sector to boost jobs, services, and welfare for the poor; provision of cash for the poor, through either a guaranteed income or "income transfers"; and the enhancement of individual opportunity. Johnson's insistence on preserving consensus militated against the redistribution of wealth implicit in the first approach and against free cash handouts. Some Great Society reforms did incorporate modest elements of both approaches, but the predominant emphasis was on opportunity enhancement. Confidence ran high in the Johnson administration, as in Kennedy's, that economic expansion could generate sufficient wealth to end poverty. The problem from its perspective was that the poor lacked the values, incentives, and skills to exploit the opportunities available in the expanding economy. Accordingly, the so-called War on Poverty program treated poverty as a largely cultural problem, rather than a predominantly economic one. Its goal was to increase the ability and the incentive of the poor to seek self-improvement. The underlying assumption was that the poor themselves, not the flaws of the economic system, were responsible for their predicament.

The centerpiece of the War on Poverty was the Office of Economic Opportunity (OEO), created in 1964. Among its responsibilities were VISTA (a "domestic Peace Corps" providing educational services for the poor); the Job Corps (residential centers offering vocational training for unskilled youngsters), and the Neighborhood Youth Corps (which provided training and some jobs for school dropouts). OEO's most innovative venture was the Community Action Program, which sought neighborhood solutions to poverty and encouraged "maximum feasible participation" by the poor themselves in developing projects. Its activities included educational programs like Head Start, family-planning advice, legal services, and day-care centers for children. All these efforts did nothing, of course, for the unemployable poor—the aged, the crippled, and nonsupported mothers with dependent children. Nor did they provide what the employable poor needed above all else—decently paid jobs. Without this incentive and hampered by the low educational background of the poor, the vocational programs ended up training their recruits for unskilled, badly paid work that did nothing for the self-esteem of the poor.

Some commentators, notably John E. Schwarz, point to the decline in the number of poor to 23 million by 1973 (11 percent of Americans) as proof of the War on Poverty's success.[5] However, the more widespread view, exemplified by Allen J. Matusow and James T. Patterson, is that far more could have been achieved by giving the poor direct cash payments and expanding public employment, possibly through a WPA-style program.[6] Based on dubious concepts, the antipoverty programs were also gravely underfunded. Annual OEO expenditures only averaged $1.7 billion in 1965–68, under 1.5 percent of the federal budget, while antipoverty features of other Great Society programs amounted to a further $5 billion yearly. National security expenditures averaged $64 billion in this period, showing where U.S. priorities still lay.

In general the Great Society bequeathed a flawed legacy of socioeconomic reform. Many other measures, notably the housing and urban programs, were underfunded because Johnson would not increase the budget deficit or raise taxes to finance more generous provision. Despite his massive 1964 reelection victory, the president was concerned about how long the public would back reform. "Hurry, boys, hurry," he told aides. "Get that legislation up to the Hill and out. Eighteen months from now ol' Landslide Lyndon will be Lame-Duck Lyndon."[7] Compromises made to expedite enactment of reforms often marred their effectiveness. In response to Republican criticisms of "socialized medicine," Medicare only provided compulsory insurance for hospital costs; to appease the American Medical Association, it also allowed doctors to determine their own fees, which contributed to rapid inflation of medical costs. By 1986 Medicare covered under half the medical expenses of the aged, who spent 15 percent of their income on health care, the same as in 1965.

Similarly, the school-aid program circumvented opposition from conservatives and local bureaucrats by not challenging local administrative control of education. This hindered federal efforts to channel special funding to low-income districts. Local authorities decided which schools in their districts received aid and often chose those with only a scattering of poor. The schools themselves selected pupil beneficiaries, usually targeting low academic achievers irrespective of economic status. In 1977 only one-third of pupils receiving special federal aid were poor.

The Great Society never recognized that "social justice required conflict between different groups or a struggle over power."[8] Whereas the New Deal "broker state" had built up the power of groups like trade unions and farmers, the War on Poverty was directed at amorphous groups of poor, almost wholly lacking in political resources and organizational traditions. A strategy of countervailing power was much more difficult in this context, but Johnson had no interest in attempting it anyway. OEO efforts to organize neighborhood groups antagonized many Democratic mayors, who felt their local power bases threatened. In response to their complaints, Johnson curbed the OEO budget, and Congress in 1967 required that OEO-funded community initiatives should be approved by the state governments.

The portion of the national income taken home by the rich, the middle classes and the poor remained the same in 1970 as in 1947. For the poor to make significant advances, some redistribution of wealth and power in American society was essential. Except in the specialized case of the civil-rights legislation of 1964–65, Johnson would not countenance this. It would have taken a leader of immense ideological resolve to have acted differently. Unlike Roosevelt, who could attack "economic royalists" and their kin because his programs brought widespread benefits in the depressed 1930s, Johnson needed the support of the majority who were not disadvantaged, to assist the minority who were, in the affluent 1960s. His predicament suggests the plausibility of the cyclical theory of American reformism, advanced by historian Arthur M. Schlesinger, Jr. According to this view, American politics alternates between long troughs of complacency and brief bursts of reform, when conservatism, apathy, and party divisions are overcome.[9] From this perspective, Johnson deserves credit, despite the limitations of his policies, for seizing the moment when some reform was possible.

By 1968 the postwar liberal consensus was unraveling under the pressure of its own contradictions. The civil-rights programs had primarily benefited Southern blacks, but in conjunction with Johnson's promise to eliminate poverty, they inevitably aroused expectations for economic equality among blacks in Northern ghettos. The limitations of change soon turned hope into frustration and rage. A wave of ghetto riots hit Northern cities during the "long hot summers" of 1965–68, while many black activists abandoned the interracialism of the civil-rights movement to embrace separatist demands for black power. In turn, white opinion was less sympathetic to black socioeconomic demands than it had been toward civil rights for Southern blacks. Congress twice rejected a civil-rights bill prohibiting racial discrimination in housing, until Johnson exploited remorse after Martin Luther King's assassination in April 1968 to push through a somewhat ineffective compromise. From 1966 onward, opinion polls revealed a growing conviction among whites that blacks were asking for too much and that liberal politicians were undermining law and order through their willingness to reward rioters with federal largesse.

Other disadvantaged groups, their consciousness raised by the civil-rights movement, stepped up social protest. The establishment of the National Organization for Women in 1966 heralded the revival of feminism and new activism in pursuit of equal rights for women. Mexican-Americans found a new champion in the National Farm Workers Association, organized in 1963 by César Chavez, which used strikes and boycotts to win some concessions for migrant farm laborers from their employers. Meanwhile, Native Americans began to protest their entrapment on impoverished reservations. In November 1969, militants seized Alcatraz Island in San Francisco Bay as "Indian land," occupying it for eighteen months.

What fundamentally undermined the liberal consensus was the escalation of American involvement in Vietnam. In 1965 Johnson effectively Americanized the war to save the crumbling Saigon regime. He acted partly out of a belief that he was honoring a moral commitment made by Kennedy, but mainly from traditional Cold War assumptions and a new concern about the power of China, which was in the process of developing nuclear capability. Mindful of the McCarthyite assault on the Fair Deal after the "loss" of China in 1949, Johnson also feared a conservative counterattack on the Great Society if South Vietnam were lost. Historiographical opinion initially criticized the morality of U.S. intervention, but communist atrocities and depredations in Southeast Asia since 1975 have put Johnson's attempt to save South Vietnam in better light. Recent criticism, focusing more on Johnson's lack of realism, regards Vietnam as an unwinnable war that did not involve vital U.S. interests, and whose costs far outweighed potential benefits.

As Larry Berman has shown, Vietnam was "Lyndon Johnson's War," not America's.[10] The episode underlined the dangers of the imperial presidency. Through subterfuge, Johnson obtained from Congress the Gulf of Tonkin Resolution of 1964, which he used as a blank check to escalate U.S. involvement without a formal declaration of war. Administration war policy was formulated by a decision-making group smaller even than Kennedy's NSC. Also, Johnson made a deliberate effort to deceive the American people in depicting the military stalemate in Vietnam as a situation promising eventual victory.

In reality, U.S. war strategy was misconceived. In 1965 a massive aerial bombing campaign was launched against North Vietnam to cut off aid to the Vietcong insurgents and destroy communist morale. American troop presence in South Vietnam was initially increased to 184,000, and eventually to over 500,000 in 1968, in pursuit of a "meat-grinder" strategy of victory through attrition. The aim was to force the communists to the peace table by inflicting losses on their forces at a rate that exceeded their ability to recruit additional troops. America's intervention did little to undermine Vietcong strength in the rural areas, but it did provoke North Vietnam's direct military involvement in the conflict, enabling communist forces to replenish their losses and match every American troop escalation. Vietnam became a sinkhole into which Johnson kept pouring more troops in the belief that the enemy would eventually succumb to superior America power. He also kept on assuring the American people that victory was at hand, even when secret intelligence reports began pointing in 1967 to the existence of a stalemate. The United States could never gain the upper hand against brave and resourceful foes, who were willing to die in large numbers for their cause. By the end of 1968 the total death toll of Vietcong and North Vietnamese soldiers exceeded 400,000, but the Americans themselves had lost 28,000 dead.

Domestic response to the war was complex, cutting across political and cultural values. In 1965, opinion polls recorded that 65 percent of Americans, including two of every three students, backed Johnson. However, a significant and highly vocal minority of college youth vigorously disputed the morality of the war. Initially their protest was peaceful, but frustration built up as the war continued, leading to draft resistance, campus disruption, and, on occasions, violence. These developments meshed with a broader questioning of a society that seemed driven by materialist and imperialist ambitions. Rejection of traditional values resulted in the emergence of the counterculture. Temporarily abandoning conventional mores, many young Americans experimented with drugs, free love, and communal living, resisted the depersonalizing effects of technology and bureaucracy, and questioned the work ethic. Underlying the counterculture was a sense of alienation, a disbelief that society could be meaningfully improved. Tastes in music changed accordingly, with the folk protest of Joan Baez and Bob Dylan giving way to a new rock music devoid of social idealism. Groups like the Beatles, Doors, and Rolling Stones celebrated youth, sex, and drugs. The youth culture also found its heroes in films like *The Graduate,* whose main character rejects the hypocrisy of his parents' generation, and *Bonnie and Clyde,* which portrayed two outlaws as rebels against conventional society.

Meanwhile, conservatism was reasserting itself across the cultural divide. Most Americans still cherished values that the counterculture scorned. In France's "May events" of 1968, which focused against Gaullist regimentation, student protesters evoked some sympathy from other groups, notably industrial workers, but the U.S. antiwar movement could not broaden its base. Much of blue-collar youth disdained student activists as a privileged, cosseted elite. Older Americans shared similar feelings and viewed the protest as a threat to law and order, even though polls showed that people over fifty were not more hawkish than those under thirty in 1968. Fears of a breakdown in social order bred a strong popular desire for leadership that would restore stability, patriotism, and traditional values.

The economic consequences of the Vietnam War also undermined the political foundations of the Great Society. Johnson had steadfastly insisted on fighting communism abroad and poverty at home without raising taxes. Initially economic growth generated sufficient revenue to pay for guns and butter, but the pressure of increasing war costs doubled the real budget deficit to $8.7 billion in 1967 and virtually trebled it to $25.2 billion in 1968. As a result the economy overheated, generating a surge in inflation. To counter this danger, Johnson eventually enacted a 10 percent surcharge on income and corporate taxes in 1968, but the support of Congressional conservatives for this had to be bought with a $6 billion cut in social programs. The combination of rising prices and increased taxes halted the growth in living standards for median-income blue- and white-collar workers. Their resentment turned not against the war but on the Great Society, which they believed was squandering hard-earned tax dollars on rebellious minorities, dissident youth, and welfare chiselers. Having consistently diverted economic resources from domestic programs, the war had now drained them of political capital too.

The communist Tet offensive of early 1968 provided indisputable evidence that Johnson's promises of imminent victory were hollow. The president himself recognized that further escalation would be militarily futile and would provoke massive disorder at home. In March 1968 he declared that he would work for a negotiated peace while continuing the war with existing resources. To assist this process, he announced that he would not seek reelection. The ensuing battle for the Democratic presidential nomination laid bare the divisions between pro-administration and antiwar factions in the party. The assassination of Robert Kennedy, probably the Democrats' best hope for unity and victory, on the night that he won the California presidential primary added to the anguish of the party and the nation. Democratic fortunes reached their nadir when Vice President Hubert H. Humphrey was nominated by the national convention at Chicago on August 28 with a pitched battle raging outside between police and antiwar demonstrators.

Despite Democratic divisions the election was surprisingly close. Republican candidate Richard M. Nixon took only 43.4 percent of the popular vote, the lowest winning percentage since 1912, while Humphrey won 42.7 percent and Governor George C. Wallace of Alabama, running on a conservative third-party ticket, won 13.5 percent, mainly from the South. Nevertheless, the political significance of the election was clear. Wallace's poor showing revealed that only a minority wanted to roll back the Great Society. Running as a harmony candidate, Nixon had eschewed outright attacks on Johnson's social programs, but his victory underlined the domestic mood that reform had proceeded far enough. Many analysts believe that the New Deal voter coalition, which had elected four of the last five presidents, fell apart forever in 1968. Humphrey, as the liberal candidate, polled 11.9 million votes fewer than Johnson in 1964. Only three out of every ten white voters supported him.

The decline of the Cold War consensus was also evident, since the election confirmed poll findings that doubts about the Vietnam War were widespread. Only Wallace ran as a pro-war candidate; Nixon declared that he had a secret plan to achieve peace with honor in Vietnam, while Humphrey's popularity had surged late in the campaign after he disassociated himself from Johnson's war policy. Since the 1940s Americans had accepted the necessity for a global struggle against communism, but by 1968 they questioned whether the rewards of hegemony justified the costs.

Nixon presided over a nation in which most people were "unpoor, unyoung and unblack; . . . middle-aged, middle-class and middle-minded."[11] By 1970 the median family income was $8,473, compared with $6,347 (in constant 1967 dollars) a decade earlier, an increase of one-third. The affluent society was increasingly a suburban one. In 1970, 37.6 percent of Americans lived in suburbs, 31.4 percent in central cities, and 31 percent in small towns; a decade earlier the corresponding figures had been 30.7 percent, 32.6 percent, and 36.7 percent. Although over a million blacks had moved into the suburbs since 1950, the suburban population was 95 percent white in 1970. Americans were also moving into the Sunbelt, the states of the South and Southwest. California replaced New York as the most populous state in 1963. Meanwhile, a "new South" was emerging, under the impact of civil rights, industrial development, and suburbanization.

As the first president from California, Nixon personified the political rise of the Sunbelt. He was no ideologue, but a pragmatic conservative whose keen intelligence made him receptive to new ideas. Nixon's presidency will always be remembered for ending in disgraced resignation owing to his misuse of presidential powers. It is also significant to the political historian as marking a transition between the consensus conservatism of the postwar era and Reaganism in the 1980s. Nixon sustained the postwar consensus in his welfare and economic policies, while heralding the new conservatism in his concern for federal devolution and the restoration of traditional social relationships and values.

Nixon had no interest in the social engineering of the Great Society, so programs like the OEO and Model Cities fell under his axe. In general, however, his aim was not to destroy the welfare state, but to improve its efficiency through changing the twentieth-century emphasis of American welfare away from service provision to income support. To this end he proposed a Family Assistance Plan (FAP) that would guarantee through direct cash payments an annual income of $1,600 (plus $860 in food stamps) for each poor family of four. This would have benefited the working poor, established national standards for aid, and reduced welfare bureaucracy, but the plan was defeated in Congress by a combination of liberals and conservatives, who respectively deemed it inadequate and excessive. Nevertheless, the FAP initiative opened the way for other income-support programs, such as supplementary security income (for the aged, blind and disabled), expanded food-stamp provision, and—most significantly—automatic cost-of-living adjustments for social security recipients. Defense spending had dominated the federal budget since 1945, but this changed under Nixon. Human resource programs were the largest expenditure item in each of his budgets, which produced a sevenfold increase in social services funding. In reality, it was Nixon, not Johnson, who was the last of the big domestic spenders.

Concern with the excessive bureaucratization of federal service provision shaped Nixon's efforts to restructure federalism. The New Federalism program, initiated in 1972, promoted the notion of revenue sharing and marked the first effort since 1933 to reverse the centralizing trend in American government. Instead of conventional categorical grants, states were provided with stringless grants, totaling some $30 billion for a five-year period, to spend as they chose on "distributive" programs, like education, manpower training, community development, and public health. The federal government retained control over income-support programs and "nondistributive" programs like energy and environmental protection. This effort to rationalize state and federal responsibilities also facilitated presidential impoundment of Congressional appropriations for services that Nixon considered more suited to state-local jurisdiction.

Nixon also took economic management a stage further than his Democratic predecessors in seeking to resolve deep-seated problems that he had inherited. To slow down the inflation-prone economy, his administration initially followed a restrictive strategy of expenditure cuts and interest-rate hikes. This abrupt change of policy provoked a recession, but failed to cure inflation. To make matters worse, in 1971 the United States suffered its first international trade deficit since 1893. With their confidence in the economy already affected by inflation, the balance-of-payments problem prompted foreigners to cash in their excess dollars for U.S. gold, thus threatening America's reserve position. Nixon responded to the recession with a full dose of Keynesianism, announcing a budget for fiscal 1972 with a built-in deficit of $23 billion, the second largest on record, and inducing the Federal Reserve to relax monetary policy. A ninety-day wage-price freeze briefly reduced inflation in 1971, but trade union anger at the fact that the restraints affected labor far more than business scuttled Nixon's plans to extend the experiment. Most significantly, Nixon devalued the dollar in 1971 to boost American exports. The dollar had been the world's major reserve currency, convertible into gold at the fixed price of $35 per ounce, since the Bretton Woods Agreement in 1944, which laid the foundations for the postwar international economy. In allowing the dollar to float on the international money markets, Nixon was recognizing that the conditions that had once made the United States financially dominant had changed with the economic rise of Western Europe and Japan.

Nixon's intention of creating a new Republican electoral coalition, based on the Sunbelt, the suburbs, Catholic ethnics, and blue-collar workers, ensured that his centrism did not extend to sociocultural issues. These groups lacked a common economic interest, but they were united in their resentment against the breakdown of social order in the 1960s. In seeking to mobilize their support, Nixon exacerbated tensions and divisions within society. With violence and street crime on the rise, administration spokesmen accused liberals of causing the crime wave by coddling criminals, and questioned the wisdom of recent Supreme Court judgments that expanded the rights of the accused. Feminists were offended and traditionalists gratified when Nixon vetoed a bill to provide a national system of child day-care centers, which he claimed would undermine the moral authority of the family. The president also declared his personal opposition to abortion. Above all, Nixon's hard line toward the anti–Vietnam War movement appealed to cultural conservatives. Campus protest reached new heights after the U.S. invasion of Cambodia in 1970, but the killing of four demonstrators at Kent State University by Ohio National Guardsmen, and of two others at Jackson State College, Mississippi, by police, did nothing to soften the administration's rhetorical attacks.

As part of its electoral strategy to recapture the South from Wallace, the Nixon administration sought to slow down progress on civil rights. Justice Department efforts to postpone school desegregation in Mississippi led to the Supreme Court ruling in *Alexander* v. *Holmes County Board of Education* (1969) that desegregation should be carried out "at once." This intensified Nixon's efforts to appoint conservative Southern justices, but the Senate twice thwarted him. Even his success in getting four moderates appointed could not divert the Supreme Court from supporting civil rights. In *Swann* v. *Charlotte-Mecklenberg Board of Education* (1971), it ruled unanimously that busing was a legitimate means to achieve school desegregation if other methods failed. With the federal judiciary plainly opposed to further delaying tactics, the administration eventually had no option other than to enforce desegregation. It even filed suit requiring Georgia to terminate its dual system of schools. By 1972, only 8 percent of black children in the South and 12 percent nationwide attended all-black schools; the comparable figures in 1968 were 68 percent and 40 percent. Nevertheless, under Nixon the presidency's symbolic and emotional attachment to the black cause was ended. For this reason the reality of school desegregation did not hinder the emergence of Southern Republicanism.

Despite the significance of his domestic initiatives, Nixon himself was convinced that his foreign policy record would determine the historical reputation of his presidency. Guided by National Security Adviser Henry A. Kissinger, he pursued a new foreign policy that recognized the limits of American power and the reality of divisions within the communist world. In general historians have praised the Nixon-Kissinger team for seeking a change of course, but they question how successful it was in achieving its aims and criticize the means used to pursue them. Arms control perfectly illustrates the strengths and weaknesses of the duo. Whereas the Kennedy and Johnson administrations had ambitions of nuclear superiority, the Nixon administration accepted the reality that the Soviets had effective nuclear parity by 1969. In recognition of this, the Moscow summit of 1972 produced the first ever nuclear arms limitation agreements, which limited antiballistic missile deployment and froze each side's current intercontinental ballistic missile strength for five years. However, Nixon and Kissinger insisted on excluding the new Multiple Independently Targeted Reentry Vehicles from the agreement, hoping to exploit U.S. technological superiority in multiwarhead missilery. The result was a new arms race in this field, which the Soviets soon showed signs of winning.

The centerpiece of the Nixon-Kissinger foreign policy was the strategy of détente, which pursued the traditional goal of containment by new and cheaper methods. This put great reliance on the idea of linkage, in other words that the Soviets, with their crumbling economy, could be persuaded to restrain their expansionist activities in return for U.S. trade and technology. The underlying assumption was that superpower relations were the core of world politics and could control developments in the Third World periphery. In essence, Nixon and Kissinger were more interested in establishing a stable world order than achieving anticommunist hegemony. To this end they recognized big-power spheres of influence. The Berlin Agreement of 1972 and the Helsinki Accords of 1975 effectively conceded Soviet hegemony in Eastern Europe, which previous Cold War presidents had denied. Similarly, Nixon opened up relations with the People's Republic of China in 1972, thereby gaining an ally against Soviet power in Asia, but also acknowledging the Beijing regime's control of the Asian mainland over the claims of the Nationalist regime in Taiwan. In anticipation of a more stable global order, the Nixon Doctrine of 1969 had announced that the United States would no longer "undertake all the defense of the free nations of the world," and would not intervene militarily abroad unless critical security interests were threatened.[12] Nevertheless, the limitations of détente as an instrument of Third World control were revealed by the failure of Vietnamization.

Withdrawal from Vietnam was essential for the restoration of domestic tranquillity and the establishment of the new foreign policy, but concern to preserve America's credibility as a world power made Nixon and Kissinger determined to achieve a peace that resembled victory rather than defeat. The Vietnamization strategy entailed gradually running down the American troop presence to 39,000 in 1972, while seeking to boost South Vietnam's self-sufficiency in defense. According to Stephen E. Ambrose, this was "one of the worst decisions ever made by a Cold War President."[13] It prolonged the war by four years at the cost of nearly 21,000 more American lives and huge loss of national treasure, increased domestic divisions, and involved the president in unconstitutional war activities, all to achieve peace terms that were hardly better than could have been gained through negotiation in 1969. The Vietnamization strategy wrongly assumed that the Hanoi regime was a Soviet client that could be brought to heel by its Moscow masters, and that a temporary expansion of the U.S. war effort could pressure it into negotiating peace. Aerial bombing of North Vietnam was resumed with increased ferocity, U.S. forces made illegal incursions into neutral Cambodia and Laos to hit supposed communist "sanctuaries" and supply lines, and in 1972 Haiphong harbor was mined. All this proved futile. The peace settlement that effectively ended U.S. military participation in the war in January 1973 clearly benefited North Vietnam, which was allowed to maintain 100,000 troops in South Vietnam after the Americans effected a full withdrawal. In reality, the United States had suffered the first military defeat in its history.

Withdrawal from Vietnam brought to an end an era that had started with Kennedy's inaugural promise of engagement and activism at home and abroad. The 1960s have gone down in

American history as a decade of disillusionment. Compared with most of their predecessors, Kennedy and Johnson had achieved a great deal, but they had also promised much more—too much, it transpired. The postwar liberal consensus, which found its ultimate expression in their policies, collapsed under the weight of its own shortcomings in the 1960s. Both Kennedy and Johnson placed too much reliance on economic growth to resolve domestic problems and overestimated American power abroad. In contrast, Richard Nixon limited the horizons of reform and the ambitions of U.S. foreign policy. A landslide victory over Senator George McGovern of South Dakota, a liberal Democrat, in the 1972 presidential election suggested that Nixon had established a new consensus in American politics, but his success proved short-lived. As his second term began, the United States was on the verge of one of the most dismal eras of its history, in which it would have to cope with the harsh realities of relative economic and international decline.

Notes

1. Carl M. Brauer, "The Endurance of Inspirational Leadership: John F. Kennedy," in *Leadership in the Modern Presidency*, ed. Fred I. Greenstein (Cambridge, Mass., 1988), p. 119.

2. Walter LaFeber, *The American Age: United States Foreign Policy at Home and Abroad since 1750* (New York, 1989), p. 572.

3. Alonzo L. Hamby, *Liberalism and Its Challengers: FDR to Reagan* (New York, 1985), p. 213.

4. Michael Harrington, *The Other America: Poverty in the United States* (New York, 1962), p. 10.

5. John E. Schwarz, *America's Hidden Success: A Reassessment of Public Policy from Kennedy to Reagan*, rev. ed. (New York, 1988), pp. 21–51.

6. Allen J. Matusow, *The Unraveling of America: A History of Liberalism in the 1960s* (New York, 1984), pp. 217–71; James T. Patterson, *America's Struggle against Poverty, 1900–1985* (Cambridge, Mass., 1986), pp. 126–54.

7. James T. Patterson, *America in the Twentieth Cen-*

tury: A History, 2nd ed. (New York, 1983), p. 391.

8. William H. Chafe, *The Unfinished Journey: America since World War II* (New York, 1986), p. 245.

9. Arthur M. Schlesinger, Jr, *The Cycles of American History* (Boston, 1986), pp. 23–48.

10. Larry Berman, *Lyndon Johnson's War: The Road to Stalemate in Vietnam* (New York, 1989), esp. pp. xi–xiii, 111–38.

11. Richard Scammon and Ben Wattenberg, *The Real Majority* (New York, 1970), p. 21.

12. Robert S. Litwak, *Detente and the Nixon Doctrine: American Foreign Policy and the Pursuit of Stability* (Cambridge, 1984), pp. 122–23.

13. Stephen E. Ambrose, *Rise to Globalism: American Foreign Policy since 1938*, 5th ed. (New York, 1988), p. 240.

Bibliography

The best overviews of the 1960s are William H. Chafe, *The Unfinished Journey: America since World War II* (New York, 1986); Godfrey Hodgson, *In Our Time: America from World War II to Nixon* (New York, 1976); and Allen J. Matusow,. *The Unraveling of America: A History of Liberalism in the 1960s* (New York, 1984). Kim McQuaid, *The Anxious Years: America in the Vietnam-Watergate Era* (New York, 1989) offers an unusual perspective on the crises of 1968–74, but it should be supplemented with the more balanced Peter N. Carroll, *It Seemed Like Nothing Happened: America in the 1970s* (New Brunswick, N.J., 1990). The era's leading political personalities are the subject of excellent essays in Alonzo Hamby, *Liberalism and Its Challengers: FDR to Reagan* (New York, 1985), and Fred I. Greenstein, ed., *Leadership in the Modern Presidency* (Cambridge, Mass., 1988). Arthur M. Schlesinger, Jr., *The Cycles of American History* (Boston, 1986) puts the sixties in wider historical perspective.

The trends in Kennedy historiography are exemplified by Arthur M. Schlesinger, Jr.'s laudatory *A Thousand Days: John F. Kennedy in the White House* (Boston, 1965); Henry Fairlie's critical *The Kennedy Promise: The Politics of Expectation* (New York, 1975); and the more balanced recent works, Herbert S.

Parmet, *JFK: The Presidency of John F. Kennedy* (New York, 1983) and David Burner, *John F. Kennedy and a New Generation* (Boston, 1988). The main biographies of LBJ are Doris Kearns, *Lyndon Johnson and the American Dream* (New York, 1976) and Paul K. Conkin, *Big Daddy from the Pedernales: Lyndon B. Johnson* (Boston, 1986), which emphasizes his personality in explaining his politics. Vaughn D. Bornet, *The Presidency of Lyndon B. Johnson* (Lawrence, Kans., 1983) is a detailed, factual, and sympathetic account. Until recently, Nixon was the preserve of psychobiographies, the best of which was Fawn M. Brodie, *Richard M. Nixon: The Shaping of His Character* (Harvard, 1983). Fortunately, the subject has been reclaimed for historians by Stephen E. Ambrose, *Nixon:* vol. 1, *The Education of a Politician, 1913–1962;* vol. 2, *The Triumph of a Politician, 1962–1972* (New York, 1987–89); and Herbert S. Parmet, *Richard Nixon and His America* (New York, 1990).

Domestic programs are covered generally by Robert A. Divine, ed., *Exploring the Johnson Years,* vol. 1 (Austin, Tex., 1981); Marshall Kaplan and Peggy Cuciti, eds., *The Great Society and Its Legacy: Twenty Years of U.S. Social Policy* (Durham, N.C., 1986); A. James Reichley, *Conservatives in an Age of Change: The Nixon-Ford Years* (Washington, D.C., 1981); and James L. Sundquist, *Politics and Policy: The Eisenhower, Kennedy and Johnson Years* (Washington, D.C., 1968). The antipoverty programs are examined in Carl M. Brauer, "Kennedy, Johnson and the War on Poverty," *Journal of American History* 69 (1982): 98–119; James T. Patterson, *America's Struggle against Poverty, 1900–1980* (Cambridge, Mass., 1981); John E. Schwarz, *America's Hidden Success: A Reassessment of Public Policy from Kennedy to Reagan,* rev. ed. (New York, 1988); and Ira Katznelson, "Was the Great Society a Lost Opportunity?" in *The Rise and Fall of the New Deal Order, 1932–1980,* ed. Steve Fraser and Gary Gerstle (Princeton, 1989), pp. 185–211. For contrasting treatments of the federal response to civil rights, see Carl M. Brauer, *John F. Kennedy and the Second Reconstruction* (New York, 1977); Manning Marable, *Race, Reform and Rebellion: The Second Reconstruction in Black America, 1945–1982* (New York, 1984); and Hugh D. Graham, *The Civil Rights Era: Origins and Development of National Policy, 1960–1972* (New York, 1990). Economic policy is discussed by Walter Heller, *New Dimensions of Political Econ-*

omy (New York, 1966), and Herbert Stein, *Presidential Economics: The Making of Economic Policy from Roosevelt to Reagan and Beyond* (New York, 1984).

Three foreign policy surveys give excellent coverage of the 1960–72 era: Stephen E. Ambrose, *Rise to Globalism: American Foreign Policy since 1938*, 5th ed. (New York, 1988); Thomas J. McCormick, *America's Half-Century: United States Foreign Policy in the Cold War* (Baltimore, 1989); and Walter LaFeber, *The American Age: United States Foreign Policy at Home and Abroad since 1750* (New York, 1989). For Vietnam, the best general study is George C. Herring, *America's Longest War: The United States and Vietnam, 1950–1975*, 2nd ed. (New York, 1981), and Gary R. Hess, *Vietnam and the United States: The Origins and Legacy of War* (Boston, 1990). The best accounts of Johnson's policy are Larry Berman's books, *Planning a Tragedy: The Americanization of the War in Vietnam* (New York, 1982), and *Lyndon Johnson's War: The Road to Stalemate in Vietnam* (New York, 1989). The most thorough account of Nixon's foreign policy is Raymond L. Garthoff, *Détente and Confrontation: American-Soviet Relations from Nixon to Reagan* (Washington, D.C., 1985). Other important studies are Robert S. Litwak, *Détente and the Nixon Doctrine: American Foreign Policy and the Pursuit of Stability* (Cambridge, 1984), and Robert D. Schulzinger, *Henry Kissinger: Doctor of Diplomacy* (New York, 1989).

The literature on the antiwar movement and the counterculture is voluminous, though there are no definitive works. Useful studies are Todd Gitlin, *The Sixties: Years of Hope, Days of Rage* (New York, 1987); James Miller, *"Democracy Is in the Streets": From Port Huron to the Siege of Chicago* (New York, 1987); and Lawrence W. Wittner, *Rebels against War: The American Peace Movement, 1933–1983* (New York, 1984). The contours of mainstream America are explored by: Kevin Phillips, *The Emerging Republican Majority* (New Rochelle, N.Y., 1969); Richard Scammon and Ben Wattenberg, *The Real Majority* (New York, 1971); and Jonathan Rieder, "The Rise of the Silent Majority" in the book by Fraser and Gerstle cited above, pp. 243–68. For the rediscovery of the poor, see Michael Harrington, *The Other America: Poverty in the United States* (New York, 1962).

7

The Age of Uncertainty: The United States since 1973

Iwan W. Morgan

Future generations of Americans may well look back on the mid-twentieth century as their country's golden age. For some thirty years, from the early 1940s onward, the United States could regard itself as the most bountiful, the most powerful, and the most democratic nation in mankind's history. During the mid-1970s this self-assurance evaporated. The United States entered an era of uncertainty, characterized by relative economic and international decline. Gone were the optimism and sense of direction of the postwar decades. In 1980 public opinion pollster Daniel Yankelevich observed, "We've gone almost overnight from being a nation of optimists to a nation of pessimists."[1] Conventional solutions were unable to remedy the nation's problems. Keynesian economic policies lost their magic, while many assumptions underlying U.S. foreign policy no longer held good. Successive Republican and Democratic administrations seemed incapable of halting America's decline in the 1970s, but President Ronald Reagan, whose inaugural address called for an "era of national renewal" in the 1980s, confidently offered a conservative cure for the malaise. Despite numerous successes, however, the so-called Reagan Revolution promised more than it delivered, and left many problems unresolved at home and abroad. As a result the age of uncertainty carried over into the presidency of George Bush.

Journalist Tom Wolfe labeled the 1970s the "me decade," because many Americans seemed intent on bettering their private worlds in the midst of public confusion. Christopher Lasch interpreted the popular indulgence in self-improvement activities like jogging, healthy dieting, and the search for personal roots as a refuge from the realities of America's decline.[2] The revival of religion, particularly evangelical Christianity, seemed to support this view. Today, some thirty million Americans call themselves "born-again Christians," most having experienced rebirth in the 1970s. Nevertheless, Peter Carroll disputes the view that public passions were exhausted during the decade, pointing to the progress of causes like women's rights, gay rights, the antinuclear campaign, and environmentalism.[3] In contrast to the theme of a popular Hollywood movie, *The Big Chill* (1983), many Americans who had been activists in the 1960s did not abandon idealism for materialism in the 1970s. Probably the real distinction between the two eras lay in the fact that the problems of the 1970s defied confident solution. The causes of this era did not have the kind of clear-cut and morally certain goals that the civil-rights and antiwar movements had pursued in the 1960s.

Looming over every other problem was the sick economy. The American self-image as a people of plenty had fundamentally shaped the national character. Economic abundance had spawned a dominant ideology, the American dream, which affirmed that hard work and individual enterprise would ensure material self-advancement. Three out of every four Americans did experience affluence in the postwar era, when the economy enjoyed a twenty-five-year boom, propelled by the automobile, construction, and defense industries. In constant dollar terms, the GNP and the average family income more than doubled between 1945 and 1970. By the end of the 1970s, however, popular expectations of everlasting economic expansion had vanished. Opinion pollsters now discovered that most people considered the present worse than the past, and expected the future to be bleaker still.

The economy had experienced previous downturns, of course, but the combination of ailments that afflicted it in the 1970s had no twentieth-century precedent. First, inflation became a serious problem, because Lyndon Johnson's policy of financing the Vietnam War through budget deficits instead of tax increases overheated the economy. Richard Nixon's first-term efforts at fine-tuning the economy created a stop-go cycle of slump and expansion that left inflation higher than ever at nearly 10 percent in 1973.

Meanwhile, the once-mighty dollar was in trouble. Already under pressure because global defense commitments and overseas investments had produced an almost continuous balance-of-payments deficit since 1945, the dollar's problems were exacerbated when the United States incurred international trade deficits in the early 1970s for the first time in the twentieth century. Productivity in the modern factories of the European Economic Community (EEC) nations and Japan was beginning to outpace what America's older industrial plants could achieve. With the benefits of heavy automation, Japanese productivity in particular grew at four times the American rate in the 1970s. Initially, the U.S. balance-of-payments deficit had benefited foreign nations in the process of postwar reconstruction. The outflow of dollars, the world's major reserve currency, had provided the liquidity to revive the international economy after 1945. With economic recovery, however, Western Europe and Japan had less need of dollars, which they began to convert into gold, at the price fixed by the Bretton Woods Agreement of 1944.

To relieve pressure on U.S. gold reserves and boost exports, Nixon suspended fixed convertibility in 1971 and devalued the dollar. Symptomatic of its new economic power, the EEC rejected American efforts to negotiate new fixed currency rates in 1973, in favor of an arrangement limited to member nations' currencies. Henceforth, global demand rather than political agreement would determine the international purchasing power of the dollar. The abandonment in 1974 of American capital controls, which was a green light for increased overseas investment, effectively ended efforts to stem the dollar drain. To some commentators, this signified that the United States was in the process of transformation from an industrial giant to a rentier nation that lived off its income from overseas assets, a metamorphosis experienced earlier by Britain.

The energy crisis of the mid-1970s caused further deterioration in America's trade balance. After being largely self-sufficient in cheap energy until the 1960s, the United States had to import one-third of its oil needs by 1973. Americans now became vulnerable to an "energy Pearl Harbor." Arab oil-producing nations imposed a five-month embargo on the United States in retaliation for its pro-Israeli position during the Yom Kippur War of 1973. Once the embargo was lifted, the Organization of Petroleum Exporting Countries (OPEC) formally quadrupled its prices. Unable to reverse its reliance on foreign oil, the United States was paying $90 billion for oil imports by 1980, compared with just $4 billion ten years earlier. The effects of higher oil prices reverberated through the economy, driving up inflation and unemployment. Worst hit was the automobile industry, the postwar giant whose profits had derived from the manufacture of big, luxurious, gas-guzzling cars. These former symbols of affluence now lost their market appeal, and the smaller fuel-efficient models in which foreign firms specialized enjoyed soaring sales. Unemployment consequently shot up in the automobile industry in 1974–75 and spread to feeder industries, notably steel, rubber and glass.

The process of adjustment to new economic conditions resulted in some deindustrialization. Although 26.5 million new jobs were created in the 1970s, compared with 12.2 million in the 1960s, much of this expansion was in low-skill work. The old "smokestack industries" continued to lay off workers, either shutting down plants or modernizing production methods through the use of computers and robots. Many unemployed factory workers had to take jobs in the low-paid service sector. Others headed off to find work in the Sunbelt states of the South and Southwest.

The regional structure of the economy had been undergoing change since World War II in response to the Sunbelt's spectacular growth, and the process intensified in the 1970s. The Sunbelt was far less vulnerable than the Rustbelt, the old industrial heartland of the Northeast and Midwest, to the new economic problems. It was the home of new industries like aerospace, defense, electronics, plastics, oil, and computer technology, which had largely developed since the 1940s. Relatively cheap energy resources, good climate, inexpensive real estate, state laws hostile to trade unions, and low state-local taxes made the region a haven for modern industry. In addition, Sunbelt politicians, who wielded great power in Congressional committees, won a disproportionate share of federal contracts for their states. These advantages even tempted many older industries to relocate to the region.

The 1980 census revealed that for the first time, southern and western states had more population than northern and eastern states. Cities like Atlanta, Houston, Phoenix, Tucson, and San Diego rode the crest of a continuing growth wave in the 1970s. In contrast, virtually every big city in the Rustbelt lost population, and some tottered toward bankruptcy under the burdens of inflation and shrinking tax bases. In 1975 New York City required federal loan guarantees before it could raise money to meet payroll and bond-repayment obligations. Three years later, Cleveland became the first city since Detroit in 1933 to default on its debts.

Developments abroad were also a source of uncertainty in the 1970s. For a quarter century, despite occasional doubts, the United States had believed itself strong enough to win a global struggle against communism. Military failure in Vietnam undermined this confidence and provoked a search for a new foreign policy. Détente proved an ineffective means of protecting American interests in the Third World. In 1975, Hanoi launched a new military offensive that brought the collapse of the Saigon regime and the unification of Vietnam under Communist control. Meanwhile, political turmoil in Africa embroiled the superpowers, notably in Angola and Mozambique, where the United States backed the losing side in local wars, and later in Ethiopia and Somalia. In the Middle East, the Soviets and Americans nearly lost control of their allies during the Yom Kippur War, resulting in a military alert that brought the world closer to nuclear confrontation than at any time since 1962.

Hawkish critics of détente insisted that defeat in Vietnam resulted mainly from a loss of will and should not deter America from reasserting international hegemony. Other voices advocated a more selective activism in world affairs that recognized the real limits of U.S. power. Finally, there were those who wanted to move away from Cold War traditions and establish American moral leadership in the quest for peace, arms control, and the resolution of Third World socioeconomic problems. None of these views had sufficient support to form a new consensus. As a result American foreign policy remained confused during the middle and late 1970s.

The other great dilemma troubling Americans during the 1970s centered on the presidency, the fount of national leadership and moral inspiration since Franklin D. Roosevelt's era. The political scandal known as Watergate confirmed popular fears, already aroused by the Vietnam War, that the modern presidency was prone to flout constitutional legality. In fact, what historian Arthur M. Schlesinger, Jr., labeled the "imperial presidency" had emerged in the 1940s. Every president from Roosevelt to John F. Kennedy sometimes made critical foreign policy decisions without Congressional authority, but their successes shielded them from retribution. Johnson took the process a stage further, leading the nation into the Vietnam débacle partly through subterfuge and misleading the people about the military situation.

The imperial presidency reached its apogee under Nixon, who sanctioned the secret bombing of Communist-held areas of Cambodia, failed to consult Congress when ordering a U.S. military incursion into this neutral nation in 1970 and U.S. air attacks in support of South Vietnam's 1971 invasion of Laos, and made a secret and unauthorized promise to protect the Saigon regime if North Vietnam violated the 1973 peace pact. Unconstitutional presidential actions also extended into domestic affairs. Nixon made excessive use of the impoundment power, refusing to spend some $15 billion that Congress had appropriated for domestic programs. More sinister was his effort, unsuccessful thanks to the opposition of FBI director J. Edgar Hoover, to establish a special committee with broad surveillance powers to investigate whether the antiwar movement was Communist-inspired. Some administration critics also became targets for a "dirty tricks" campaign by presidential aides. What finally undid Nixon was his involvement in efforts to cover up the illegal activities of his reelection campaign organization. The incompetent burglars who broke into the Democratic National Committee headquarters in the Watergate building in Washington in June 1972 had been financed by the Committee to Reelect the President (CREEP). After nearly two years of persistent investigation, involving journalists, judges, Justice Department officials, and Congress, the net closed around Nixon. In August 1974, facing certain impeachment, he became the first American president to resign office.

The wrongdoings of Johnson and Nixon provoked Congressional action to curb the misuse of presidential power. Legislation was enacted to prohibit the president from making secret executive agreements with foreign governments, to limit presidential use of the CIA in covert operations, to regulate executive powers during national emergencies, to expand freedom of information, to curb the impoundment power, and to constrain the president's war-making powers.

The power and the authority of the presidency diminished under the combined impact of these measures and the Watergate disgrace. Unfortunately this occurred when the United States needed strong leadership, wisely and legitimately exercised, more than at any time since FDR's presidency. Congress could hardly fill the void. Its cumbersome procedures were more responsive to the particularist interests of constituents and pressure groups. Unlike the presidency, it could not speak for the nation with one voice, an intrinsic weakness aggravated by post-Watergate reforms. Following revelations of CREEP's activities, the 1974 Campaign Finance Law limited contributions by Political Action Committees (PACs) to five thousand dollars per candidate in federal elections, but placed no restrictions on the number of such organizations from which a candidate could take money. Within six years PACs had quadrupled in number, and congressmen tended to show greater concern for these special interests than for the national agenda of party programs. The leadership vacuum that developed in the 1970s indubitably made America's economic and international problems more difficult to resolve and intensified the nation's sense of drift.

What fundamentally hampered government efforts to cure the economy, however, was the irrelevance of conventional remedies. Since 1945, Democratic and Republican administrations had managed the economy to keep unemployment and inflation low. To counteract slumps in the business cycle, federal spending was increased, taxes were cut, the money supply was expanded, and interest rates were lowered. When the economy showed signs of overheating, the opposite policies were implemented. Contrary to normal trends, the economy experienced simultaneous high inflation and unemployment in the 1970s, a condition known as stagflation. Efforts to alleviate one problem exacerbated the other, forcing politicians to decide their priorities. This dilemma further weakened the domestic consensus that had shaped post–New Deal politics.

Since inflation affected everyone, it became the predominant political issue. Conservatives in both parties branded it the inevitable result of the explosion of domestic federal expenditure in the 1960s and early 1970s. The issue even divided liberal Democrats along what William E. Leuchtenburg called a "generational fault line."[4] The postwar expansion of the welfare state had largely been financed from the incremental revenues generated by economic growth. Older liberals, like Senator Edward M. Kennedy of Massachusetts, insisted that the Democratic party should remain true to its traditional concerns in the economically stagnant 1970s, even at the cost of growing budget deficits. In contrast, many younger Democrats, like Senators Gary Hart of Colorado and Paul Tsongas of Massachusetts, disputed that New Deal solutions were applicable to modern problems. More concerned with economic renewal than recovery, these so-called "neoliberals" wanted to address the issues of inflation, declining productivity and industrial restructuring.

The federal government's war against poverty ran out of steam in the middle and late 1970s. Although expenditure on existing social programs continued to increase, there was no effort to address the changing nature of poverty and the needs of an emergent underclass. Economic growth, the civil-rights programs, and the Great Society reforms had helped to raise living standards for many members of traditionally underprivileged groups in the 1960s. Others still remained trapped in poverty, lacking any prospect of escape in the economically stagnant 1970s without new federal programs to assist them.

The experience of African-Americans illustrated this dichotomy. In the 1960s the proportion of black families earning over $10,000 annually had increased from 13 to 31 percent. The growth of the black middle class continued in the 1970s, now assisted by equal-employment programs, affirmative action, and better educational qualifications. The number of black college students increased from 282,000 in 1966 to 1.1 million in 1977, when one-third of black high-school students were going on to college, the same proportion as for whites. Meanwhile, open-housing rules enabled middle-class blacks to escape from the ghettos to the suburbs. Black advancement caused many whites to complain of "reverse discrimination." To meet federal nondiscrimination requirements, some colleges and companies operated affirmative action programs that established quotas for the number of nonwhites and women they took on, and often accepted lower qualifications from these groups than from white males. In a complicated split decision, *Regents of the University of California* v. *Bakke* (1978), the Supreme Court ruled that race could be used as one of the qualifications in the selection process, but that explicit minority-group quotas could not be established. Busing was another white grievance and provoked violence in several cities in 1975–76, notably Boston and Louisville.

Nevertheless, economic advancement remained a hopeless dream for millions of blacks. In 1978 27.5 percent of black families lived in poverty, compared with 6.7 percent of white families. Lower-income blacks were caught in a vicious circle of inner-city and industrial decline. Blue-collar job opportunities were decreasing and good education was the key to well-paid white-collar jobs. The declining economy hurt young blacks worst of all. In 1979–80 unemployment among this group reached 50 percent in some cities and nationwide it surged by 6.3 percent for every 1 percent increase in overall unemployment. Compounding black problems was the high number of female-headed black families, which increased 130 percent between 1960 and 1975. Welfare or low-paid service jobs were generally their only source of income. Moreover, in contrast to the 1960s, there was no coherent voice of black protest. The middle classes, the natural leaders of the black community, did not share the problems of the underclass, and as suburban dwellers they had lost touch with the plight of the ghettos. Several commentators now argued that two black Americas had emerged, one relatively affluent and the other hopelessly poor. Writing in 1980, sociologist William Julius Wilson claimed that "the life-chances of blacks have less to do with race than with economic class affiliation."[5]

Women were another group among whom the benefits of recent change fell unevenly. By 1980 the number of women in employment was nearly double that in 1960. Many were establishing a career before raising a family, a reversal of the postwar trend. For the college-educated there were breakthroughs into prestigious professional and business jobs that gender discrimination had previously denied to women. By contrast, women whose low-income background saddled them with poor educational qualifications found it virtually impossible to achieve economic mobility and had to provide cheap labor in the service industries. In some ways the sociocultural changes of the 1960s also helped to increase the feminization of poverty. With divorce now easier and traditional male obligations to the family weaker, the number of female-headed families increased by 72 percent in the 1970s. It was small wonder that by 1986 two-thirds of the adult poor were women. Children raised in a female-headed family had one chance in three of being poor, while those from two-parent families had one in nineteen.

Also swelling the ranks of the new underclass were newcomers to the United States. About four million immigrants and probably about eight million illegal aliens entered the country in the 1970s, the greatest influx in any single decade in U.S. history. They came mainly from Mexico, Cuba, Vietnam, South Korea, and Taiwan. The Hispanics, whose total number included 20 million official residents and 8 to 12 million illegal aliens, were the fastest-growing racial minority, but they were ill-equipped to cope with the economic conditions of the 1970s. In addition to the disadvantages of race and class, they suffered from a linguistic barrier that inhibited their educational progress. Only 30 percent of Hispanic high-school students graduated, and fewer than 7 percent finished college. Median income for Mexican-American families in 1979 was $11,400, compared with $16,300 for whites, and 19 percent lived in poverty. Puerto Ricans were even worse off, with a median income of $8,300 and 30 percent living in poverty. Hispanics found it even more difficult than blacks to organize themselves to demand better conditions, owing to divisions between Mexicans, Cubans, Puerto Ricans, and others. Whatever their national origins, newcomers with marketable skills or private resources could still find the good life in the United States of the 1970s. For the others, the pursuit of the American dream was a daunting task.

The federal government's failure to resolve the problems of the underclass was not offset by success in breaking the stagflation cycle. President Gerald R. Ford, who succeeded Nixon, pursued a restrictive economic policy that reduced inflation from 12 percent to 5 percent, but also pushed unemployment to a post-Depression high of 9 percent in 1975. Under pressure from the Democrats, who controlled Congress, the Republican administration loosened federal purse-strings, but the combination of higher spending and the tax-revenue loss resulting from the recession swelled the budget deficit to a record $66.4

billion in 1976. Nevertheless, the party of Roosevelt fared little better when it recaptured the White House.

Jimmy Carter, an agribusinessman, born-again Christian, and former governor of Georgia, emerged from relative obscurity to win the 1976 presidential election. Owing to Watergate, Carter's status as an outsider and his promise that he would never lie to the American people were his main attractions. His banner issue was his pledge to curb the "imperial presidency," which he largely fulfilled. In many ways, however, Carter's presidency epitomized the age of uncertainty, lacking as it did the kind of unifying theme and sense of direction that had characterized previous Democratic administrations. He never associated his name with a popular reform slogan, breaking a Democratic tradition that ran from Woodrow Wilson's New Freedom to Johnson's Great Society. His political values seemed rooted in contradiction. A liberal on social issues, Carter promised to fight for the underprivileged, but he also wanted to reduce federal expenditure and balance the budget by 1980. Reconciling these aims proved impossible, and in practice his fiscal conservatism prevailed. The aura of confusion permeating the Carter era was compounded by the post-Watergate context of American politics. Congress was in no mood to be compliant to the new president, who also lacked the political skills to save some of his major programs from defeat.

Scholarly opinion initially rated Carter an abject failure as president, but a revisionist view now suggests that he has been underestimated. Political scientist Erwin Hargrove depicts Carter as the legatee of southern Progressivism, for whom good government was based on expertise rather than popular politics, morality rather than power, public goods rather than particularist interests.[6] These values constituted both the strength and weakness of his presidency. Carter's outlook enabled him to break away from the conventional New Deal agenda and respond to the new issues of the late twentieth century, such as energy conservation, environmentalism, and tax reform. A willingness to innovate underlay his main domestic and international achievements, and his leadership gave the Democratic party a centrist image more in tune with the current political climate than traditional liberalism. Nevertheless, Carter's personal philosophy, which eschewed political horse-trading and accommodation of interest groups, ensured a stormy relationship with his party in Congress. Similarly, it prevented him from developing and appealing to the kind of popular constituency that had sustained his Democratic predecessors. When unmanageable problems, which were more the result of bad luck than misjudgment, blighted the final year of his presidency, he had no reservoir of public and political support to cushion him from the effects of economic and international failures.

Economy, efficiency, and equity in government were Carter's main domestic concerns. In line with his promise to restore fiscal integrity, he abandoned the "full-employment budget," initiated by Kennedy, in favor of the traditional method of calculating public finances. Convinced that the welfare system was unfair and wasteful, Carter proposed to amalgamate various income-transfer programs under a single budget, in order to target antipoverty spending more effectively without increasing the costs. This fell foul of Congress, where conservatives wanted expenditure cuts and liberals the opposite. To improve policy-making and administration in two crucial areas of modern government, Carter created new cabinet-level departments of Education and Energy. Major civil-service reforms that provided reward for merit were also implemented. To encourage domestic energy production, Carter decontrolled oil and natural-gas prices, but this was only enacted after an eighteen-month tussle with Congress. Adjunct proposals for a crude-oil tax, intended to encourage energy conservation and to finance energy grants for low-income families, and a windfall-profits tax on oil companies were lost because legislators responded to special-interest lobbies. To encourage competition, Carter also deregulated the airline, trucking, and railroad industries. Major environmental reforms met the requirements of equity and efficiency, and included controls over strip-mining, a superfund for chemical waste cleanup, and the establishment of the Arctic National Wilderness Reserve, which protected 100 million acres of Alaska from development and oil drilling.

Carter's greatest domestic problem remained the economy. Recovery from the "Ford recession" had brought a new inflationary cycle whose effects were compounded by the credit explosion of the mid-1970s, when many Americans had taken advantage of the fact that interest rates were not climbing as rapidly as prices. Between 1974 and 1979 total business and household borrowing soared from $94 billion to $328 billion.

Credit-card usage also became universal in this period, with the number of MasterCard holders alone leaping from 32 million to 57 million.

To correct this situation, Carter cut domestic program expenditure in 1979–80 and the Federal Reserve introduced draconian tight-money measures that sent the prime lending rate skyrocketing to an unprecedented 20 percent. Business retrenchment inevitably followed, with the automobile and construction industries suffering most. Already reeling from foreign competition, the giant Chrysler Corporation headed for bankruptcy until it was bailed out in 1980 by federal loan guarantees of $1.5 billion, made partly conditional on employees taking salary cuts. Economic recession depressed tax revenues, destroying Carter's hopes of balancing the budget, but rising unemployment was not accompanied by reduced inflation. Loan repayments became dearer and price decontrol pushed up energy costs. To make matters worse, a new revolutionary government in Iran cut off oil supplies to the United States, a close ally of the deposed shah. OPEC exploited this opportunity to raise its prices, which helped to double the cost of crude oil in 1979. With the discomfort index (inflation and unemployment) approaching a record 20 percent in 1980, many Americans judged Carter's economic policies a hopeless failure.

Meanwhile, Carter's early foreign policy successes were overshadowed by crushing reverses during his final fifteen months in office. Voicing the national sense of decline, the journal *Business Week* lamented in 1980: "For the first time in its history, the United States is no longer growing in power and influence among the nations of the world."[7]

The post–Vietnam War challenge facing the United States was to exercise world leadership without hegemony. In addressing this, Carter manifested a Wilsonian emphasis on international cooperation and peace. His greatest triumph was in personally negotiating the Camp David Accords of 1978, which laid the foundation for an Egyptian-Israeli peace treaty. While this left the Palestinian problem unresolved and did not include Syria, it still stands as the most significant contribution to the search for peace in the Middle East. Carter's efforts to increase U.S. moral influence in the Third World also marked a departure from Cold War traditions. Some attempt was made, albeit with limited success, to pressure Latin American dictatorships into better observance of human rights, support for racist regimes in Namibia and Zimbabwe was terminated, and following a tough battle for Senate ratification, a treaty scheduled the Panama Canal's restoration to native control in the year 2000. Also, though more from indecision than idealism, the Carter administration eschewed intervention when pro-U.S. dictatorships in Iran and Nicaragua were threatened by revolution and finally overthrown.

Nevertheless, Carter was too bound by recent orthodoxy to establish truly new foundations for U.S. foreign policy. The Cold War was reinvigorated following the Soviet invasion of Afghanistan in 1979. Already weakened by a renewed arms race, superpower rivalry in Africa, and Carter's criticism of Soviet human rights, détente was now in ruins. Some analysts, like George F. Kennan, considered the Soviets' action a defensive measure against the spread of Islamic fundamentalism along their southern borders, but the administration saw it as an expansionist threat to Western oil supplies. The Carter Doctrine proclaimed that the United States would intervene, militarily and unilaterally if necessary, to prevent further Soviet advances toward the Persian Gulf. In addition, Carter announced a defense program designed to restore U.S. military superiority, signifying what historian Gaddis Smith called a "return to militarism."[8] In reality, the roots of Ronald Reagan's defense buildup lay in Carter's military budgets, which sanctioned the largest new weapons programs in nearly thirty years.

This response did not dispel the popular conviction that Carter had allowed American power to decline to unacceptable levels. His failure to compel Soviet withdrawal from Afghanistan and OPEC's continued excess were viewed as evidence of U.S. weakness. The most humiliating episode of all was the Iranian hostage crisis. In November 1979, militants seized the U.S. embassy in Tehran and held its personnel hostage for 444 days, in an effort to force Carter to send home for trial the deposed shah (who was in New York for medical treatment) and apologize for past U.S. involvement in Iran. Moral suasion, economic pressure, and an abortive military rescue mission failed to secure the hostages' release. The crisis left Americans yearning for a leader who would restore their power and prestige in world affairs.

The problems that engulfed Carter at home and abroad

resulted in his landslide defeat in the 1980 election by Ronald Reagan, whose coattails also produced the first GOP Senate majority since 1952 and substantially increased Republican strength in the House. Conservatives viewed the election as a turning point similar to that of 1932 and anticipated that Reagan would be the "Roosevelt of the Right." Liberalism, the fount of new ideas throughout the twentieth century, had run out of intellectual steam in the face of America's economic and international decline. In contrast, the U.S. Right, like its counterpart in Britain under Margaret Thatcher, had rediscovered its intellectual vigor in the late 1970s and transformed itself from a reactionary into an innovative force. Appalled by the results of diplomacy and conciliation, conservatives were adamant that American interests abroad could only be protected by an expansion of military power. They were also in fundamental agreement that less government involvement in the economy was the road to salvation.

Many conservatives wanted deep cuts in the welfare state to balance the budget and finance tax reduction. Grass-roots support for this view was manifest in 1978 when California voters approved the Proposition 13 referendum to reduce property taxes and put stringent limits on state expenditure for social programs. Others on the right wanted to go much further than Jimmy Carter had done in rolling back the regulatory state, which they considered a drag on the competitiveness of American business. Finally, and most importantly, supply-side economics gained respectability in place of neo-Keynesian doctrines, first among segments of the academic community, and then with Republicans like Congressmen Jack Kemp of New York and David Stockman of Michigan. This theory bore some resemblance to the trickle-down economics popular in the 1920s, but the supply-siders believed that tax cuts should precede a balanced budget. Their game plan also envisaged expenditure cuts across the board rather than in selected programs, though it did accept the necessity for a welfare safety net for the poor. The essence of supply-side doctrine was that tax cuts for corporations and high earners would boost investment, thereby reviving the economy to the benefit of all groups in society. Prosperity would also bring greater tax revenues for government, thus eliminating the budget deficit in conjunction with expenditure reductions.

The conservative resurgence also drew strength from the growth of religious fundamentalism. In the late 1970s the Christian Right began to flex its muscles against the forces of modernism, demanding a reassertion of traditional values and behavior. With crusading zeal, it initially attacked the sociocultural legacies of the 1960s, notably feminism, the permissive society, and secularism. Unlike previous outbursts of fundamentalist protest such as that of the 1920s, however, the new movement made no distinction between moral and political issues. The Christian Right stood for the conservative rebirth of the nation and its government. A healthy economy was deemed a moral imperative, for which lower federal expenditures and a balanced budget were essential prerequisites. Fundamentalists were equally adamant that higher defense spending was a vital antidote to the international expansion of godless communism.

New organizational and technological developments enabled the modern Right to propagandize its messages very effectively. A host of conservative interest groups sprang up in the 1970s, the most famous being the National Conservative Political Action Committee, an ideological organization whose activities in the 1980 election helped to defeat prominent liberal senators, and the Moral Majority, which had over two million members and articulated the political aims of the Christian Right. These organizations, small and large, reached out to the grass roots and acquired substantial funding through the new techniques of computerized mailing lists. Cable television development also led to the establishment of religious broadcast networks, through which TV evangelists, like Pat Robertson, could preach to a total audience of some thirty million.

The standard-bearer of the New Right, Ronald Reagan, a former Hollywood actor and two-term governor of California, became the most popular president of recent times. A master communicator, he articulated conservative goals in a manner that appealed to a wide audience, and his engaging style and supreme optimism helped to restore national self-confidence. On the other hand, Reagan was no master of detail and sought only to shape the general direction of his administration's programs. Aides and cabinet department heads assumed responsibility for detailed policy-making. The shortcomings of this system of delegation were revealed by the Iran-Contra affair, an illegal arms-for-hostages deal that National Security Council officials apparently arranged without the president's knowledge. Critical of Reagan's hands-off leadership style, some observers, particularly foreign analysts, saw him as a bumbling incompetent, whose popularity was the result of skillful public relations rather than substantive achievement. By contrast, British political scientist David Mervin adjudges Reagan the most effective president since Roosevelt, in terms of his success in changing the course of public policy, his legacy as party leader, and his revitalization of the presidency.[10] This assessment is certainly closer to the truth than the highly negative view of Reagan, but it is important not to exaggerate the extent and success of the "Reagan Revolution."

The scale of change that Reagan brought about in American government does not appear to match the transformation achieved by Roosevelt in the 1930s. Nor, for that matter, is it comparable to the contemporary "Thatcher Revolution" in Britain, which encompassed tax reduction, privatization of publicly owned industries, substantial reduction in public expenditure, major reform of the National Health Service and the educational system, abolition of the "metropolitan county" tier of government, reform of local-government finance, and reduction of trade unions' rights.

Doubts persist about the American economy, despite the disappearance of stagflation. The supply-side experiment was launched by the Economic Recovery Tax Act of 1981, which provided for universal income-tax reduction, averaging 23 percent over a three-year period (with the top rate coming down from 70 percent to 50 percent). Before its benefits took effect, however, the economy plunged deeper into recession under the impact of high interest rates and foreign competition. By October 1982, unemployment was 10.1 percent nationwide, the post-Depression peak, and 15.6 percent among industrial workers. The pattern of "smokestack" factory closures continued, the most notable victim being the world's biggest steel plant at Lackawanna, N.Y. At least inflation did fall, from 12.4 percent in 1980 to 3.8 percent in 1983, but how far this was due to Reagan is in dispute. The halving of interest rates by the independent Federal Reserve authorities did more to boost the economy and reduce inflation than any fiscal action by the administration. The tax cuts helped to generate recovery in 1983, but two pieces of unanticipated good fortune did much to prevent an accompanying increase in inflation. World commodity prices fell, particularly for foodstuffs, and an oil glut forced price restraint on OPEC.

By 1984 the economy was booming, the rise of 6.8 percent in GNP being the highest annual increase since 1951. The main beneficiaries were the wealthy. The richest 1 percent of Americans owned 14.9 percent of national wealth by 1988, compared with 8 percent in 1980. The middle classes also did well out of "Reaganomics," which helped to create a new class of young, upwardly mobile professionals, the so-called yuppies. However, the trickle-down of supply-side benefits petered out at the lower end of the income scale. Poverty was manifestly on the increase, rather than in decline. According to official statistics, 14.4 percent of Americans were poor in 1984, compared with 11 percent in 1979. Nor was all well among the nonpoor. Hurt by the decline of old industries and unable to organize new ones, trade unions were less able to win substantial pay increases for their members. Chief executive officers of big corporations, who earned on average forty times as much as their workers in 1980, earned ninety-three times more in 1988. Meanwhile, farm foreclosures reached a post-Depression high. Farm debt had tripled in the 1970s, when high food prices tempted farmers into borrowing money to expand their operations. The international decline in food prices made loan repayment difficult in the 1980s. By the end of the decade annual interest obligations on farm debt nearly matched net annual farm income.

Regardless of general prosperity, some long-standing economic problems intensified in the 1980s. The annual trade gap climbed steadily past the $100 billion mark. Until 1981 U.S. overseas investments had produced more than enough income to counterbalance the export shortfall. However, the need to finance the massive growth in federal deficit spending led the United States to borrow abroad, mainly from Japan and Western Europe. In 1985, the United States became a debtor nation for the first time since 1914. When Reagan left office, Americans owed foreigners a total of $400 billion, making them the world's most indebted people.

The budget deficit, which Reagan promised to eliminate by the end of his first term, climbed instead from $59.6 billion in fiscal 1980 to an astronomical $211 billion in fiscal 1985. Reagan's huge defense buildup, with projected expenditures of

$1.7 trillion over eight years, strangled the supply-side budget-balancing strategy of tax reduction and across-the-board expenditure cuts at birth. Congress finally despaired of corrective action from the president. In 1985 it enacted the Balanced Budget and Emergency Deficit Control Act, better known as Gramm-Rudman-Hollings, which scheduled automatic yearly spending reductions in virtually all programs to balance the budget by 1991. This was reduced to advisory status in 1986, virtually ensuring its ineffectiveness, after the Supreme Court ruled that Congressional action in mandating automatic spending cuts was unconstitutional. The problem of how to regain control over public finances was unresolved when Reagan left office. The dangers of prolonging this fiscal drift were clearly signaled by the stock-market crash of October 1987, Wall Street's worst panic since 1929, which many commentators attributed to business concern about the long-term effects of diverting national resources from the improvement of trade and productivity to the financing of the budget deficit and national debt.

Reagan enjoyed only partial success in other areas of domestic policy. As Richard Polenberg notes, his efforts to roll back the welfare state had more impact on Great Society programs than on programs tracing their pedigree to the New Deal.[11] In 1981–82, Reagan's honeymoon period with Congress, some $35 billion was cut from social programs, particularly those benefiting the poor and relatively powerless client groups. The story was different when it came to programs benefiting constituencies like retired people and veterans, who had some political clout. In 1981, administration efforts to cut social security benefits, especially early retirement and disability income protection, were rejected ninety-six to zero in the Republican-controlled Senate. After the midterm elections of 1982 boosted Democratic strength, Reagan found it virtually impossible to cut welfare further. The core of the administration's supposedly revolutionary New Federalism program, a structural transfer of federal responsibilities for programs like Aid to Families with Dependent Children and Food Stamps to the states, went down to defeat in 1983. Democratic congressmen and a bipartisan coalition of state and local officials were adamant that only the federal government had the means to finance these costly programs. Probably the best indication of the lack of change under Reagan is the fact that federal transfer payments to individuals still constituted around 45 percent of the budget in 1988, compared with 47 percent in 1980.

Reagan's record in reducing the regulatory state was also unimpressive. Some environmental protection standards were relaxed, but a counterattack by environmentalists blocked further rollbacks from 1983 onward. The administration's most important action was the deregulation of the savings and loan (S & L) industry, but this had disastrous consequences. Caught up in the get-rich-quick mentality of the 1980s, the once staid S & L institutions made unwise stock-market and other investments, which nearly bankrupted the entire industry. A federal bailout became necessary in 1990, at a possible cost to taxpayers of $500 billion over the next twenty years.

Reagan's rhetorical support for the Christian Right's goals, notably the outlawing of abortion and the legalization of school prayer, was not converted into legislative results. In this field, however, he may have laid foundations for future change. Presidential control over appointments to the Supreme Court and the federal judiciary has resulted in the promotion during the 1980s of judges who were likely to interpret the Constitution to the liking of conservatives on social issues.

It was in foreign policy that Reagan could claim greatest success. Whereas his immediate predecessors had been searching for ways to manage the Cold War, he was out to win it. Reagan's main priority was to deal with the Soviet Union from a position of strength, not parity. As a result the national security state reached its apogee. Reagan accelerated the Carter defense buildup to bring about the greatest expansion of military power in American peacetime history. He also approved development of the Strategic Defense Initiative (SDI), popularly known as Star Wars, to build a space-based defense system over the United States as a high-tech defensive shield against missile attack. This project was intended to restore the level of security that had been enjoyed in the 1940s when only America possessed atomic weaponry. Critics doubted that absolute security was scientifically possible in the nuclear age and warned that Star Wars might provoke the Soviets into developing new weapons to counter it, thereby setting off an endless arms race. By contrast, Reagan, who had a strong personal abhorrence of nuclear weaponry, was confident that the SDI plan would be instrumental in forcing the Soviets into arms reduction negotiations. The achievement of the 1988 Intermediate Nuclear Force Treaty, in which the superpowers agreed to eliminate their short- and medium-range missiles based in Europe, appeared to prove him right. Moscow also gave way to the United States on a number of regional issues, notably in its decision to pull out of Afghanistan in 1988. Reagan had been fortunate that Soviet leader Mikhail Gorbachev, who came to power in 1985, was anxious to reduce superpower tensions in order to concentrate on reform and economic restructuring at home. Nevertheless, his strategy had borne fruit and America was on the verge of Cold War victory in Europe when he left office.

The lack of comparable success in the Third World served to underline the reality that the United States had not regained global hegemony. The Reagan Doctrine went beyond containment in announcing a new rollback strategy in support of indigenous rebel groups seeking to overthrow Third World governments aligned with the Soviet Union. In 1983 U.S. marines invaded the Caribbean island of Grenada to prevent it from falling into the Cuban-Soviet orbit. In most instances, however, Reagan intended only to support "freedom fighters" with economic aid and military supplies. This policy proved effective in the case of the Afghan mujaheddin, but not with regard to U.S.-backed forces in Angola and Central America. The president's application of the domino theory to the latter region made it a new Cold War battleground. Despite massive U.S. aid appropriations, El Salvador's right-wing government could not destroy the challenge of a left-wing guerrilla insurgency. Nor did U.S. aid to the contra rebels result in the military overthrow of Nicaragua's Sandinista regime, though the economic chaos resulting from the prolongation of the civil war ultimately contributed to the electoral defeat of the supposedly antidemocratic government of Daniel Ortega in 1990.

The Reagan Doctrine proved irrelevant in the Philippines, where a wave of popular discontent overthrew the Marcos regime in 1987. Reagan's determination to reassert U.S. power in the Middle East also yielded uncertain results. American marines went to civil war—torn Lebanon in 1982 as part of an international peacekeeping force. Their mission ill-defined, they were sucked into the conflict and a terrorist bomb attack on a marine barracks killed 240 servicemen. Soon afterward, behind the smokescreen of victory in Grenada, Reagan withdrew his forces from Lebanon, having in reality suffered a greater defeat than had Jimmy Carter over Iran. His intervention had also made U.S. residents in Lebanon vulnerable to being taken hostage by terrorist groups. The attempt to free them through illegal arms deals manifested the limitations of American power and nearly destroyed the Reagan presidency. The bombing of Libya by U.S. jets in 1986, in retaliation for its government's support of terrorists, was a piece of saber-rattling that ultimately did nothing to curb Middle Eastern terrorism, which was the product of complex political, historical, and national forces.

Claims that Reagan's presidency marked the emergence of a new and dominant conservative voter coalition are also unconvincing. Reagan was one of several beneficiaries of an international swing to the right in the late 1970s and early 1980s, but he only had support from 27.6 percent of the total potential electorate in the low-turnout 1980 election. His soulmate Margaret Thatcher in Britain in 1979 and Christian Democrat Helmut Kohl in West Germany in 1983 ran better than this, and even Valéry Giscard d'Estaing was supported by some 35 percent of the entire French electorate when he became one of the few losing conservatives of this era in the 1981 presidential election. In his landslide reelection victory of 1984, when he carried every state except Minnesota to win the second greatest electoral college majority in history, Reagan was supported by only 32.3 percent of the potential electorate. This was less than the victorious candidate won in every presidential election from 1952 to 1972, barring 1968.

Moreover, Republican presidential success has not been matched by Congressional success. The Democrats increased their strength in Congress in 1982 and 1984, finally regaining control of the Senate in 1986. They also held a majority of governorships and two-thirds of state legislatures in this period. This success did not signify the resuscitation of the New Deal voter coalition, as woeful Democratic performances in presidential elections made clear. Walter Mondale's liberalism held little appeal in 1984, while in 1988 the bland Michael Dukakis could find no effective response to George Bush's "L-word" strategy that portrayed him as a liberal. The Democrats' search for a winning theme in national elections must go on. One of the principal features of the age of uncertainty has therefore continued throughout and beyond the Reagan era. In contrast to the prevalent electoral trend in the first two-thirds of the twentieth century, there has been no majority party in American politics since 1968.

Finally, any assessment of Reagan must acknowledge that he has returned the presidency to its central role in American politics. Unlike Carter, he exercised decisive leadership and manifested a clear sense of purpose. Without doubt he restored public demand for strong national, party, and executive leadership, and has provided a yardstick against which his successors will be judged. Equally clearly, his experience has confirmed that Americans do not want the imperial presidency back. Reagan's failure to break popular fear of foreign military involvement, the so-called Vietnam syndrome, was evidence of this. Despite his warnings of a communist threat in the U.S. backyard, the public firmly opposed military intervention in Central America. Memories of presidential escalation of the Vietnam War from small beginnings remained strong. Nevertheless, the deployment of U.S. forces in Lebanon and Grenada, the naval intervention in the Iran-Iraq war in 1987 to keep the Persian Gulf open to international shipping, and the Iran-Contra arms-for-hostages deal were proof that the legislative constraints of the 1970s had not shackled presidential activism in foreign affairs. The Reagan record suggests that the late-twentieth-century presidency has still not adjusted fully to the optimum parameters of its power.

Without doubt Reagan restored the heroic image of the presidency. In line with this, historians like Garry Wills and Michael Rogin have depicted Reagan and the political culture he represents as the products of the Hollywood films that founded modern America's mass culture.[9] Interestingly, the films of the 1980s point, by contrast, to the ambiguities of Reagan's America. *Red Dawn* and *Rocky IV* celebrated American patriotism and anticommunism in a manner unthinkable in the era of Vietnam and Watergate, while films like *Top Gun* implicitly lauded American military power. "Teen" movies like *Back to the Future* had incipient yuppie heroes; the rebellious cult figures characteristic of the 1950s and 1960s were gone from the screens. On the other hand, "save-the-farm" movies, notably *Places in the Heart, Country,* and *The River,* depicted the grim plight of rural America. The materialism and greed of the new entrepreneurial culture came under critical scrutiny in *Wall Street*. Movies also offered differing views of the Vietnam War. Sylvester Stallone's Rambo films portrayed this as a good cause and attributed America's defeat to national loss of will. In contrast, *Platoon* and *Full Metal Jacket* emphasized the brutal and brutalizing aspects of the conflict.

Whatever the shortcomings of Reagan's achievements, the American people overwhelmingly endorsed his legacy and voted for continuity in electing Vice President George H. Bush to succeed him in 1988. Over the next eighteen months, cataclysmic events in Eastern Europe brought about the collapse of the Soviet Union's communist satellite regimes. Further superpower discussions also laid the basis for new arms reduction agreements. In 1990, President Bush pronounced the Cold War over. "End-of-empire" theories, popular with commentators when American power was in decline during the 1970s and 1980s, were replaced by an "end-of-history" theory, according to which liberal democracy's triumph over communism signifies the end of the ideological conflict that had shaped world history in the twentieth century. However, the apparent eclipse of the Soviet empire has not encouraged assumptions, even among the most optimistic analysts, that the "American Century" is back on the course forecast by Henry Luce in 1941.

In the early 1990s the United States can claim to be the world's sole superpower, but its relative power is not comparable to what it was in the immediate postwar era. Military superiority is no longer accompanied by economic superiority. Though still the world's richest nation, Americans face a growing challenge from Japan, a united Germany, and an integrated European Community, all of which have greater resources than the United States to improve civilian productivity because they spend so much less on military needs. America's future economic well-being also depends on its ability to bring under control the massive national debt, which increased from $907 billion to $2,602 billion under Reagan. In 1990 over one in five federal tax dollars was consumed by interest repayments on this debt, compared with one in eight in 1980, and the burden will grow unless the budget is balanced. Hard choices face the nation's leaders in the 1990s about where to cut domestic and military programs, and whether to increase taxes. The signs of this are already evident. The president ordered parts of the federal government shut down in October 1990 after negotiations between the White House and the Congressional Democrats over how to reduce a projected $293.7 billion deficit failed to produce a budget agreement before the 1991 fiscal year started. By then Bush's famous pledge of "no new taxes," which had helped to elect him, had a hollow ring to it.

The passing of the Cold War should yield a "peace dividend" of military budget cutbacks in the 1990s. It also creates the opportunity for the United States to launch a new foreign policy attuned to its long-term needs into the twenty-first century. With Soviet-American relations seemingly on a stable and cooperative basis, the greatest threat to global stability will probably emanate from Third World countries. Recent history has shown that the United States cannot control these nations. Its successful military intervention to oust Panamanian leader and international drug dealer Manuel Noriega in 1989 is unlikely to be replicated elsewhere in the world. America's response to Iraqi leader Saddam Hussein's annexation of Kuwait, though swift, recognized that it could no longer operate alone as an unpaid global policeman. The Bush administration made the U.S. the sheriff of a world posse, building up an international coalition through the United Nations to provide political, financial, and military support for American policy toward Iraq.

The Gulf War may mark the end of America's "Age of Uncertainty." Unlike Vietnam, this was a conflict that could be and was won by technologically superior military power. The speed of victory and its low cost in terms of Allied casualties boosted American national self-confidence, inducing President Bush to declare that the "Vietnam syndrome" had finally been laid to rest. Bush and Secretary of State James Baker also predicted that Allied success in the war had laid the foundations for the emergence of a new international order, in which a world coalition—led by the United States, but not solely dependent on its resources—would work together to ostracize and defeat regional aggressors. Nevertheless it is clear that military victory in the Gulf has not yet resolved the fundamental problems of the Middle East, which continue to threaten regional peace and global stability. The future of the new world order is also uncertain. Military power alone cannot build this. Its emergence requires the United States and the economically powerful nations of Western Europe and Japan to address the social and economic problems of the Third World in a more committed and systematic fashion than before. Whether the political will exists for such an endeavor remains to be seen.

The new confidence in international affairs suggests that the American mood of uncertainty is passing away. The United States has experienced and overcome previous bouts of national uncertainty, of course. The desire for normalcy in the 1920s reflected anxiety about the changes of the Progressive era. Uncertainty about the economy prevailed throughout the 1930s. Cold War fears engendered McCarthyism, and the Soviet technological triumph in launching the Sputniks triggered concern that consumer-culture values had sapped American strength, initiative, and vitality. Nevertheless, these periods of doubt were a response to rapid change or temporary failures. The uncertainty of the 1970s and 1980s was intrinsically different because it was the product of a new sense of limitations. Whatever the future holds, the optimism and certainty of the mid-twentieth-century mood are unlikely to be recaptured. The United States cannot fully reverse the relative international and economic decline that it experienced in the 1970s and 1980s. The challenge it faces as a new century beckons is how to exercise world leadership and deal with domestic problems within the realistic limits of its power and resources.

Notes

1. Quoted in Mary Beth Norton et al., *A People and a Nation: A History of the United States*, 2nd ed. (Boston, 1986), p. 973.

2. Christopher Lasch, *The Culture of Narcissism: American Life in an Age of Diminishing Expectations* (New York, 1978), esp. pp. 4–6; see too his essay "The Narcissistic Society," *New York Review of Books*, September 30, 1976, pp. 8–9.

3. Peter Carroll, *It Seemed Like Nothing Happened: America in the 1970s* (New Brunswick, N. J., 1990), pp. ix–xiii.

4. William E. Leuchtenburg, *In the Shadow of FDR: From Harry Truman to Ronald Reagan*, rev. ed. (Ithaca, N. Y., 1985), p. 244.

5. William Julius Wilson, *The Declining Significance of Race: Blacks and Changing American Institutions*, rev ed. (Chicago, 1980), p. 152.

6. Erwin C. Hargrove, *Jimmy Carter as President: Leadership and the Politics of the Public Good* (Baton Rouge, La., 1988), especially pp. 6–32.

7. Quoted in Walter LaFeber, *The American Age: United States Foreign Policy at Home and Abroad since 1750* (New York, 1989), p. 666.

8. Gaddis Smith, *Morality, Reason, and Power: American Diplomacy in the Carter Years* (New York, 1986), p. 9.

9. Michael P. Rogin, *Ronald Reagan, the Movie and Other Episodes in Political Demonology* (Berkeley, Calif., 1987); Garry Wills, *Reagan's America: Innocents at Home* (New York, 1988), especially pp. 440–60.

10. David Mervin, *Ronald Reagan and the Presidency* (New York, 1990), especially pp. 1–11, 175–222. See also his article "Ronald Reagan's Place in History," *Journal of American Studies* 23 (1989): 269–86.

11. Richard Polenberg, "Roosevelt Revolution, Reagan Counterrevolution," in *The Reagan Revolution?* ed. B. B. Kymlicka and Jean V. Matthews (Chicago, 1988), p. 52.

Bibliography

The best overview of the 1970s is Peter N. Carroll, *It Seemed Like Nothing Happened: America in the 1970s* (New Brunswick, N.J., 1990). The national mood of the era is covered by Christopher Lasch, *The Culture of Narcissism: American Life in an Age of Diminishing Expectations* (New York, 1978), and Daniel Yankelevich, *New Rules: Searching for Self-Fulfillment in a World Turned Upside Down* (New York, 1981).

Economic problems of the 1970s are analyzed by Richard Barnet, *The Lean Years: Politics in the Age of Scarcity* (New York, 1980); Barry Bluestone and Bennett Harrison, *The Deindustrialization of America* (New York, 1982); Lester Thurow, *The Zero-Sum Society* (New York, 1980); and Alan Wolfe, *America's Impasse: The Rise and Fall of the Politics of Growth* (New York, 1981). Attendant social problems are discussed by John Crewden, *The Tarnished Door: The New Immigrants and the*

Transformation of America (New York, 1983); Rochelle Gatlin, *American Women since 1945* (London, 1987); Michael Harrington, *The New American Poverty* (New York, 1984); and William J. Wilson, *The Declining Significance of Race: Blacks and Changing American Institutions*, rev. ed. (Chicago, 1980).

The problems of the presidency are covered by Arthur M. Schlesinger, Jr., *The Imperial Presidency* (Boston, 1973); James L. Sundquist, *The Decline and Resurgence of Congress* (Washington, D.C., 1981); and Theodore White, *Breach of Faith: The Fall of Richard Nixon* (New York, 1975). For the Republican administrations of the 1970s, see A. James Reichley, *Conservatives in an Age of Change: The Nixon-Ford Administrations* (Washington, D.C., 1981), and the admittedly partisan *RN: The Memoirs of Richard Nixon* (New York, 1978), and Gerald R. Ford, *A Time to Heal* (New York, 1979).

The best surveys of Carter's presidency are M. Glen Abernathy, Dilys M. Hill, and Phil Williams, eds., *The Carter Years: The President and Policymaking* (London, 1984); and Erwin C. Hargrove, *Jimmy Carter as President: Leadership and the Politics of the Public Good* (Baton Rouge, La., 1988). These can be supplemented by Jimmy Carter, *Keeping Faith: Memoirs of a President* (New York, 1982). William E. Leuchtenburg, *In the Shadow of FDR: From Harry Truman to Ronald Reagan*, rev. ed. (Ithaca, N.Y., 1985), and Thomas Ferguson and Joel Rogers, *Right Turn: The Decline of the Democrats and the Future of American Politics* (New York, 1986) deal with the Democratic party's adjustment to the conservative climate of the 1970s and 1980s. Indispensable for foreign policy are Gaddis Smith, *Morality, Reason and Power: American Diplomacy in the Carter Years* (New York, 1986); and Raymond Garthoff, *Détente and Confrontation: American-Soviet Relations from Nixon to Reagan* (1985). Stimulating assessments from a radical perspective are offered by Fred Halliday, *The Making of the Second Cold War*, 2nd ed. (London, 1986), and Thomas J. McCormick, *America's Half-Century: United States Foreign Policy in the Cold War* (Baltimore, 1989).

A challenging, if not always persuasive, assessment of the Reagan presidency is David Mervin, *Ronald Reagan and the American Presidency* (New York, 1990). The works cited above by Garthoff and McCormick are also useful for foreign policy in the 1980s. These should be supplemented by Coral Bell, *The*

Reagan Paradox: American Foreign Policy in the 1980s (London, 1989); William G. Hyland, ed., *The Reagan Foreign Policy* (New York, 1987); and Robert Tucker, "Reagan's Foreign Policy," *Foreign Affairs* 68 (1988–89). For a highly critical, journalistic account of the Iran-Contra scandal, see Jane Mayer and Doyle MacManus, *Landslide: The Unmaking of the President, 1984–1988* (Boston, 1988). A host of useful essay collections assessing Reagan's legacy has appeared since he left office. For the perspective of British scholars, see Dilys Hill, Raymond Moore, and Phil Williams, eds., *The Reagan Presidency: An Incomplete Revolution* (New York, 1990); and Joseph Hogan, ed., *The Reagan Years* (Manchester, 1990). Among the best overviews by North American scholars are Charles O. Jones, ed., *The Reagan Legacy: Promise and Performance* (Chatham, N.J., 1988); and B. B. Kymlicka and Jean V. Matthews, *The Reagan Revolution?* (Chicago, 1988).

Economic issues are dealt with in Michael J. Boskin, *Reagan and the Economy: The Successes, Failures and Unfinished Agenda* (San Francisco, 1989); and Henry Aaron et al., *Economic Choices* (Washington, D.C., 1987). The socioeconomic consequences of Reaganism are critically discussed in Robert Lekachman, *Visions and Nightmares: America after Reagan* (New York, 1987), and Kevin Phillips, *The Politics of Rich and Poor* (New York, 1990).

Fascinating but impressionistic studies of the connection between politics and culture in the 1980s are Robert Dallek, *Ronald Reagan and the Politics of Symbolism* (Cambridge, Mass., 1984); Michael P. Rogin, *Ronald Reagan, the Movie and Other Episodes in Political Demonology* (Berkeley, Calif., 1987); and Garry Wills, *Reagan's America: Innocents at Home* (New York, 1988).

For contrasting views of America's twenty-first-century prospects, see Paul Kennedy, *The Rise and Fall of the Great Powers: Economic Change and Military Conflict from 1500 to 2000* (New York, 1987), and Joseph S. Nye, Jr., *Bound to Lead: The Changing Nature of American Power* (New York, 1990).

8

American Women in the Twentieth Century

Jay Kleinberg

A generation ago a collection of essays such as this would not have contained a chapter on women. Indeed there might have been no mention of women in the entire book or only a passing reference in the chapter on the Progressive era in the context of settlement houses and campaigns against drink and for the vote. A few famous women, typically Jane Addams and Eleanor Roosevelt, might also have been discussed. But times have changed; our interests in the present inform our concerns about the past and the questions we ask of it. The feminist movement of the 1960s and 1970s led to women's being written back into the past. This does not alter what happened then, but it does modify historical discourse and our understanding of it.

As an area of investigation, the history of women has evolved quickly through two stages. The first concentrated upon organized women, obtaining the vote, women in trade unions, articulate and middle-class women. Many excellent studies appeared with pioneering works by Eleanor Flexner, Aileen Kraditor, Gerda Lerner, and Anne Firor Scott. The focus then shifted to wider social and economic inquiries as the historical profession, prodded by the political concerns of the 1960s, began writing about matters of race, ethnicity, class, and gender, the unorganized and inarticulate, the masses as well as the elite.

Some of the writing in this second stage has questioned the extent to which changes in women's lives indicate progress.

Did the vote, World War I, or World War II emancipate women and free them from gender constraints or, as some analysts have suggested, were these instances in which liberation was more apparent than real? To what extent did objective changes in women's circumstances over the course of the twentieth century, for example smaller families and higher rates of employment, actually alter the socially defined behavior patterns governing relations between the sexes, or are gender roles in some profound sense immutable?

By 1900 American women's lives had changed in many respects from those of their preindustrial predecessors. They undertook a broader variety of activities outside the home, but produced fewer goods within it. They were much more likely to live in cities and to buy, rather than make, their basic necessities. Many young women held jobs, and a few undertook advanced education. Women from disparate backgrounds and age groups participated in social, literary, benevolent, and political societies, seeking companionship and asserting their own vision of order in a world that was itself changing rapidly. Over the course of the twentieth century, women's roles evolved, their range of employment grew, and their social and political participation widened, but as the women's liberation movement of the 1960s and 1970s showed, women did not achieve parity with men in any sphere. This chapter examines the demographic, economic, and social changes in women's lives and briefly reviews the political responses to women's situation at critical junctures in the last hundred years. It is intended to provide an overview of the female experience in the context of the developments that characterized American society in the twentieth century.

The century began with many women trying to reform their political and social roles. The struggle for the vote was but one of a number of activities through which women sought to express their opinions and to move from the world of the home to participation in more varied experiences. It was part of a larger struggle to alter women's legal status from dependence to independence. However, it was not directly related to the increase in women's participation in the labor force with which it coincided, since many of the most active suffragists were not employed outside the home. By the turn of the century most states had passed married women's property legislation which gave married women the same legal control over property enjoyed by single women and all men. Property and citizenship rights did not, however, give women the franchise. Women could vote for federal and state officials only in four western states, Wyoming, Utah, Colorado, and Idaho, although some other states permitted them to vote in local and school board elections.

As the United States urbanized and industrialized and its ethnic base diversified, fundamental questions were raised as to whose values should predominate in the emerging nation. Both the campaign for the vote and women's participation in the temperance, club, and reform movements should be seen in the context of the controversies of the day and as part of the Progressive movement. Women's quest for suffrage began in the 1840s when women involved in the great crusades of their era, namely temperance and abolition, realized that their political opinions were not taken seriously because of their sex. After the Civil War a split occurred among the group of reformers that supported abolitionism and women's rights over the contentious issue of whether women's suffrage should be included in the constitutional amendment to provide voting rights for freedmen. Disappointed by the exclusion of women from this amendment, Elizabeth Cady Stanton and Susan B. Anthony spearheaded the formation of the National Woman Suffrage Association in 1869 with the sole aim of pressuring Congress into granting the vote to women. Their more moderate sisters in the abolitionist and women's rights struggles formed the American Woman Suffrage Association, campaigning on a state-by-state basis for the vote. Neither group achieved much success and the two factions united in 1893 to form the National American Woman's Suffrage Association.

The second generation of suffragists came to the movement from a wide range of reformist backgrounds. While some were interested only in suffrage, others regarded the vote as a means to achieve their particular ends, be these temperance, the reform of corrupt politics, better housing, or peace. Many had been active in other organizations including the Women's Christian Temperance Union, the General Federation of Women's Clubs, the Progressive movement, the National Association of Colored Women, and various literary and social clubs. Although there were some militant feminists among them, this generation based their campaign on the results to be expected once women got the vote, on the reforms that would ensue, and on women's superiority to men in areas of social reform and social housekeeping—the skills and concerns of motherhood transferred to the public arena. They believed that women needed the vote in order to protect both their immediate families and the community as a whole from corrupt influences.

Not surprisingly, suffragists were opposed in their campaign by those corrupt influences and by those with a conservative view of women's proper social roles. The liquor industry feared that women's suffrage would result in prohibition, a realistic fear given that the Women's Christian Temperance Union was one of the largest women's organizations in the United States. Many women joined the WCTU through their churches, becoming aware of reform issues through it. A number moved from temperance to social reform generally, and saw the vote as a means of accomplishing their aims. The WCTU had a large following in the Presbyterian and Methodist churches, small towns and rural areas, and among the native-born, white middle classes. As with the suffrage movement generally, these women legitimized their political and reform activities as extensions of their roles as mothers and Christians. They sought to impose their religiously based temperance viewpoint upon the immigrants who did not share their dry perspective. Issues of social control thus became intertwined with the quest for the vote.

The Catholic Church and urban political machines also opposed women's suffrage. The church believed that women's place was in the home, and political bosses took the reformist sympathies of suffragists seriously, worrying that enfranchised women would vote them out of office. Some women also opposed the campaign to widen the franchise because they feared that such a break with the established order threatened the family, tainted women with political corruption, or impaired their ability to crusade for social justice. Ida Tarbell, the muckraking political journalist, wrote that nature assigned women to motherhood, a more important role in society than that of public life. Although sympathetic to women's rights as a young woman, she regretted that she never married or had children, and was not entirely in favor of suffrage for women.[1] In contrast, many other reformers, including Jane Addams, the founder of the Hull House Settlement in Chicago, believed that suffrage would further the cause of social justice.

Women campaigned for the vote on the grounds that they

were morally superior to men, and that if they voted they could protect their homes from corrupt influences. The suffrage campaign itself became intertwined with Progressivism. By 1914, all major women's organizations had joined the bandwagon. Suffrage parades dramatized their quest, as did picketing the White House, arrests, and force-feeding in jail. There has been considerable debate among historians whether this new militancy or women's role in keeping the economy and home fires burning during World War I actually led Congress to pass the Nineteenth Amendment. The combination of the reform movement and increased public roles during the war which demonstrated women's capabilities in nondomestic roles certainly helped persuade some of those men previously reluctant to enfranchise women; other men were swayed by the successes of the suffrage movement at the state level.

Although the fear of change led many to oppose the vote, in fact the enfranchisement of women in 1920 did not alter the conduct of American politics dramatically. Many women assumed that the vote would lead to a more just world. When it did not, they retreated from activism in disappointment. Women identified themselves with the ethnic and class groups from which they came rather than as women. As a result of these tendencies, women did not vote as a group, their turnout at the polls was lower than men's, and the women's movement itself became divided. Many women dropped out, believing they had accomplished what they set out to do. The League of Women Voters succeeded the National American Woman's Suffrage Association and dedicated itself to educating women to vote and to promoting good citizenship within the entire community. A small group led by Alice Paul formed the Women's party to agitate for an equal rights amendment. Thus divided, the movement lost its momentum.

Progressive women's concerns became part of American social politics and welfare systems in the early twentieth century. Various state and federal departments conducted social surveys such as the 1911 inquiry into women and children's health by Emma Duke, which demonstrated that poor nutrition and maternal overwork deprived immigrant and working-class children of a good start in life.[2] Such concerns eventually translated into schemes for mothers' pensions and ultimately into the Aid to Dependent Children provision of the Social Security Act.

Reformers such as Grace Abbott became part of the welfare infrastructure when she accepted the post of chief of the Children's Bureau in the Department of Labor in 1921, a position she retained until 1934.

Despite some political successes, the new woman of the 1920s was more socially than politically concerned. Women rebelled against constraints upon their behavior, but where in the Progressive era this rebellion took the form of political activism, by the 1920s the main areas of contention were over public and private social behavior. The flapper epitomized female leisure time rather than political or economic concerns. She wanted the same social freedom as men to drink in speakeasies, smoke cigarettes, and engage in freer sexual behavior. Her short skirts, cigarettes, and cocktails gave her a sexually daring image. The women who moved into Greenwich Village's Bohemian life-style and those who acquired the consumer durables and delights of the 1920s believed they had achieved emancipation. Premarital intercourse increased, as did the use of birth-control devices. Women participated in more athletic activities and were movie stars, but there were few women directors or producers; women rarely controlled the content or finance of the movies. Some women such as Mary Pickford were well paid; nevertheless roles open to women were very limited. They were either vampish seductresses or innocent child-women. If women of color got parts at all they were maids or other stereotyped figures.

Although the acquisition of the vote produced few dramatic political effects, both demographic and economic changes altered the daily circumstances of women's lives throughout the twentieth century. Falling family sizes, increased longevity, and higher rates of participation in the labor force meant that over the course of the twentieth century succeeding generations of women cared for fewer people for a shorter proportion of their lives than previously. There are many fewer large families in contemporary America. Households typically consist only of family members, rather than including boarders or resident domestic servants as they did a century ago. Two centuries ago, 36 percent of all households contained seven or more members. By the end of the nineteenth century that proportion decreased to 23 percent. In 1970, only 5 percent of all families had that many people. As the number of large families decreased, the number of small household units increased. It was very rare indeed for anybody to live alone at the end of the nineteenth century or even as part of a couple, without children, relatives, boarders, or servants. In 1800, only 4 percent of all households consisted of one person while 12 percent contained two people. In 1970, 17 percent of all households consisted of a single person and 29 percent of a couple.

A number of factors have contributed to the increased number of one- and two-person families. Rising standards of living have made it possible for many more people to support themselves and sustain a separate dwelling unit on a single income. Childbearing is now bunched into a few years rather than continuing across a woman's entire potential childbearing span. The birth rate itself fell steadily from 1800 until just after World War II, when it surged for two decades, only to return to its downward trend in the mid-1960s. Women today have half as many children as did their grandmothers, and one-fourth as many as their great-great-grandmothers. The average age at marriage, having fallen from 23 to 20 during the first half of the century, climbed back to 23 by 1984. Thus, except for the era immediately after World War II, the trend has been toward smaller families. There is also evidence to suggest that some women today are delaying childbearing, thus reducing their commitment to a family-oriented life-style by trying to combine motherhood with careers.

At the same time that family size is shrinking, life expectancy at birth has risen by about twenty years for whites and thirty years for blacks. As the number of children per marriage has declined, the child-free period at the end of the life cycle has increased. In the middle of the nineteenth century most women who had children spent their entire adult lives caring for their families. At the beginning of the twentieth century, women averaged about ten to fifteen years between the time their youngest child left home and their own deaths. By 1970, that interval had more than doubled, leaving more than thirty years of "empty nest." One of the consequences of falling family size and the shift of production from inside to outside the home has been the increased presence of married and older women in the labor force.

The rising rate of divorce in the twentieth century also contributed to the number of such women who undertook gainful employment. In 1860 there was one divorce per 1,000 married couples. In 1900, there were 9 divorces per 1,000 marriages, and by 1980 there were 22. If present trends continue about half of all new marriages will end in divorce.

Once a marriage ends, the former husband and wife experience different prospects. Divorced women are less likely to remarry than their former spouses. Over the course of the twentieth century the ratio of divorced women to men has risen from 119 divorced women for every 100 divorced men in 1910 to 156 divorced women per 100 divorced men in 1970. Census studies in the early 1980s found that about one-third of all divorced women did not remarry. Since fewer than one-quarter of all divorced fathers actually contribute substantially to their children's maintenance, divorce has two consequences for women and children: it significantly lowers their standard of living and results in the increased employment of women when mothers seek to provide for their children without help from their former partners. Increased postwar divorce rates resulted in a corresponding rise in the proportion of families maintained by women without male partners. In 1960, women on their own supported 7 percent of all families with children; by 1985, women sustained one-quarter of all families. The proportion of female-headed families was highest among African-Americans. Over half of all African-American and one-fifth of all European-American families with children are supported by women. Many of these families live well below the poverty line.

Both before and after divorce and regardless of participation in the labor force, women had, and retain, primary responsibility for house and child care, although industrialization and urbanization altered the nature of that care. Increased production of goods and services outside the home and smaller families within it abolished many of the tasks which preindustrial women performed. Items previously made by women in the home could, as a result of industrial production and distribution methods, be purchased more cheaply. Almost no women made their own cloth in 1900, and many bought ready-made clothes. As Americans moved off the farms and into the cities, they relied more and more upon store-bought food as well. Thus jobs opened up in industry replacing some of the work done by women in the homes. Many young women, who in an earlier generation would have helped their mothers spinning, weaving, sewing, gardening, baking, cooking, washing clothes, and looking after numerous younger brothers and sisters, took jobs outside the home. This contributed to the steadily increasing number of women in the labor force between 1870 and 1940, but it also concentrated domestic responsibilities to an unprecedented extent upon married women working in isolation in their own homes.

Housework has changed in a number of significant ways over the course of the twentieth century. At the turn of the century most middle-class women relied upon the assistance of paid helpers to care for their homes. In 1900, about 10 percent of all families had servants; by 1920, about 5 percent did so; and by 1960, only 3 percent. Moreover, in 1900 most of these servants lived in their employers' households, while in 1960 they came to work by the day. Two factors explain the decline in household help. The growing availability of household technology lessened the amount of physical labor involved in doing housework, making it more acceptable to middle-class women. Second, the supply of servants declined as other, more socially acceptable jobs became available.

At the turn of the century, and certainly by 1920, urban middle-class homes had indoor plumbing, hot and cold running water, electricity and gas, central heating, and perhaps a few electrically powered appliances such as an iron, a washing machine, and a vacuum cleaner. The typical city worker's house after World War I had indoor plumbing; by the start of the Depression most had electricity. Rural families acquired domestic technology later, many not benefiting from electricity until the electrification programs of the Depression itself. The new suburban housing developments after World War II contained fully equipped kitchens, so that refrigerators, stoves, and dishwashers became standard items, as did laundry rooms with automatic washers and clothes driers. Women in the suburbs spent increasing amounts of time chauffeuring their children, delivering them to an expanding group of activities, and driving to shopping centers rather than walking to the stores or having their groceries delivered. The dispersion of technology also made working and middle-class women's daily routines more similar over the course of the century.

Although the widespread availability of domestic technology eased the physical burden of housework, it did little to lessen the amount of work done. Most studies of housework have suggested that the time spent on household tasks has remained essentially static over the century. Standards of cleanliness have risen, encouraged by advertisers seeking to sell their products. Family advisers over the course of the century have told women that they alone can care for their children. Where previously women divided their attention between household production and child care, mothers were expected to devote themselves entirely to their offspring. Despite a decline in family size, twentieth-century mothers spent more time in looking after children than previously. In addition, as Ruth Cowan and others have pointed out, some so-called labor-saving devices actually make more work: when an automatic pasta maker replaces store-bought noodles the end result is more, rather than less work.[3] Food processors make more complicated recipes possible and increase work and washing up even though they make quick work of the chopping. The net effect is to increase the time spent in food preparation.

Household labor, moreover, has remained women's work. Even in homes where the wife is employed in the labor force, there is little evidence to suggest that the amount of housework done by husbands has increased very much. Husbands contribute about 15 percent of the household labor and daughters do about twice as much as sons. There are also sharp distinctions in the sort of housework done by males and females. Men's jobs are episodic, have a high leisure content, and are rarely time-pressured. Men mow lawns, shovel snow, play with children, and do minor household repairs. Women do the repetitive, time-stressed tasks: the cooking, cleaning, and laundry. When wives work, they spend less time on housework, but retain responsibility for running the home. Regardless of social class most men have strenuously resisted any increase in their own domestic responsibilities; by default, women have retained theirs.

Women's labor-force participation rates have risen dramatically over the course of the century. The type of women taking paid employment has also altered over the last hundred years. In 1870, 14 percent of all women of working age had jobs. The proportion climbed steadily through the Great Depression (27 percent in 1940), surged during the wartime emergency to 37 percent, fell to 30 percent in the immediate postwar years, but regained its wartime level by 1960. The war itself provided opportunities for women to work in traditionally male preserves including heavy industry and munitions manufacturing, but women rarely moved into supervisory positions. There is some controversy about the rapid decrease in women's employment at the end of the war: did women leap eagerly from the factory to family life, or did a combination of returning soldiers, hostile unions and employers, and advertising campaigns for new products push them from jobs they enjoyed to domesticity? Social surveys taken at the time suggest that a majority of women wished to retain their positions, but also wished to start families. They resolved this conundrum by leaving the labor force, but returning a decade later when their children were safely ensconced in school.

The last two decades have seen a sharp rise in female employment to 41 percent in 1970, 51 percent in 1980, 55 percent in 1985, and still rising. Mothers of young children account for much of this increase. The proportion of working mothers with children aged six to eighteen has more than doubled since 1950, jumping from 29 percent in that year to 65 percent in 1985. The increase among mothers of very young children is sharper still. In the same interval it shot up from 12 percent to 50 percent.

A century ago the typical female worker was young, single, an immigrant herself, or the daughter of immigrants, and worked as a domestic servant. Forty-one percent of all single women had jobs, but the proportion varied by ethnicity. While only 28 percent of native-born white women with native-born white parents had jobs, 44 percent of those with foreign-born parents did so. Among unmarried foreign-born women, the employed proportion was 70 percent. The overall labor-force participation rates of African-American women were far higher than those of white women. At the turn of the century, one-fifth of all white women over the age of sixteen had jobs, compared with more than two-fifths of all African-American women. Three-fifths of all single black women were in the labor force. The contrast between the races is sharply etched in the employment experiences of married women. In 1890, only 2 percent of all married white women worked, compared with 23 percent of all African-American married women.

The higher rates of employment among women of the African-American community are explained by the racially based poverty that they endured. Because the men found it difficult to get decent jobs or to move up the employment hierarchy, the women were propelled into the labor force at an early age and stayed there throughout their adult lives. The sharp drop in the proportion of married African-American women who undertook employment in the decade immediately following emancipation undermines the hypothesis that working patterns under slavery strongly influenced their presence in the labor force. The subsequent increase in female labor-force participation among African-Americans would seem to suggest that they perceived female employment as a necessary expedient rather than as intrinsically desirable or a direct legacy from slavery times.

As the twentieth century progressed, the experience of women as workers has converged across status and racial divisions. The proportion of white married women workers rose steadily during the first half of the twentieth century, from 6 percent in 1900 to 25 percent in 1950. Between 1950 and 1980, married women's labor-force participation has doubled, so that half of all wives work. Married women's labor-force participation rates among both races are also more similar. In 1985, 64 percent of married African-American women and 53 percent of married white women worked. There is also less discrepancy now in the rates of employment among married and single women. In 1980, about three-fifths of all single women had jobs, as did more than half of all married women. Current trends point to a continued rise in married women's employment.

Why have the employment experiences of these groups of women converged when, at the turn of the century, they differed so drastically? Part of the explanation is demographic. As families got smaller, women sought other activities to absorb their energies. Smaller families mean fewer people to help carry the financial burden of the remaining family members. Previously, money crises could be resolved by sending more family members out to work. But after the turn of the century, as more and more states made school attendance to the age of sixteen mandatory, the burden of adding to the family income fell more directly on married women. Moreover, the way in which these women could help meet their families' financial needs has changed over the course of the century. At the turn of the century, many poor and some middle-class families took boarders and lodgers into their homes. Particularly for immigrant families, this enabled women to make a significant financial contribution without going into the labor force. While this practice was commonplace at the turn of the century, it became much less so by the Depression and hardly exists today. A greater desire for familial privacy, smaller homes, decreased immigration, and rising real incomes made this practice less attractive to potential lodgers and landladies. This foreclosed one possible source of income for married women and decreased the size of households themselves.

Another part of the explanation behind rising female labor-force participation is rooted in the nature of consumer society. Desires have proliferated as more goods became available and advertisers played upon people's emotions to entice them into purchasing. Many families perceived their income as insufficient to keep up with the Joneses and pay for the college education that would enable their children to join the middle class. Over the course of the twentieth century married women increasingly filled this gap through activities within the labor market. As the economy itself became more oriented toward paperwork and marketplace services, and the hours required in the workplace dropped (from about sixty hours per week at the turn of the century to about forty hours per week today), married women have been more willing to venture outside their own homes in search of income.

The type of work undertaken by women workers has altered as more socially acceptable jobs have proliferated. Domestic servants formed the largest group of employed women at the turn of the century, followed closely by textile mill operatives and textile workers (including seamstresses and dressmakers), farm laborers, and farmers. But while doing housework at home for one's own family was regarded as a labor of love, doing it for pay was stigmatized, and women sought other work in preference to it. Domestic servants had little autonomy, did the heaviest jobs in the household, worked very long hours, and typically had only half a day off each week. The nature of domestic service changed in response to pressure from the workers themselves. Fewer white women undertook service work, preferring jobs that either required some education or were regarded as clean and "ladylike," such as office and sales work. Housework became a residual employment, which women undertook only if they could not find other jobs. Increasingly domestic service became the province of African-American women, many of them married, who resented the restrictions imposed by living away from their own families and communities under the watchful and frequently prejudiced eyes of their employers. Thus daily work replaced living in, and employers had to do more of the work previously undertaken by servants on call twenty-four hours a day.

The shift from domestic employment, first to manufacturing jobs, then to white-collar and non—household service occupations, has been underway since the United States Census Bureau began keeping detailed records on women's occupations. Domestic service, which occupied more than half of all employed women in 1870 and one-quarter in 1920, now accounts for 1 percent of employed women. Agriculture experienced a similarly drastic decline, from one-quarter of the women workers in 1870 to half that level after World War I to a handful of women today. Manufacturing (primarily textiles, cigar and tobacco factories, food, and clothing) accounted for 19 percent of all women workers in 1870, peaked at 26 percent in 1900, and fell gradually to 12 percent in 1982. In 1870, these three categories accounted for 94 percent of all women's employment. By 1920, about 60 percent of all women had jobs in these fields. In 1982, about 13 percent did.

The growth in women's employment has occurred in white- and pink-collar jobs. In 1870 a mere handful of women had clerical positions. By 1920, 16 percent of gainfully employed women did so, rising to 38 percent in 1982. Women also represent a larger proportion of professional and managerial workers than they did a century ago. In 1870, the smattering of women who had such positions were teachers or trained nurses. By 1920, about 10 percent of all women had such jobs. By 1982, 20 percent of all women worked in professional and technical capacities while another 8 percent were managers and administrators. White-collar jobs now account for about two-thirds of all women's occupations. Another 12 percent of employed women work in "other services," a catchall category that includes beauticians, waitresses, cleaners in hotels, and cooks.

Rising educational levels have enabled women to move into the higher echelon white-collar jobs in growing numbers and help explain why women persist longer in the labor force today than they did a century ago. Throughout the early decades of the century, women depended upon their individual rather than group efforts to improve their own situation. Many consciously chose to remain longer in school, taking commercial and academic courses in the expanding high-school system in order to obtain white-collar jobs when they graduated. As women have deliberately sought advanced educational training in order to prepare themselves for careers, they have become reluctant to give up their positions upon either marriage or childbearing.

In 1870, there were thirteen women college graduates for every one hundred men with degrees. Women's degrees as a proportion of men's peaked in 1920, following the intense activism of the suffrage campaign, then fell away under the constraints of the Depression and began rising again only after World War II. By 1982, there were ninety-five women graduates per one hundred men of equivalent status. An increasing number of women have taken advantage of civil-rights legislation that forbade discrimination in educational institutions to obtain professional credentials in occupations in which women were once drastically underrepresented. In 1960, women accounted for only a handful of the medical, dental, legal, and engineering degrees awarded. In 1982, 25 percent of the doctors, 15 percent of the dentists, 33 percent of the lawyers, and 11 percent of the engineering graduates were women. At the preprofessional level, there has also been some shift of women out of the arts and into the science and business courses.

Although the type of work women do today has changed greatly from that of their grandmothers, they still tend to be concentrated in a small number of job categories and tend to work with other women rather than in mixed groups. All during the twentieth century between three-quarters and four-fifths of all women workers toiled in jobs in which women were disproportionately represented. This means that although the number of employed women has increased and the types of jobs women do have changed, most women still work in a segregated labor market in which their sex, rather than their occupational qualifications or interests, determines which jobs they will do.

The range of women's employments remains narrower than men's. Thus more than one-third of all women workers today are clerical workers, but no single occupational category accounts for more than a few percent of men's employment. One survey of occupational segregation in California conducted by the United States Employment Service between 1959 and 1979 found that of a possible segregation index of 100 (no men in "women's" jobs and no women in "men's" jobs), the average index of segregation was 93.4 in the firms surveyed. Two-thirds of the establishments were absolutely segregated, that is, men and women worked at jobs in which no members of the opposite sex also worked. Although there is some evidence to suggest that occupational segregation has decreased in the 1970s and 1980s, it still remains a considerable force in the American economy.

One consequence of the segregation of the economy into men's and women's jobs has been that women's jobs pay much less than men's. Even where women and men do the same work (true only of a limited number of jobs), women's wages are lower than men's. Comparing only full-time, year-round workers (and thus controlling for women's greater tendency to work part-time and seasonally), women's median earnings were 64 percent of men's in 1955. As more women entered the labor market, their median earnings fell relative to men's, to 57 percent in 1974. Women's earnings were 61 percent of men's in 1978; 64 percent in 1983, and 69 percent in 1990. Women college graduates earn about 80 percent as much as their male counterparts, but do not get comparable promotions and wage increases. As a result even the income of highly educated women falls behind men's.

Although more women now retain their jobs after having a baby, the difficulty of finding adequate child care and the assumption that women will be the primary caretakers of young children still leads many to drop out of the labor market, even if only for a few years. Some conservatives have maintained that they, rather than feminists, are "pro-family," opposing publicly funded day-care centers in order to protect the traditional family. Richard Nixon vetoed the Comprehensive Child Development Act of 1971, claiming that day-care centers would lead to a breakdown in family life. In 1976, working parents got the right to claim part of the costs of child care as a credit against their tax bill. The value of this tax credit is undermined because informal arrangements with baby-sitters who do not wish to declare the income they receive are not eligible. It subsidizes those in work, but excludes those who are not currently in the labor market, for example women on welfare, who would benefit from child-care assistance in order to upgrade their education and training in order to obtain jobs.

Few children have places in public nurseries. State-funded or licensed day-care centers can accommodate less than one-eighth of all children under six whose mothers work. Many working mothers rely upon a precarious hodgepodge of informal arrangements using relatives, neighbors, and friends to look after their children. If these arrangements break down the children are either left alone or their mothers miss work. The lack of child-care facilities has a negative impact on women's job and promotion prospects and tends to lower their lifetime earnings, particularly if women choose to work part-time in order to fit in with children's school hours. Part-time jobs pay poorly and provide few benefits such as medical insurance or pensions which are vital to family welfare.

A number of factors demonstrate that women and men occupy different niches in the labor market, including lower wages and occupational segregation. So, too, do the attempts to protect women as workers. Male workers organized themselves through labor unions to work together for higher wages and better working conditions. But although women attempted to follow this route, ultimately they relied upon the legislative process rather than solidarity for protection from rapacious employers. The reasons for this are rooted both in contemporary attitudes toward women and the realities of their laboring lives.

Although some of the earliest labor unions organized women and men (notably in the textile and shoe industries), by the end of the nineteenth century most unions were composed of skilled male workers who regarded women as competitors for their jobs rather than as potential comrades. This tendency is partially explained by employers' use of women as semiskilled and unskilled minders of the machines that increasingly replaced skilled craftsmen. The nature of the female labor force in this era exacerbated the potential conflict between the sexes in the workplace. Because many of the women workers were young, single, desperately poor, from backgrounds without a union tradition, and in the labor force for a relatively brief period, they were unlikely to sacrifice their short-term needs and those of their families for long-term goals. In this they resembled other unskilled workers who changed jobs frequently and eked out a bare living.

Employers regarded women as a disposable cheap labor force and strenuously resisted their attempts to organize. Male unionists' patriarchal values and desire to limit competition for their jobs led them to reject women's efforts to be part of the labor movement, or to include them only halfheartedly. Most male union members believed that the world would be a better place if women stayed in the home. Thus a combination of employers' and male unionists' attitudes and the nature of women's jobs and brief employment life span meant that women were largely unorganized at the turn of the century. Certain women's occupations such as domestic service were also notoriously difficult to organize. There were sporadic attempts by washerwomen and domestic servants to raise wages and improve working conditions in the late nineteenth and early twentieth centuries. At the end of World War I domestic servants in ten cities managed to affiliate with the American Federation of Labor, but the isolated nature of housework and the ability of employers simply to fire their domestic help rapidly broke these unions.

Women working in groups had more success in organizing, but met with tepid support from unions and the American Federation of Labor. About 3 percent of all women industrial workers were organized in 1900, as were about 7 percent two decades later. By contrast, in 1920 about 20 percent of male industrial workers belonged to unions. About half of the women trade unionists worked in the garment industry, while one-fourth were in the printing trades. In order to combat the paucity of protection, a coalition of women union activists and middle-class reformers formed the Women's Trade Union League at the turn of the century. This organization provided assistance at the local level to women seeking to improve their wages and working conditions.

The halting and largely ineffective efforts to organize in the workplace led many working women and their middle-class allies to agitate for legislation to protect them from the worst abuses. Some northern and western state legislatures attempted to regulate wages, hours, and working conditions, but these usually failed in the face of judicial opposition. Turn-of-the-century reformers believed that the conditions under which women worked endangered their health and their ability to bear children and be good mothers. In *Muller* v. *Oregon* in 1908, the Supreme Court accepted the argument put forward by reformers that women were fundamentally weaker than men and lacked the stamina to complete a full working day. According to this judicial decision, the state had a vested interest in protecting women from the full rigors of employment so that they might fulfill their maternal destiny. A rash of legislation ensued, restricting the number of hours women could work in various industries, although not in domestic service or agriculture.

Despite these limitations, women's share of the labor force continued to grow, largely because the new jobs that women took were outside the factory, in offices and shops. Although the proportion of women in the labor force only rose from 23 to 24 percent in the 1920s, more middle-class and married women joined the ranks of women working in these new environments. They did so for a complicated set of reasons. The example of feminist professional women encouraged women to look beyond the home front. They wanted to contribute to the family economy as children stayed longer at school. The new consumer items available, automobiles, refrigerators, and hot and cold running water, were all expensive to purchase. Women's employment helped their families to improve their standard of living.

When the Depression set in, various groups questioned the legitimacy of married women occupying space in the labor market. Employed married women were criticized for "taking" jobs away from others who felt they were more entitled to them, notably all men and single women. Pundits such as Norman Cousins made simple-minded equations between the overall numbers of unemployed and women in the labor force, concluding that if no women worked there would be no unemployment. As the number of job openings fell, women clung desperately to their positions, some working for a mere pittance.

Some New Deal legislation, far from improving women's employment situation, actually worsened it by legitimizing wage differentials between women and men in the same occupations and permitting employers to pay women workers (but not men) less than the minimum wages established by the various National Industrial Recovery Act (NIRA) boards. Yet NIRA legislation did incorporate some concerns of women activists; child labor and home work were banned. Despite the attempts by organized women's groups and Eleanor Roosevelt to ensure equity for women, they were excluded from many federal employment projects. Particularly in the Southeast, black women suffered sexual and racial discrimination in obtaining relief employment as did Mexican-American women in the Southwest.

Federal relief programs enshrined and exacerbated the prejudices against married women's employment (and by logical extension, the employment of all women) by stipulating that only one family member could be enrolled and that one had to be the principal breadwinner of the family. Some states interpreted this narrowly to exclude married women altogether. Additionally, many states passed legislation prohibiting the employment of married women in publicly funded jobs. Federal offices fired married women; more than three-quarters of the nation's school systems refused to hire married teachers and half of them fired those who got married. By the end of the Depression, more than half the states passed or were contemplating legislation barring women from public-sector employment. Nevertheless, a number of women held important federal posts during the Roosevelt administration, including Frances Perkins (secretary of labor), Lucille Foster McMillan (civil service commissioner), and Marion Glass Banister (assistant treasurer of the United States).

Women's organizations defended women's right to employment in domestic rather than personal terms, trying to legitimize women's presence in the labor force through reference to maternal obligations. Family circumstances rather than individual preference became the criterion upon which women's, but not men's employment was to be judged. Where women's employment had previously been discussed in terms of widening horizons and utilizing training, now constant reference was made to family need. Work became an additional service that women performed for their families rather than themselves. Thus different standards were applied to women's and men's presence in the labor force. Nevertheless, the proportion of women in the labor force actually rose from 23.6 percent to 27.6 percent between April 1930 and March 1940. Many women clearly rejected patriarchal notions of gender roles in order to see their families through the emergency.

During World War II women were positively encouraged to work, not for their families' sake, but for the nation's. The mobilization of labor power led to campaigns aimed at women to encourage them to work for the war effort in the shipyards, steel mills, and aircraft factories. Women were lured into war work through higher rates of pay and better working conditions than they could obtain elsewhere. Black women, in particular, benefited from access to jobs hitherto denied them in industry and stores. Nevertheless, men retained the skilled and supervisory jobs, tolerating women's presence in the workplace only as a wartime expedient. Unions remained uninterested in organizing them or promoting equality in employment, and at the end of the war sought to evict women from their wartime jobs in previously male industries. Women's employment levels rose rapidly during the war, but fell from 37 to 30 percent as the men returned home. There were two separate reasons for this. In many cases women were pushed out of their higher-paying, more interesting jobs when preference was given to returning veterans. Management also reverted to its traditional hiring practices of choosing men over women. Additionally, many women wanted to start or care for their families. The long-term impact of World War II on women in the United States is hard to gauge, but it may be that the increased responsibility that women enjoyed during the war, suppressed though it was in the postwar era, underpinned the resurgence of the feminist movement in the 1960s.

There was a broad consensus at the end of the war that women with children, particularly young children, should be at home looking after them, rather than in the labor force. Earlier arguments that had legitimized married women's work in terms of the family now rebounded. The real level of men's wages paid rose, enabling them to support families on a single income. There were active campaigns to persuade women to leave the labor force, or at least the higher-paying jobs that they had held during the war. Women who wanted to retain their wartime jobs in heavy industry received little support from labor unions or the general public. Opinion polls conducted at the end of the war found that few women or men believed that the sexes should have an equal chance at jobs. Manufacturers wishing to ensure a ready market for the consumer goods flooding into the stores depicted women at home, using the products to care for their families. Women's magazines, which depended upon advertising revenues from these manufacturers to sustain them, hammered home the message that women achieved happiness by embracing domesticity rather than competing with men in the working world. The number of employed women dropped dramatically as women turned inwards, looking to their families for fulfillment.

As women left the labor force, the population boomed. Young white families left the cities in droves, seeking a better life in the suburban developments that sprawled across the United States encouraged by low-interest mortgages, veterans' benefits, and mass highway building programs. New homes made a wide range of domestic technologies available to suburban housewives. They came furnished with central heating, hot and cold running water, complete bathrooms, and fitted kitchens. But postwar American architecture also isolated women in anonymous neighborhoods with no obvious gathering places, no places to meet and greet and get to know each other. Suburban developments were segregated by income (all houses cost nearly the same) and by race. Lacking public transportation and marooned in neighborhoods zoned only for housing, women devoted themselves to driving their children to and from the vast array of activities now deemed necessary for their development, including scouts, music and dancing lessons, Little League, band practice, and after-school clubs.

Although the household technology available to postwar families meant that housework required less physical effort, it did not result in any less time being spent on housework. Standards of cleanliness rose, prompted in no small measure by manufacturers seeking outlets for a panoply of cleansing devices and agents. Advertisers used the powerful medium of television to convey their message: American women could only retain their husbands' love by using a certain brand of coffee, cake mix, or vacuum cleaner. In a reprise of magazine advertisements at the turn of the century, modern mothers were told that their children would not love them unless they used the right mouthwash or toothpaste. The 1950s version implied that if mother supplied the wrong toothpaste, the little one's gleaming smile would be full of holes. Television depicted women as housewives and mothers, serving their families, but rarely venturing outside the domestic scene and almost never being in a position of authority. Women functioned as consumers, buying goods for their family and in order to obtain their family's love, but they did not exist outside the family context.

In an updated version of the cult of domesticity, women became responsible for their children's happiness. Supposed child-care experts told women that they alone could meet their offspring's every need. They bore not only the children, but responsibility for their well-being. Some social commentators blamed women's work outside the home or neglect of their proper duties for rising rates of juvenile crime, delinquency, alienation, drinking, smoking, or drug taking, laying the ills of modern society in the maternal lap. Others, such as Philip Wylie, blamed women for smothering their children, for devouring them, and preventing their sons from achieving independence. Writing just after the war, Ferdinand Lundberg and Marynia Farnham lambasted women for seeking fulfillment outside the home and rejecting their supposedly feminine, passive, dependent nature.[4]

Pundits on all sides lashed out at women in the postwar decade. College presidents wanted to revise the courses that women studied in order to enhance their domesticity. Freudian psychiatrists declared that women could either follow their female destiny or become neurotic career women. It was not possible to be well-adjusted and employed. Despite the intensity of the message, women's employment rose steadily throughout the 1950s as more women returned to the labor force when their children entered school, provoked by a concern to maintain consumption levels, a growing awareness of the cost of providing a college education for their offspring, and boredom brought on by tending highly technologized homes in isolation. Employers facing staff shortages, especially in the burgeoning clerical fields, also became less reluctant to hire married women. Both women who entered the labor market and those who did not experienced conflicts over their proper roles, questioning what they should do with their time and energies, and wondering why they did not find fulfillment in waxing the kitchen floor.

Betty Friedan articulated many of these concerns in her landmark book, *The Feminine Mystique*, written in 1963. She described the problem that had no name, the emptiness and lack of satisfaction perceived by numerous women despite the acquisition of what they believed to be the American dream: a husband, children, a new home in the suburbs, a station wagon in which to ferry the children and fetch the groceries, and the unprecedented affluence that made possible the purchase of a host of labor-saving devices.[5] In spite of the postwar emphasis on domesticity, women commonly felt they were "nothing but a housewife." In so saying, they captured an essential truth: propaganda notwithstanding, the tasks they performed were valued neither by themselves nor by society. They resented living their lives vicariously through their husbands and their children.

Friedan's book ignited the women's liberation movement, a diffuse protest movement, whose goal has been to obtain equity for women in all spheres of life. Like the suffrage movement before it, this feminist movement grew as a result of women's participation in a number of reform activities. Only the Woman's party had continued in existence from the 1920s, and it was soon to be superseded by new groups. In the late 1950s and 1960s many women joined Women Strike for Peace, an organization composed largely of middle-class housewives led by Dagmar Wilson, concerned about the prospects of nuclear war and radioactivity in the atmosphere. Black and white women had also been active members of the civil-rights movement. The year-long bus boycott in Montgomery, Alabama, was sparked off in 1955 when Rosa Parks, a seamstress and secretary of the local chapter of the National Association for the Advancement of Colored People, refused to give up her seat on a segregated bus to a white man. She and other women were much involved in the formation of the Southern Christian Leadership Conference, and the civil-rights movement in general. Almost half the early civil-rights protesters were women and some, like Fannie Lou Hamer in Mississippi, were prominent as leaders. Women were also involved in the student movement and Vietnam protests of the 1960s. Female activists in these movements frequently found their contributions trivialized and marginalized to the typewriter and coffee pot. Although women constituted well over a third of its membership, no woman held a major position in Students for a Democratic Society (SDS) until 1966. Nonetheless, the radicalism of the 1960s combined with a reaction against the domesticity of the 1950s to produce the feminist movement.

In 1966 Friedan, Aileen Hernandez, and others founded

the National Organization for Women (NOW) to end discrimination against women. Along with more radical groups NOW sought to raise women's consciousness about their common problems and to fight on many fronts for equality. Professional and academic women were involved in the Women's Equity Action League formed in 1968, while Bella Abzug, Gloria Steinem, and Fannie Lou Hamer fought to open politics to women through the Women's Political Caucus. Other, more radical groups such as the Redstockings, formed in 1969, took a more extreme position and tried to have as little to do as possible with men, whom they perceived as the enemy. All the new feminist theorists questioned gender roles, highlighting the relationship between personal life and politics, the systematic discrimination against women in all aspects of American life, and the pervasive nature of sexism. In the last twenty years women's rights groups have focused on discrimination against women in education, the workplace, and retirement and pensions; the negative portrayal of women in the media, in literature, and in language; and the unfair treatment of women by the courts.

As women's employment, especially that of mothers with young children, skyrocketed in the 1970s and 1980s the public provision of child-care facilities became an issue. Married women joining the labor force discovered that traditional assumptions about who did the housework meant that they had two jobs: one in the workplace, the other in the home. As the divorce rate increased, the feminization of poverty alarmed many. Single mothers and women over sixty-five were overrepresented among the ranks of the poor as were minority women. The welfare system refused to provide assistance to families with an unemployed adult male present, which encouraged men to leave their families. Minority women have lower remarriage rates than white women, so this exacerbated African-American poverty in particular.

The civil-rights movement led to the passage of the Civil Rights Act in 1964, which prohibits discrimination in hiring based upon an individual's race, color, religion, sex, or national origin. The act does permit employers to distinguish between potential employees where sex, religion, or national origin (but not race) is a bona fide occupational qualification. The courts have interpreted this clause narrowly, so that average capabilities cannot be used as a means of discriminating against individuals. The argument that women are generally weaker than men and therefore should not be employed in positions where heavy weights might need to be lifted has been rejected on the grounds that the individual should be judged on her own abilities. Protective legislation has been declared invalid, opening up more jobs to women. Given the segregation of employment by sex, feminists have pressured for pay levels to be based on comparable worth rather than just on equal pay for equal work. In the 1980s some cities and firms reevaluated the education needed for certain jobs and the levels of responsibility within them. In the process they have raised women's wages in recognition of their training and the significance of the work they do. The expansion of women's employment opportunities has reduced the supply of labor available for traditionally female occupations and led to some improvement in working conditions and wages for secretaries and nurses among others.

The women's liberation movement also led to Title IX of the Education Amendments of 1972 which prohibited discrimination on the basis of sex in federally funded educational programs, including athletics. This had the effect of increasing the amount of money devoted to women's athletic activities and widening the participation of women in high-school and college athletic programs. Although Title IX has increased the amount of spending on women's athletic programs, it has not eliminated the disparity in funding levels between men's and women's athletics and was gutted by a 1984 Supreme Court decision (*Grove City College* v. *Bell*) which maintained that the nondiscriminatory provisions applied only to the department actually in receipt of federal funds. This prompted Congress to consider legislation to overturn this decision.

Other recent Supreme Court decisions have also closely affected women. In 1973, the Court decided (in *Roe* v. *Wade*) that abortion in the first trimester of pregnancy is a private matter between a woman and her physician. This controversial decision has been opposed by conservative individuals and religious and political groups who maintain that the foetus has a right to life independent of the mother's wishes and needs. They have attempted to overturn *Roe* v. *Wade* and cut off publicly funded abortions for women on welfare. In 1989, the Supreme Court undermined *Roe* v. *Wade* by ruling that states could regulate abortion. This has led Louisiana, among others, to pass highly restrictive abortion legislation. In other states, notably Virginia, voters turned against antichoice politicians.

The attempt on the part of women's groups to include the Equal Rights Amendment in the Constitution has also sparked concerted opposition from conservative groups. Congress passed the Equal Rights Amendment in 1972, but the bill failed to obtain the necessary support in state legislatures, even though a majority of Americans support its main provision: "Men and women shall have equal rights throughout the United States and every place subject to its jurisdiction."

Some women opposed the Equal Rights Amendment because they genuinely feared that changes in the sexual status quo would affect their own lives negatively. Women who devoted themselves to caring for their families worried that husbands would no longer be responsible for the families' financial well-being. One unintended consequence of the women's liberation movement is that judges and legislatures have assumed that in case of divorce the ex-husband did not need to provide support for his ex-wife or children. Other women, including Republican activist Phyllis Schlafly, have combined opposition to women's rights with a wide-ranging conservatism, which has led them to oppose abortion, civil rights for homosexuals, and big government. Although the ERA is not necessarily related to any of these other issues, they have become conflated as threats to the existing social and economic systems.

Even without the Equal Rights Amendment, a limited number of women are moving into nontraditional jobs. There are more women serving in the armed forces, police, and fire-fighting services than ever before. There are now women coal miners, construction workers, and truck drivers. But they comprise only a tiny proportion of women wage earners, frequently encounter serious discrimination and harassment on the job, and do not enjoy the same promotion prospects as men. Women who take these jobs do so because they pay better than traditionally female jobs, but in many cases they have had to fight through the courts in order to gain access to them.

The proportion of women in unions has increased as labor unions began organizing white-collar workers and the service industries, prompted by the decline in their traditional constituencies. The formation of the Coalition of Labor Union Women in 1974 gave women trade unionists a national presence in the labor union movement and made it easier for them to act as a pressure group within their own locals. Unions have supported their women members' concerns for pay equity, an end to sexual harassment, and the provision of adequate child care.

The number of women candidates and elected officials at all levels of government has risen particularly at the local level since the feminist movement, although not all women elected are feminists. Women in the United States now vote in greater numbers than men and tend to be somewhat more liberal in their voting behavior. The Democratic party recognized this in its campaign strategies, selecting Geraldine Ferraro as its vice presidential candidate in 1984. Her presence on the ticket attracted controversy and interest, but not sufficient votes to beat Ronald Reagan. Reagan appointed the first woman to the Supreme Court, Sandra Day O'Connor, but his overall record on feminist issues and female appointments was worse than that of his recent predecessors in the White House. His drastic cutbacks in expenditure on social-welfare programs had a negative impact on women, while George Bush's pledge not to raise taxes suggested that there would be little expansion in federal programs for the disadvantaged, the majority of whom are women and children.

Many feminists view electoral politics, the Supreme Court, and the public arena as crucial for women's well-being. They have protested vigorously when the police and the courts blamed rape victims for somehow attracting the attack upon themselves through their dress, behavior, or previous sexual conduct. The complex issues of rape and family violence seem to be linked by a common factor: the perpetrators feel that they have the right to impose their will upon their victims, regardless of their protests. Feminist theorists such as Andrea Dworkin believe that a society that tolerates pornography showing women and children as the victims of sexual violence sends a message to men that such behavior is acceptable.[6] A major item on the feminist agenda, therefore, is to change men's attitudes towards women, so that gender relations no longer contain suppressed or explicit violence.

Betty Friedan's latest book, *The Second Stage*, posits that feminism has failed women by assuming that the male model of career combined with children somewhere along the way is appropriate in contemporary society. If women put career first, children and family may suffer. Friedan calls on feminists to transcend the polarization between the sexes in order "to achieve the new human wholeness that is the promise of feminism, and get on with solving the concrete, practical problems of living, working and loving as equal persons. This is the personal and political business of the second stage."[7] Friedan believes that, as countless millions of women have discovered, liberation dislocates traditional family life. However, Friedan has failed to root her quest for human wholeness in historical context. Women assumed complete responsibility for household and child care only when men moved out of the home to work in the factories and workshops of the industrial era. With the postindustrial era, women have also moved out of the household, so it seems logical that the functions of the household itself must change.

If liberation means becoming Superwoman, trying effortlessly to blend career, children, spouse, and community activities with no adjustments on the part of society, spouse, or children, then the goals of the women's liberation movement are impossible. But women's liberation means an equal chance for all people to participate fully in life regardless of gender, sexual orientation, race, or class. The rest of society must accommodate groups previously hindered by those characteristics. Although child care has been viewed as an issue for working mothers, society as a whole benefits from equity, equal opportunity, and the social care of children. The labor of the young pays for the retirement and care of the increasing number of elderly. As the birth rate falls, those who have not had access to employment become more important to the smooth running of the economy. Whether inadequate child care, racism, or sexism constrain that access, the effects on an aging society could be devastating.

The feminist agenda for the last decade of the twentieth century includes issues of equity in relationships, the law, employment, education, and political representation. But that agenda goes beyond those concerns to the structure of society, to consider how families and the community will adjust to the challenges of rising employment levels among married women, increased divorce rates, prolonged life spans, and lower birth rates. The devastating poverty of many women supporting children on their own links many of these issues together. Feminists also express concern about the images of women in contemporary life, whether in television, movies, or pornographic magazines. Insofar as these media legitimize violence against women the question of censorship or self-censorship will be raised, querying whether freedom of the press protects depictions of grown men having intercourse with little children or sexually abusing women.

While attitudes toward women's roles in society have changed, feminism still presents challenges to American society in the late twentieth century. The aim of the women's liberation movement is a critical reassessment of American culture in order to achieve a world free from assumptions about gender relations and gender roles. Feminists seek to remove the element of force from relations between the sexes and to return to women control over their sexuality. There is great diversity within the feminist movement, but all feminists agree that gender should not be the fact that dictates one's life chances or life style.

Many men and some women have viewed women's efforts to end gender discrimination as threatening traditional family relationships. Massive social change brings uncertainty in its wake and discomforts those groups who have benefited from the established order. Demographic and economic shifts have interacted with political awareness to transform women's and men's lives and relationships. Rising educational, employment, and divorce levels coupled with falling fertility levels have changed the daily content of women's lives. Over the course of the twentieth century women have moved out of the private world of the home and into the public worlds of work, politics, and sports. They have not achieved equality with men, but few Americans now believe that inequality is either natural or right.

Notes

1. Ida Tarbell, *The Business of Being a Woman* (New York, 1912).

2. Emma Duke, *Infant Mortality: Results of a Field Study in Johnstown, Pa., Based on Births in One Calendar Year* (Washington, D.C., 1915).

3. Ruth Schwartz Cowan, *More Work for Mother: The*

Ironies of Household Technology from the Open Hearth to the Microwave (New York, 1983).

4. Philip Wylie, *A Generation of Vipers* (New York, 1942); Ferdinand Lundberg and Marynia Farnham, *Modern Woman: The Lost Sex* (New York and London, 1947).

5. Betty Friedan, *The Feminine Mystique* (New York, 1963), pp. 7, 14, 27, 37.

6. Andrea Dworkin, *Pornography: Men Possessing Women* (New York, 1981).

7. Friedan, *The Second Stage* (New York, 1981), p. 24.

Bibliography

General introductions to this period and overviews of women in the twentieth century include William Chafe, *The American Woman: Her Changing Social, Economic, and Political Role, 1920–1970* (New York, 1972); Carl Degler, *At Odds: Women and the Family in America from the Revolution to the Present* (New York, 1980); Jacqueline Jones, *Labor of Love, Labor of Sorrow: Black Women, Work and the Family from Slavery to the Present* (New York, 1985); Mary P. Ryan, *Womanhood in America from Colonial Times to the Present* (New York, 1975); Anne Firor Scott, *The Southern Lady: From Pedestal to Politics, 1830–1930* (Chicago, 1970).

For statistical and economic guides to women in the twentieth century see Nancy Barrett, "Women and the Economy," *The American Woman, 1987–1988: A Report in Depth*, ed. Sara E. Rix (New York, 1987), pp. 100–49; Barbara Bergmann, *The Economic Emergence of Women* (New York, 1986); Suzanne M. Bianchi and Daphne Spain, *American Women in Transition* (New York, 1986); William T. Bielby and James M. Barron, "A Woman's Place Is with Other Women," in *Sex Segregation in the Workplace*, ed. Barbara F. Reskin (Washington, D.C., 1984); Claudia Goldin, *Understanding the Gender Gap: An Economic History of American Women* (New York, 1990); Alice Kessler-Harris, *Out to Work* (New York, 1982); Valerie Kincade Oppenheimer, *The Female Labor Force in the United States* (Berkeley, Calif., 1970); United States Bureau of the Census, *Statistics of Women at Work, 1900* (Washington, D.C., 1907); United States Bureau of the Census, *Historical*

Statistics of the United States from Colonial Times to 1970 (Washington, D.C., 1975); United States Department of Labor, *1965 Handbook on Women Workers* (Washington, D.C., 1965).

More specialized studies on women's employment include Margery Davies, *Women's Place Is at the Typewriter* (Philadelphia, 1982); Nancy Schrom Dye, *As Equals and as Sisters: Feminism, the Labor Movement and the Women's Trade Union League of New York* (Columbia, Mo., 1980); Joan Jensen, *With These Hands: Women Working on the Land* (Old Westbury, N.Y., 1981); Mary Lindenstein Walshok, *Blue-Collar Women: Pioneers on the Male Frontier* (Garden City, N.Y., 1981).

For studies of family relations and housewifery see S. J. Kleinberg, *The Shadow of the Mills: Working Class Families in Pittsburgh, 1870–1907* (Pittsburgh, 1989); Ruth Schwartz Cowan, *More Work for Mother: The Ironies of Household Technology from the Open Hearth to the Microwave* (New York, 1983); S. J. Kleinberg, "Escalating Standards: Women, Housework and Household Technology in the Twentieth Century," in *Technology in the Twentieth Century*, ed. Frank J. Coppa and Richard Harmond (Dubuque, Iowa, 1983); Glenna Matthews, *"Just a Housewife": The Rise and Fall of Domesticity in America* (New York, 1987); Helena Z. Lopata, *Occupation: Housewife* (New York, 1971); Robert Lynd and Helen Merrell Lynd, *Middletown* (New York, 1929); Elizabeth Pleck, *Domestic Tyranny* (New York, 1987); Linda Gordon, *Heroes of Their Own Lives: The Politics and History of Family Violence* (New York, 1988).

There are a number of studies focusing on single topics or a narrower time span. On women and war see Karen Anderson, *Wartime Women: Sex Roles, Family Relations, and the Status of Women during World War II* (Westport, Conn., 1981); D'Ann Campbell, *Women at War with America: Private Lives in a Patriotic Era* (Cambridge, Mass., 1985); Maurine Honey, *Creating Rosie the Riveter: Class, Gender, and Propaganda during World War II* (Amherst, Mass., 1984). Chronological studies include Rochelle Gatlin, *American Women since 1945* (Basingstoke, 1987); Lois Scharf and Joan Jensen, *Decades of Discontent: The Women's Movement, 1920–1940* (Westport, Conn., 1983); Susan Ware, *Beyond Suffrage: Women in the New Deal* (Cambridge, Mass., 1981).

Works that focus on women's situation as affected by race and gender include Angela Davis, *Women, Race and Class* (New

York, 1981); Bell Hooks, *Ain't I a Woman: Black Women and Feminism* (Boston, 1981); Gloria T. Hull, Patricia Bell Scott, and Barbara Smith, eds., *All the Women Are White, All the Blacks Are Men, But Some of Us Are Brave: Black Women's Studies* (Old Westbury, N.Y., 1982); Joyce Ladner, *Tomorrow's Tomorrow: The Black Woman* (Garden City, N.Y., 1972); Gerda Lerner, ed., *Black Women in White America* (New York, 1973); Alfredo Mirande and Evangelina Enriquez, *La Chicana: The Mexican-American Woman* (Chicago, 1979); Carol Stack, *All Our Kin* (New York, 1974).

The literature on women, politics, and feminism is voluminous. The books listed represent only a fraction of those available. Kirsten Amundsen, *A New Look at the Silenced Majority: Women and American Democracy* (Englewood Cliffs, N.J., 1977); Susan Brownmiller, *Against Our Will: Men, Women and Rape* (New York, 1976); Ellen Carol Dubois, *Feminism and Suffrage* (Ithaca, N.Y., 1978); Andrea Dworkin, *Pornography: Men Possessing Women* (New York, 1981) and *Right-Wing Women* (New York, 1983); Cynthia Fuchs Epstein, *Women in Law* (New York, 1983); Sara Evans, *Personal Politics: The Roots of Women's Liberation in the Civil Rights Movement and the New Left* (New York, 1979); Shulamith Firestone, *The Dialectic of Sex: The Case for Feminist Revolution* (New York, 1981); Eleanor Flexner, *Century of Struggle: The Woman's Rights Movement in the United States* (Cambridge, Mass., 1975); Betty Friedan, *The Feminine Mystique* (New York, 1963) and *The Second Stage* (New York, 1981); Judith Hole and Ellen Levine, *The Rebirth of Feminism* (New York, 1971); Aileen Kraditor, *Up from the Pedestal: Selected Writings in the History of American Feminism* (Chicago, 1968); Kate Millett, *Sexual Politics* (New York, 1970); Robin Morgan, *Sisterhood Is Powerful* (New York, 1970); Anne Firor Scott and Andrew McKay Scott, *One Half the People: The Fight for Woman Suffrage* (Philadelphia, 1975).

9

Black Americans in the Twentieth Century

Neil A. Wynn

"The history of American democracy," wrote Ralph Barton Perry in 1944, "is a gradual realization, too slow for some, and too rapid for others, of the implications of the Declaration of Independence."[1] Until fairly recently the history of African-Americans in the twentieth century often echoed this view and presented the black experience as a slow but steady, and probably inevitable, movement from discrimination and segregation toward equality and integration, culminating in the period of civil-rights protest and reform from the mid-1950s to the late 1960s. This story of progress might end with the example of Jesse Jackson, the black candidate for the Democratic party's presidential nomination in 1984 and 1988, who triumphantly announced "We can move from the slave ship to the championship, from the guttermost to the uttermost, from the outhouse to the courthouse, from the state house to the White House."[2] However, more than twenty years after the death of Martin Luther King, the achievements of the protest movements and legislation of the 1960s are being reassessed, and the assumption of a history of progress is being questioned and qualified with them.

If, as the young black educator and emerging leader W. E. B. Du Bois could write in 1903, "the problem of the twentieth century is the problem of the color line," then to some extent that problem still remains. Jackson's candidacy and relative success in the 1988 campaign notwithstanding, the optimism of earlier decades has been replaced by a growing pessimism and an awareness of the continuity of racism through American history. Nonetheless, certain aspects of black life have clearly changed, and so have prevailing attitudes among whites. The problem is to assess the extent of these changes and determine their causes.

While any notion of a simple upward linear development is now questioned, it is still possible to divide twentieth-century black history into four rough periods or phases: the 1890s to 1930s, 1930s to mid-1950s, 1950s to late 1960s, and 1960s through to the present. Each of these different periods charts something of the complex interaction of black and white Americans amid changing social, economic, and political conditions. The first period, from the 1890s through to the 1930s, may, as David G. Nielson has suggested, have been when "modern black America came into being" in terms of social and demographic changes and black attitudes,[3] but it saw little in the way of political recognition of the black plight and much to indicate the persistence of entrenched white racism. The second period, from the 1930s to the 1950s, through a combination of depression, reform, war, and political factors, witnessed further socioeconomic changes in the position of African-Americans, a growth in support for black civil rights among some whites, a degree of recognition for blacks at the federal level, and raised expectations of further change. When those expectations were frustrated, the third phase—of civil-rights protest and increasing militance—began, leading to the legislation, but also the racial violence, of the 1960s. The final period, from the end of the 1960s through to the 1990s, has been marked by both conservative white reaction and an improvement in the position and status of middle-class blacks. As a result direct black protest has been displaced by activity in the political arena. Increasingly, however, the 1980s and 1990s have also witnessed a growing awareness that the situation for African-Americans at the lower end of the social and economic scale may be little different in some respects from that at the start of the century.

Clearly, the response of blacks to their situation was not constant. Varying in time and place, it swung from apparent acquiescence and acceptance through to challenge and protest and beyond to outright rejection. It has been said that blacks were most optimistic about integration when whites seemed most sympathetic, and more pessimistic and inclined to separation when whites were hostile, but always there was to be something of an ambiguity about black attitudes. Richard Wright, a leading black author of the 1930s and 1940s, explained the black situation in his well-known essay "How 'Bigger' Was Born":

> . . . because . . . blacks were so *close* to the very civilization which sought to keep them out, because they could not *help* but react in some way to its incentives and prizes, and because the very tissue of their consciousness received its tone and timbre from the strivings of that dominant civilization, oppression spawned among them a myriad variety of reactions, reaching from outright blind rebellion to a sweet, otherworldly submissiveness.[4]

It is worth remembering, too, that the black population rarely acted in total unison. Just like any other group of people, they could be, and sometimes were, divided along lines of class and status, town and country, North and South. Just as there have been black radicals, so, as Wright suggested, there have also been black conservatives.

Black spokesmen have always had to face the difficulty of mediating between black wishes and white concessions. At the beginning of the twentieth century, black leaders were in fact in conflict over directions and strategies to follow in response to their second-class place in America. The dominant voice was still that of Booker T. Washington, the founder and principal of Tuskegee Institute in Alabama. Washington, a former slave, had seemingly counseled a policy of accommodation in his famous Atlanta Exposition address in 1895, urging that blacks should concentrate on self-help and vocational development rather than social arrangements, voting rights, or politics. It is hard to see what else he might have said in the South and survived, and his position did win him white financial assistance and considerable influence—some of which he used secretly to support legal cases testing discrimination. Nonetheless, before his death in 1915 Washington was increasingly being challenged by black leaders of the growing northern, urban black communities, of whom W. E. B. Du Bois was to become the most famous.

For most of the nine million Americans of African descent who constituted almost 12 percent of the population of the United States in 1900, the outlook for the new century must have seemed bleak. With the end of Reconstruction and the "redemption" of the South at the close of the 1870s, racism had been institutionalized in a pattern of living that ensured that blacks were exploited economically, segregated socially, and increasingly disenfranchised politically. This subordinate position was reinforced throughout the South by violence or the threat of violence—over 750 lynchings were recorded in the first decade of the twentieth century alone—and fear was a constant part of black life.

The situation in the North was only marginally better for the 10 percent of blacks who lived there. Most were confined to separate areas of towns and cities, worked in menial jobs, experienced some discrimination, and were also increasingly likely to be the victims of violence. Throughout America, North and South, white attitudes toward blacks hardened and were sustained by the expressions of racial difference and white superiority. Such views were articulated in numerous books ranging from Charles Carroll's *The Negro Is a Beast* (1900) through to Madison Grant's *Passing of the Great Race* (1916). On stage, and increasingly on screen, blacks were portrayed at best as foolish minstrel figures in the Sambo mold and at worst, as in D. W. Griffith's film *Birth of a Nation* (1915), as threatening, sexually depraved monsters.

While Progressivism did nothing specifically for blacks, the general mood of reform encouraged Du Bois and others, like Monroe Trotter, the editor of the *Boston Guardian*, and James H. Hayes of the National Negro Suffrage League, to call for more positive action than the "accommodationism" of Washington. Another more powerful cause, however, was the disillusionment with the moderate approach in a period of mounting race violence and deteriorating conditions for blacks generally. In 1905 twenty-nine black delegates, the majority from the North, met together at Niagara to call for an end to racial discrimination in America. In 1909 this small group joined with whites shocked by the riot in Springfield, Illinois, the previous year in which two black people had been killed in a conference on the Negro question, and the following year formed the National Association for the Advancement of Colored People. Oswald Garrison Villard, grandson of abolitionist William Lloyd Garrison, was the NAACP's first president, and Du Bois became secretary and editor of the journal, *Crisis.*

The NAACP was to be the most important civil-rights organization until the late 1950s, and its campaign to end discrimination by means of court action was to have a major influence on later events. In the early years, however, it had little direct impact on racial policies. The new organization could do little to prevent the spread of segregation in the federal civil service under the Wilson administration, nor in the end, despite its initial optimism, was it able to do much to end discrimination during World War I.

When America entered World War I in 1917, most black Americans responded loyally. The majority of black leaders saw the war as an opportunity, as Du Bois wrote in the NAACP's magazine *Crisis,* "to emphasize their American citizenship." While he urged blacks "to forget [their] special grievances,"[5] others saw it as an ideal moment to press their claims for equality. Little, however, was done to meet those claims. The 400,000 blacks who served in the army were in segregated regiments, largely confined to noncombatant roles; those who fought at the front did so beside French troops. Despite awards for valor from the French government, black servicemen were not generally recognized as heroes back home but were instead either despised or feared. Returning black troops were often the targets of race violence, and at least ten black soldiers were lynched in 1919.

There was a widespread outbreak of racial conflict at the end of the war, and while this in part reflected the general instability of the immediate postwar years, it was also a reaction to a significant change in black demography—the mass migration of blacks from the South. The extent of the Great Migration has often been exaggerated, but between 1910 and 1920 the black population of the North rose by almost 700,000, and cities like Chicago, Detroit, and Philadelphia experienced an enormous influx of black southern migrants. This movement was encouraged by the job opportunities that opened with the boom in war industries and the decline in immigration, coupled with the push of poverty, deprivation, and suffering in the South. With the imposition of immigration controls and continued industrial growth this movement continued in the 1920s, and by 1930 almost one million blacks had left the South.

The consequences of this shift in population were enormous. Although 75 percent of African-Americans still remained in the South, the focus in race relations had begun to shift to northern centers. Equally significant, a black working class was being formed as African-Americans moved into the meat-packing, steelmaking, and auto industries rather than just the domestic service work that had previously been their main occupation in the North. In 1900 over 50 percent of the black labor force worked in agriculture and 33 percent were in domestic service; by 1930 these figures had fallen to 44 percent and 20 percent respectively, while employment in industry over the same period rose from 7 percent to 22 percent. Earnings, educational opportunities, and social conditions often improved too, but equally, blacks now confronted a whole host of new problems.

If the northern ghettos had been evident before 1914, they became more widespread and obvious during and after the war as a result of the endemic prejudice faced by black newcomers. Segregated in overcrowded and poor areas of the industrial cities, the migrants were resented by whites because of pressure on housing and competition for employment. Both factors contributed to the race riot in East St. Louis in 1917 in which forty-seven people were reported killed, and to the massive outbreak in Chicago in 1919 in which thirty-eight died. But there were race riots elsewhere too—some twenty-five in total in 1919, the locales ranging from Longview, Texas, to the national capital itself. While there were some instances of black violence against whites, if only in self-defense, most of the riots reflected a desire among whites to keep black Americans "in their place." Although the spate of rioting was to subside, racial violence continued throughout the twenties and more than two hundred blacks were lynched in that decade.

It may be hard to discern any note of progress in this period, but significant changes had occurred. The northern centers were to provide the locus for what Du Bois called "a new, radical Negro spirit" born in France and in the postwar reactions of whites. For Du Bois the war marked a growing realization that political and social equality would not be easily won but would come only as a result of "grim, determined, everyday strife."[6] This spirit of militance was evident in the black resistance to white attacks during the riots in St. Louis and Washington, D.C.; it was also apparent in the surge in membership of the NAACP—from 10,000 in 1918 to 62,000 in 1919.

While the experience of World War I served to sharpen some blacks' efforts to achieve equal integration into American society, for others it fostered a sense of disillusionment and support for separatist movements, the most significant of which was Marcus Garvey's Universal Negro Improvement Association (UNIA). Garvey, a West Indian, arrived in the United States in 1916. He had hoped to meet Booker T. Washington whom he greatly admired, but the Wizard of Tuskegee died the year before. In some ways this was fortunate, for while Garvey accepted notions of self-help and economic enterprise he did so in an altogether different fashion. Rejecting any hint of accommodation or subservience, he preached race pride and the solidarity of all African peoples. With the cry "Up, you mighty race!", he remained in New York to establish an organization that was to have followers in America and the West Indies and even an influence in parts of Africa through the medium of the newspaper *Negro World*. Actual membership of the UNIA was always disputed: Garvey claimed millions, his detractors suggested thousands. While paid-up members probably only numbered between 25,000 and 50,000, there were doubtless many more who followed or were influenced by the charismatic leader. The UNIA had seven hundred branches in thirty-eight states including the South, but its strength lay in the appeal to the new black northern urban working population. Through parades, conventions, colorful uniforms, and a variety of organizations ranging from the Black Cross to the ill-fated Black Star Shipping Line, Garvey mobilized black Americans in a movement that combined economic, religious, and cultural nationalism in a manner not to be repeated until the 1960s.

Using the "Back to Africa" slogan to create race pride, and using religious language and metaphors, Garvey gave his movement an almost messianic dimension. Despite the opposition of "respectable" blacks and the business failings that led to his jailing for fraud in 1923 and deportation in 1927, various splinter groups survived in different cities and formed groups such as the Peace Movement of Ethiopia, the Ethiopian Pacific Movement, the Brotherhood of Liberty for Black People, and the Black Muslims.

Although in many ways a unique phenomenon, Garvey's movement was also part of a much more general mood among black Americans. Even his most severe critics shared some common ground with the self-proclaimed president of Africa.

Black socialists like A. Philip Randolph regarded Garvey as a menace and urged "Garvey Must Go," yet Randolph was just as determined an opponent of white racism and also stressed black self-help in the union he built up through the twenties, the Brotherhood of Sleeping Car Porters, or later in 1941 in the March on Washington Movement. His aim, though, was integration, not separation. Similarly, Du Bois despised Garvey for his vulgarity and bombast, and described the West Indian as fat, ugly, and "the most dangerous enemy of the Negro race in America" because of his separatist views. However, Du Bois also stressed black unity in Pan-Africanism, and eventually he, too, argued that blacks must find their own salvation even to the point of developing their own economic institutions. This apparent change of direction caused a rift with the NAACP and Du Bois resigned in 1934. He subsequently moved further leftward and at the same time maintained his Pan-Africanism. He died in Africa in 1963, more respected there than in his own country.

These differing views, while revealing the internal debate within the black community, were also indicative of the vitality of black life. Their common elements reveal the awakening of self-awareness and race consciousness which the experience of war, the move northward, and following disillusionment seemed to bring. This mood was also made manifest in the literary–cultural movement known as the Harlem Renaissance which sprang up in the twenties.

If, as one of the most famous of this group of writers, Langston Hughes, suggested, the Renaissance had little to do with "ordinary Negroes," but was confined to what his friend Wallace Thurman called the "niggerati," it nonetheless shared many of the concerns of less elevated movements such as the UNIA. While the young black writers threw off old racial stereotypes and wrote proudly as blacks, they also asked "What is Africa to me?", and debated "The Negro in Art: How Shall He Be Portrayed?", and often came up with different answers. Hughes himself wrote of ordinary blacks and used dialect and blues idioms in his poetry—and was criticized at the time for doing so; others stressed the exotic and emphasized the African past. In part this reflected the demands of the audience: the Renaissance was often dependent upon white patronage and interest— "the Negro was in vogue" as whites sought to escape from or rebel against what they saw as a repressive or sterile mainstream culture. The many whites who flocked to Harlem to listen to jazz at the Cotton Club or to watch black vaudeville rarely had any appreciation of the realities of black life and indeed often perpetuated stereotypes of blacks as joyful, primitive, and sensual. Some white writers, however, went beyond this and used black subject matter in a sympathetic and sensitive fashion: Carl Van Vechten's *Nigger Heaven* (1926), and Eugene O'Neill's plays *The Emperor Jones* (1921) and *All God's Chillun Got Wings* (1923) being among the best examples.

If, as the black scholar Alain Locke suggested in *The New Negro* (1925), African-American writers had come of age in the twenties, they still had a long way to go before they were accepted by the general reading public. Equally, the black population as a whole was still a long way from acceptance as equals by whites. The differences beten Garvey, Du Bois, and others, or between different literary schools, were part of an internal debate among blacks and as such hardly impinged upon white consciousness. Old racial stereotypes still prevailed, and were carried over into the new media. The *Amos 'n' Andy* radio show perpetuated comic images of blacks—played by whites—and in the movies blacks were generally portrayed in menial roles of the Stepin Fetchit variety. The film celebrated as the first talkie appropriately had white performer Al Jolson appear in a black minstrel role singing "Mammy." Blues and jazz were still largely confined to speakeasies and "race records"—separate labels produced for a black market.

Blacks did not find any greater recognition at the level of national politics. Despite meeting with James Weldon Johnson, the leader of the NAACP, President Harding did nothing to indicate that a return to Republican government would change official policies. Segregation increased in the federal civil service, and the president said publicly that he stood uncompromisingly against any suggestion of social equality. Neither he nor his successors took any steps to prevent lynching, and antilynching measures were allowed to die in Congress.

The situation grew worse through the decade. In an attempt to capitalize on Democratic defections in 1928 and build a political base for the Republican party in the South, President Hoover "appointed almost no blacks to federal office, closed down the Negro Division of the Republican National Committee, and made fewer public statements on race than any other president in the century."7 Already some black voters and organizations such as the National Democratic Negro Conference Committee had cause to consider a change in political allegiance, but when faced with a choice between the bad and the worse in the form of a Democratic party dominated by white southerners, the vast majority of black voters remained within the Republican fold.

The picture at the level of local politics was not quite as bleak. One consequence of the northern migration was an increase in black influence in urban politics. In Chicago, where neither major party had a clear majority, the black vote was crucial and ensured victory for Republican Mayor Bill Thompson. In return, black Chicagoans, who represented 7 percent of the population, held 25 percent of postal jobs and 6 percent of civil-service posts. In 1928 the black ward organizer Oscar De-Priest was elected to Congress, the first black congressman since 1901. Blacks also held a variety of local offices in Cleveland, Detroit, New York City, and Philadelphia.

Such gains as these offered only little hope for the black electorate in the 1920s. In the next decade, however, there was to be significant change. During both the 1930s and the 1940s African-Americans gained in influence at national and local levels, made significant legislative and economic advances, and shifted in political affiliation. Paradoxically, a period of depression and war was to bring greater progress than at any time previously.

That the thirties and forties should be marked by advances in race relations was far from clear at their onset. On the contrary, the crash and Depression had an even worse effect on blacks than whites. Last hired and first fired, blacks suffered an unemployment rate twice as high as among whites. National figures suggested that 50 percent of blacks were unemployed, but in some places the situation was worse. In 1935 65 percent of black workers in Atlanta and 80 percent in Norfolk, Virginia, were on relief. Even those in work or on the land suffered as wages were pushed down or crop yields fell. Two-thirds of black cotton growers in the South made no profits at all from their crops, and they and many of their city counterparts were reduced to scavenging and begging in order to avoid starvation.

The Depression not only intensified the poverty of African-Americans, but also brought an increase in the overt racism they experienced. In 1930 white extremists in Atlanta urged "No Jobs for Niggers Until Every White Man Has a Job," and the *New Republic* reported in July 1931 that "dust had been blown from the shotgun, the whip, and the noose, and Ku Klux practices were being resumed in the certainty that dead men not only tell no tales but create vacancies."[8] The number of lynchings rose in the early thirties from eight in 1932 to twenty-eight in 1933, fifteen in 1934, and twenty in 1935.

Driven by violence and the collapse of tenant farming, or by natural disaster such as the flooding of Mississippi, many southern blacks migrated to the city and the North. Over 100,000 black sharecroppers left the land, and by 1940 over 36 percent of the southern black population was urban. Nationally 48 percent of the black population was classed as urban, and despite the high unemployment, 400,000 blacks still moved to northern cities. This was only half the number of the previous decade, but the migration speeded up again during the war years. By 1940 77 percent of blacks lived in the South; by 1950 this had fallen to 68 percent, while the black urban population had risen to 62 percent.

This continued demographic shift undoubtedly contributed to the growing political recognition of African-Americans, but it was to be a combination of forces that marked this as a period of dramatic change. The return of a Democratic administration in 1932 did not initially augur well for blacks. Franklin Roosevelt had never spoken on behalf of blacks nor was he prepared to jeopardize southern support by doing so once in the White House. However, the general humanitarian emphasis of the New Deal almost inevitably meant that blacks would eventually feel some benefit. The return of liberal reformers and social workers to Washington, D.C., and their concern for the "forgotten man," helped to place the plight of African-Americans on the agenda. Individuals like Secretary of the Interior Harold Ickes, Secretary of Labor Frances Perkins, Emergency Relief Administrator Harry Hopkins, and Will Alexander of the Farm Security Administration appointed blacks to various advisory positions in their agencies, creating a "black cabinet" of people like Mary McLeod Bethune, William Hastie, and Robert C. Weaver. Eleanor Roosevelt also proved to be enormously sympathetic to the black cause and personally provided access to the president for black leaders. In 1939 when the Daughters of the

American Revolution refused to allow the black singer Marian Anderson to perform at Constitution Hall, Mrs. Roosevelt publicly resigned her membership and helped to organize an alternative concert at the Lincoln Memorial.

While such gestures had an enormous impact on black morale, New Deal legislation brought some direct assistance although the picture was uneven and marked by persistent discrimination. The administration of relief and recovery agencies was very much in the hands of local officials and subject to prevailing racial attitudes. Relief payments in the South were consistently lower for blacks than whites, and agencies like the TVA and NRA excluded blacks from many positions and permitted discriminatory levels of pay. The Civilian Conservation Corps (CCC) initially only offered 3 percent of its places to blacks, and although this was increased to 6 percent after protests, black workers served in segregated camps. The NRA, in setting minimum wage levels, also unintentionally encouraged some employers to replace black labor with machines. For many blacks NRA stood for "Negroes Ruined Again." Federal policy generally, but the Agricultural Adjustment Administration (AAA) in particular, also contributed to the collapse of tenant farming in the South and so seriously affected the plight of blacks.

However, as Raymond Wolters observed, "Despite its deficiencies the New Deal offered Negroes more in material benefits and recognition than had any administration since the era of Reconstruction."[9] Over one million blacks held jobs on the Works Progress Administration (WPA), 30 percent of black families received federal relief, and one-third of federal housing and almost one-quarter of FSA loans went to blacks. The political consequences were obvious: in 1932, 72 percent of black voters had supported Hoover; in 1936, 75 percent voted for FDR. It was with this development in the 1930s that blacks became important members of the new Democratic alliance, and their influence was to grow to the point that eventually in the 1980s Jesse Jackson could declare that hands that had picked cotton could now pick the president.

The black vote was not given then (nor in the eighties) uncritically or without reservation. Black organizations, encouraged by the more receptive mood, lobbied continually against discrimination within the New Deal and in the country at large. The thirties produced a greater militance and organization as once again apparent disadvantages produced positive developments. Few civil-rights bodies were able to maintain their income or membership at previous levels, and both the NAACP and National Urban League (NUL) had to struggle to survive in the years immediately after the crash. Increasingly such groups were forced to cooperate, and also to direct their attention more to economic than to political or social matters. This change of emphasis brought considerable debate within the NAACP, but the wider concerns and more aggressive approach were to have results as membership, which had slumped to 21,000 in 1929, rose to 54,000 in 1939.

Part of the new approach of the civil-rights organizations was to encourage black trade unionism. Both NAACP and NUL campaigned to end discrimination in the AFL and supported CIO membership drives. Within the unions A. Philip Randolph, head of the Brotherhood of Sleeping Car Porters, capitalized upon federal legislation to build up his union and gain recognition in the AFL. Despite his constant pressure, the AFL still tolerated segregated union locals and did little to extend black membership. The industrial unions that formed the CIO promoted a much more egalitarian policy and with the aid of other groups were able to organize black steel workers, auto workers, meat packers, and longshoremen. Although there was always some white resistance and black reluctance, even after American entry in the war, by 1945 700,000 blacks were union members and they constituted 5 percent of total union membership.

Unions were only a part of the wider support for civil-rights causes that emerged during the Depression as a variety of white organizations widened their programs in the more radical climate of the times. While groups like the American Civil Liberties Union lobbied to end discrimination in government or supported antilynching legislation, individual whites joined pickets, protests, and demonstrations in support of black causes. Most notable of these causes was the case of the Scottsboro boys, nine black youths charged with raping two white women on a freight train in Alabama in 1931. An all-white jury found the youths guilty despite the flimsy evidence, and all but the youngest were sentenced to death. Communist groups, seeking to recruit black members, seized upon the case and turned it into an international cause célèbre. Other bodies, including the NAACP, joined with them and were able to save the lives of the Scottsboro boys and secure their eventual release.

Crimes, real or supposed, involving interracial sex could still result in horrific consequences. In 1934 Claude Neal, a black man arrested in Marianna, Florida, for the murder of his white mistress was seized from a jail by a mob in Alabama where he had been sent for safety. After hours of brutal torture he was finally killed. Similar outrages continued through into the postwar years, but legal penalties were also exacted upon blacks in a manner reflecting prejudice: "Of the 455 men executed for rape between 1930 and 1969 in the United States, 405 or 89 percent were black."[10]

Such facts and figures are salutary reminders that whatever the impressions of progress, discrimination, prejudice, and violence were to remain a feature of American society well beyond the 1930s. Perhaps nowhere was this more evident than in the field of employment. As America became the "Arsenal of Democracy" after 1940 its economy began to recover in response to Allied needs. Blacks, however, remained last hired and first fired, and their numbers unemployed stayed constant while those for whites fell dramatically. Faced with overt discrimination in defense industries, African-Americans immediately began to protest. In 1941 A. Philip Randolph initiated a call for a march of 10,000 blacks on Washington that was to secure presidential action in the form of an executive order prohibiting discrimination in defense plants. Black lobbying also won concessions in military policy, and segregation in the armed forces was to be severely challenged by the forces of war.

The mood of black militance never totally disappeared even after Pearl Harbor. Fighting for a "double V"—victory at home and abroad—the black press and civil-rights organizations used the war against fascism to point up the contradictions between American practices and principles. One man, Winfred Lynn, refused to serve in a segregated army until forced to do so by the courts. Some groups went further and refused to participate altogether—the Black Muslim leader Elijah Muhammad and several followers were jailed for draft resistance. Frustration with continued discrimination led to race violence in Harlem in 1943, while white resistance to change led to riots in a number of other cities. Such outbreaks served to highlight the issue of race, and many whites began publicly to question American race relations in "the American century" and to ponder what Gunnar Myrdal called in his world-famous study published in 1944, *An American Dilemma.*

These trends continued when the war ended. As Malcolm X was to remark, "Stalin kept up the pressure put on by Hitler,"[11] and while America's overseas commitments helped to ensure almost full employment, its international position enabled civil-rights campaigners to insist on democracy at home. The reintroduction of the draft in 1947 brought the threat of a civil-disobedience campaign from A. Philip Randolph unless segregation in the armed forces ended. This was one of the factors that forced President Truman to order the beginning of integration, and political considerations coupled with a genuine concern led the president to establish a committee on civil rights and to speak out against race violence.

As the Cold War progressed the climate of opinion became less conducive to open struggle and protest. On the one hand continued progress in employment and the inclusion of civil rights as a major issue in national politics in 1948 encouraged optimism, while on the other hand the mood of anticommunism restrained liberal/progressive tendencies. Equal rights were too easily equated with radicalism in the McCarthyite period. The great black singer and actor Paul Robeson was labeled a "black Stalin" by the House Un-American Activities Committee in 1948 because of his communist sympathies, and he was denied a passport for ten years. In 1951 W. E. B. Du Bois, who had stood for election as a candidate of the left-wing American Labor party and spoke against the war in Korea, was arrested for aiding a foreign power, but was acquitted. He left the United States in 1961 and died in Ghana two years later. Civil-rights organizations, like trade unions, deliberately worked to avoid being charged with communist sympathies, and so became more conservative in outlook. Nonetheless, the NAACP continued its less public legal struggle to remove segregation from American life. As a result a succession of Supreme Court rulings was issued through the 1940s against white primaries, segregation in housing, interstate transport, and higher education, and in 1954 in *Brown v. Board of Education, Topeka,* the Supreme Court declared segregated schools to be unconstitutional. In 1955 the Court urged that integration be implemented with "all deliberate speed."

These landmark decisions had enormous consequences.

Initially African-Americans were most encouraged, and expectations of a dramatic transformation of American society seemed fully justified. The southern white response, however, did much to crush those hopes. While one hundred southern congressmen issued a manifesto sanctioning defiance of the laws, local politicians put resistance into practice. When obstruction, intimidation, and other methods failed to prevent the admission of black children, the authorities simply closed the public schools as they did in Little Rock, Arkansas, from 1958 to 1959. In 1960 not one school in South Carolina, Georgia, Alabama, Mississippi, or Louisiana had been integrated.

The issue of the desegregation of schools had two mutually reinforcing effects. First, it sparked off a mood of widespread resistance among whites to any racial changes at all, and was followed by a revival of groups such as the Ku Klux Klan and White Citizens' Councils. Second, it heightened the sense of disappointment and frustration among blacks and strengthened their insistence upon equality. Other factors increased this tendency. The youth of many participants in civil-rights protest pointed to a generation with different experiences and expectations from their elders: theirs was a sense not so much of progress as of failure to live up to wartime or Cold War rhetoric or to keep pace with changes elsewhere. Television not only enabled blacks to see what was happening within different parts of the United States, but also kept them abreast of events outside. The wave of decolonization that brought independence to thirty-six African states between 1957 and 1965 led black writer James Baldwin to observe acidly that the whole of Africa would be free before black Americans could even get a cup of coffee. Such restrictions were increasingly galling to a black population that had moved off the land and into the cities in search of a better life—between 1940 and 1960 the percentage of blacks in farm labor fell from 32 to 8 percent, and by 1960 80 percent of the black population was urban. Although almost 50 percent of blacks now lived in the North or West, it was in the South that protest began, and led to the civil rights revolt that dominated America in the late 1950s and 1960s.

The bus boycott that began in Montgomery, Alabama, in 1955 when Rosa Parks was arrested for failing to give up her seat to a white person was not the first to occur, but it was an instance when uncompromising whites met determined and united opposition from blacks with a strong organizational base and a charismatic leader. Rosa Parks was herself an active member of the local NAACP and the Women's Political Council which was active in planning the boycott; E. D. Nixon, the early leader of the Montgomery Improvement Association, was also head of the local NAACP and Brotherhood of Sleeping Car Porters. Nixon stood down in favor of the newly arrived young minister Martin Luther King, who emerged from the success of Montgomery to become the president of the new Southern Christian Leadership Conference (SCLC) and, of course, a civil-rights leader of national prominence.

King's role has been subject to considerable reevaluation since his assassination in 1968. Internationally recognized, voted *Time* magazine's Man of the Year, and awarded the Nobel Peace Prize in 1964, King was to be elevated almost to sainthood amid the riots and eulogies which followed his death. Later, in the cold light of hindsight and with an awareness of how much still remains unaccomplished, a more critical view emerged aided by FBI revelations about King's personal life, and by claims for recognition from other black leaders.

There is little doubt that King had personal failings (who has not?), and yet he also had enormous strengths that outweighed everything else. Despite his doubts, uncertainties, fears (he was jailed nineteen times, his home was dynamited, he was stabbed and attacked on several other occasions), and in the knowledge that the FBI was using wiretapped information to gain leverage over him, King showed great courage in maintaining his assault on discrimination. A great orator, he combined religious and emotional appeal with intellectual and rational argument not only to move masses, but to hold together a ramshackle movement that defied organization. His famous "I have a dream" speech at the march on Washington in 1963 remains a powerful and moving expression of African-American hopes: his letter from a Birmingham jail justifying his actions to critical white clergymen is an impressive statement of Christian activism. Through his speeches and personal charisma King was able to appeal to whites and yet also maintain a large black following in a way that no black leader was able to do before or since.

But King was more than the "great exhorter." He was a shrewd tactician who carefully and sometimes ruthlessly planned campaigns, learned from his mistakes, and exploited confrontational situations. Although his willingness to negotiate or compromise with local or federal officials brought criticism from more militant groups, it also secured important victories. The successes in Montgomery, Birmingham (1963), and even Selma (1965), helped pave the way for the integration of public facilities in the South and the passage of civil-rights legislation in 1964 and 1965. Just before his death King was moving beyond the issues of race to attack the fundamental problems of economic inequality affecting *all* the dispossessed. Coupled with his increasingly outspoken opposition to the war in Vietnam, this new stance alienated some whites, including President Johnson, and more conservative black leaders such as Roy Wilkins of the NAACP. Nonetheless, in broadening his appeal he was to pioneer the route followed by later black leaders such as Jesse Jackson.

Of course, King and the SCLC were not alone and it would be ridiculous to ascribe every success to a single individual. As one participant pointed out, "the movement made Martin rather than Martin made the movement."[12] Indeed the fact that King had a power base in the southern black population was one of the unique features of the SCLC. But other groups helped arouse that constituency too and may even claim to have taken the initiative in starting positive action to confront segregation, rather than reaction as in the case of the boycotts. The sit-ins and freedom rides begun by the Student Nonviolent Coordinating Committee (SNCC) and Congress of Racial Equality (CORE) mobilized an enormous number of people in confrontational protest and voter registration drives. From the first sit-in in Greensboro, North Carolina, in 1960 the movement rapidly spread to one hundred cities in twenty states in 1961 and involved over 50,000 people; in 1963 there were more than 10,000 demonstrations of one sort or another against race prejudice.

Members of other movements were often resentful of King's personal domination and his moderate policies. Frustrated by lack of success and angered by continued violence, both SNCC and CORE demanded a more militant approach. In 1966 members at these groups began to call for "Black Power," an ambiguous and emotional cry for race pride, self-defense, and self-determination in the face of persistent white racism and violent attacks such as the murder of James Chaney, Andrew Goodman, and Michael Schwerner, three civil-rights workers killed in Mississippi in 1964. Black Power was the response of individuals impatient with reforms that provided too little too late. Although it originated in the South, the slogan had particular appeal in the North where the civil-rights movement had little effect on a deteriorating black situation.

While King and others could confront and expose de jure segregation and overt prejudice in the South, they found it less easy to deal with the de facto segregation and insidious discrimination of the ghetto. When King tried to mobilize a direct-action campaign against slum housing and poverty in Chicago in 1966 he faced black apathy, white intransigence, and the powerful political machine of Mayor Daley, and was forced to retreat. It was the only time SCLC campaigned outside the South.

The mood in the black northern centers was much more inclined toward disillusionment, despair, and violence than in the South, and more militant bodies than the SCLC had stronger appeal. Many of those blacks who had migrated north had seen the promised land and were disappointed. Blacks entered the industrial cities as whites were moving out to the suburbs, taking jobs and tax revenues with them. Prejudice and economic inequality restricted black movement, and thus blacks were confined to decaying inner-city areas experiencing industrial decline.

Concentrated in slum areas of impoverished cities, the black urban population faced a rise in unemployment that compounded their misery. Black unemployment reached 12.6 percent in 1958 and rarely fell below 10 percent through the sixties—and was always double white unemployment rates. Statistics revealed that the advances made in the 1940s had not continued—African-Americans were primarily concentrated in poorer jobs with lower incomes. In 1960 20 percent of whites and 9 percent of blacks had skilled jobs, while 48 percent of black males were in semiskilled or laboring categories. Black women fared little better: although the gap between black and white female earnings narrowed considerably, black women were still in the lowest categories of work, and over one-third were still employed as domestics. With 50 percent of black families living in poverty, and unemployment among black youth at more than 20 percent, it is not surprising that many northern blacks rejected King's integrationist "dream," but turned instead to the separatism of black nationalist and religious groups.

The 1960s saw the dramatic rise to prominence of the Nation of Islam or Black Muslims. Though they were still led by Elijah Muhammad, it was the head of the New York Temple, Malcolm X, who projected the Muslims into the headlines with his fiery speeches and blistering attacks on white society. Malcolm was severely critical of Martin Luther King and the non-violent revolution which he disparagingly referred to as the "Negro revolution." While Malcolm better represented the anger of the ghetto dweller, he was never able to mobilize an organized movement, and although membership of the Muslims rose his own personal success led to a split with Elijah Muhammad in 1964. Shortly afterwards Malcolm established the Organization of Afro-American Unity, a body reminiscent of Garvey's UNIA, but in 1965 Malcolm was assassinated. He had, however, radicalized other blacks and inspired other movements.

The Black Panther party developed out of the Black Power movement and shared some of Malcolm X's views. Formed in the postwar ghetto of Oakland, California, by Bobby Seale and Huey Newton in 1966, the Panthers demanded black self-determination, full employment, and the right to self-defense. They became known for their resistance to police attacks and for the open display of weapons and an increasingly revolutionary language. By 1968 they had over five thousand members nationally and had recruited some of the former leaders of SNCC. In the event the Panthers were to be victims of their own militant rhetoric and white repression, and they were consumed in the flames of the race riots that swept America in the late 1960s.

The riots began in 1964 in Chicago and New York, exploded in Watts, Los Angeles, in 1965 when thirty-four people died, and continued through the long hot summers of the decade. In 1967 sixty-five cities experienced riots, and in 1968, following King's murder, there were more than one hundred riots. Between 1964 and 1972 over 250 people were killed and millions of dollars' worth of damage was done in these eruptions of black anger and bitterness. The National Advisory Commission on Civil Disorders (Kerner Commission) located the causes of the riots firmly in the socioeconomic environment of racial deprivation, and stated categorically, "White racism is essentially responsible for the explosive mixture which has been accumulating in our cities since the end of World War II."[13] Nonetheless, it was tempting to blame groups that used militant language and adopted slogans such as "Burn, baby, burn!" The Panthers particularly became subject to a repressive white backlash—between 1968 and 1971 more than thirty Panthers died in shoot-outs with the police and FBI agents, over 750 were jailed, others went into exile, and the movement virtually ceased to exist. The Black Muslims became more moderate after the death of Elijah Muhammad in 1975, and attempts to take a more radical line by people like Louis Farrakhan in the 1980s found little support.

It is hard to determine what, if anything, such movements contributed to the black cause in the long term. Certainly they helped to create a stronger feeling of racial awareness and race pride—the "Black is beautiful" movement was an important psychological development of the period. It could also be argued that in posing more frightening alternatives the Muslims and the Panthers contributed to Martin Luther King's success by emphasizing the essential moderation of his vision of harmony achieved through nonviolence. But at the same time the militants contributed to the fragmentation of the civil-rights movement in the latter part of the decade as various groups differed over ends and means. Divided over strategies to follow in the wake of legislative successes and over the position to be adopted on national issues such as the war in Vietnam, the mainstream movements such as SNCC, CORE, and the SCLC lost their sense of direction, and after King's death, any unifying leadership. With the change in political climate and return to conservatism ushered in by the election of Richard Nixon, the Second Reconstruction came to an end.

The civil-rights revolt ended in part because of its successes. Much had been accomplished in ten to fifteen years. The social and political patterns of the South, and indeed of the whole nation, had been affected by the move toward integration and political participation. In a sense the movement had achieved its objectives at the moment when Lyndon Johnson, a white southern president, appeared on television on March 15, 1964, and declared in the words of the civil-rights song, "We shall overcome." Where the 1957 and 1960 Civil Rights Acts had been limited to investigation of the denial of voting rights, the 1964 Civil Rights Act specifically guaranteed access to places of public accommodation, provided for protection of voting rights, and continued the desegregation of schools. This legislation was further strengthened in 1968 by a bill prohibiting discrimination in housing. As a consequence, segregation virtually ceased to exist in public places, and school integration accelerated.

Between 1968 and 1970 the number of African-Americans in all-black schools fell from 68 percent to 18 percent, and the number in college rose 85 percent. In addition blacks now gained access to public office on an unprecedented scale. In 1964 only 6 percent of blacks in Mississippi and 19 percent in Alabama were registered to vote; following the passage of the Voting Rights Act (1965) and the subsequent voter registration drives in the South, by 1969 these figures had risen to 66 percent and 61 percent respectively. The number of black elected officials rose from a total of 103 in 1964 to 3,500 in 1974, and even former race-baiters like Governor George Wallace moderated their approach to appeal to black voters—Wallace was elected governor of Alabama in 1982 with some black support. It was hardly surprising, then, that Andrew Young, a future mayor of Atlanta and former SNCC worker, could say that "politics is the civil rights of the seventies."[14]

However, political success brought its problems too, as Young was to discover. Some 130 black mayors were elected to office in the 1970s, but in a number of the northern cities particularly, such as Cleveland and Newark, the new administrations found that they had come into power at the worst possible moment. They faced a declining tax base because of white flight and industrial relocation, combined with high expenditures due to rebuilding and welfare programs. In both North and South, black city politicians had to overcome inherited racial problems in their civil services, deal with delicate matters such as policing, and confront racial opposition from the white electorate.

Faced with enormous financial burdens and political difficulties, the black mayors and city workers also had to deal with a less sympathetic federal administration. Richard Nixon skillfully appropriated the Black Power slogan to urge the development of black capitalism and free enterprise so as to reduce dependency upon federal government; a White House memo leaked to the press suggested that race matters might benefit from a period of "benign neglect." The president himself spoke out against busing, encouraged attempts to amend the Voting Rights Act, and tried to appoint southern conservatives with dubious records on racial issues to the Supreme Court. His successors were little better. Even the return of the Democrats with Jimmy Carter proved to be a disappointment for the black voters who had given him overwhelming support. The first Democrat to be elected from the Deep South since the 1840s, Carter represented the new, post-civil-rights, moderate South. However, while he did nothing to strike down civil rights, he did little to advance them either. His early actions suggested otherwise: the appointment of Andrew Young as U.S. ambassador to the United Nations and of other black activists to federal posts seemed to indicate major advances. Young's appointment, however, proved short-lived, and Carter's conservative economic policies had disastrous consequences for blacks dependent on federal aid. According to Manning Marable, "Carter was probably the most conservative Democratic president since Woodrow Wilson,"[15] a fact registered in the decline in his black support from 94 percent in 1976 to 85 percent in 1980. In the "Reagan revolution" that followed, black Americans were even more adversely affected by the cuts in employment and training programs, the food-stamp programs, Aid to Dependent Children, child nutrition programs, and student loan programs. Reagan also continued the Republican southern strategy by emphasizing states' rights and making conservative appointments to the Supreme Court.

Black protest, however, seemed confined to voter apathy. In the 1980s there was even a fall in black voter registration in both North and South, and the turnout among southern blacks fell to a mere 41 percent in 1984. Those who might have led protest movements seemed to have little inclination to do so. Incorporated within the decision-making processes, they had become part of a sizeable black middle class of governmental, educational, and professional employees. This was evident in the media where blacks appeared in all television roles and "The Cosby Show," starring Bill Cosby as head of a very middle-class black family, was one of the most successful programs of the eighties. Equally indicative was the manner in which advertisers targeted blacks as consumers. That blacks had finally been admitted to the mainstream of society also seemed evident from the widespread incorporation of black influences into white popular music and the success of black performers in their own right. One of the most successful pop stars of the late eighties was Michael Jackson (who also advertised and was in turn sponsored by Pepsi Cola), while in film the young black comedian Eddie Murphy was a huge box-office success in a number of films that had little or nothing to do with race. In the literary world the protest literature of the 1960s, dominated by Ralph Ellison, James Baldwin, and others, had given way to concerns within the black community, particularly those relating to gender. In dealing with the issue of sexual exploitation writers such as Maya Angelou, Toni Morrison, and Alice Walker were able to reach a much wider audience than blacks alone to gain a place among the major American writers of the eighties.

Even the number and proportion of blacks classed as poor declined—from 9.9 million (55 percent) in 1959 to 7.6 million (30 percent) in 1978. These optimistic figures do not, however, tell the whole story. While a considerable proportion of blacks have now joined middle-class American society, beneath them remain a large number trapped in an "underclass" of poverty: black representation among the poor actually increased from 33 percent to 50 percent of the total. A report by the National Research Council in 1989 found a general deterioration in the economic status of blacks since the 1960s. The irony of modern black history was that the areas blacks had moved to in hope and expectation were the very areas of industrial and economic decline in the seventies and eighties. As auto plants and steel manufacturing closed, northern cities became known as the Rustbelt; growth in light industries, in high-tech and electronic engineering, now took place in the South and was centered on places like Dallas, Houston, and Atlanta. Black unemployment, meanwhile, was two and sometimes three times as high as that of whites, running at 14—18 percent (and as high as 22 percent in 1983). Lacking marketable skills, detached from society at large, and politically apathetic, many jobless African-Americans seemed to face a hopeless future.

For young blacks the unemployment figures were higher still, and this fact lay behind a widespread number of related problems that reinforced their outsider status as part of an "underclass"—drug abuse, violence, crime, and family-related problems. In the 1960s Daniel Moynihan had created a furor when he suggested in *The Negro Family* that the problems faced by blacks were largely a consequence of the breakdown of the black family.[16] Twenty years later it was evident that on the contrary, the problems faced by blacks were *causing* a breakdown of the family with over 40 percent of black families classed as female-headed single-parent, compared with 15 percent of white families. (In 1960 the comparative figures had been 21 percent for blacks, 6 percent for whites.) In 1983 almost 55 percent of black babies were born to unmarried mothers, many of whom were very young. For those black women in particular, life was an unremitting circle of poverty and exploitation.

It was to those excluded from the gains of the sixties and seventies that Jesse Jackson appealed for support in building his Rainbow Coalition in 1984 and 1988. Consciously trying to pick up Martin Luther King's mantle as black leader, Jackson attempted to overcome voter apathy among the poor, African-Americans, and Hispanics in order to capture the Democratic party's presidential nomination. A series of bold initiatives in foreign affairs, including securing the release of an American airman shot down over Syria in 1983, helped to project Jackson onto the national and international stage. Although he was unsuccessful in the 1984 primary campaign, his often inspirational appeal won considerable support in 1988 when he ran second to the eventual Democratic nominee, Michael Dukakis. Jackson scored some significant victories en route, but suffered in states like New York as a result of his support for the Palestine Liberation Organization, and for some widely publicized anti-Semitic remarks. His failure to disassociate himself from Louis Farrakhan, who also took an extreme anti-Israeli position, did not help either. However, Jackson continued to keep a high profile and in 1990 he went to South Africa to greet the ANC leader, Nelson Mandela, on his release from prison and also won election as senator at large for the District of Columbia.

Other African-Americans scored electoral successes in 1989. Coleman Young was reelected to an unprecedented fifth term as mayor of Detroit, and David Dinkins became the first black mayor of New York City after beating the incumbent Ed Koch for the Democratic nomination. However, by 1991 the financial problems of the city suggested that Dinkins's term might be a short one, and despite such victories voting patterns pointed to the persistence, even revival of white racism. In politics blacks are still underrepresented—the number of black elected officials is still only 1 percent of the total. The election of Douglas Wilder as governor of Virginia in 1989 marked a major breakthrough, but he was still the only black state governor. So strong was the sense of political powerlessness that for some African-Americans, the arrest and subsequent jailing on drug charges of former civil-rights leader and long-time mayor of Washington, D.C., Marion Barry, following an undercover FBI operation in 1990, was evidence of a conspiracy against black politicians.

Whatever the political changes, in some parts of the South segregation still survives. In certain towns white children have been withdrawn from public schools and placed in all-white private colleges, leaving public schools as virtually all-black institutions. In the North, too, the problem of busing remains a controversial and unresolved issue in a number of cities. Violence against blacks has also continued at horrific levels, North and South: in 1979 five Communist party workers taking part in a march in Greensboro, North Carolina were gunned down by members of the Ku Klux Klan—a group that, although still small, had grown in membership. In 1981 there were "at least 500 documented cases of random white teenage violence" against blacks. [17]

Racial conflict seemed to achieve greater prominence as the 1980s wore on. In 1987 white youths were tried and convicted for running down and killing a young black in the Howard Beach section of Queens in New York City. Two years later a white gang attacked and killed one of four young African-Americans who had strayed into Bensonhurst, a largely Italian neighborhood in Brooklyn; subsequent black protest demonstrations were met with abuse from white onlookers. Equally whites were shocked in 1989 when a white woman jogger was brutally beaten and raped in an apparently motiveless attack by black teenagers in New York's Central Park. The subsequent trials and convictions of a number of the young blacks in 1990 ensured that racial tension remained high, and were the subject of widespread media interest. Outbreaks of violence between African-Americans and Koreans in New York City in 1989, and between African-Americans and Hispanics in Miami and Wash-

272

ington, D.C., in 1989 and 1991 also pointed up basic divisions within elements of the Rainbow Coalition.

If the continuation of acts of violence against blacks indicates how little has changed for African-Americans in the twentieth century, the public reactions indicate how much has changed. In 1900 race violence would rarely be considered newsworthy, let alone subject to such intense public outcry and debate. Nonetheless these incidents and the various other statistics indicate that race remains an important issue in American life. For those subjected to such violence or experiencing economic hardship because of their color, "the American century" continues as something to be suffered rather than celebrated. Although Jesse Jackson appeared able to mobilize some white as well as black, Hispanic, and other minority support in 1984 and 1988, the possibility of his inclusion on the Democratic ticket as the vice-presidential candidate in 1988 was still perceived as a vote loser on grounds of both his race and his radicalism. Given such problems it remains to be seen whether the black "underclass" will provide the basis for a further integrationist drive or follow the separatist route advocated by others before them. It also remains to be seen whether the full meaning of the Declaration of Independence will ever be realized for African-Americans in the twentieth century.

Notes

1. Ralph Barton Perry, *Puritanism and Democracy* (New York, 1944), p. 133.

2. Jesse Jackson, quoted in John White, *Black Leadership in America 1895–1968* (London and New York, 1985), p. 149.

3. David C. Nielson, *Black Ethos: Northern Urban Negro Life and Thought, 1890–1930* (Westport, Conn., and London, 1977), p. xiii.

4. Richard Wright, introduction to *Native Son* (New York, 1940), p. xii.

5. *Crisis*, May 1918, p. 7; July 1918, p. 111.

6. Du Bois, "An Essay Toward a History of the Black Man in the Great War," ibid., June 1919, p. 72.

7. Harvard Sitkoff, *A New Deal for Blacks* (New York, 1978), p. 28.

8. Ibid., p. 36.

9. Raymond Wolters, "The New Deal and the Negro," in *The New Deal: The National Level*, ed. John Braeman, Robert H. Bremner, and David Brody (Columbus, Ohio, 1975), p. 170.

10. Mary Frances Berry and John Blassingame, *Long Memory: The Black Experience in America* (New York, 1982), pp. 124–25.

11. Malcolm X, *The Autobiography of Malcolm X* (Harmondsworth, Middlesex, 1965), p. 344.

12. David J. Garrow, *Bearing the Cross: Martin Luther King and the Southern Christian Leadership Conference* (New York, 1986), p. 625.

13. Kerner Commission, *Report of the National Advisory Commission on Civil Disorders* (New York, 1969), p. 203.

14. Young quoted in William Issel, *Social Change in the United States, 1945–1983* (London, 1985), p. 188.

15. Manning Marable, *Race, Reform, and Rebellion: The Second Reconstruction in Black America, 1945–1982* (London, 1984), p. 183.

16. Daniel P. Moynihan, *The Negro Family in America: The Case for National Action* (New York, 1965).

17. Manning Marable, *How Capitalism Underdeveloped Black America* (London, 1983), p. 240.

Bibliography

For general surveys of twentieth-century black American history the relevant chapters of John Hope Franklin's *From Slavery to Freedom*, 3rd ed. (New York, 1968) still provide a good basic narrative of events, as does Mary Ellison's shorter *The Black Experience: American Blacks since 1865* (London, 1974). Otherwise, there is not as yet a single-volume history of the period. Economics are covered generally in William H. Harris, *The Harder We Run: Black Workers since the Civil War* (New York and Oxford, 1982).

The changing black response to their situation is dealt with in August Meier, Elliott Rudwick, and Francis Broderick, *Black Protest Thought in the Twentieth Century* (New York,

1971). David G. Nielson's *Black Ethos: Northern Urban Negro Life and Thought, 1890–1930* (Westport, Conn., and London, 1977) includes more cultural and social material. Different individual black leaders are discussed in John Hope Franklin and August Meier, eds., *Black Leaders of the Twentieth Century* (Urbana, Ill., Chicago, and London, 1982), and John White, *Black Leadership in America, 1895–1968* (New York and London, 1985). On the leading civil-rights organizations and black movements, see Charles F. Kellogg, *NAACP: A History of the National Association for the Advancement of Colored People, 1909–1920* (Baltimore, 1967); and the less academic Langston Hughes, *Fight for Freedom: The Story of the NAACP* (New York, 1962); Nancy J. Weiss, *The National Urban League, 1910–1940* (New York, 1974); Adam Fairclough, *To Redeem the Soul of America: The Southern Christian Leadership Conference and Martin Luther King* (Athens, Ga., and London, 1987); August Meier and Elliott Rudwick, *CORE: A Study in the Civil Rights Movement, 1952–1968* (New York, 1973); Clayborne Carson, *In Struggle: SNCC and the Black Awakening of the 1960s* (London, 1981); E. U. Essien Udom, *Black Nationalism: The Rise of the Black Muslims in the USA* (Chicago, 1962); and C. Eric Lincoln, *The Black Muslims in America* (Boston, 1973).

The situation of blacks at the turn of the century is dealt with in Rayford Logan, *The Betrayal of the Negro from Rutherford B. Hayes to Woodrow Wilson* (New York and London, 1965), and C. Vann Woodward, *The Strange Career of Jim Crow* (New York and London, 1966). Du Bois is the subject of two excellent biographies by Francis L. Broderick, *W. E. B. Du Bois: Negro Leader in Time of Crisis* (Stanford, Calif., 1966), and Elliott M. Rudwick, *W. E. B. Du Bois: Propagandist of the Negro Protest* (New York, 1969).

Black migration and urbanization is the focus of Allen H. Spear, *Black Chicago: The Making of a Negro Ghetto, 1890–1920* (Chicago, 1967), Gilbert Osofsky, *Harlem: The Making of a Ghetto* (New York, 1968), and Kenneth L. Kusmer, *A Ghetto Takes Shape: Black Cleveland, 1870–1930* (Chicago and London, 1978). For the race riots that followed see Elliott M. Rudwick, *Race Riot at East St. Louis, July 2, 1917* (Carbondale, Ill., 1964), W. Tuttle, *Race Riot: Chicago in the Red Summer of 1919* (New York, 1977), and Arthur I. Waskow, *From Race Riot to Sit-in: 1919 and the 1960s* (Garden City, N.Y., 1967).

There are no good general surveys of black life in the 1920s, and one has to look at the separate aspects of the subject. On Garvey and Garveyism, the older E. David Cronon, *Black Moses: The Story of Marcus Garvey and the Universal Negro Improvement Association* (Madison, Wis., 1955) needs to be balanced with Theodore Vincent, *Black Power and the Garvey Movement* (San Francisco, 1972), and Judith Stein, *The World of Marcus Garvey: Race and Class in Modern Society* (Baton Rouge, La., and London, 1986). A. Philip Randolph and the BSCP are the subject of William H. Harris, *Keeping the Faith: A. Philip Randolph, Milton P. Webster and the Brotherhood of Sleeping Car Porters, 1925–1937* (Urbana, Ill., Chicago, and London, 1977). The Harlem Renaissance is not the subject of as many studies as might be imagined, but is left to literary studies of various authors. Nathan I. Huggins, *Harlem Renaissance* (New York, 1971) is the best overall account, while Victor A. Kramer, ed., *The Harlem Renaissance Reexamined* (New York, 1987) consists of a useful collection of essays.

Blacks in the thirties are dealt with in B. Sternsher, ed., *The Negro in Depression and War* (Chicago, 1969), John B. Kirby, *Black Americans in the Roosevelt Era* (Knoxville, Tenn., 1980), Harvard Sitkoff, *A New Deal For Blacks: The Emergence of Civil Rights as a National Issue: The Depression Decade* (New York, 1978), and Raymond Wolters, *Negroes and the Great Depression* (Westport, Conn., 1970). New Deal policies and their effects on African-Americans in the South are dealt with in Gavin Wright, *Old South, New South* (New York, 1987). The war years are also often seen as pivotal: see especially Neil A. Wynn, *The Afro-American and the Second World War* (New York and London, 1976).

The story then jumps to the 1950s. Early works of interest include Louis Lomax, *The Negro Revolt* (London, 1963) and Benjamin Muse, *The American Negro Revolution: From Nonviolence to Black Power* (Bloomington, Ill., 1968). More up-to-date accounts can be found in Harvard Sitkoff, *The Struggle for Black Equality, 1954–1980* (New York, 1983) and Manning Marable's provocative *Race, Reform, and Rebellion: The Second Reconstruction in Black America, 1945–1982* (London, 1984). On Black Power see Stokely Carmichael and Charles V. Hamilton, *Black Power: The Politics of Liberation in America* (New York, 1967), John H. Bracey, August Meier, and Elliott

Rudwick, eds., *Black Nationalism in America* (Indianapolis, 1970), and James Forman, *The Making of Black Revolutionaries* (New York, 1972). On the Black Panther party Bobby Seale's *Seize the Time* (New York, 1970) gives a good idea of the origins and aims, and Malcolm X, *The Autobiography of Malcolm X* (New York, 1965) remains one of the best books on postwar black life as well as the rise of the Black Muslims.

There are now a considerable number of books on the life of Martin Luther King. The early and less critical studies include David L. Lewis, *King: A Critical Biography* (London, 1970), and Stephen B. Oates, *Let the Trumpet Sound: The Life of Martin Luther King, Jr.* (London, 1982). More recently the detailed studies by David J. Garrow, *Bearing the Cross: Martin Luther King, Jr. and the Southern Christian Leadership Conference* (New York, 1986), and Fairclough, *To Redeem the Soul of America* (cited above, p. 275) have provided thoroughly documented and critical accounts.

The race riots of the 1960s are dealt with in Robert M. Fogelson, *Violence as Protest: A Study of Riots in Ghettos* (Westport, Conn., 1969), James W. Button, *Black Violence: The Political Impact of the 1960s Riots* (Princeton, N.J., 1978), and the Kerner Commission, *Report of the National Advisory Commission on Civil Disorders* (New York, 1969).

The period from the late 1960s on is dealt with in Michael B. Preston et al., eds., *The New Black Politics: The Search for Political Power* (New York and London, 1982), Sar A. Levitan et al., *Still a Dream: The Changing Status of Blacks since 1960* (Cambridge, Mass., 1975), and Manning Marable, *How Capitalism Underdeveloped Black America* (London, 1983).

10

Constitutional Change and the Courts in the Twentieth Century

David J. Barling

In 1987 Americans celebrated the bicentennial of their Constitution. Over the previous two centuries the United States had evolved from an agrarian, coastal, sparsely populated, fledgling republic into a transcontinental industrial giant and global superpower. Nevertheless the form of the original Constitution has largely survived this metamorphosis. On the other hand the interpretation of the document's relatively brief contents has changed dramatically. Writing in 1888, British political scientist Viscount James Bryce commented that the Constitution was "a judicious mixture of definiteness in principle with elasticity of detail," which afforded the United States a framework of government that was both stable and capable of operating in accordance with changing historical standards.[1] Ever since the Supreme Court established the right of judicial review early in the nineteenth century, it has been in the forefront of constitutional interpretation and reinterpretation. In many ways the establishment of the judiciary as the third and coequal branch of government constituted America's most distinctive contribution to the science of government. Conventionally, treatment of the Supreme Court is the preserve of political science, but the judiciary's contribution to the major constitutional changes in

"America's century" makes it an important topic of historical analysis too.

The Constitution symbolizes the American belief in the authority of a "higher law" that can stand above statute law and the immediate manipulation of human desire. Paradoxically, the American republic itself emerged from the human desire to establish popular sovereignty in place of regal authority. It is hardly surprising, therefore, that the Constitution has had to adapt to changing political pressures in the course of its two-hundred-year history. Many of its principles remain constant: a federal system; limited but effective national government; three separate and balanced branches of national government; and the primacy of certain individual liberties. Within this framework, however, there has been important scope for change. To date the judiciary's role in promoting such change during the twentieth century has gone through four fairly distinct phases, each of which bore a close relationship to contemporary political developments. Until 1936 the Supreme Court adhered to a conservative interpretation of the Constitution that sought to limit the growth of regulatory government at state and federal levels during the Progressive and New Deal eras. This phase of judicial history gave way to a transitional era, lasting until the mid-1950s, when the Court shifted its concern from economic issues to civil liberties. Later, from 1954 to the early 1980s, judicial activism was at its peak and did much to nationalize the Bill of Rights (below, p. 288). Finally, the advent of Ronald Reagan to the presidency in 1980 testified to a conservative trend in American politics to which the federal judiciary has not been immune.

The principles of judicial supremacy and judicial review enable the Supreme Court to hold the laws and actions of the federal and state governments unconstitutional and make its decisions binding on them. The importance of judicial interpretation of the Constitution has inevitably engendered political and legal controversy between advocates of a strict-construction approach and those who favored a looser, activist concept of the Constitution. American jurisprudence has reflected this debate throughout the twentieth century. The traditional approach to judicial decision-making, inherited from the nineteenth century, was the "declarative" or "legal mechanical" method which regarded legal interpretation as a technical, mechanical process. According to its precepts, judges could reach an objective conclusion regarding a case through a process of purely legal deduction based on the original and only meaning of the law. This tradition was challenged from the turn of the century by the "sociological" view, which held that the law was not part of a body of fixed principles and rules, but was constantly shaped and changed by social pressures. According to this credo, judges acted as agents in the process of change, but did so objectively, interpreting the law according to the social mores and values of their day. The Constitution was seen as a set of rules that evolved and changed to meet the differing needs of different times. The "legal realists," whose views emerged in the 1920s, took this approach a stage further. They felt that objectivity was impossible in judicial decision-making, and hence that judges could adopt a clear legislative and policy-making role in adjudication. The "legal realists" advocated a more loosely constructed or "living" Constitution.

In 1907 Charles Evans Hughes, future Republican presidential candidate and chief justice, claimed: "We live under a Constitution, but the Constitution is what the judges say it is."[2] Twentieth-century history has not borne him out, as judicial decision-making is circumscribed in certain ways. Operating in a legal environment, judges must generally make decisions in the context of an established body of previous legal rulings. Most of the Court's jurisdiction is appellate; it can only choose litigation cases on appeal, which limits the range of its activity. Furthermore the Court lacks enforcement powers, as illustrated by Southern resistance to implementation of the school desegregation rulings in the 1950s and 1960s. Political influences upon the Court further shape the context within which judges decide, for interest groups often use litigation to seek favorable legal rulings. The process of judicial selection is also highly political and reflects presidential needs. The president nominates judges to the Supreme Court and the federal judiciary but the Senate must grant approval. The approval process can lead to conflict when the Senate majority disagrees with the president's aims. For example, President Richard Nixon's attempt to place two conservative strict-constructionist justices on the Court was frustrated with the rejection of Clement F. Haynesworth (1969) and G. Harrold Carswell (1970), as was Ronald Reagan's effort to appoint Robert H. Bork (1987). Even the confirmation of the president's nominee does not guarantee subsequent judicial compliance. Both presidents Dwight D. Eisenhower and Harry S. Truman expressed dismay at the outcome of certain appointments they had made. Truman recalled, "when you ask me what was my biggest mistake, that's it. Putting Tom Clark on the Supreme Court of the United States."3 Finally, the process of selection has tended to reflect, in a symbolic manner, the pluralistic nature of American society in the twentieth century. Today there are a female and a black justice on the Court, whereas in previous years there were both a Jewish and a Roman Catholic seat on the bench.

Hence the Supreme Court is a judicial body operating in a political world. Its role is both judicial and political, but the interaction is complex, and generally frustrates the ability of observers to predict future decisions with great accuracy. Consensus is the dominant characteristic of the twentieth-century American polity, but the nature of this consensus has changed over time. The Court has sometimes sought to resist the emergence of a new consensus, as in the mid-1930s, and it has sometimes tried to hasten its development, as the Warren Court did in the 1950s. Nonetheless, the Court will rarely stray too far from the prevailing political mood for too long a period, for to do so would jeopardize its constitutional authority.

Continuing the pattern that it had established during the late nineteenth century, the Supreme Court played an activist role in interpreting the Constitution from a conservative perspective in the first phase of the twentieth century. Its concerns were to defend the primacy of private property against government regulation, to preserve state government jurisdiction against federal expansion, and to restrict the power of labor organizations. The social and economic effects of rapid industrialization and urbanization in the late nineteenth century had motivated Populists and later Progressives to demand stronger government regulation of private enterprise. The expansion of regulatory government, particularly at the federal level, became a durable feature of America's development for most of the twentieth century, but the Supreme Court fought a determined rearguard action against this trend until the late 1930s. Aware of the strength of reformist sentiment, the Supreme Court acted cautiously, and usually only when its intervention could be justified by legal arguments concerning substantive due process, the commerce clause, or the Tenth Amendment.

The due-process clauses of the Constitution are contained in the original Fifth Amendment, a procedural guarantee of certain rights in criminal proceedings, and the Fourteenth Amendment, which stipulated that the states could not "deprive any person of life, liberty or property, without due process of law." Based on this, the concept of substantive due process was developed by the Supreme Court during the late nineteenth century in a long series of decisions and minority opinions. It held that the Court could impose a substantive limit upon any economic legislation seeking to dispossess persons of their economic liberty or property in a manner considered arbitrary, a term that came to mean virtually whatever the justices decided. The commerce clause, which gave Congress the power to "regulate commerce with foreign nations, and among the several states," was eventually employed to justify the expansion of federal regulatory power, but conservative judges initially resisted this development by interpreting its provisions narrowly. The strict constructionists' third weapon was the Tenth Amendment, which states that "the powers not delegated to the United States by the Constitution, nor prohibited by it to the states, are reserved to the states respectively, or to the people." Taking its cue from Chief Justice Roger Taney's seminal ruling in *Charles River Bridge* v. *Warren Bridge* (1837), the Court used this amendment to invalidate a variety of federal encroachments during the early twentieth century.

The significance and scope of each approach were illustrated by three famous decisions. In *Lochner* v. *New York* (1905), the Court ruled on a New York law regulating work conditions in the baking industry that included a limitation on working hours in order to protect workers against adverse conditions such as the inhalation of flour dust. Arguing that conditions in the baking industry did not justify such regulation, the Court contended that the real purpose of the law was "to regulate the hours of labor between the master and his employee . . . in a private business," an unconstitutional interference with the liberty of contract as protected by the Fourteenth Amendment. The Court's stand against the regulation of working hours aroused great controversy, and was repeated two decades later in *Adkins* v. *Children's Hospital* (1923) which struck down a statute setting up a board with authority to regulate minimum wages for women and child workers in the District of Columbia. In the famous majority opinion, Justice George Sutherland declared that the law violated the liberty of contract under the due-process clause of the Fifth Amendment. Finally, in *Hammer* v. *Dagenhart* (1918), the Court struck down a federal law prohibiting the interstate passage of goods produced by child labor. In a much disputed opinion, the majority specified that the law interfered with production, which was deemed to be subject to the police power of the states under the Tenth Amendment (itself misquoted in the opinion), rather than commerce, which came under Congressional jurisdiction.

Of course the Supreme Court could not always stem the Progressive tide. The reformers achieved some of their goals through the process of constitutional amendment. Political democracy received a boost from the Seventeenth Amendment (1913), which mandated the popular election of U.S. senators instead of their selection by state legislatures, and the Nineteenth Amendment (1920) which gave the vote to women. Furthermore, the Eighteenth Amendment (1919) introducing Prohibition enhanced federal regulatory power, while the Sixteenth Amendment (1913), which established the legality of a federal income tax, superseded a previous Supreme Court ruling of 1895 (*Pollock* v. *Farmers Loan and Trust Co.*) that the federal government did not have the constitutional power to impose a direct tax.

The Supreme Court itself had to make some concessions to the Progressives in recognition of political reality. It broadened the federal commerce power in *Champion* v. *Ames* (1903), a ruling that recognized the federal police power and upheld Congressional legislation prohibiting the use of mails for the dispatch of lottery tickets. In *National Securities Co.* v. *U.S.* (1904) the Court upheld and reestablished the force of the Sherman Antitrust Act (1890), which forbade all restraints of trade. The *Muller* v. *Oregon* decision (1908) even supported the cause of organized labor and modified the Lochner ruling by allowing interference with the liberty of contract when it could be interpreted as protecting public health. Despite such examples of accommodation, the general trend of Court decisions in the early twentieth century was antiregulatory. This pattern was strengthened in the 1920s when the Progressive impulse waned and Republican President Warren G. Harding appointed three new justices to the Court who showed a preference for limited government.

However, the political agenda changed when Franklin D. Roosevelt entered the White House committed to use federal powers to pull the United States out of the Depression. He introduced a plethora of legislation during his first hundred days in office, much of which delegated considerable quasi-legislative power to the executive by allowing it to enact regulations through the use of executive orders. The New Deal legislation also allowed for unprecedented federal government intervention in state and private economic affairs during peacetime. Although Congress was initially compliant to the president's aims, nobody expected that the Supreme Court would be.

Within a short time business interests sought judicial redress against new government regulations. In its response the Court tended to rule in favor of state as opposed to federal regulatory powers, in line with the police-power-of-states doctrine. Its decisions in *Home Building and Loan Association* v. *Blaisdell* (1934) upheld a Minnesota law imposing a moratorium on mortgages, despite the perceived threat to the obligation-of-contract clause. Even more significantly, in *Nebbia* v. *New York* (1934) the Court sustained a state board's right to set milk prices (and overturned the hallowed protection that business prices had received in previous judgments) by arguing that any business was subject to reasonable regulation. By contrast, during a sixteen-month period from January 1935 onwards, the Supreme Court decided against New Deal statutes in eight cases and upheld them only twice. It invalidated Section 9(c) of the National Industrial Recovery Act (NIRA), the NIRA itself, the Railroad Pension Act, the Farm Mortgage Law, the Agricultural Adjustment Act (AAA), the AAA amendments, the Bituminous Coal Act, and the Municipal Bankruptcy Act. Only the Tennessee Valley Authority Act and the Emergency Banking Act of 1933 received the judicial seal of approval, albeit in circumscribed fashion.

The New Deal statutes were held unconstitutional on a variety of grounds. In *Panama Refining Co.* v. *Ryan* (1935), the Court struck down section 9(c) of the NIRA by a vote of eight to one, declaring that Congress had delegated power to the executive without setting sufficiently specific limits or standards for its use. Similarly, in *Schechter Poultry Corporation* v. *U.S.* (1935), the Court unanimously held invalid many of the main provisions of the NIRA as an excessive delegation of power from

Congress to the president. The decision also concluded that the National Recovery Administration's codes of fair competition for the poultry industry attempted to regulate transactions within the states, thereby exceeding the federal government's powers under the commerce clause. On similar grounds the Court ruled, in *Carter* v. *Carter Coal Co.* (1936), that the Bituminous Coal Act's attempt to control the working conditions of miners and to fix prices for the sale of coal was unconstitutional, as coal mining was a productive rather than a commercial activity. Employing another traditional argument, in *U.S.* v. *Butler* (1936) the Court invalidated the AAA on the grounds that Congress was transgressing upon the Tenth Amendment, which reserved such powers of regulation to the individual states. The due-process clause was also invoked in *Louisville Joint Stock Land Bank* v. *Radford* (1935), which found the Federal Farm Bankruptcy Act to be a violation of the due-process guarantee.

A great deal has been written about the nine justices on the New Deal Court, who have often been classified according to ideological grouping. First, there was the bloc of four conservatives in Sutherland, James C. McReynolds, Pierce Butler, and Willis Van Devanter; second, a group of three liberals sympathetic to the New Deal in Louis A. Brandeis, Harlan Fiske Stone, and Benjamin N. Cardozo; and finally a swing group of Chief Justice Hughes and Owen J. Roberts. However, a closer study of the votes on the cases shows that all of the justices were reluctant to agree with the degree of legislative delegation that the president assumed in the New Deal statutes. The majority also rejected the federal government's attempt to extend its control over production through either the commerce, taxation, or general-welfare clauses of the Constitution. The trio of liberals, Brandeis, Stone, and Cardozo, did support such control to an extent, but even they voted down the NIRA. On the other hand, the liberal group criticized the Court's tendency to play a super-legislative role in invalidating many of the New Deal programs. In *U.S.* v. *Butler* (1936) the minority opinion, written by Justice Stone and supported by Brandeis and Cardozo, attacked the majority decision as being a "tortured construction of the Constitution," and criticized the Court's legislative tendencies: "Courts are not the only agencies of government that must be assumed to have the capacity to govern."[4] In essence this was a plea for judicial restraint in place of the Court's activism in opposition to government intervention in the economy over the previous half-century. By the 1930s it was becoming increasingly clear that the nineteenth-century judicial insistence on limited government regarding socioeconomic issues was outdated in the modern, interdependent, and complex economy of the twentieth century. The flexibility and political pragmatism eventually manifested by the Supreme Court from 1937 onwards prevented a severe constitutional crisis over the New Deal and allowed the Constitution to adapt to the needs of the twentieth century.

Bowing to change, in the late 1930s the Court entered an era of transition, and shifted from a predominantly conservative defense of laissez-faire interests to a more liberal advocacy of the civil rights and liberties of the component parts of the New Deal political coalition. In 1937 a judicial U-turn on New Deal legislation reinterpreted the constitutional clauses regarding the powers of Congress, notably the commerce clause but also the taxation and general-welfare clauses. This legitimized whole new areas of federal regulation, particularly economic management, regulation of labor relations and working conditions, and support for the unemployed and aged. The judicial branch effectively abandoned its role as adjudicator of statutes, ceding its authority on these matters to the elected branches of government. Adopting the doctrine of the preferred freedoms or double standard (below, p. 288) in judging constitutional cases, the Court became preoccupied with the civil rights of the individual and, in turn, of the various minority groups.

The turning point followed Roosevelt's record-breaking 1936 reelection victory, which the president considered an unqualified public endorsement of the New Deal legislative program. Emboldened to confront the judiciary, he introduced the so-called "court-packing" legislation, which allowed the president to appoint a new judge to the federal courts for each incumbent who reached the age of seventy and refused the opportunity to retire. A total limit of fifteen members was put on the Supreme Court and an appointment limit of fifty additional judges for the federal judiciary as a whole. Had the bill become law, the president could have appointed a clear pro–New Deal majority to the Supreme Court. Nevertheless, Congress, including many Democrats, opposed this aspect of the bill which seemingly threatened the constitutional separation of powers.

Public opinion was also hostile, particularly as totalitarian developments in Europe heightened fears of possible presidential dictatorship. For once, Roosevelt had made a grave political error. Although the divisions on the Court were quite complicated, Roosevelt seemed to have developed a legal realist view that appointment on an ideological basis was sufficient to control the direction of its decision-making. In fact it was the New Deal Court itself that proved him incorrect, and in so doing vindicated the public's faith in the Supreme Court as guardian of the Constitution and began a new era in the constitutional role of the Court.

"A switch in time saved nine" became the popular, if slightly misleading aphorism, as the Court began to alter many of its established stances on New Deal legislation at the very time that Roosevelt's court-packing plan was being considered by Congress. In March 1937 (before the court-packing plan became known), the Court had voted five to four in *West Coast Hotel Company* v. *Parrish* to overturn the line of reasoning employed in the Lochner and Adkins decisions regarding the constitutionality of state minimum-wage laws. In this case, the Court upheld a minimum-wage law of the state of Washington, and Chief Justice Hughes, writing the majority opinion, altered the Court's view on the freedom of contract, claiming that the due-process clauses sought, not liberty of contract, but "liberty in a social organization which requires the protection of the law against the evils that menace the health, safety, morals, and welfare of the people."[5] In April, again by a five-to-four vote, the Court upheld the National Labor Relations Act in *NLRB* v. *Jones and Laughlin Steel Corporation*. The majority opinion concluded that the commerce clause gave Congress the power to legislate for collective bargaining, a fundamental right of the employee. Soon afterwards, in *Steward Machine Co.* v. *Davis* and *Helvering* v. *Davis*, the Court upheld two of the benefit programs within the Social Security Act of 1935, employing a broad interpretation of Congress's tax power and the general-welfare clause. Although the conservative bloc of four generally voted against the decisions, its ranks were soon thinned by death and retirement. In fact, within five years, Roosevelt was able to appoint a total of seven new justices and a new chief justice. This period was a pivotal point in twentieth-century constitutional development. As Robert McCloskey observed:

"Constitutional doctrine emerged from those months of crisis profoundly altered. The Court's relationship to the American polity had undergone a fundamental change."[6]

Abandoning its traditional precepts, the Court also began carrying out the constitutional role that would eventually become its major preoccupation during the second half of the twentieth century. This was the application of the national Bill of Rights, enshrined in the first ten amendments, to the individual states under the due-process clause of the Fourteenth Amendment. Earlier decisions, such as *Chicago B.&Q.R.* v. *Chicago* (1897), *Gitlow* v. *New York* (1925) and *Near* v. *Minnesota* (1931) had already raised this issue on a piecemeal basis. The conceptual coherence of the Court's position on the subject received its most significant expression in *Palko* v. *Connecticut* (1937). Written by Cardozo, the majority opinion stated that through a "process of absorption," some, but not all, of the rights of the first ten amendments had become binding upon the states under due process. The mood of judicial restraint was still strong, for Cardozo only defined rights such as freedom of thought and speech and freedom of the press as "fundamental principles of liberty and justice which lie at the base of all our civil and political institutions."[7] Over the next thirty years, however, the Court slowly but surely changed the standard for determining whether or not a Bill of Rights guarantee was fundamental. By 1969, most of these guarantees had been found applicable to the states. Formal recognition of this was made by the final decision of the Warren Court, *Benton* v. *Maryland* (1969), which overturned the *Palko* decision's limited definition of fundamental rights.

The preferred-freedoms doctrine became the Court's principal vehicle for the nationalization of the Bill of Rights. This was promulgated by Justice Stone in a footnote to the majority opinion in *U.S.* v. *Carolene Products Co.* (1938). Stone contended that the Court should concern itself with the constitutionality of those statutes that threatened personal liberties as enumerated in the Bill of Rights. In questions of the infringement of economic liberty, the Court would presume the statute to be valid, leaving the challenger to prove otherwise. "There may be narrower scope for operation of the presumption of constitutionality when legislation appears on the face of it to be within a specific prohibition of the Constitution, such as those of the first ten Amendments, which are deemed equally specific when held to be embraced within the Fourteenth."[8] This double standard was necessary since infringement of the basic freedoms threatened the very operation of the political process, while laws that threatened economic liberty did not, since the political process could redress these itself. Hence, Stone set forth the new direction for Supreme Court activism.

The Court only slowly displayed this activism in the 1940s. In *U.S.* v. *Darby Lumber Company* (1941), it upheld the Fair Labor Standards Act of 1938, which had prohibited child labor and set maximum hours and minimum wages for workers in interstate commerce. As a result, it reversed its previous ruling of *Hammer* v. *Dagenhart* (1918) which had placed child labor beyond the reach of the commerce clause, and now gave this clause a broader definition. The Darby ruling also had the effect of abandoning the freedom-of-contract doctrine and established that the Tenth Amendment, from which the states derived their police powers, was of no relevance to questions of federal power. In 1939–40, other Court decisions struck down state law and city ordinances restricting labor activity, as infringements of First Amendment rights.

World War II interrupted these developments while the executive branch expanded its emergency and war powers. As McCloskey observes: "The Court tacitly acknowledges an informal but very real limit on its jurisdiction; the most explosive issues are nonjusticiable. Sometimes (as in war) the most explosive issues will also be the most important, and then the Court is likely to play a rather modest role in national affairs."[9] This was the case during both world wars when the Court conformed to the "balanced-test" approach to judicial decision-making which accepted that it was sometimes necessary to restrict liberty in order to maintain authority and to promote the general good. This was an outlook that carried over into the Cold War era. During the outburst of McCarthyite anticommunism, the Court displayed a schizoid tendency, showing restraint on the kind of individual-liberty issue that would later appear on the forefront of the judicial agenda.

Examples of judicial activism in defense of civil rights are not prominent in the 1940s. Indeed, the Court complied with one of the most flagrant cases of disregard for rights in twentieth-century history, the enforced relocation of Japanese-

Americans from their West Coast homes to inland internment camps. The only qualification came in *Korematsu* v. *U.S.* (1944), which adjudged that restrictions on the rights of a single racial group are automatically suspect and must be subject to very close scrutiny. The Court also reversed itself on decisions regarding the daily pledging of allegiance to the American flag by schoolchildren and the public distribution of minority religious material by Jehovah's Witnesses, eventually declaring unconstitutional state and local actions that enforced the first and prevented the second. However, continuing its deference to national security imperatives, the Court upheld various anticommunist statutes in the Cold War years, despite claims that they contravened the First Amendment. In *American Communications Association* v. *Douds* (1950), it upheld a clause in the Taft-Hartley Act requiring labor union leaders to swear that they were not Communist party members. Later, *Dennis* v. *U.S.* (1951) upheld the conviction of eleven members of the Communist party under the Smith Act, which had made it unlawful to promote or teach the violent overthrow of the U.S. government or to belong to an organization dedicated to the achievement of this end.

Only in one notable instance was the executive's assertion of its emergency powers challenged. In 1952, following a labor dispute in the major steel companies, President Truman seized control of the steel mills in order to prevent a strike and avoid disruption of steel production during the Korean War. In this instance national security justifications proved inadequate. The Supreme Court ruled in *Youngstown Sheet and Tube Company* v. *Sawyer* (1952) that Truman's actions had exceeded the constitutional limits of presidential power.

By the mid-1950s the decline of Cold War tension, the ending of the Korean War, and the waning of McCarthyism produced a more relaxed national mood that enabled the Supreme Court to resume its defense of civil rights and liberties. In many respects the era from 1954 to 1986 witnessed the zenith of liberal constitutional interpretation. Chief Justice Earl Warren (1953–69), who regarded the Constitution as a living organism responsive to social change, took the lead in promoting the new activism. Chief Justice Warren Burger (1969–86) followed this tendency, though in a more limited fashion. The Warren Court took the lead in some policy areas, reaching decisions that preceded action by the legislative and executive. During this activist period major decisions in the areas of racial discrimination, minority advancement, electoral-district reapportionment, criminal justice procedures, birth control and contraception, women's rights, school prayer, and libel law combined to have a dramatic effect on American society. Changes resulting from these judicial decisions benefited many elements of the liberal New Deal coalition, notably blacks, women's groups, the poor, the media and artistic sectors, and government employees. According to Martin Shapiro, "The preferred position doctrine with suitable additions and appurtenances served as a gigantic umbrella and a blueprint for transferring Supreme Court political services from Republican to Democratic clienteles. . . ."[10]

Decisions in the area of national security and communist subversion illustrated this more liberal trend. *Slochower* v. *Board of Education* (1956) determined that a state could not automatically dismiss employees because they invoked their Fifth Amendment right to remain silent when questioned by Congressional committees. More importantly, the Smith Act was emasculated in *Yates* v. *U.S.* (1957), which ruled that only advocacy of subversive activity rather than of subversive doctrine could be penalized without contravening the First Amendment.

The Court's most significant advancement came in the field of civil rights, in particular racial discrimination and school desegregation. The *Brown* v. *Board of Education, Topeka* rulings of 1954 and 1955 came to symbolize this new phase of activism. According to traditional doctrine since *Plessy* v. *Ferguson* (1896), racial segregation was legal as long as it was separate but equal in its public provision. The Court had begun to insist that equal facilities actually be provided in order for separation to continue in state education with the decisions of *Sweatt* v. *Painter* and *McLaurin* v. *Oklahoma State Regents* (both 1950). Finally, the first *Brown* decision rejected the *Plessy* views in a unanimous opinion, which concluded "that in the field of public education, the doctrine of 'separate but equal' has no place." Warren, who wrote the opinion, asserted that "separate educational facilities are inherently unequal."[11] He based his decision upon social-science evidence that separate education, because it gave black students a psychological feeling of inferiority, made for inequality. As a piece of legal reasoning this opinion is open to judicial doubt, but as an example of legal realism and of judicial policy-making in an area where there was a clear policy vacuum, it proved highly effective.

Brown showed the strengths and weaknesses of the new Court. It set in train de jure desegregation in the South, but this process proved slow and painful. The second *Brown* decision in 1955 addressed the implementation of the new standard and declared that desegregation in public schools should be carried out with "all deliberate speed."[12] Lacking any enforcement mechanism, however, the Court had to rely upon the cooperation of other federal institutions and the state governments themselves. Many of the states and schools fiercely resisted implementation, seeking to gain exemption through the lower courts on a variety of grounds, or simply refusing to comply. The most extreme example was in Little Rock, Arkansas, where Governor Orval E. Faubus and his National Guard prevented black pupils from entering a white high school in 1957. In response President Eisenhower mobilized the army to ensure their admission, but in most instances he was reluctant to use federal power to enforce state and local compliance with Supreme Court decisions on school desegregation.

Having served as the catalyst for school desegregation, the Court took a back seat in promoting the civil-rights revolution that *Brown* had helped to engender. Presidential and Congressional activism eventually came to the forefront in the 1960s. However, following the election of President Richard M. Nixon who sought to slow down the already halting pace of desegregation, the Court made a crucial ruling in *Alexander* v. *Holmes County Board of Education* (1969). This opinion abandoned the weak wording of "all deliberate speed" and ruled that "the obligation of every school district is to terminate dual school systems at once, and to operate now and hereafter only unitary schools."[13]

The Court also became active in upholding the voting rights of citizens where they were adversely affected by legislative reapportionment. The question of voting rights was brought under judicial review by a 1962 ruling that a state had violated the Fifteenth Amendment in gerrymandering a district to exclude black voters. Subsequently, in *Baker* v. *Carr* (1962), the Court ruled that the malapportionment of voters in a legislative district in Tennessee violated the Fourteenth Amendment guarantee of equal protection. In *Gray v. Sanders* (1963), the majority opinion declared that "one person, one vote" was the standard for judging the constitutionality of reapportionment plans; and the principle was extended to U.S. Congressional districts and both houses of state legislatures in two rulings in 1964. These decisions on reapportionment had the effect of weakening the traditional rural conservative hold on state legislatures and some Congressional districts, and allowed for greater representation from the urban, liberal interests of the Democratic electoral coalition.

The issue of civil rights entered a new dimension when affirmative action programs were promoted by federal and state authorities in a bid to provide blacks with positive help in overcoming de facto segregation and racism. The Burger Court upheld some of these policies in areas such as school integration, employment practices, and college admissions. As a result the equal-protection clause was extended beyond the rights of the individual to include the rights of minority groups, giving this clause a clear racial application. In *Swann v. Charlotte-Mecklenberg Board of Education* (1971) the Court unanimously approved a variety of means, including busing, to achieve a proper racial mix in public schools. But recognition of public hostility to busing compelled Burger to qualify his opinion, notably by requiring that existence of some form of de jure segregation be proven and that busing should not risk the health of children or disrupt the educational process. The ruling also stipulated that rigid racial quotas in the school system were not constitutionally acceptable. Nonetheless the Court hesitated in supporting busing plans where de facto school segregation existed in northern and western metropolitan areas, such as Denver, Detroit, and Dayton. However, in 1979, in *Dayton Board of Education v. Brinkman*, the majority opinion abandoned the distinction between de jure and de facto segregation, and approved an integration plan for Dayton that involved the busing of some 15,000 students.

In college admissions and employment practices, the affirmative action approach established racial preference quotas to encourage the admission and hiring of minority students and employees. This practice came before the Court for judgment in *Regents of the University of California v. Bakke* (1978).

A white student who had been denied entry to the medical school, despite scoring higher points on the entry examination than minority students who were admitted, claimed that he had been denied his right to equal protection under the law. The Court's conclusion was complex, as it issued two judgments with differently composed majorities, both being approved by a five-to-four margin. On the one hand it agreed that the medical school's policy for admission was an unconstitutional denial of Bakke's right to the equal protection of the law according to the Fourteenth Amendment and Title VI of the 1964 Civil Rights Act. Meanwhile the second ruling declared that such racial quotas could be acceptable, although the justices comprising the majority issued different opinions as to when such quotas were acceptable. Hence the *Bakke* decisions confirmed both the rights of the individual and the rights of a specific racial group, providing a good example of the balanced style that marked the decisions of the Burger Court.

The liberal agenda was also advanced in the area of criminal procedures concerning the rights of the accused when the Court began to apply the various due-process requirements of the Bill of Rights to state laws and procedures, instead of confining them as previously to federal procedures. Important decisions made states adhere to the Fourth Amendment guarantees of security against unreasonable search and seizure; the Fifth Amendment right against self-incrimination; the right to speedy trial and regulation of wiretapping and surveillance under the Fourth Amendment; and the right to a jury trial and the provision of an attorney for all defendants charged with serious crimes. However, the most controversial decision was *Miranda* v. *Arizona* (1966) when the Court decided, by a majority of five to four, that the police could not interrogate a suspect in custody without first informing him of his rights to silence and to consult a lawyer. Statements obtained from suspects who had not been read their rights constituted inadmissible evidence.

The Court was also instrumental in advancing women's rights, which became a core issue of the liberal agenda in the 1960s. The nationalization of the Bill of Rights was extended to birth control and abortion. State legislation prohibiting the use of contraceptives and provision of birth-control information to married couples was outlawed as an invasion of the constitutional right to privacy in *Griswold* v. *Connecticut* (1965). The landmark ruling on abortion was *Roe* v. *Wade* (1973). A Texas law making it a crime to obtain an abortion was struck down as a violation of a woman's right to privacy, which was held to be embraced within personal liberty protected by the Fourteenth Amendment's due-process clause. The Court issued a complex ruling that the abortion decision was the woman's during the first trimester of pregnancy, while states could restrict but not prohibit abortion in the second semester. Only in the final trimester could the states regulate or prohibit abortion, and even then it was legitimate if necessary to protect the mother's life. This decision projected the judiciary into the forefront of the controversy over abortion in the 1970s and 1980s. The right-to-life lobby won a small concession when *Maher* v. *Roe* (1977) upheld a Congressional amendment prohibiting Medicaid funding of abortion unless it was necessary to save life.

In the area of gender discrimination the Court upheld a variety of antidiscrimination statutes enacted by Congress in the 1960s, and struck down various state laws prejudicial to gender equality under the due-process and equal-protection clauses. In this field, however, it eschewed the activist approach adopted against racial discrimination and took each instance on a more rational case-by-case basis. The Court's preoccupation with the rights of the individual may explain its limited response to one of the most significant constitutional developments of the modern era, the excessive growth of executive power. In 1968 and again in 1970 it spurned the opportunity to pronounce on the legality of the Vietnam War by refusing to give an opinion on whether the president could constitutionally commit American troops to protracted action in Southeast Asia without a Congressional declaration of war. On a more limited matter, however, the Court did strike a blow at the imperial presidency in its 1971 ruling against the Nixon administration's efforts to prevent the publication by the *New York Times* of the Pentagon Papers, classified documents showing that President Lyndon B. Johnson had misled Congress and the public to secure support for the escalation of the Vietnam War. A more decisive judgment followed in *U.S.* v. *Nixon* (1974), which rejected the president's claim of executive privilege to justify withholding from Congressional investigators the so-called Watergate tapes. In general the Supreme Court played a supporting role to the lead part taken by Congress in trimming presidential power. Nevertheless, the revival of constitutional issues regarding executive power compelled the judiciary to address issues that it had largely ignored since the 1930s. Recent evidence, however, gives some indication that the Court believes that Congressional constraints on presidential power have gone far enough. *Chadha* v. *I.N.S.* (1983) ruled the so-called legislative veto, which Congress has recently incorporated into a number of statutes, an unjustifiable method of bypassing the president's constitutionally guaranteed veto power.

With the nationalization of the Bill of Rights, the Warren and Burger Courts significantly advanced the interests of racial minorities, furthered women's rights and individual liberties, and facilitated federal control over state actions and laws. A more open and democratic society evolved under the influence of judicial decisions on racial desegregation, affirmative action, voting and abortion rights, inadmissibility of evidence, and relaxation of libel and obscenity laws. Although it did not achieve these changes alone, of course, the Court often blazed a trail for later executive and Congressional action. Its reinterpretation of the commerce clause, once the linchpin of judicial conservatism, provided constitutional justification for new federal laws regulating areas such as voting, consumer product safety, occupational health, and environmental and pollution standards.

Nonetheless, by the late 1960s many conservatives believed that the Court had become instrumental in the breakdown of traditional moral and legal order. Nixon exploited these fears in his 1968 and 1972 election campaigns. In particular he advocated the need for a return to a strict-constructionist approach by the judiciary and promised to use his powers of appointment to place like-minded justices on the Supreme Court. Like other conservatives, Nixon advocated a narrow conception of the constitutionality of national legislative power, a retreat from the nationalization of the Bill of Rights, a return of authority to the individual states, a less open and liberal interpretation of the Constitution, and greater judicial restraint; in short, a more conservative Court. Despite Nixon's sudden fall from grace over Watergate, the revival of opposition to judicial liberalism continued to gain strength and eventually shaped President Reagan's political agenda in the 1980s.

In sharp contrast to the prevailing trend of constitutional reinterpretation over the previous decades, Reagan favored an avowedly conservative approach to judicial issues. He voiced support for conservative and Republican demands for constitutional amendments to prohibit abortion, sanction prayer in public schools, and compel the balancing of federal budgets. While these were not forthcoming in the 1980s, the Reagan administration did seek to redirect the actions of the Supreme Court. Attorney General Edwin Meese exhorted the Court to return to a conservative view of the Constitution and replace a "jurisprudence of idiosyncrasy" with a "jurisprudence of original intent" based on the aims of the Founding Fathers in writing the Constitution and its amendments. Of course the Founding Fathers may well have intended the "living Constitution" envisaged by Warren rather than a clear and fixed set of prescriptions. The conservative approach to jurisprudence itself veiled a subjective interpretation concerning which areas were suitable for either judicial review or judicial restraint. The Reagan administration itself endorsed judicial activism for the ends it favored: to redefine the relationship between federal and state legislation, and to denationalize the Bill of Rights and thus reverse the liberal trends in relation to abortion, school prayer, affirmative action, and criminal procedure.

The administration devised two main strategies to achieve this agenda. First, it appointed judges to the federal bench who were sympathetic to its constitutional preference. During his presidency Reagan had the opportunity to appoint more than half the 750 federal judges. An elaborate screening process subjected all nominees to an ideological litmus test. In addition Reagan filled three vacancies on the Supreme Court with conservatives and appointed a new chief justice in 1986, William H. Rehnquist. With the replacement of Justice Lewis F. Powell by Anthony Kennedy in 1988, Reagan's legacy was a Court with a conservative majority of five-to-four. The second feature of the administration's judicial strategy was its carefully orchestrated litigation and advocacy campaign to seek specific rulings on selected test cases. Following some initial hesitancy there were clear signs of a conservative shift in constitutional adjudication by the end of the 1980s.

The Burger Court had begun showing some conservative tendencies even before 1980. Most notably, *National League of*

Cities v. *Usery* (1976) was the first ruling in forty years against Congressional use of the commerce power. During the Reagan era the Burger Court also gratified critics of affirmative action with its ruling in *Firefighters Local Union No. 1784* v. *Stotts* (1984), while advocates of school prayer took heart from the *Lynch* v. *Donnelly* decision (1984). Nevertheless both rulings fell short of ultimate conservative objectives. Meanwhile the administration continued to suffer outright setbacks. The Burger Court reaffirmed the constitutionality of abortion in *Akron* v. *Akron Center for Reproductive Health* (1983), and overturned its 1976 *National League of Cities* ruling that the Tenth Amendment protected states from federal laws regulating the wages and hours of state and local government employees in *Garcia* v. *San Antonio Metropolitan Transport Authority* (1984). Even the Rehnquist Court has shown independence by ruling against the executive in upholding the constitutionality of the Ethics in Government Act.

However, the conservative group of five often ruled as a majority since 1988, resulting in an erosion of some of the liberal gains of the former era. This trend seemingly signals an end to the Court's former policy-making role, and suggests that future advances on social issues are more likely to be achieved through the political process rather than through the judicial one. In civil-rights and affirmative action cases, the Court has made it more difficult to prove discrimination and to obtain preferential treatment. The rights of the defendant have been interpreted less liberally, particularly in drug cases. The erosion of the nationalized Bill of Rights was illustrated by the *Webster* v. *Reproductive Health Services* ruling (1989) which gave the individual state greater power to regulate abortion facilities. Conversely, the justices have maintained a tolerant view on First Amendment rights to free speech in cases relating to the burning of the national flag and to telephone pornography. At the midpoint of President Bush's first term, Justice Sandra Day O'Connor remained a swing vote on cases involving abortion and religion, but retirement had already started to thin the ranks of liberal justices, three of whom were over eighty years of age. The replacement of William Brennan by David Souter in 1989 enabled Bush to begin strengthening the conservative majority on the Court.

The twentieth century imposed new economic, social,

and political pressures on the Constitution. After initially being a bulwark against change, the Supreme Court came to play a vital role in assisting constitutional adaptation to the forces of modernization. Its role in the field of economic management and regulation was permissive rather than promotional, effectively legitimizing measures already taken by the executive and Congress. The judiciary's most distinctive contribution to constitutional change lay in the fields of civil and individual rights. By effectively nationalizing the Bill of Rights, it helped to ensure the survival of the Constitution and strengthen American democracy. As the United States moves toward the twenty-first century, the Court's activist role is entering a period of restraint. Nonetheless the Supreme Court will still be the final arbiter of the federal-state relationship and the balance between the executive and legislative branches of government, continuing to play the crucial role in the shaping of the American polity that it has fulfilled so far in the making of "America's century."

Notes

1. James Bryce, *The American Commonwealth,* abridged ed. (New York, 1896), p. 14.

2. Alpheus T. Mason, "Myth and Reality in Supreme Court Decisions," in *Theory and Practice in American Politics,* ed. William H. Nelson and Francis L. Loewenheim (Chicago, 1964), p. 64.

3. Merle Miller, *Plain Speaking: An Oral Biography of Harry S. Truman* (New York, 1975), p. 225.

4. Peter H. Irons, *The New Deal Lawyers* (Princeton, 1982), pp. 195–96.

5. Stanley I. Kutler, ed., *The Supreme Court and the Constitution: Readings in American Constitutional History,* 3d ed. (New York, 1984), p. 388.

6. Robert G. McCloskey, *The American Supreme Court* (Chicago, 1960), p. 177.

7. Robert F. Cushman, *Leading Constitutional Decisions,* 15th ed. (Englewood Cliffs, N.J., 1977), p. 209.

8. M. Glenn Abernathy, ed., *Civil Liberties under the Constitution,* 4th ed. (Columbia, S.C., 1985), p. 388.

9. McCloskey, *The American Supreme Court*, pp. 111–12.

10. Martin Shapiro, "The Supreme Court: From Warren to Burger," in *The New American Political System*, ed. Anthony King (Washington, D.C., 1978), p. 173.

11. Abernathy, *Civil Liberties under the Constitution*, p. 483.

12. Ibid., p. 485.

13. Cushman, *Leading Constitutional Decisions*, p. 419.

Bibliography

For a complete and comprehensive account of constitutional development, see Alfred H. Kelley, Winifred A. Harbison, and Herman Belz, *The American Constitution: Its Origins and Development*, 6th ed. (New York, 1983). Briefer, but still useful, alternatives are Forrest McDonald, *A Constitutional History of the United States* (New York, 1982); Archibald Cox, *The Court and the Constitution* (Boston, 1987); and David P. Currie, *The Constitution of the United States: A Primer for the People* (Chicago, 1988). For studies with a twentieth-century focus see William F. Swindler, *Court and Constitution in the Twentieth Century*, 2 vols. (Indianapolis, 1969–70); Glendon Schubert, *The Constitutional Polity* (Boston, 1970); Paul L. Murphy, *The Constitution in Crisis Times, 1918–1969* (New York, 1972); and Alpheus T. Mason, *The Supreme Court from Taft to Burger* (Baton Rouge, La., 1979).

Elder Witt, ed., *Congressional Quarterly's Guide to the U.S. Supreme Court* (Washington, D.C., 1979) offers a comprehensive guide to Supreme Court decisions. Robert G. McCloskey, *The American Supreme Court* (Chicago, 1960) is a well-written and stimulating history, and is well complemented for post-1960 developments by Richard Hodder-Williams, *The Politics of the U.S. Supreme Court* (London, 1980). Archibald Cox, *The Role of the Supreme Court in American Government* (New York, 1976) offers a defense of judicial activism, while Alexander M. Bickel, *The Supreme Court and the Idea of Progress* (New Haven, Conn., 1978) provides a critical perspective. On relationships with the executive branch, see Henry J. Abraham, *Justices and Presidents: A Political History of Appointments to the Supreme Court* (New York, 1974) and John D. Lees, "The President and the Supreme Court: New Deal to Watergate," *British Association of American Studies Pamphlet 3* (1980).

The New Deal Court is analyzed in Bernard Schwarz, *The Supreme Court: Constitutional Revolution in Retrospect* (New York, 1957); William E. Leuchtenburg, "The Origins of Franklin D. Roosevelt's 'Court-Packing' Plan," in *The Supreme Court Review, 1966*, ed. Philip B. Kurland (Chicago, 1966), pp. 352–99; Michael E. Parrish, "The Hughes Court, the Great Depression and Historians," *The Historian* 40 (1975): 286–308; and Richard Maidment, "The New Deal Court Revisited," in *Nothing Else to Fear: New Perspectives on America in the Thirties*, ed. Stephen W. Baskerville and Ralph Willett (Manchester, 1985).

Two studies by Bernard Schwarz, *Super Chief: Earl Warren and His Supreme Court: A Judicial Biography* (New York, 1983) and *The Unpublished Opinions of the Warren Court* (New York, 1985) provide a thorough and favorable account of the Court in the 1950s and 1960s. For a critical perspective, see Richard Maidment, "Policy in Search of Law: The Warren Court from Brown to Miranda," *Journal of American Studies* 9 (1975): 301–20. Vincent Blasi, ed., *The Burger Court: The Counter-Revolution That Wasn't* (New Haven, 1983), and Herman Schwarz, ed., *The Burger Years: Rights and Wrongs in the Supreme Court, 1969–1986* (New York, 1987) are the best studies of the Burger Court. Other useful studies of the modern period are Stephen L. Wasby, *Continuity and Change: From the Warren Court to the Burger Court* (Pacific Palisades, Cal., 1976); Richard Y. Funston, *Constitutional Counterrevolution? The Warren Court and the Burger Court: Judicial Policy Making in Modern America* (Cambridge, Mass., 1977); and two essays by Martin Shapiro, "The Supreme Court: From Warren to Burger," in *The New American Political System*, ed. Anthony King (Washington, D.C., 1978), pp. 179–211, and "The Supreme Court from Early Burger to Early Rehnquist," in *The New American Political System: Second Version*, ed. Anthony King (Washington D.C., 1990), pp. 47–85. For evaluations of the Reagan era, see Elder Witt, *A Different Justice: Reagan and the Supreme Court* (Washington, D.C., 1986) and Richard Hodder-Williams, "Ronald Reagan and the Supreme Court," in *The*

Reagan Years: The Record in Presidential Leadership, ed. Joseph Hogan (Manchester, 1989), pp. 143–63.

On the specific issue of racial desegregation, the most useful studies are Stephen L. Wasby, Anthony d'Amato, and Rosemary Metrailer, *Desegregation from Brown to Alexander: An Exploration of Supreme Court Strategies* (Carbondale, Ill., 1976), and J. Harvie Wilkinson III, *From Brown to Bakke: The Supreme Court and School Integration, 1954–1978* (New York, 1979). For civil rights and liberties the best study is Henry J. Abraham, *Freedom and the Court: Civil Rights and Liberties in the U.S.* (New York, 1987).

11

The Foreign Policy of a World Power

Geoff Stoakes

> As America enters dramatically upon the world scene, we need most of all to seek and bring forth a vision of America as a world power which is authentically American and which can inspire us to live and work and fight with vigor and enthusiasm. . . . It is in this spirit that all of us are called, each to his own measure of capacity, and each in the widest horizon of his vision to create the first great American Century.
>
> Henry Luce, 1941

Henry Luce's famous _Life_ editorial crystallized the debate over the role America ought to play as a world power, which had been keenly contested at least since 1898 when it acquired an empire. The immediate cause of Luce's invocation of a new era in American history was an attempt to dispel the isolationist mood that still gripped the country some eighteen months after the outbreak of war in Europe. Luce called upon Americans to accept wholeheartedly "our duty and responsibility as the most powerful and vital nation in the world" and to intervene in the war and, simultaneously, to start planning the postwar peace.[1] However, in addition to being a decisive rejection of the isolationist cause in favor of a century of American internationalism, Luce's editorial also reflected the missionary idealism that has so often imbued American perceptions of the nation's world role. In the new century, America would have "to assume the leadership of the world" and specifically to take over from Britain the primary responsibility for maintaining world peace. This vision of a _Pax Americana_ was not entirely devoid of self-interest, however: it would facilitate the extension of the American system of free enterprise to the rest of the world. Not surprisingly, Luce's critics promptly accused him of arrogant imperialism, and in May 1942 Vice President Henry A. Wallace, a liberal Democrat, countered Luce's capitalist vision with a more radical one of his own: the next hundred years could and must, he said, be "the Century of the Common Man."[2]

Luce's editorial and the response to it exposed the tensions underlying the American people's approach to foreign affairs in the twentieth century, notably the dichotomies between isolationism and internationalism, ideals and self-interest, and anticolonialism and imperialism. This chapter will evaluate the significance of these guiding principles in fashioning American diplomacy in the twentieth century.

Orthodox historians have tended to describe American foreign policy in terms of fluctuations between the competing forces of isolationism and internationalism. However, both concepts are ill-defined. Indeed, their meaning has altered considerably over time at the hands of politicians and historians alike, and they need to be handled with care. Isolationism was one of the oldest traditions in American history and was closely bound up with the New World's rejection of the Old. In essence, it consisted of the avoidance of entangling alliances with foreign powers and a policy of abstention as far as possible from the affairs of Europe. Many historians also interpret the Monroe Doctrine's prohibition of further European encroachment in the Western Hemisphere as symptomatic of an isolationist America's desire to quarantine itself from Old World diseases such as war, poverty, and oppression.

The internationalist tradition is rather more recent. In its original form, it entailed a willingness to project American power and influence in the world, specifically to accept a share in the responsibility for maintaining world peace and to engage to that end in systems of collective security. Recently, some historians have muddied the waters by attributing the desire to interfere in the affairs of other nations and for economic penetration of other societies to internationalism. Thus the Spanish-American War of 1898 has been interpreted as evidence of *both* isolationism (the New World's desire to eradicate European imperialism) and internationalism (America's assumption of sphere-of-influence responsibilities). This clearly indicates the confusion now surrounding the terms.

In fact, the Spanish-American War is more accurately portrayed as the quite distinct product of a volatile mixture of the anticolonial and imperialistic traditions: the compulsion to free Cuba from Spanish rule coinciding with the drive for an American overseas empire. The Teller Amendment (1898), declaring that the United States was not going to war to conquer territory, and the Platt Amendment (1901), reserving for America important controls over supposedly independent Cuba, together with the retention of the Philippines, Puerto Rico, and Guam, taken from Spain in the war, testify to what has been aptly labeled America's "imperial anticolonialism." To revisionist historians, the acquisition of overseas empire was no novel departure because the United States was by its very nature an expansionist power: overseas colonization followed naturally on the conquest of the American continental interior.

So-called Open Door revisionists, on the other hand, have been keen to represent the events of the 1890s and 1900s as evidence of a new global dimension in American foreign policy. America's thrust for empire was dictated, they argue, by surplus agricultural and industrial production in search of overseas markets. According to William A. Williams, "The capitalist economy is inherently imperialistic."[3] In his view, Secretary of State John Hay's Open Door Notes of 1899 and 1900, which committed the United States to defend for the world the principle of equal and impartial trade with all parts of the Chinese Empire, were a prescription for ultimate dominance by the United States of the entire world marketplace.

But it is very doubtful whether the attempt to create this kind of "informal empire" became the crucial determinant of American diplomacy at this time. The American economy remained home market–, not export market–oriented, at least until 1914. The Open Door notes were limited to China and designed not so much to expand America's economic control as to prevent Germany, Russia, and Japan from developing their own exclusive spheres of influence. Furthermore, America's commitment to defend the Open Door principle (and Chinese sovereignty) ultimately crumbled in face of the Japanese annexation of Korea in 1910.

This failure, and the hostile response of many in America

to Theodore Roosevelt's attempt to mediate between the European great powers at Algeçiras in 1906 and to increase the size of the U.S. Navy, together with a general reluctance to consider the expansion of its formal empire, all testify to the continued refusal of most Americans to accept that the United States was destined to play a larger international role. Thus neither America's newly acquired imperial status, nor the presumed need to promote overseas economic expansion, nor Theodore Roosevelt's flirtation with internationalism effected any immediate and irreversible change in America's outlook on the world.

Woodrow Wilson is generally identified with a crusade for internationalism. His attempt to secure U.S. participation in his beloved League of Nations at the cost of his own health has helped to establish him as the tragic hero of the postwar world, trying but ultimately failing to educate the American people about the duties and responsibilities of America's position as a world power. Realist historians have criticized Wilson's tendency to enunciate universal principles and ideals rather than to define and defend the American national interest. On the other hand, more sympathetic historians have suggested that his overt idealism disguised a "higher realism." New Left historians have also described Wilson as a realist, but one whose goal was the creation of a peaceful "liberal capitalist world order," secure against both traditional imperialism and revolutionary socialism.

However, it has to be remembered that Wilson was not committed to the idea of collective security at the start of his presidency or even at the outbreak of war in Europe in 1914. In fact, his call for Americans to be "impartial in thought as well as in action," his ban on loans to belligerents, and his defense of neutrals' shipping rights were all perfectly consistent with the traditions of American isolationism. His espousal of collective security was not, therefore, the result of long-held and deeply rooted Christian convictions. It was a response to wartime developments, in particular the loss of American lives as a result of Germany's tactic of unrestricted submarine warfare, and of the delivery of his own virtual ultimatum to Germany demanding the policy's discontinuance in the *Sussex* crisis. It is really no coincidence that Wilson's first public endorsement of U.S. participation in a League of Nations on May 27, 1916, came in the wake of this crisis. His commitment to postwar collective security was, perhaps, partly at least an attempt to encourage the Allies to negotiate an early peace. Certainly Wilson's abandonment of isolationism was at least as much pragmatic as idealistic.

It has been suggested that the desire to realize his vision of a new postwar world order provided Wilson with a reason to take the United States into World War I; in order to secure an influential seat at the peace conference, America needed to be a belligerent. This seems rather farfetched. It was only the German resumption of unrestricted submarine warfare in January 1917, in flagrant disregard of the *Sussex* pledge, that compelled Wilson to contemplate intervention. Even then he hesitated. It was only when actual German-American naval clashes occurred and the Zimmermann Telegram raised the possibility (however remote in reality) of an extension of the war to the American continent that Wilson requested a declaration of war from Congress. His war message of April 2, 1917, justified intervention in terms of the need to make the world safe for democracy, but this was hardly the *casus belli*. Wilson's rhetoric was arguably intended to reassure pacifists and progressives by tying intervention to a crusade for a liberal world order.

The debate over the Versailles treaty and America's entry into the League of Nations is usually presented as a climactic confrontation between the traditional forces of isolationism and the new doctrine of internationalism. However, this scenario, while no doubt based on Wilson's own perception of it—and partly because it is based on this—underestimates the complexity of the treaty flight. Specifically, it assumes first that Wilson was an unqualified advocate of internationalism and second that his Republican opponents were dyed-in-the-wool isolationists. Both assumptions have been questioned recently by Lloyd Ambrosius.

Most historians, whether impressed by Wilson's "higher realism," critical of his blindness to the national interest, or alienated by his liberal-capitalist values, have generally accepted that his single-minded attempt to secure the Senate's acceptance of the League of Nations Covenant without reservations indicated his total rejection of the isolationist mentality. Ambrosius, by contrast, stresses that the entire concept of "new diplomacy" embodied in the covenant was based on a conscious rejection of "Old World" power politics and diplomatic alignments with which isolationists could easily identify. Furthermore, the unanimity principle enshrined in the covenant, which ensured a national veto on all decisions in the league's council, preserved American sovereignty. Hence "[Wilson's] conception of the league which would have involved the United States in global obligations while allowing it alone to defend them,"[4] combined both internationalism and isolationism.

Historical assessments of the motives of the league's Republican opponents in the Senate have also been sharply divergent. Some have portrayed Henry Cabot Lodge, chairman of the Senate Foreign Relations Committee, as an unprincipled partisan politician who insisted on attaching the Fourteen Reservations to the covenant in order to prevent an outright Democratic victory in the peacemaking process. Others have rejected this portrait, arguing that Lodge was genuinely concerned to defend American national interests and that he favored not isolationism, but "prudent involvement" in world affairs. Unqualified acceptance of the covenant, and in particular Article 10's commitment to defend the territorial integrity and political independence of member states, would place the United States under the control of an international organization that could legitimately request that it protect all countries against external aggression. The league might also interfere in the affairs of the Western Hemisphere in defiance of the Monroe Doctrine. Lodge's reservations, which included the unconditional right of the United States to withdraw from the league and exclusive American rights to decide which questions were within the league's jurisdiction, were thus designed to protect America's independence within the league. Hence "the question of control," according to Ambrosius, "not isolationism versus internationalism, was the central issue in the treaty fight."[5]

Also at issue in the conflict was the question of who controlled America's foreign policy. While still an academic at Princeton in 1908, Wilson had written that the president's power was "very absolute" in the area of foreign policy and that he could negotiate treaties that effectively committed the nation, thereby making Senate ratification almost a formality.[6] The high-handedness of Wilson's presentation of the Treaty of Versailles to the Senate in July 1919, when he essentially invited the Senate not to study the document but to sign it, seemed to reflect this belief in presidential treaty-making. Lodge's campaign against the treaty was motivated in part by the desire to reassert Congressional influence in foreign affairs.

So was the treaty fight really the great test of America's willingness to accept its responsibilities as a world power? If it was, in part, a battle between the White House and Congress over the control of foreign policy, and if Wilson cannot be considered to be a full-fledged internationalist and his major opponent was not intrinsically isolationist, then was the debate really over isolationism and internationalism, or over the form that American internationalism should take? Lodge's stated preference was certainly for a cautious internationalism, whereby the league had to defer to member states' sovereignty in decision-making. But, it must be stressed, the covenant already ensured this (as the later history of the league proved). All things considered, the treaty debate was about appearances more than reality. However, this assessment should not obscure the fact that in failing to ratify the Versailles treaty the Senate in effect rejected an entangling alliance—the Anglo-American guarantee of France's frontiers. In failing to join the League of Nations (for whatever reason) the United States absented itself from the system of collective security. In these respects, the decision was a victory for isolationism.

The defeat of Wilsonianism in 1920 could not, however, disguise the fact that America's standing in the world had been altered irreversibly by World War I. Like it or not, it was a major world power. By 1919 its fleet was large enough to challenge Britain's long-vaunted naval supremacy, and its merchant marine was second only to that of Britain in size. Its wartime loans to the Allies had turned the net debtor nation of 1913 into a net creditor by 1919. Thus many of the preconditions of isolationism had been eroded, and it is not surprising to find historians referring to the "legend of isolationism" in the 1920s.

In the diplomatic sphere, the term *isolationism* could be applied only in its narrowest sense, and then only relatively. The United States continued in the 1920s to avoid entangling alliances and to a large degree evade the responsibility for collective security, observing the activities of the league but refusing to join in. However, American governments did, on occasion, act in the spirit of internationalism. For example, Secretary of State Charles Evans Hughes threw the weight of the United States behind the cause of naval arms limitation at the Washington

Conference (November 1921–February 1922). Two of the result-
ant Washington treaties—the Four-Power Treaty, by which Britain, America, Japan, and France agreed to respect each other's
rights in the Pacific and to consult in the event of a dispute in
the area, and the Nine-Power Treaty, which guaranteed Chinese
sovereignty and the Open Door principle in respect to trade,
created an embryonic system of regional collective security.
Hughes defended the treaties against charges of Wilsonianism
by some critics, pointing out that they were conducted within
limitations defined by the American government and contained
no binding commitment to act. But it was undeniable that he
had placed the authority of the United States behind the territorial status quo in the Pacific. In reality, the isolationists'
strict code of practice was now confined to Europe.

In the economic sphere it is misleading to use the term
isolationism at all, since by the 1920s America was inextricably
enmeshed in the world marketplace. American involvement in
the Dawes and Young plans to scale down German reparations
payments and the refloating of the German economy after 1924
by American loans were not entirely altruistic, in view of the
expected returns regarding Allied debt repayments and increased international trade. Nevertheless they also constituted
an enlightened gesture of internationalism, which committed
the United States to assist Western Europe's economic recovery.

Some historians argue that the key to understanding
American diplomacy of the 1920s is the realization that it was
based on the coming of age of the Open Door policy.[7] But save
for the Nine-Power Treaty's reiteration of the Open Door principle, there is little evidence to suggest that the search for foreign
markets was the dominant motive behind American foreign
policy. Indeed, American insistence on Allied debt repayments
and the raising of tariff barriers to their highest-ever level in
1922 would appear flatly to contradict the idea. Foreign nations
could hardly buy American goods if they were deprived of foreign currency by debt repayments and/or unable to earn dollars
in the American market because of prohibitive tariffs. Protectionism, therefore, hampered rather than helped the development of foreign markets. Although there is no doubting the
desire for overseas markets, it can hardly have been the decisive
consideration in American diplomacy in the 1920s.

One area where economic interests were often paramount

was Latin America. America's commitment to internationalism did not normally extend here. The Monroe Doctrine, by denying Europeans the right to intervene in the Western Hemisphere, had implied an exclusive American sphere of influence. In 1904 Theodore Roosevelt's corollary to the Monroe Doctrine made this explicit by claiming for the United States the right to exercise "international police power" in Latin America "in flagrant cases of wrongdoing or impotence." Since 1904 the United States had intervened militarily in the Dominican Republic, Panama, Haiti, Nicaragua, and Mexico in defense of American strategic and financial interests. However, in the 1920s successive American governments tried to halt this trend. By 1930, apart from a temporary reversal in the case of the Nicaraguan revolt of 1927, American troops had been withdrawn. The State Department's *Memorandum on the Monroe Doctrine*, drafted in 1928 and published two years later, expressly disavowed the Roosevelt Corollary as an alibi for American intervention and paved the way for Franklin D. Roosevelt's Good Neighbor policy. Despite this, the Monroe Doctrine remained the guiding principle of American diplomacy toward Latin America.

American foreign policy in the 1920s defies easy categorization. Internationalism, in the form of the Washington system of collective security in the Far East, coexisted with pervasive isolationist hostility toward the League of Nations. High tariff barriers sought to protect the American economy from being swamped by European imports, while increased trade with Latin America was sought by the retreat from informal empire and the fostering of improved diplomatic relations.

The economic depression of the 1930s brought the high tide of isolationism as a political force. It undercut the cautious internationalism of the Washington system in a number of very direct ways. First, the need to revive overseas trade as a means of stimulating economic recovery ruled out serious consideration of American economic sanctions against Japan, despite the latter's flagrant breach in the Manchurian incident of the Four- and Nine-Power treaties. Stimson's nonrecognition doctrine was a poor substitute. Second, the need to secure the passage of New Deal legislation to tackle the Depression through a Senate still dominated by isolationists prevented meaningful American participation in collective security. At the World Disarmament Conference in 1933 U.S. representatives could only assure the great powers that if peace were threatened, America would not interfere with league sanctions against an aggressor provided that it felt them justified. Third, the Depression led to the passage of what is often seen as the first piece of neutrality legislation, the Johnson Act of 1934, which made it illegal for Americans to raise loans for those governments (principally Britain and France) that had defaulted on their debt repayments to the United States as a result of the Depression. Finally, suspicions that big business had caused the Wall Street crash of October 1929 in part at least inspired the so-called merchants-of-death theory that munitions manufacturers had paved the way for American intervention in World War I by pressuring Wilson into supplying arms to the Allies. A Senate committee inquiry led by Gerald P. Nye of North Dakota found little concrete evidence to support this but did add bankers who loaned money to the Allies to the list of possible culprits. Though Walter Millis's best-selling *Road to War: America 1914–1917* (1935) depicted the defense of traditional neutral trading rights as the main *casus belli*, there is little doubt that suspicion of corporate business convinced many Americans of the need to take precautions to ensure their nation's genuine neutrality in any future conflict.

The result was three Neutrality Acts, enacted between 1935 and 1937 in the face of escalating international tensions provoked by the Italian invasion of Abyssinia in 1935, the outbreak of the Spanish Civil War in 1936, and the renewed Sino-Japanese hostilities of 1937. The acts banned the sale of arms to and the raising of loans for belligerents, prohibited the export of nonmilitary goods to belligerents except on a cash-and-carry basis, and forbade American citizens from sailing on vessels belonging to belligerent nations. Designed to prevent the repetition of the circumstances that led to America's intervention in 1917 while, at the same time, ensuring that it could still take advantage of the expansion of trade in wartime, these acts created only the "illusion of neutrality." This was made plain when the U.S.S. *Panay* was attacked by Japanese planes in December 1937. In the ensuing war scare, however, isolationist sentiment reached its peak with the Ludlow Resolution, which proposed that except in the case of invasion, declarations of war be subject to national referenda rather than a vote in Congress.

This proposal was only narrowly defeated by 209 votes to 188 in the House of Representatives on January 10, 1938.

Franklin D. Roosevelt's role in this flurry of wishful anti-war thinking has been much debated. Some historians have portrayed him as a committed isolationist, disillusioned by his support for Wilson in 1919–20, who did not try effectively to combat the forces of isolationism. Others have suggested that he played an equivocal role, floating with the tide of isolationist opinion initially but later attempting, albeit rather tentatively, to educate the American people in their responsibilities for maintaining world peace. Robert Dallek, on the other hand, regards Roosevelt as a loyal Wilsonian pursuing internationalist policies but frustrated by Congress and discouraged by the European powers.[7]

Some of these conflicts of opinion result from the by now familiar tendency to present all American diplomatic activity in terms of the isolationist-internationalist dichotomy. For example, Dallek interprets the diplomatic recognition of the Soviet Union in 1933 as evidence of a continuing commitment to collective security, inspired by the necessity not only to revive Soviet-American trade but also to deter Japanese aggression against the USSR. By contrast, British historian A. J. P. Taylor treats it as collaboration between isolationists.[8] The fact is, of course, that economic necessity, not isolationism or internationalism, stimulated this piece of détente. This was also true of Roosevelt's controversial decision to reject an international agreement to reduce tariffs and to stabilize currency exchange rates, which scuttled the World Economic Conference in 1933.

Some of the conflicts of opinion are also more apparent than real, resting on only slightly different assessments of the amount of pragmatism and idealism in Roosevelt's maneuverings. For example, he conciliated isolationist opinion by encouraging the Nye Committee to consider neutrality legislation, but he also bowed to collective security ideals in his unsuccessful efforts to acquire discretionary powers to impose sanctions only against an aggressor. Realizing that the neutrality laws provided the green light to aggressors, since victims as well as perpetrators of aggression would be subject to a U.S. arms embargo, he refused to activate the legislation in the Sino-Japanese War after 1937. In the quarantine speech of October

1937 he sought to promote American participation in collective action against aggression but, fearing lack of domestic support, he restrained the American delegation to the Nine-Power Conference in Brussels in November 1937 from offering concrete backing for sanctions against Japan. In reality, what the British regarded as another example of Roosevelt's empty rhetoric was a misguided attempt to throw the moral authority of the United States behind the cause of collective security in a situation where he knew his actions could not match his words.

Whether Roosevelt favored appeasement is still in dispute and will always remain so, since the rejection of the so-called Roosevelt Initiative by British Prime Minister Neville Chamberlain kept the American president one stage removed from direct negotiations with the European dictators. In all probability, however, Roosevelt's suggestion to Britain in 1937 for an international conference to establish new rules of international law and a convention to implement its recommendations was an attempt to add Washington's imprimatur to Western European efforts to conciliate the Axis. United States economic policy in the 1930s has also been interpreted as evidence of appeasement. Yet American efforts to wean Britain off the system of Imperial Preference and to entice Britain and Germany, which had negotiated bilateral deals after 1933, back into the multilateral economy were backed by both pro- and antiappeasement elements in the U.S. government. It is therefore likely that pressure on Britain to return to the fold was primarily intended as a means to revive the international economy rather than as a response to Nazi aggression.

The Roosevelt Initiative failed because the British preferred to hold bilateral talks with Adolf Hitler. Meanwhile, the Nazi dictator reacted scornfully to Roosevelt's peace messages of September 1938 and April 1939. These responses underlined the fact that the United States could not wield international influence without military power and political commitments. But it is evident that the 1930s can no longer be considered simply as years of unrelieved isolationism. Roosevelt pursued internationalism in this era alongside policies of economic liberalization and political detachment.

It has been suggested by Selig Adler that "the isolationist cause had been lost before the Japanese bombed Pearl Harbor."[9] Roosevelt's successive infringements of American neutrality after September 1939—the repeal of the arms embargo, the "destroyers for bases" deal, Lend-Lease, and the convoy system (each move justified in terms of all-out aid to Britain short of war) were bitter blows to the isolationist cause. Yet there is good reason for doubting that they were fatal ones. First, the arguments of the America First movement, established in September 1940 with support from famous personalities like Henry Ford and Charles Lindbergh, carried some weight with public opinion. The Fortress America policy of this organization envisaged a massive buildup of home defense in order that the latest Old World conflict could be ignored with impunity. Henry Luce's "American Century" editorial was partly intended to rebut this concept, but had to stop short of open advocacy of intervention in recognition of the isolationists' popular appeal.

Second, the majority of Americans still wanted to believe what the president was telling them: it was possible to keep America out by keeping Britain in the war. Third, the outbreak of hostilities between Germany and the Soviet Union in June 1941 seemed to diminish the likelihood of an Axis victory quite markedly. Roosevelt's apparently devious manipulation of Germany into an undeclared naval war in the Atlantic in the autumn of 1941, together with his inability to request a declaration of war on Germany even after Pearl Harbor, testify to the constraints still imposed on him by the isolationists.

Ironically, war came in the Far East, and in retrospect, the isolationists can be seen as having bolted the front door while leaving the back door open. Europe was the traditional isolationist *bête noir*. Roosevelt had been left relatively free after 1937 to respond to Japanese aggression. The results were the abrogation of the Japanese-American Trade Treaty in 1940, aid to Chiang Kai-shek's forces in China, and ultimately, the freezing of Japanese assets in the United States in July 1941. Controversy still rages over whether Roosevelt was deliberately provoking the Japanese to enable him to take America into the war in Europe or merely trying to deter Japan from further acts of aggression. On balance, it is most likely that Roosevelt was convinced that the Japanese would capitulate under American financial and diplomatic pressure. It is equally likely that what may have been intended in Washington as a deterrent was regarded in Tokyo as provocation. It is important to note also that the United States was acting here on the basis of that brand of American internationalism designed in Washington in 1921–22 and reinforced by the Stimson Doctrine, which rejected any territorial change based on force.

The events of December 1941 seemed to destroy the preconditions for the isolationism that had so dominated American diplomacy in the 1930s. Pearl Harbor punctured for all time the myth of American strategic invulnerability. The German declaration of war on America on December 11 proved that Woodrow Wilson had been right all along when he had argued that there could be no neutrality when the peace of the world was at stake. Even the Republican party, the seedbed of isolationism, became converted to collective security. Former presidential candidate Wendell Willkie's book *One World* (1943), the most influential internationalist text of the decade, and political expediency—the 1944 Congressional elections proved to be a graveyard for unrepentant isolationists—may have contributed to this change of heart. However, the Republicans, faithful to Lodge's position in 1919–20, favored only "*responsible* participation by the United States in [a] postwar cooperation organization among *sovereign* nations."[10] The conversion to internationalism in early 1945 of Senator Arthur Vandenberg of Michigan, the ranking Republican in the Senate Foreign Relations Committee, while ensuring bipartisan support for collective security in the immediate postwar period, was effected without infringement of his fervently nationalistic principles.

World War II was, therefore, the second chance for internationalism. Roosevelt talked of a new system of collective security that would avert the possibility of a future war, and he stressed that collaboration between the "Four Policemen" (the United States, Soviet Union, Britain, and China) would provide the surest guarantee of lasting peace. Roosevelt has been criticized for being naïve about the prospects of continued U.S.–Soviet cooperation and for engendering false hopes with the rhetoric of liberal internationalism. In fact, he was quite level-headed, but perceived that the American people had been gripped by a missionary idealism generated by wartime propaganda, Luce's call to internationalism, and Willkie's enthusiastic hymn of praise to the Soviet Union in *One World*. The president could not puncture this mood of optimism without destroying the postwar consensus for internationalism.

In private, Roosevelt was skeptical about the chances of postwar collaboration with Stalin. Soviet involvement in the United Nations was achieved only after much hard bargaining in conferences at Tehran (November 1943), and Yalta (February 1945). At Yalta, the United States had to concede a national veto on decisions in the Security Council and three seats for the Soviet Union in the General Assembly. Roosevelt also had to acquiesce in Soviet territorial gains at Polish expense in return for Stalin's promise of free elections in the European countries "liberated" by the Red Army. The fact that arrangements for a postwar settlement could not be separated from the strategy of winning the war caused further complications. At Yalta Roosevelt made territorial concessions to the Soviet Union in Europe and Asia in order to secure its pledge to participate in the war against Japan within three months of Germany's surrender in Europe—a crucial commitment at a time when the atomic bomb was still untried.

Roosevelt's wartime policy toward the Soviets was shaped by practical necessity rather than naïve idealism. Without doubt the overriding concern to keep the Soviets in the war dictated concessions at Yalta that affected the postwar balance of power in Europe and Asia. Paradoxically, Roosevelt's policy of accommodation has been criticized both as a territorial sellout to communism and as a cause of the Cold War (since he did not make clear to Stalin the limits of American tolerance of Soviet expansionism in Europe). In reality, the Yalta concessions, though objectionable from the perspective of national sovereignty, concerned territories that were beyond American control. Furthermore, to blame Roosevelt for causing the Cold War not only belittles his attempts to integrate the Soviet Union into the postwar international community but also oversimplifies the nature of the conflict. The roots of confrontation can be traced back to Lenin's ideological declaration of war on the capitalist world in November 1917 and to the Allied intervention in Russia of 1918–20, which evolved in its latter stages into something akin to an anti-Bolshevik crusade. The retreat of the United States and the Soviet Union into relative isolationism in the 1920s and 1930s and the rise of Fascist states in Central Europe prevented the conflict reaching its full potential immediately. However, the eclipse of the Axis powers in 1945 eliminated the common enemy whose destruction had necessitated the shotgun marriage of the leading capitalist and communist nations in World War II.

This is not to argue that the Cold War was inevitable. Competing state ideologies can coexist. The catalyst that transformed the incipient rivalry into outright political and military confrontation is still hotly debated. The orthodox school of historians points to Soviet aggression in Eastern Europe and the refusal to hold the free elections promised at Yalta. The revisionists, on the other hand, blame American provocation of various kinds. Open Door theorists cite pressure on the Soviet Union to allow equal access to trade in Eastern Europe, but there is no evidence of serious U.S. economic interest in the area. President Truman has been accused of dropping the atom bombs on Hiroshima and Nagasaki in an attempt to browbeat the Russians; but while this may have been seen by some as a useful by-product, precipitating the Japanese surrender was surely his main purpose. Truman's tough response to the Soviet failure to honor the Yalta accords is another cause of revisionist criticism.

The case for U.S. provocation presupposes a keenness to confront the Soviet Union that did not exist. In fact, the rapid demobilization of the U.S. armed forces in 1945–46 seemed, irrespective of American membership of the United Nations, to herald a revival of isolationism in the form of a withdrawal from Europe. This was what Western European governments, especially the British, suspected and feared. In fact, American officials were deeply divided over the nature of the Soviet threat. Daniel Yergin has referred to the "Riga and Yalta axioms" to highlight the differences between those who considered the Soviet Union to be driven by an expansionist ideology and bent on world conquest (Riga) and those who saw it as a traditional great power whose ambitions could be accommodated, as at Yalta.[11] In light of this debate, it is important not to predate American enthusiasm for containment.

A distinctive Cold War policy finally emerged in response to several factors; the Soviet imposition of Communist-dominated regimes in Eastern Europe; Soviet pressure on Iran and Turkey; and Britain's inability to maintain military aid for the Greek government against indigenous Communist guerrillas. In March 1947, Harry S. Truman delivered a vague, imprecise, and sweeping promise to support "free peoples" against communist aggression. This became known as the Truman Doctrine. Its fundamental principle was given a name by George F. Kennan, the State Department's leading Soviet expert, whose anonymous article in *Foreign Affairs* in July 1947 recommended "a long-term, patient but firm and vigilant containment of Russian expansive tendencies."[12] The Marshall Plan for U.S. financing of a European Recovery Program, unveiled in June 1947, though motivated initially by the desire to restore world trade, was to become the financial arm of containment. The restoration of the Western European economies was intended in part to undercut the political appeal of indigenous Communists, especially in Italy and France. The Soviet-inspired coup in Czechoslovakia in February 1948 and the year-long Soviet blockade of Berlin that began later in March finally overcame residual Congressional suspicions about European entanglements. The Western European nations responded to the renewed Soviet threat with the Brussels Mutual Defense Pact (signed in 1948 by Britain, France, and the Benelux countries), which formed the basis for the North Atlantic Treaty Organization (NATO). The Senate's ratification of the NATO treaty in 1949 signified a decisive break with America's isolationist traditions. Furthermore, American membership in a mutual defense system indicated that the USSR was now appraised as a direct threat to the security of the United States.

America's NATO commitments were clear enough, but the policy of containment as a whole was largely undefined. Whom would the United States defend and how? The uncertainty about this was partly deliberate—to deter Soviet aggression—but it also reflected continuing disagreement in the American camp over the nature of the Soviet menace. Kennan's *Foreign Affairs* article was seen by Truman and others as identifying a Soviet military threat to the United States. Kennan has since claimed that he was misinterpreted and that he did not consider Russia to be a military threat at all, given the devastation of the country caused by World War II. What he feared was that the Soviets, with their prestige enhanced by the war, might be able to manipulate an indigenous Communist party into a takeover in a Western European country or Japan, which would have materially affected American security. Kennan did not advocate the commitment of U.S. armed forces to prevent this. Instead he favored political and financial aid of the type envisaged by the Marshall Plan in order to shore up governments in Greece and China that were hostile to local communist movements. Thus he supported political containment and rejected the military emphasis in the Truman Doctrine as well as its sweeping generality.

The events of 1949–50, however, widened the scope of containment in Asia and strengthened the hand of those who believed in military intervention. In August 1949 the successful Russian atom-bomb test destroyed America's nuclear monopoly. The stunning Communist victory in the Chinese civil war the following month, and the North Korean invasion of South Korea in June 1950, were taken as furthering the cause not of Asiatic nationalism but of Soviet expansionism. The Truman administration conceived an early version of President Dwight D. Eisenhower's domino theory that a Communist victory anywhere in Southeast Asia would lead in an unbreakable chain reaction to the loss of the whole area to communism. It persuaded Congress to vote financial aid to the French "anticommunist" forces in Indochina (political containment) and to back the president's decision to send American troops into Korea (military containment). In accepting a defense budget in line with the hawkish recommendations of National Security Council Paper 68 (NSC-68), however, Congress seemed to create the potential for a worldwide containment policy, in which military aid would increasingly take precedence over financial aid.

Congress had already unwittingly provided the institutional underpinning of the policy of military containment by the passage of the National Security Act of 1947, which sought to make the executive more responsive to the demands of the Cold War. Among its creations were the Department of Defense (DOD), a new cabinet office with oversight over all matters relating to national defense, the Central Intelligence Agency (CIA) to centralize intelligence-gathering, and the National Security Council (NSC), designed to coordinate foreign and defense policy for the president. In the first flush of Cold War bipartisanship, Congress thereby accelerated the trend toward an "imperial presidency" in the area of foreign affairs and, arguably, helped to increase the influence of those who favored military containment. In the next twenty-five years, as the threat of force or the actual resort to force became the order of the day, the military Joint Chiefs of Staff through the DOD would undermine the State Department's traditional authority in external policy-making; the CIA, through its covert activities, would develop into an unofficial agency of presidential interventionism; and the NSC would become the main means by which presidents would manipulate the foreign and defense policy establishment. While the Cold War consensus held, Congress willingly surrendered the initiative in foreign policy to the executive. For the same period also, the potential of the mushrooming foreign policy bureaucracy to thwart presidential ambitions remained largely hidden.

During the 1950s security treaties with Japan and the Philippines (1951) and the ANZUS (1952), SEATO (1954) and CENTO (1958) mutual assistance pacts extended America's formal alliance system. However, Eisenhower's secretary of state, John Foster Dulles, believed that the United States should go beyond containment and should strive to "liberate" those people suffering under Communist rule. In the event, American action did not match Dulles's bombast. During the Polish and Hungarian risings of 1956 there was no serious effort to advance the cause of "liberation."

The assumptions about a global communist menace that sustained containment policy to a large extent explain the American involvement in Vietnam. But the commitment of U.S. ground troops after 1965 was the product of nearly twenty years of deepening involvement and it is important to understand the reasons for each stage in the process.

In 1945 American intelligence officers collaborated with the Vietnamese nationalist leader Ho Chi Minh in ridding Indochina of the Japanese occupation force and were opposed to the return of French colonial rule. In 1950 President Truman agreed to a package of $20 million in military aid to the French forces fighting Ho's Vietminh. Clearly anticommunism had supplanted anticolonialism as the major American priority in Vietnam. Truman's decision was taken at the very moment he was dispatching American troops to South Korea and a year after the "loss" of China to the Communists, which Senator McCarthy was busy attributing to Communist infiltration of the State Department. At stake, therefore, was the credibility of containment. Truman's decision would be difficult to reverse since, in the logic of containment, the advance of communism anywhere (whether in Korea or Vietnam) was a setback for freedom everywhere.

Despite U.S. financial assistance, the French will to resist was broken by the siege of Dien Bien Phu in 1954. The Geneva accords attempted to disguise the French defeat by temporarily dividing Vietnam into two zones (the North under the Vietminh), with the proviso that the country be reunited after a general election to be held within two years. President Eisenhower is sometimes praised for not intervening militarily to prevent France's defeat, particularly for resisting advice to use atomic power, but he did collaborate with the new regime of Ngo Dinh Diem in repressing opposition in the South and connived in its failure to hold elections. By 1960 there were 685 American noncombatant military advisers in South Vietnam and the United States had contributed $2 billion in military aid to the war against South Vietnamese rebels and their North Vietnamese supporters. Eisenhower's policy, like Truman's, was designed to avert a victory for the Vietminh.

President John F. Kennedy presided over an increase in the number of military advisers from 685 to over 16,000, and a proportional increase in military assistance. The growing unpopularity of the Catholic Diem regime, horrifically displayed by the self-immolation protests of Buddhist monks, and the continued civil war with the National Liberation Front of South Vietnam led the United States to acquiesce in Diem's overthrow and assassination in November 1963. Kennedy was considering a U.S. withdrawal at the time of his own assassination, but it seems unlikely that he would have reversed his policy and permitted a communist takeover in South Vietnam in view of his conviction that the Third World was becoming the major battleground of the Cold War and his belief in the domino theory.

In August 1964 after two apparent attacks on U.S. warships in North Vietnamese waters, President Lyndon B. Johnson persuaded Congress to pass the Tonkin Gulf Resolution authorizing him to take "all necessary measures to repel any armed attacks against the forces of the United States and to prevent further aggression." This was almost certainly designed as a show of unity and conviction for the benefit of Hanoi but it did, of course, give the president carte blanche to expand the scope of the American involvement should he decide that it was necessary. In April 1965, following the North Vietnamese raid on the American base at Pleiku in February, Johnson made American cobelligerency overt by commencing the Rolling Thunder campaign of aerial bombardment of the North. Soon afterward, American ground troops were committed to defend American air bases and the process of escalation was in full swing.

It is now clear that the Tonkin Gulf incidents were fabricated and that the Pleiku raid itself occasioned rather than caused the introduction of Rolling Thunder. A consensus had already been reached among Johnson administration foreign policy decisionmakers by the end of 1964 that a carefully orchestrated bombing campaign was vital to raise South Vietnamese morale, to deter Hanoi from sustaining the Viet Cong and, most importantly, to prevent imminent South Vietnamese defeat. South Vietnam had descended into political chaos in mid-1964 and the war was going badly. The decision to commit ground troops followed when Rolling Thunder failed to halt the Communist offensive. There was, as General Westmoreland was to put it, "no solution . . . other than to put our own finger in the dike."[13]

No president since World War II can be exonerated from a share of the responsibility for the American involvement in Vietnam. It resulted from a series of incremental decisions that made the reversal of policy progressively more difficult. Blind anticommunism rather than any real strategic or economic interest led America into the Vietnam quagmire.

American military failure in Vietnam made it clear that global containment was impracticable. However, for twenty years containment reflected the so-called Cold War consensus. It is important, therefore, to assess its impact on American foreign policy. The first point to stress is that containment to a large extent hijacked the internationalist cause. During World War II a modus vivendi was found between nationalism and internationalism, which facilitated bipartisan support of the U.N. Later, anticommunism seemed to fuse internationalism and interventionism. There appeared to be little difference between America's involvement (to varying degrees) in multilateral diplomacy under the U.N.'s auspices during the crises in Korea (1950–53), Suez (1956) and the Congo (1960), and its unilateral actions over the Bay of Pigs (1961), the Cuban missile crisis (1962), the Dominican revolt (1965), and, of course, Vietnam. All appeared to serve the cause of containment.

Essentially, liberal internationalism had become a hostage to containment. The fate of Kennedy's Alliance for Progress (AFP) in Latin America is a good example. The AFP-s ten-year aid program to encourage social, economic, cultural, and political development originated in the Eisenhower administration's decision to try to stimulate democratic forces in the region. Its origins predated the emergence of a communist regime in Cuba. Nevertheless, after 1961 the AFP became a means of containing the Cuban revolution and its humanitarian principles were largely forgotten as aid was given to anticommunist dictatorships. Thus aid to Third World countries, like the Marshall Plan earlier, became another weapon in the Cold War. Containment effectively shackled internationalism and interventionism into an unholy alliance.

The second point to stress about the containment policy is that it combined idealism and self-interest in a highly combustible mixture. In abandoning their historical ambivalence toward internationalism after 1945, American politicians frequently propounded the nation's global mission to preserve and extend democratic principles of government. President Kennedy, for example, announced in his inaugural in 1961 that "we shall pay any price, bear any burden, meet any hardship, support any friend, oppose any foe to assure the survival and success of liberty." Of course, such idealism did not prevent the United States from backing undemocratic governments in Spain, Portugal, the Dominican Republic, South Korea, South Vietnam, and Iran, where perceived American interests were at risk from revolutionary change. This has led some to conclude that American foreign policy is essentially counterrevolutionary. This judgment is somewhat unfair. As Kennedy explained when Rafael Trujillo, long-time dictator of the Dominican Republic, was assassinated in 1961: "There are three possibilities in descending order of preference: a decent democratic regime, a continuation of the Trujillo regime, or a Castro regime. We ought to aim at the first, but we really can't renounce the second until we are sure that we can avoid the third."[14] The United States would, in principle, have preferred democratic change to continued dictatorship but was afraid of a Communist takeover.

When idealism and pragmatism conflicted head-on, there was little doubt which had to take precedence. Containment was not concerned primarily with the advancement of democratic government.

At the end of the 1960s the Cold War consensus finally collapsed. For the first time in twenty-five years, the identification of American national interest with an anticommunist world order was questioned. This meant not only the collapse of bipartisanship, which had been based on this article of faith, but also the end of Congressional tolerance of presidential initiative in foreign affairs. In cutting military assistance programs and in passing the War Powers Act of 1973, requiring the president to consult Congress within forty-eight hours of the commencement of hostilities and forcing him to seek specific Congressional authorization within sixty days, the legislature attempted to reassert the principle of codetermination of foreign policy. Whereas the former tactic could be successful for particular appropriations, the latter turned out to be a flawed instrument of general control. In the absence of a Congressional veto over presidential warmaking, the act unintentionally gave the chief executive greater powers to commit the United States to hostilities. As a result the Congressional backlash proved to be lacking in real substance.

It is often suggested that the evolution of détente and the American inability to end the war in Vietnam prompted a thorough-going reevaluation of America's self-image as a world power. Open clashes between Soviet and Chinese forces on the Manchurian frontier in 1969 made indisputable what had been suspected for some time, namely that the communist world was not monolithic. Sino-Soviet tension combined with the burgeoning costs of the arms race and the pioneering efforts at East-West conciliation by West German chancellor Willy Brandt paved the way towards détente. President Richard M. Nixon's visits to Peking in February and Moscow in May 1972 marked the official American acceptance of a multipolar world and of the need for peaceful coexistence and arms control.

The shift from confrontation to détente, capped by the signing of the Strategic Arms Limitation Treaty in May 1972, was dramatic. Whether it signified the abandonment of containment is debatable. Détente was based on the idea of "linkage"; increased trade and the exchange of technological expertise were offered in return for Soviet good behavior. As National Security Adviser (later Secretary of State) Henry Kissinger, the chief architect of détente, recognized, it was a carrot-and-stick approach. Détente did not mean the end of containment but the continuation of containment by other means.

If the evolution of détente did not dramatically alter official perceptions of America's global role, the Vietnam War certainly did. The Tet offensive of 1968 put the lie to all the confident predictions of impending American victory and revealed with unmistakeable clarity the limitations of American power. At Guam, on a tour of Southeast Asia in July 1969, President Nixon gave the first indication of a retreat from globalism. While promising that America would honor all existing commitments, he stressed that "except for the threat from a major power involving nuclear weapons," it would expect Asiatic nations to take primary responsibility for their own security. The Vietnamization of the war in Indochina reflected the same shift in attitude and constituted a marked withdrawal from the global containment of the Truman Doctrine and NSC-68.

The "no more Vietnams" syndrome in the 1970s has been interpreted as evidence of a new isolationism; but, in reality, it represented a rejection of American interventionism, not of internationalism. The War Powers Act of 1973 was intended primarily to ensure that there would be no repeat of the unchecked escalation of the war in Vietnam nor of the unauthorized extension of the conflict to Cambodia and Laos by Nixon in 1969. Carter administration foreign policy testified to the endurance of internationalism. The espousal of human rights, the pursuit of better relations with the Third World, the negotiation of the Camp David Accords, and the imposition of an embargo on grain sales to the Soviet Union in response to the invasion of Afghanistan in 1979 were all clear indications that Wilsonianism was at large in the White House. However, Carter's internationalism was vulnerable to domestic criticism from conservatives, especially in 1979–80 when it appeared to reap a harvest of failure. The approach of the 1980 election induced Carter to appeal to the anticommunist instincts of the American people by ordering a huge defense buildup and engaging in tough anti-Soviet rhetoric. This led George Kennan to observe that "never since World War II has there been so far-reaching a militarization of thought and discourse in the capital."[15]

Ronald Reagan proved better able to orchestrate the resurgence of anticommunist internationalism. The Reagan Doctrine abandoned the search for rapprochement with the Third World. Deeming the containment strategy of the Truman Doctrine inadequate, this mandated the provision of assistance in the form of economic aid and weaponry to rebel groups attempting to overthrow Third World regimes aligned with the Soviet Union. As a result the United States furnished aid to the Nicaraguan Contras and to anticommunist forces in such places as Afghanistan, Angola, Kampuchea, and Nicaragua. Overall, however, Reaganite policy manifested no interest in reconciling the unnatural marriage of internationalism and interventionism, which the early Cold War had ordained, but which the Vietnam War had split asunder.

Meanwhile, Reagan presided over the greatest arms buildup in American peacetime history in a bid to reestablish military superiority over the Soviets. The president's aim was to prove to the Soviet Union that it lacked the economic power to compete in a new arms race and thereby force it to the negotiating table in order to achieve nuclear arms reduction. This policy led ultimately to the INF treaty of 1988 which banned further production of intermediate range nuclear missiles and required the destruction of all existing intermediate range missiles possessed by both superpowers (1,752 by the Soviets, 859 by the U.S.). Reagan's personal abhorrence of nuclear weaponry is well documented, and seemingly imbued his foreign policy with world peace ideals. However, national security considerations were of far greater significance in shaping Reagan's policy on arms reduction. Further evidence of this was his insistence on the development of the Strategic Defense Initiative (SDI), a plan for a shield of high-tech weaponry to be raised above the United States as defense against nuclear missile attack.

Reagan's tough anti-Soviet policy did not have unanimous support within NATO. The internationalist features of American foreign policy since 1945 had generally found favor with Western European nations, who regarded the United States as integral to their own defense. Only France had manifested resentment of American leadership of the West. It claimed, in the wake of Eisenhower's refusal to support the Anglo-French intervention in Suez in 1956, that the global interests of the United States were too often at variance with

European regional interests. This attitude precipitated France's withdrawal from participation in NATO in 1966 (though it remained a member). Despite occasional disputes, relations between the U.S. and the rest of Western Europe remained good until the intensification of the Cold War in the early 1980s.

Widely regarded as trigger happy, Reagan was deeply unpopular with Western European public opinion, a factor that contributed to the reemergence of peace movements in Britain and West Germany in particular. NATO allies were also outraged by the lack of consultation over SDI, especially as this did not offer them protection. In these circumstances the support of British prime minister Margaret Thatcher, the most anti-Soviet of the European leaders, was important in helping Reagan to preserve the unity of the alliance. Exhausted by its efforts in World War II, Britain had effectively ceased to be a great power in 1945, but had mistakenly assumed that it would continue to exert significant influence on world affairs through the close relationship that it had developed with the United States in wartime. The so-called special relationship did not survive the 1950s because American interests required the establishment of close links with other Western European nations in addition to Britain. The Thatcher-Reagan relationship appeared to resuscitate the relationship, giving Britain a new influence in international affairs that its limited power did not merit. However, the revived Anglo-American relationship lost its significance for the U.S. once the decline in Soviet-American tensions paved the way for arms reduction. In future, the principal axis of the transatlantic relationship is likely to be between the United States and the newly united Germany, whose influence rests on its economic power and political leadership within the European Community.

The collapse of communism in the Soviet Union's East European satellites in the *annus mirabilis* of 1989 heralded the apparent passing of the Cold War. Reagan's anticommunist policies appeared vindicated, but his political legatee and successor, George H. Bush, now had the opportunity to pursue different internationalist ideals in shaping a new world order. In view of the disappearance of the Soviet Union as a global enemy, regional aggressors are the most likely threat to peace and American interests in the post–Cold War world. Although the United States now stands indisputably as the solitary military superpower, the lessons of Vietnam and the realization of the economic limits of its military power will probably deter it from acting as a lone policeman. Instead, the United States will probably seek to build a peaceful and stable world order by placing itself at the head of an international coalition to outlaw regional aggression. The prosecution of the Gulf War as a United Nations collective security action, albeit under American military leadership, supports the view that the internationalist-interventionist paradigm could be restored in a new guise.

Whatever the future holds, nationalist considerations will continue to have some influence on U.S. policy. The limits of internationalism in the Gulf War were evidenced by Bush's insistence that he only needed a Congressional rather than a U.N. mandate to commence actual hostilities. Similarly, Bush's hesitant actions in giving protection to Kurdish and Shiite rebels, who had been encouraged to rise up against Saddam Hussein during the war and whose fate following the conflict has horrified world opinion, reflect America's interest in preserving Iraq as a counter against Iran in the oil-rich Persian Gulf.

The Gulf War offers further proof that the only consistent theme in twentieth-century American foreign policy has been the desire to maintain freedom of action. This concern has been shared by isolationists, nationalists, and internationalists alike. Otherwise, modern American diplomacy defies neat conceptualization. It has been the product of diverse forces, which often coexisted despite their contradictions. In the 1930s, for example, internationalist aspirations and isolationist instincts were both in evidence, as was economic nationalism which was essentially distinct from both. After 1945, isolationism did not have a constituency in the United States, other than among the uninterested and ill-informed mass public. The isolationist politicians of the 1930s were converted to the nationalist lobby. Yet even those policymakers who followed Henry Luce's advice and influenced world affairs by intervention and internationalism after 1941 did so very much on American terms.

Ideals and self-interest have contributed and continue to contribute to the making of American foreign policy because they reflect two vital necessities—first, for America to espouse ideals worthy of its self-image as a "beacon lighting for all the world the paths of human destiny" (Ralph Waldo Emerson), and second, to protect the nation from external threats to its security. The two are crucial in securing support from different constituencies, but they frequently end up on collision course and produce the moods of disillusionment that have periodically punctuated the twentieth-century American attitude to world affairs.

It is difficult to accept that American foreign policy in this century has been determined primarily by imperialism. Equally, there can be little doubt that America has enjoyed an "informal empire," not colonial in inspiration but often with the trappings of empire. Thus, it has sustained clients in the Caribbean, Southeast Asia, and elsewhere, and benefited from this patronage in terms of special trading and investment privileges. But whether economic gain was always the primary motive, as the Open Door theorists suggest, is debatable. In the case of pre-Castro Cuba or the Dominican Republic, it may have been; but in Korea and South Vietnam the dictates of anticommunism were clearly paramount.

The United States has done more than any other nation to shape twentieth-century world politics. It played a vital role in the victorious coalitions that fought World War I and World War II. In the second half of the century it was instrumental in the economic reconstruction of the postwar Western world and engaged in a forty-year global struggle against communism that it appears to have won. No single set of guiding principles or even dichotomies—isolationism versus internationalism, ideals versus self-interest, anticolonialism versus imperialism—is sufficient to encapsulate twentieth-century American foreign policy. "America's Century" in global terms has been the product of complex American views on world affairs. The future is likely to express the same pattern as the past in this respect, regardless of whether the next century is an American century or not.

Notes

1. Henry Luce, "The American Century," *Life*, February 17, 1941, p. 61.

2. Norman D. Markowitz, *The Rise and Fall of the People's Century: Henry A. Wallace and American Liberalism, 1941–1948* (New York, 1973), pp. 48–50.

3. Quoted in Henry Abelove, ed., *Visions of History* (Manchester, 1983), p. 139.

4. Lloyd E. Ambrosius, *Woodrow Wilson and the American Diplomatic Tradition: The Treaty Fight in Perspective* (New York, 1987), p. xii.

5. Ibid., p. 162.

6. Woodrow Wilson, *Constitutional Government in the United States* (New York, 1908), p. 77.

7. Robert Dallek, *Franklin D. Roosevelt and American Foreign Policy, 1932–1945* (New York, 1979), see especially pp. 35–97, 529–38.

8. Ibid., pp. 78–81; A. J. P. Taylor, *The Origins of the Second World War* (Harmondsworth, U.K., 1964), pp. 95–96.

9. Selig Adler, *The Isolationist Impulse: Its Twentieth-Century Reaction* (London 1957), p. 280.

10. Kirk H. Porter and Donald B. Johnson, eds., *National Party Platforms, 1840–1956* (Urbana, Ill., 1956), pp. 407–8.

11. Daniel Yergin, *Shattered Peace: The Origins of the Cold War and the National Security State* (Boston, 1978), pp. 17–69.

12. Mr. X (George F. Kennan), "The Sources of Soviet Conduct," *Foreign Affairs* 25 (1947): 580.

13. Quoted in George C. Herring, *America's Longest War: The United States and Vietnam, 1950–1975* (New York, 1979), p. 132.

14. Arthur M. Schlesinger, Jr., *A Thousand Days: John F. Kennedy in the White House* (Boston, 1965), p. 769.

15. Gaddis Smith, *Morality, Reason and Power: American Diplomacy in the Carter Years* (New York, 1986), p. 247.

Bibliography

On the cyclical nature of American foreign policy, see Geir Lundestad, "Uniqueness and Pendulum Swings in American Foreign Policy," *International Affairs* 62 (1986): 405–21; Arthur M. Schlesinger, Jr., *The Cycles of American History* (Boston, 1987); and Charles W. Kegley and Eugene R. Wittkopf, *American Foreign Policy: Pattern and Process*, 3d ed. (New York, 1987). For a British overview of policy-making, see John Dumbrell, *The Making of U. S. Foreign Policy* (Manchester, 1990)

A number of general surveys reflect various schools of thought on American foreign policy. For the orthodox interpretation see Foster R. Dulles, *America's Rise to World Power, 1898–1954* (New York, 1955), and John Spanier, *American Foreign Policy since World War II* (New York, 1985). The revisionist school is exemplified by Lloyd Gardner's two books, *Imperial America: American Foreign Policy since 1898* (New York, 1976) and *A Covenant with Power: America and World Order from Wilson to Reagan* (New York, 1983); Stephen E. Ambrose, *Rise to Globalism, American Foreign Policy since 1938*, 5th ed. (New York, 1988); and Walter LaFeber, *The American Age, United States Foreign Policy at Home and Abroad since 1750* (New York, 1989). On the Open Door thesis see two books by William A. Williams, *The Tragedy of American Diplomacy* (New York, 1972) and *Empire as a Way of Life* (New York, 1980); and Gabriel Kolko, *The Roots of American Foreign Policy* (Boston, 1969). The main expressions of the realist viewpoint are George F. Kennan, *American Diplomacy, 1900–1950* (Chicago, 1951); Robert E. Osgood, *Ideals and Self-Interest in America's Foreign Relations* (Chicago, 1953); Hans J. Morgenthau, *In Defense of National Interest* (Lanham, Md., 1983); and Norman A. Graebner, *America as a World Power: A Realist Appraisal from Wilson to Reagan* (Wilmington, Del., 1984).

Useful on the early twentieth century are Ernest R. May, *Imperial Democracy: The Emergence of America as a Great Power* (New York, 1961); Walter LaFeber, *The New Empire: An Interpretation of American Expansion, 1860–1898* (Ithaca, N.Y., 1962); Howard K. Beale, *Theodore Roosevelt and the Rise of America to World Power* (New York, 1962); and Frederick W. Marks III, *Velvet on Iron: The Diplomacy of Theodore Roosevelt* (New York, 1982).

Scholars of the Wilson era fall into three fairly distinct categories. Realist works critical of the president's failure to develop clearly defined American interests include (in addition to Kennan, Morgenthau, and Osgood noted above): Norman A. Graebner, ed., *Ideas and Diplomacy* (New York, 1964), and John A. Thompson, "Woodrow Wilson and World War I," *Journal of American Studies* 19 (1985): 325–48. Studies depicting Wilson as having a shrewd grasp of political reality include two books by Arthur S. Link, *Wilson the Diplomatist* (Princeton,

N.J., 1957) and *The Higher Realism of Woodrow Wilson and Other Essays* (Princeton, N.J., 1971); Ernest R. May, *The World War and American Isolation, 1914–1917* (Cambridge, Mass., 1959); and Daniel W. Smith, *The Great Departure: The United States and World War I* (New York, 1965). New Left criticism of Wilson's liberal-capitalist values is exemplified by Arno J. Mayer's two studies, *Political Origins of the New Diplomacy, 1917–1918* (New Haven, 1959), and *Politics and Diplomacy of Peacemaking: Containment and Counter-Revolution at Versailles, 1918–1919* (New York, 1967); and N. Gordon Levin, Jr., *Woodrow Wilson and World Politics* (New York, 1968). A major recent study breaking with the "Wilsonian perspective" that according to its author has colored all previous debate is Lloyd E. Ambrosius, *Woodrow Wilson and the American Diplomatic Tradition* (New York, 1987).

For the 1920s, the most helpful study is Warren I. Cohen, *Empire Without Tears: America's Foreign Relations, 1921–1933* (1987). For a useful overview of different perspectives, see John M. Carroll, "American Diplomacy in the 1920s," in *Modern American Diplomacy*, ed. John M. Carroll and George C. Herring (Wilmington, Del., 1986), pp. 53–70.

For an insightful survey of the debate over Franklin D. Roosevelt's foreign policy, see Lloyd Gardner, "Isolation and Appeasement," in *The Origins of the Second World War Reconsidered: The A. J. P. Taylor Debate after Twenty-five Years*, ed. Gordon Martel (Boston, 1986), pp. 210–26. In his own book, *Economic Aspects of New Deal Diplomacy* (Madison, Wis., 1964), Gardner argues that FDR did not "yearn for an active role" in Europe. Robert A. Divine, *The Illusion of Neutrality* (Chicago, 1962) presents FDR as "equivocal," while Robert Dallek, *Franklin D. Roosevelt and American Foreign Policy, 1932–1945* (New York, 1979) portrays him as a frustrated internationalist. For Asian affairs, see Herbert Feis, *The Road to Pearl Harbor* (New York, 1950); Dorothy Borg and Shumpei Okamoto, eds., *Pearl Harbor as History: Japanese-American Relations, 1931–1941* (New York, 1973); and Akira K. Iriye, *The Origins of the Second World War in Asia and the Pacific* (Chicago, 1987). Important studies of isolationism include Selig Adler, *The Isolationist Impulse: Its Twentieth-Century Reaction* (New York, 1957); Robert A. Divine, *Second Chance: The Tri-*

umph of Internationalism in America during World War II (New York, 1967); and Wayne S. Cole, *Roosevelt and the Isolationists, 1932–1945* (Lincoln, Neb., 1983).

The historiography of the Cold War is increasingly difficult to categorize. Representative of the orthodox school, which blames Soviet expansion, are Dean Acheson, *Present at the Creation: My Years at the State Department* (New York, 1969), and Herbert Feis, *From Trust to Terror: The Onset of the Cold War, 1945–1950* (New York, 1970). For a revisionist survey, see Walter LaFeber, *America, Russia, and the Cold War, 1945–1975* (New York, 1976). However, the revisionists are a disparate group, linked only by their desire to apportion some of the blame for the Cold War to the U.S.: Gar Alperowitz, *Atomic Diplomacy: Hiroshima and Potsdam—The Use of the Atomic Bomb and the American Confrontation with Soviet Power,* rev. ed. (New York, 1985) blames Truman's atomic "saber-rattling"; Joyce and Gabriel Kolko, *The Limits of Power* (New York, 1972) blames U.S. attempts to restructure the world along capitalistic lines; and Diane Clemens, *Yalta* (New York, 1970) stresses U.S. misreading of Soviet promises at Yalta. The classic statement of the "realist" position, viewing the Cold War as the inevitable outcome of World War II, is Louis J. Halle, *The Cold War as History* (New York, 1967); see too the general surveys by Morgenthau and Graebner, cited above. The postrevisionist school, which accepts that the Soviets did not act according to any plan for world conquest, and that the U.S. has to share responsibility for the Cold War, is represented by John L. Gaddis. *The United States and the Origins of the Cold War, 1941–1947* (New York, 1972), and Daniel Yergin, *Shattered Peace: The Origins of the Cold War and the National Security State* (Boston, 1978).

The historiography of the Vietnam War is rather unusual. The war was largely discredited before it ended, so the orthodox view (i.e. the one generally accepted at the time) was sharply critical of American involvement on grounds of both morality and necessity. This is exemplified by Arthur M. Schlesinger, Jr., *Bitter Heritage: Vietnam and American Democracy, 1941–1966* (Boston, 1967); David M. Halberstam, *The Best and the Brightest* (New York, 1967); and George M. Kahin, *Intervention: How America Became Involved in Vietnam* (New York, 1986). For a New Left variation see Gabriel Kolko, *Anatomy of a War* (New York, 1986). The revisionist backlash in the 1970s came from those who defended America's policy, if not always its tactics and strategy. The classic expression of this viewpoint is Richard M. Nixon, *No More Vietnams* (New York, 1982); also important is R. B. Smith, *An International History of the Vietnam War: The Kennedy Strategy* (New York, 1985). A postrevisionist case has not yet been fully formulated, but for now try George C. Herring, *America's Longest War: The United States and Vietnam, 1950–1975* (New York, 1979).

On the evolution and decline of détente, the best studies are Stanley Hoffman, *Primacy or World Order: American Foreign Policy since the End of the Cold War* (New York, 1978); Robert S. Litwak, *Détente and the Nixon Doctrine: American Foreign Policy and the Pursuit of Stability* (Cambridge, 1984); and Raymond S. Garthoff, *Détente and Confrontation: American-Soviet Relations from Nixon to Reagan* (Washington, D.C., 1985). The conflict between internationalism and nationalism in Carter administration policy is effectively analyzed by Gaddis Smith, *Morality, Reason and Power: American Diplomacy in the Carter Years* (New York, 1986). The dust has not settled sufficiently on the momentous international events of the 1980s, so there are no clearly discernible trends in Reagan era historiography as yet. Nevertheless, suggestive overviews are provided by William G. Hyland, ed., *The Reagan Foreign Policy* (New York, 1987), and I. M. Destler, "Reagan and the World: An Awesome Stubbornness," in *The Reagan Legacy*, ed. Charles O. Jones (Chatham, N.J., 1988), pp. 241–61. For arms control see Coit D. Blacker, *Reluctant Warriors: The United States, the Soviet Union and Arms Control* (New York, 1987).

Conclusion

_____ _Iwan W. Morgan_

America's twentieth-century experience manifests a certain symmetry. In the early years of the century the Progressives sought to address the political, economic, and social problems resulting from massive industrial growth, and had to give direction to the seemingly unlimited U.S. potential for expansion at home and abroad. By contrast, America's difficulties in the twilight of the century have largely to do with constraints, limits, and relative decline. Insofar as it ever existed in the manner anticipated by Henry Luce, the "American Century" lasted for about a quarter-century. The exceptional circumstances of World War II and its aftermath led to a period of American military and economic dominance that lasted until the late 1960s. The combination of failure in Vietnam and the economic challenge of foreign nations who had rebuilt their war-torn economies brought this era to an end.

Nevertheless, the United States has arguably done more than any other nation to shape world history over the entire course of the twentieth century. In this more limited sense it is possible to label the twentieth century as the "American Century." The United States became the model followed by other nations in pioneering the transformation from the old basic industries to the new high-tech industries, from the producer economy to the consumer economy, and from the industrial society to the information society. American scientific breakthroughs included putting man on the moon, major improvements in medicine such as the Salk polio vaccine, and the more dubious legacy to mankind of the atomic and thermonuclear bombs. The United States has also been the principal actor in world politics for most of the twentieth century. Among America's greatest achievements were its role in the destruction of Nazism, the assistance it rendered to the reconstruction of postwar Western Europe, the lead that it took in the creation of a vast global marketplace after World War II, and ultimate success in its superpower rivalry with the Soviet Union.

American influence extended into other spheres. No other nation has done as much to shape the mass popular culture of the Western world. America was the birthplace of jazz, blues and rock, the core ingredients of twentieth-century "pop" music. Hollywood pioneered the development of popular cinema and created a world audience for American movies. For better or worse, the United States also led the way in the development of television culture. Meanwhile, America was the progenitor of consumer-culture values that took root in the burgeoning suburbs and were quickly absorbed by other Western nations harvesting the fruits of economic recovery after World War II. So great was America's cultural impact that some European commentators warned of U.S. cultural imperialism and bemoaned the "Americanization" of Europe, a concept that has never been satisfactorily defined but which embodies a readily recognizable symbolism. [1]

In some areas, of course, the United States has not been in the forefront of innovation. The consensual nature of American politics has restricted radical change throughout the twentieth century. In comparison with most Western European nations, the United States was slow to build a welfare state, and the model developed under the aegis of the New Deal, Fair Deal, and Great Society was a relatively limited one. Conversely, the limited gains of the "Reagan Revolution" served to restrict the international influence of U.S. conservatism in the 1980s. The model that the East European nations sought to emulate when transferring from communism to capitalism was Thatcherism, not Reaganism. Civil liberties, civil rights, and equal-employment opportunity and affirmative action programs for racial minorities and women constitute America's most internationally influential domestic policy initiatives. By contrast, U.S. efforts to deal with the endemic social problems of the late twentieth century, notably the education system's shortcomings, violent crime, drug problems, inner city decay, and deprivation among a large "underclass" have reaped limited success and made little impact abroad. It must be borne in mind, however, that no Western nation has so far perfected solutions for these problems.

It is improbable that any single nation can play in the twenty-first century the kind of role played by the United States in the present century. The diffusion of economic power and the increasing interdependence of nations, trends that became evident in the late twentieth century, are likely to militate against this. Moreover, the international agenda is changing with the emergence of so-called intermestic issues that have both a foreign and domestic policy dimension, such as control of drugs, environmental protection, trade agreements, and financial management. Superpower leadership cannot resolve these issues, which must be dealt with through international cooperation and domestic initiatives on the part of many nations.

On the other hand, many Europeans seem premature in predicting a precipitous decline in America's global influence. Typifying this viewpoint, Jacques Attali, a key aide to President François Mitterrand of France and director of the new multilateral bank that has been established to assist the economic reconstruction of Eastern Europe, has recently argued that the future will be dominated by a European bloc and a Japanese-led Pacific bloc.[2] The implication of this argument is that the world is entering a multipolar era in which economic power is of greater significance than military power. American critics of this "declinist" thesis take heart from the Gulf War, in which the United States not only played the dominant military role but also exercised political leadership in persuading the United Nations to take a stand against Iraq's invasion of Kuwait. According to Joseph S. Nye, Jr., this success shows that the United States "is still the largest possessor of both 'hard' power—the ability to command others, usually through the use of tangible resources such as military and economic might—and 'soft' power—the ability to coopt rather than command, to get others to want what you want."[3]

The nineteenth century could be labeled the "British Century" in view of Britain's status as the first industrial nation and the principal colonial power. By the eve of World War I, however,

Britain was on the verge of the long decline that would characterize its twentieth-century history. It is evident that late-twentieth-century America is not at a comparable turning point. Unlike Britain in 1914, the United States in the 1990s still possesses the world's largest economy and greater military power than any other nation. It has the resources to exercise world leadership in the twenty-first century, albeit in constrained fashion that recognizes the realistic limits of its military power. However, America's capacity to sustain such a role in the long term is likely to depend on its domestic success. Problems that threaten to erode the foundations of its economic power, namely slow growth, declining productivity, burgeoning trade and budget deficits, the disrepair that afflicts many public services, the need for better education, and urban decay and poverty, have to be addressed. Throughout its history, the United States has shown a remarkable capacity to rebuild itself, most notably after the Civil War, and during the Progressive and New Deal eras. As America's twentieth century comes to an end, the United States again faces the task of political and economic renewal in order to meet the challenges of and exert its influence on the twenty-first century.

Notes

1. For an example of this, see Ralph Willett, *The Americanization of Germany, 1945–1949* (London, 1989).

2. Jacques Attali, *Lignes d'Horizon* (Paris, 1990).

3. Joseph S. Nye, Jr., "Against 'Declinism'," *The New Republic*, October 15, 1990, p. 13.

Notes on Contributors

The Editors

IWAN W. MORGAN is Principal Lecturer in Politics and Government at the City of London Polytechnic. He has written numerous articles on state and local responses to the Great Depression and New Deal. His book, *Eisenhower versus "The Spenders": The Eisenhower Administration, the Democrats and the Budget*, appeared in 1990.

NEIL A. WYNN is Head of History at the University of Glamorgan. Formerly editor of the British Association for American Studies *Newsletter*, he has published articles and reviews on twentieth-century American history, black American history, and war and social change. His books *The Afro-American and the Second World War* (1976) and *From Progressivism to Prosperity* (1986) were both published by Holmes and Meier.

The Contributors

DAVID J. BARLING is a Lecturer in Politics in the School of Humanities, Thames Valley University. His main interest is in Congressional politics, and he is currently writing on the U.S. Congress and the legislative process.

JOHN DUMBRELL is Senior Lecturer in Politics in the Department of Social Science, Manchester University. He is the author of *The Making of U.S. Foreign Policy* (1990) and the editor of *Vietnam and the Anti-war Movement: An International Perspective* (1989).

STUART KIDD, formerly Head of United States Studies at Bulmershe College of Higher Education, is now a Lecturer in History at the University of Reading. He has published a number of articles and reviews dealing with the history and culture of America in the 1930s.

Jay Kleinberg is Head of American Studies at West London Institute of Higher Education. She has written articles on women's work, household technology, aging, working-class mortality, and women in the U.S. economy. She is the author of *Retrieving Women's History* (1988), *The Shadow of the Mills: Working Class Family Life, Pittsburgh, 1870–1907* (1989), and *Women in American Society, 1820–1920* (British Association for American Studies Pamphlet 20, 1990).

Alun Munslow is Senior Lecturer in the Department of Humanities at Staffordshire University. He is editor of the British Association for American Studies *Newsletter*, and has written a number of articles on American studies and on culture and ideology. His book on cultural creation in late-nineteenth-century America is forthcoming.

Ian Purchase is Principal Lecturer at Manchester Metropolitan University (Alsager). He is chairman of the Council for National Academic Awards' forum on American studies in Britain, and has published reports and articles on American studies in the United Kingdom as well as a variety of articles and reviews in twentieth-century American history.

Geoff Stoakes is Head of American Studies at the University College of Ripon & York St. John, York. As well as writing and teaching on American history, he works in the field of German history and is the author of *Hitler and the Quest for World Dominion* (1986).

Index